WORKING BELOW CAPACITY

Also by Derek Bosworth

PRODUCTION FUNCTIONS
THE EMPLOYMENT CONSEQUENCES OF TECHNOLOGICAL CHANGE
WORK PATTERNS (*with P. Dawkins*)

Also by David F. Heathfield

THE ECONOMETRIC STUDY OF THE UNITED KINGDOM (*with K. Hilton*)
PRODUCTION FUNCTIONS
TOPICS IN APPLIED MACROECONOMICS
THE ECONOMICS OF CO-DETERMINATION
INFLATION: Models and Policies

Working Below Capacity

Edited by

Derek Bosworth
Principal Research Fellow
Institute for Employment Research, University of Warwick

and

David F. Heathfield
Senior Lecturer in Economics
University of Southampton

MACMILLAN
PRESS

© Derek Bosworth and David F. Heathfield 1987

All rights reserved. No reproduction, copy or transmission
of this publication may be made without written permission.

No paragraph of this publication may be reproduced, copied
or transmitted save with written permission or in accordance
with the provisions of the Copyright Act 1956 (as amended),
or under the terms of any licence permitting limited copying
issued by the Copyright Licensing Agency, 7 Ridgmount Street,
London WC1E 7AE.

Any person who does any unauthorised act in relation to
this publication may be liable to criminal prosecution and
civil claims for damages.

First published 1987

Published by
THE MACMILLAN PRESS LTD
Houndmills, Basingstoke, Hampshire RG21 2XS
and London
Companies and representatives
throughout the world

Typeset by Macmillan India Ltd., Bangalore 25

Printed in Hong Kong

British Library Cataloguing in Publication Data
Working below capacity.
1. Industrial capacity—Great Britain
I. Bosworth, Derek L. II. Heathfield,
David F.
338.5'144   HC256 6
ISBN 0-333-41388-1

Contents

Notes on the Contributors — x
List of Participants — xiv
List of Tables — xvii
List of Illustrations — xv
Editors' Preface — xxi

PART I CAPACITY MEASURES

1 The CBI Industrial Trends Survey and Capacity Working — 3
B. C. Rosewell

Introduction — 3
The CBI Survey — 3
Interpretation — 5
Appendices: — 15
A1.1 Monthly Trends Enquiry — 19
A1.2 Industrial Trends Survey

2 Trend-Through-Peaks Methods of Estimating Capacity Utilisation — 23
Richard Harris and Jim Taylor

Capacity Output — 24
Methods of Estimating Capacity Utilisation — 25
Measuring the Capital Stock — 31
Estimating Capacity Output Using the Production Function Approach — 33
Estimates of Capacity Utilisation Based on the Wharton Method, the Capital Productivity Method and the Production Function Method — 38
Conclusion — 41
Appendix: Trend Increase in Capital Utilisation — 42

v

3 Capacity Utilisation and Below-Capacity Working 45
J. H. Ll. Dewhurst

Introduction	45
The Theoretical Model	46
Empirical Exercise: 1	49
Empirical Exercise: 2	53
Conclusion	56

4 Alternative Aggregate Measures of Capacity Utilisation Based on a MACE Production Function 58
John Helliwell, Peter Sturm and Gérard Salou

Introduction	58
The MACE Production Function	59
Alternative MACE Indicators of Capacity Utilisation	62
Interpretation and Comparison of Results	72
Appendix: The Production Structure: Specification and Parameter Deviation	75

5 Capacity Utilisation in a Vintage Model of United Kingdom Manufacturing 79
J. Ansar, A. Ingham, H. Leon, M. Toker and A. Ulph

Introduction	79
Capacity Utilisation in a Vintage Model	81
Estimating a Putty-clay Model	87
Calculating the Vintages Used and Quasi-rents	97
Further Work and the Need for a Putty-semi-putty Model	105

PART II LABOUR

6 The Dough, the Doughnut and the Hole: Unemployment, Labour Utilisation and Labour Market Accounting 119
Chris de Neubourg

The Utilisation of Labour Resources: Concepts and Measurement	120
A System of Labour Market Accounts	166
Appendices:	
A6.1 Labour Force, Employment and Unemployment: the ILO Definitions	199

A.6.2	Calculation of 'Aggregate Hours Lost by the Unemployed' and Aggregate Hours Lost by Persons on Part-time for Economic Reasons'	200
A6.3	Sources for Table 6.7	202
A6.4	Basic Sources and Data for the Netherlands: Labour Market Account	203
A6.5	Basic Sources and Data for the United States: Labour Market Account	207
A6.6	ILO Definition: 'Actual Hours Worked per Person Employed'	211

7 Full-Capacity Employment, Unemployment and Labour Hoarding — 219
Joan Muysken

Introduction	219
The Nature of Unemployment: an Analytical Framework	221
The Nature of Unemployment in the Netherlands 1967–81	230
Concluding Remarks	238
Appendix: Data for Chapter 7	240

8 Aggregate Unemployment and Labour Slack as Indices of Labour Utilisation — 246
Chris de Neubourg

Shortcomings of the Unemployment Rate as Guidelines for the Definition of Aggregate Labour Slack	247
Labour Slack Estimates in the Literature	250
The Definition of Labour Slack	255
Empirical Application of the Labour Slack Estimate: Some Preliminary Results	258
Conclusions	264
Appendices:	
A8.1 Definitions of the Summary Figure and Ratios in Terms of the Labour Market Accounts for the United States	266
A8.2 Summary Figures and Ratios for the Netherlands 1973–81	270

Contents

9 Average Weekly Hours of Work in the United Kingdom 1948–80: A Disaggregated Analysis — 276
A. J. Neale and R. A. Wilson

Introduction — 276
A Model of the Demand for Hours — 281
Data and Estimation — 285
Results — 289
Conclusions — 301

10 Estimating the Relationship Between Output and Hours Worked in United Kingdom Manufacturing and Production Industries — 304
Richard T. Baillie and Mick Silver

Introduction — 304
Some Evidence From Econometric Studies — 305
Inter-industry Variation in the Marginal Productivity of Hours Worked — 309
Expanding the Model — 312
Conclusion — 314

11 Industrial Capacity and Employment Promotion in Developing Countries: Some Conclusions — 317
N. Phan-Thuy

Concepts of Under-Utilisation of Industrial Capacity and Measurement Problems in Developing Countries — 317
Policy Guidelines for Promoting Employment Through Fuller Utilisation of Industrial Capacity — 321
Conclusion: Suggestions for a Programme of Action — 323

12 The Percentage Utilisation of Labour Index (PUL) — 326
A. Bennett and S. Smith-Gavine

Introduction — 326
Findings of the Index of PUL — 336
Uses of the Index Result to the Firm — 348
Foundation of the Index Data in Factory Procedures — 353

PART III CAPITAL

13 Capital Utilisation, Capacity and Scrapping   367
David F. Heathfield

Introduction   367
The Need to Measure Capital Utilisation   367
Scrapping and Capacity   373
Capital Utilisation Measures   375
Summary and Conclusion   378

14 Electricity-Based Measures of Capital Utilisation by United Kingdom Manufacturing Industry   380
Derek Bosworth and Tony Westaway

Introduction   380
Fuel Consumption and Capital Utilisation   381
Data and Sources   388
Empirical Results   390
Indices of Capital Utilisation   396
Conclusions   399
Appendix: The Multi-tier CES Function   401

15 Capital Utilisation: Time Intensity Utilisation Rates in the United Kingdom Chemicals Industry   406
Derek Bosworth

Introduction   406
TIUR Measures: a Review of the Existing Literature
  Theoretical Considerations   407
TIUR Measures for the United Kingdom Chemicals Industry   411
Conclusions   417
Appendix: Data for Chapter 15   419

Author Index   431
Subject Index   435

Notes on the Contributors

Jasmin Ansar is Lecturer in Economics and Econometrics at City University.

Richard Baillie, Lecturer, University of Birmingham, is currently Visiting Professor at University of California, San Diego and has previously been Visiting Associate Professor at University of Toronto and at State University. He has published articles in *Econometrica, Journal of the American Statistical Association, Journal of Econometrics, Oxford Economic Papers* and other major professional journals.

Alan Bennett is Senior Lecturer in Business Economics at the Aston University Management Centre. Formerly a foundry manager and director of Delta Diecastings Ltd and Cronite Ltd, he has written extensively on the economics of the foundry industry. His current research concern is productivity and its measurement in manufacturing industry.

Derek Bosworth is Principal Research Fellow at the Institute for Employment Research, Warwick University, Coventry. He was formerly Senior Lecturer in Economics at Loughborough University and Professor and Head of School at the Polytechnic of Central London. He has published a number of articles and books in the areas of optimal capital utilisation, employment and the economics of work patterns.

J. H. Ll. Dewhurst has from 1969 to the present been Lecturer in Economics and Social Statistics at the University of Kent and the University of Dundee.

Richard Harris, Lecturer in Economics at Queen's University, Belfast since 1980, has published in various journals, including the *Economic Journal*.

David F. Heathfield is Senior Lecturer in Economics at the University of Southampton. After ten years in engineering he graduated in economics and joined the Econometric Model Building Unit at Southampton. He has taught in America and was a DAAD visitor to Kiel in 1984. He has published several books and articles on production and econometric models.

John Helliwell is Professor of Economics at the University of British Columbia, a Research Associate at the NBER and author of several books and articles.

Alan Ingham has been Lecturer in Economics at Southampton since 1973. Visiting appointments include Université Catholique de Louvain, and University of British Columbia. His main research interests lie in resource economics and models of production. At present he is a member of a research group working for the United Kingdom Department of Energy.

H. Leon is Lecturer in Economic Development at the University of Kent at Canterbury, having previously worked at Southampton University both as a Research Assistant and Temporary Lecturer.

Joan Muysken was appointed Professor of Economics at the University of Limburg in 1984. He has published several papers on the aggregation of production functions.

Adrian Neale is a Research Officer at Nuffield College, Oxford, having previously been employed at the Institute for Employment Research, University of Warwick, and briefly at the Department of Employment. He has worked and published on various areas of the labour market, economic forecasting and policy and more recently has been engaged in a major econometric research project.

Chris de Neubourg lectured at the University of Groningen (Netherlands) and is now teaching economics at the University of Limburg, Maastricht (Netherlands). He has published a number of books and articles on labour markets.

N. Phan-Thuy worked in North American universities before joining the International Labour Organisation (ILO) in 1974. She is now Chief of the Evaluation Unit in the Bureau of Programming and Management.

Notes on the Contributors

Bridget Rosewell worked for five years as a research officer in the Institute of Economics and Statistics at Oxford. Prior to this she spent three years as a tutor in economics at Oriel College, publishing in the area of labour economics. In 1984 Mrs Rosewell joined the CBI as Head of the Economic Trends Department. In January 1986 she became Deputy Director. She was responsible for the running and analysis of the CBI Trends Survey as well as for the preparation of forecasts and the analysis of the current economic situation. She has since left to work for CISI-Wharton Econometric Forecasting Associates Ltd.

Gérard Salou joined the OECD, Paris, in 1982.

Mick Silver is Lecturer in Industrial Economics and Statistics and Director of Postgraduate Research at the School of Management, University of Bath. He has previously worked as a Lecturer in Applied Statistics at the Management Centre, University of Aston. His publications have generally related to the application of statistics to problems in economics and management, for example productivity systems, price variation and inflation, industrial development in LDCs and management training surveys. He has also been active in consultancy at the firm and national level.

Sydney Smith-Gavine is an Honorary Member of Leicester Polytechnic and attached to the School of Economics and Accounting (where he was previously a research and teaching member). He has been on the staff of Hull, Manchester and Aberdeen Universities. He was also in industry as an economist and work study officer. An early publication was 'A Percentage Measure of Standardisation', Special Number 1963, Productivity Measurement Review (OECD). Together with the Index of PUL this reflects his interest in productivity and the use of internal factory data to the economist.

Peter Sturm worked in North America before joining OECD, Paris, in 1974.

Jim Taylor is Professor of Economics at the University of Lancaster and has also taught at the Universities of Pennsylvania and British Columbia. He has published many articles on unemployment, labour hoarding, inflation, regional policy and the employability of graduates. His books include *Unemployment and Wage Inflation* and *Regional Economics and Policy* (jointly with Harvey Armstrong).

Notes on the Contributors

Mehmet Toker joined the Department of Economics at Southampton University as a Temporary Lecturer in 1985.

Alistair Ulph joined the Economic Department at Southampton University in 1979 as Lecturer, and subsequently became Senior Lecturer, and in 1985, Professor of Economics. Previously he had been a Research Fellow in Resource and Environmental Economics at Australian National University, Canberra, for three years, following a four-year period as Lecturer in Economics at the University of Stirling.

Tony Westaway is Lecturer in Economics at Loughborough University of Technology and he has also lectured at the University of Nottingham. He has contributed to several journals and is an author or contributor to several books including *Macroeconomics: Theory, Evidence and Policy* (joint author), *The British Economy in the 1970s* and *Case Studies in Public Sector Economics* (joint author).

Robert Wilson is a Senior Research Fellow at the Institute for Employment Research at the University of Warwick. He is responsible for running the macroeconomic model used as the main tool in conducting the Institute's regular assessments of the United Kingdom's labour market, and is on the Editorial Board of the *Review of the Economy and Employment* where the results of these exercises are published. He has published numerous papers in the field of labour economics and policy analysis.

List of the Participants

O. Al-Wattar   University of Southampton
R. Baillie   University of Birmingham
A. J. Bennett   University of Aston
J. H. Crawshaw   Textile Institute, Manchester
J. H. Ll. Dewhurst   University of Dundee
R. Harris   Queen's University, Belfast
David F. Heathfield   University of Southampton
A. Hickling   NEDO
O. Hooker   Welsh Office
A. Ingham   University of Southampton
M. A. Landesmann   DAE, University of Cambridge
J. Lewis   Wolverhampton Polytechnic
S. Madhavan   Polytechnic of Central London
D. K. Miles   Bank of England
J. Muysken   University of Limburg, Netherlands
A. J. Neale   Nuffield College, Oxford
C. de Neubourg   University of Limburg, Netherlands
Mrs Phan-Thuy   ILO, Geneva
M. Riese   University of Linz, Austria
B. Rosewell   CBI
M. S. Silver   University of Bath
S. A. N. Smith-Gavine   Leicester Polytechnic
P. Sturm   OECD, Paris
G. M. P. Swann   University of Bath
G. F. Thompson   Open University
G. Wenban-Smith   British Gas Corporation
A. J. Westaway   University of Loughborough

Institute for Employment Research, University of Warwick

D. G. Blanchflower
D. Bosworth (IER Associate Fellow; Polytechnic of Central London)
P. N. Junankar
R. M. Lindley
R. A. Wilson

Administration

M. Birch (Executive Officer, IER)

List of Illustrations

1.1	Manufacturing output comparisons	7
1.2	Survey data comparisons	9
1.3	Skilled labour shortages	10
1.4	Reported output volume and capacity utilisation: manufacturing	11
1.5	Reported output value and capacity utilisation: manufacturing	11
1.6	Reported output volume and capacity utilisation: capital goods	12
1.7	Reported output value and capacity utilisation: capital goods	13
2.1	Estimated capacity output	26
2.2	Time pattern of capital stock	32
2.3	Estimated capacity utilisation rate	39
2.4	Estimated capacity utilisation rate	40
3.1	Plot of U against W	51
3.2	Capacity utilisation: Scottish manufacturing	52
3.3	INSEE: French industry capacity utilisation	54
3.4	French industry: 'estimated' and 'actual' capacity utilisation index	55
3.5	French industry: published data	56
4.1	MACE model: labour efficiency index	61
4.2	MACE model: intensity of factor utilisation	65
4.3	MACE model: real labour cost gap	73
5.1	*Ex post* and *ex ante* isoquant: unit output level	82
5.2	Choice of technique: *ex ante* and *ex post*	83
5.3	Choice of vintages in relation to output	85
5.4	Choice of vintages in relation to profitability	87
5.5	Ratio of marginal variable cost to price VRi	103
5.6	Energy demand	104
5.7	Labour demand	105
5.8	Index of capacity utilisation	109
5.9	Deflated wage index	111
5.10	Real energy price index	112
5.11	Outputs and inputs per unit of time (I)	113
5.12	Outputs and inputs per unit of time (II)	113

List of Illustrations

5.13	Switching of vintages	114
5.14	Cost-dominant vintage	114
6.1	United States: labour force time lost and unemployment rate	157
6.2	United States: employment–population ratio	161
6.3	The Netherlands: deployment of persons 15 or older	162
6.4	Simplified outline for labour market flow accounts	173
6.5	Deployment of total population	175
6.6	Labour market utilisation account	176
6.7	The Netherlands: Deployment of labour force time	193
6.8	United States: Deployment of people 15 and older	195
6.9	United States: Deployment of labour force time	197
7.1	The employment function and the UV curve	223
7.2	The employment function	223
7.3	Decomposition of unemployment	229
7.4	Estimations of capacity demand for labour	232
7.5	Estimations of unemployment due to labour market imperfections	235
7.6	The Netherlands: employment and unemployment	236
8.1	The Netherlands: aggregate unemployment and plots of LST	259
8.2	The Netherlands: standardised estimates of registered unemployment and labour slack time	260
8.3	The Netherlands: unemployment rate and percentage labour slack	261
8.4	The Netherlands: components of labour slack	262
12.1	PUL sub-indices of consumer, intermediate and capital goods	327
12.2	PUL and output	328
12.3	Output per operative hour; PUL and 'technological' productivity; gross fixed investment in plant and machinery	329
12.4	Average weekly hours worked per operative; PUL; employment	330
12.5	Index of net work put in	335
12.6	Behaviour of total output	346
15.1	TIUR: weekly and annually	413
15.2	Annual holiday entitlements	416

List of Tables

2.1	Estimated production functions for four United Kingdom industry groups	35
4.1	Parameter values of the aggregate production structure	63
4.2	Natural rates of unemployment (%)	64
4.3	Output supply equations	66
4.4	Assumptions underlying alternative potential output measures	67
4.5	Alternative measures of capacity utilisation	68
5.1	Estimates for equation [3.8], using instrumental variables	94
5.2	Regression results	97
5.3	Sorting calculations (first 5 periods) $A = 1$, $\beta = 1$	100
5.4	Marginal vintages used and their variable cost $A = 1$, $\beta = 1$	102
5.5	Sorting calculations (first 3 periods) $A = 2$, $\beta = 0.95$	106
5.6	Marginal vintages used and their variable cost $A = 2$, $\beta = 0.95$	107
5.7	Marginal vintage details and total output produced when mark-up held constant $A = 1$, $\beta = 1$	108
6.1	Comparison of registration and survey unemployment rates (1959–80)	125
6.2	United States: estimates of 'discouraged workers' (1967–81)	129
6.3	United States: labour force time lost due to unemployment and involuntary part-time work (1967–81)	132
6.4	Hours worked per employee (1870–81)	137
6.5	United States: voluntary part-time employed as percentage of total employed (1955–82)	138
6.6	Voluntary part-time employed as percentage of total employed by sex (1973–9)	139
6.7	Size of the birth cohort entering the population of working age (1950–81)	141
6.8	Labour force participation rates	146
6.9	United States: unemployment rate, employment–population ratio, and yearly change in employment–population ratio (post-1945)	164

6.10	Average actual hours worked per person in employment (1960–81)	169
6.11	The Netherlands: labour market utilisation account in persons (1980)	180
6.12	United States: labour market utilisation account in persons (1980)	182
6.13	The Netherlands: labour market utilisation account in hours (1980)	184
6.14	The Netherlands: labour market utilisation account in hours (1980)	186
6.15	United States: labour market utilisation account in hours (1980)	188
6.16	United States: labour market utilisation account in hours (1980)	190
A6.4	The Netherlands: labour market utilisation account in persons and hours (1960)	204
A6.5	United States: labour market utilisation account in persons and hours (1960)	208
7.1	The Netherlands: decomposition of unemployment (1970–6)	221
7.2	Components of unemployment	230
7.3	The Netherlands: Components of unemployment and labour hoarding (1967–81)	238
A7.1	Data for Chapter 7	241
8.1	Germany: utilisation of labour capacity (1970–81)	251
8.2	The Netherlands: annual changes in standardised LST and $NELR^u$ (1974–81)	261
8.3	The Netherlands: $NULT^p$, $NULT^h$ and $NULT^u$ as percentages of LST (1973–81)	262
8.4	Summary figures and ratios (1981)	264
9.1	Results for manual males	290
9.2	Full-time manual females	292
9.3	Results for all workers	296
10.1	Estimation of industry level production functions by OLS	309
10.2	Estimation of industry level production functions by SURE	310
10.3	Results for textiles and paper, printing etc. industries	313
11.1	Capital utilisation rates	318
14.1	Notation and definitions	389
14.2	Regression results: two-tier CES	391

List of Tables

14.3	Regression results: three-tier CES	392
14.4	Two- and three-tier results for components of bricks, pottery, glass and cement	395
14.5	Index of capital utilisation: two-tier CES	397
14.6	Index of capital utilisation: three-tier CES	398
15.1	Weekly and annual TIUR series	414
A15.1	Comparison of holiday entitlements	420
A15.2	Holiday entitlements by industry	421
A15.3	Basic holiday entitlements, public and customary holidays, and long-service holidays	422
A15.4	Public and customary holidays in the chemicals industry	424
A15.5	Average holiday entitlements	425

Editors' Preface

The contributions to this volume were presented at the Conference on Capacity Utilisation held at Arden House, the University of Warwick in January 1985. The Conference was organised jointly by the Institute for Employment Research (IER) and the European Production Study Group (EPSG).

INTRODUCTION

According to Robbins, economics is the study of the allocation of scarce resources among competing ends. The resources are the labour, capital and land currently available for use in production, and are said to be scarce because they are in fixed or quasi-fixed supply and yet face insatiable demands.

This would seem something of a puzzle to the layman since many – if not all – of those resources are seen to experience various degrees of idleness. Factories are often in operation for only 40 hours per week and shut down altogether for Summer and Christmas holidays. Labour in employment is not always offered the amount of overtime they would like, and some labour is not in work at all.

There are many explanations of this idleness which – as a first rough classification – may be divided into planned idleness and unplanned idleness.

Planned idleness comes about partly because labour has a preferred work period and to persuade labour to work outside those hours it is necessary to offer higher wage payments. It may therefore, be more economical to have two plants operating for only 'normal' hours rather than have one plant operating for twice the normal hours. A second, and less important, explanation, is the Chamberlinian monopoly effect which implies that profit-maximising monopolists operate at less than minimum cost levels of output.

Unplanned idleness, on the other hand, is explained either as due to unexpectedly low demand (in aggregate this would be the Keynesian explanation) or due to the unexpected shortage of one necessary (complementary) input. The latter may be of particular importance in the context of developing economies.

This implies that there are two questions to be addressed. First, what is meant by – and what determines – 'capacity' output? Second, what determines the extent to which actual output falls below its capacity level?

Of these two questions it is the second which is emphasised in this volume, and in particular that aspect of idleness which is unplanned – or was unintended – when the plant or process was originally set up.

The chapters fall into three broad groups. First there are those which seek to measure the extent of under-capacity working without paying too much attention to the possible underlying causes. Second there are those which concentrate on the idleness of labour. These chapters raise questions of labour hoarding, work patterns and the various forms of unemployment. Thirdly, and finally, there are those chapters which concentrate on the idleness of capital (capital utilisation).

STRUCTURE OF THE BOOK

(a) Capacity Utilisation

Perhaps the most direct way of measuring capacity utilisation is to ask the industrialists by how much they are working below their capacity. This is essentially what is done by the CBI (United Kingdom) in its Survey of Industrial Trends. Rosewell describes this approach, and argues that although the questions could perhaps now be improved upon there is much to be said for consistency, particularly when the series is to be used for comparisons over time and when the response rate relies entirely on the goodwill of the firms in the sample. In order to keep the replies simple they are often couched in qualitative rather than quantitative terms (e.g., 'Are you working below/above/at capacity?').

There are a number of ways in which these qualitative responses can be converted into a quantitative measure. Dewhurst suggests one such transformation.

A less direct approach to measuring capacity utilisation is by way of a production function. Once the production function is known it is possible to isolate short-run deviations from the long-run 'efficient' relationship between inputs and outputs. There are three chapters dealing with this approach.

Harris and Taylor's chapter estimates two input neo-classical functions by selecting 'peak' output data from historical input and output measures. This is akin to (and an improvement on) the Wharton School approach of linking selected peaks with straight lines and measuring deviations away from these lines as under-utilisation. The choice of peaks is problematical in both cases, particularly at the beginning and end of periods, and the measure is subject to revision as the future unfolds and reveals new peaks in place of the old.

Two other production function approaches are covered in these chapters. A more general production function approach to the measurement of capacity utilisation involves a more obvious and central role for energy (as is the case with a number of the studies of capital utilisation). The specification of the production function – and, in particular, the ease of substitution between capital, fuel and labour – thus come to the force.

The chapter by Helliwell and Sturm is based on a three-factor, nested constant elasticity of substitution (CES) function. While the technology adopted is more general, a number of the primary parameters are estimated from observed average input and output quantities, rather than from fitting the production function in the normal way. Clearly, the approach does not yield the normal statistical tests for the goodness of fit of the production function. On the other hand, the authors are able to construct a variety of measures of capacity utilisation for seven OECD countries.

The chapter by Ansar, Ingham, Leon, Toker and Ulph adopts a putty-putty vintage production function, where the ease of substitution is allowed to differ *ex ante* and *ex post*. The advantages are tempered by the enormous difficulties experienced in empirical testing of such models. This chapter is no exception, although further improvements can be expected as the research progresses from this early, initial stage.

(b) Labour Utilisation

This particular aspect of under-capacity working offers a rich variety of questions. On an aggregate (national) level there are the problems of classifying unemployment according to whether it is voluntary or involuntary, taking into account early retirement and potential participation rates. For those in employment, interest focuses on the number of hours and shifts worked and – less obviously – the intensity of work effort expended during working hours.

Joan Muysken's paper distinguishes between unemployment caused by market imperfections and that due to a shortage of demand, leading to a shortfall in the demand for labour below the full employment level.

The author thereby attempts to decompose labour under-utilisation into cyclical, structural and demand-deficient unemployment and – knowing full employment output and actual output – can distinguish labour hoarding. This approach involves a traditional UV curve in order to isolate unemployment caused by market imperfections. Full-capacity employment is defined by a vintage production model. Cyclical unemployment thus results from deviations in capacity utilisation and from the level of full capacity due to changes in effective demand.

De Neubourg indicates a general preference for developing multiple indicators of labour utilisation but in this chapter recognises the need – in certain circumstances – to have a single indicator (e.g., for econometric modelling purposes). He argues overt unemployment to be unsatisfactory because of changes in overtime, labour hoarding and early retirement. The author reports on the need to develop more complex functions, such as 'labour slack time'. However, even these have to be used with considerable care. This was particularly true in the case of international comparisons, because of major differences brought about by different social security policies. The author reports estimates of 'aggregate labour slack' for five countries after 1973.

Neale and Wilson report on the explanation of hours of work at the disaggregated industry level and by different skill or occupational categories. The authors isolate a number of reasons why employees may work longer than normal hours, even in the long run. Overtime working appears to be a major means of adjustment to unanticipated changes in output in the short term. In the long term, however, hours worked are largely independent of output. This raises the question whether the different dimensions of hours ought to be separated (e.g., short time and overtime), perhaps even with different models for different dimensions.

The Baillie and Silver chapter also focuses on the explanation of hours of work. They are particularly concerned with the question of the marginal product of an extra hour's work in the production function, which has often been found to exceed unity. The main thrust of the Baillie and Silver chapter is empirical, to see if the separation of individual industries (rather than using cross-section or time series cross-section pooled data) throws any light on the returns to hours phenomenon. They are able to show that the assumption of constant elasticities for hours across industries is not valid, and that the elasticities with respect to hours exceed unity.

The question of measuring work effort is taken up by Bennet and Smith-Gavine. Their Percentage Utilisation of Labour (PUL) index is the end product of detailed, painstaking data collection and computation, drawing on information which is widely available from work measurement departments in industry. When demand falls, the first response is not generally a reduction in the size of the work force, nor even a cut in working hours, but a fall in the intensity of working. The PUL measure thus provides an index reflecting this initial response via work effort to the changing situation.

The contribution of Phan-Thuy is unique insofar as it considers utilisation in the context of developing countries. The chapter has been included under the labour utilisation section because of its policy orientation towards employment creation. However it raises a number of much broader questions. In particular, it considers the special problems of measurement that researchers have to face in dealing with developing countries. In addition, it raises the crucial question – from a development point of view – of the distinction between intended and unintended idleness of capital. It argues that employment creation might take place by a switch from single- to two-shift working.

(c) Capital Utilisation

This final section of the book looks at idle capital. This has attracted far less attention than idle labour, but nonetheless does represent a major omission from production function and productivity studies. It is also a possible waste of an acutely scarce resource in many parts of the world.

Heathfield's chapter examines three related issues. The first concerns whether it is necessary to include a measure of capital utilisation when estimating the production function or isolating a measure of productivity. The second is the important distinction between 'idle' and 'scrapped' capital. Certainly the two notions are quite separate in that the existence of idle (but 'unscrapped') capital determines the maximum capacity of the industry. Finally, Heathfield argues in favour of electricity-based measures of capital utilisation and extends this to argue that, under fairly weak assumptions, electricity consumption may provide a useful overall measure of capital services, independent of the normal errors of measurement of the capital stock.

Bosworth and Westaway's chapter estimates a series of regression equations to obtain measures of capital utilisation based on information about electricity consumption per unit of capital. They show how electricity-based measures need to take into account switches between fuels as well as moves to less energy-intensive methods of production. The empirical results taking these revisions into account are encouraging. On the other hand, while the approach using regression techniques helps to overcome these problems, it has an inherent omitted variable problem. In addition, like certain earlier measures, the choice of technology which governs the chosen specification should be consistent with any uses to which the resulting series are put. Finally, further improvements might result from using unpublished data on capital prices, as well as working at a more disaggregated level.

Finally, Bosworth reports a 'time intensity utilisation rate' (TIUR) measure for the United Kingdom chemicals industry, based on information about shift working and average hours of work per employee. In effect, this measure indicates the number of hours workers are present in the plant. To be useful as a measure of capital utilisation, a further assumption – that capital is continuously manned – is required. In addition, the construction of the TIUR measure requires certain restrictive assumptions about the underlying technology and, again – in common with a number of the alternative measures – it is an interesting question whether the assumed technology is consistent with the production function in which the index is later used. One conclusion that can be drawn from the chapter is that there are grounds for a direct survey of the operating hours of capital.

CONCLUSIONS

Once measures of capacity utilisation are established, all kinds of analyses can be undertaken, ranging from international comparisons of total economies – such as the work of de Neubourg – to estimates of the marginal productivity of overtime hours for particular industries – such as the work of Baillie and Silver and Neale and Wilson.

In spite of the difficulties of measurement, information on capacity utilisation is essential for numerous aspects of the economic planning, such as an improved infrastructure of public services, investment programmes, and the possible need for changes in the pattern of shift working.

The measurement of capacity utilisation is particularly difficult in developing countries, where cottage industries often exist alongside organised ones. The ILO delegate, Dr N. Phan-Thuy, drew attention to the importance of 'unintended under-utilisation' in developing countries, caused by bottlenecks of various kinds (e.g., raw material inputs, road transport problems, electricity supplies, etc.). This kind of under-utilisation is quite distinct from the predominant 'intended under-utilisation' found in developed economies, which is a consequence of deliberate managerial action in the face of market conditions.

Even within the terms of reference adopted by the conference, there were a number of areas which are not covered or discussed in any depth.

One such topic concerns comparisons between alternative measures of utilisation. This deficiency arises in part because, generally, each author reports on only one type of measure.

A second omission was associated with non-market work and leisure. Some concern was expressed by participants that labour utilisation indices would show an inherent downward trend as hours of work fall, holidays increase, retirement ages are brought down, etc. Reductions in utilisation in the paid market employment sector may be, to some extent, offset by increases in utilisation in the unpaid, non-market, possibly home environment.

These omissions aside, the conference raised a number of important issues and made some progress towards wider understanding of the many-faceted problems thrown up by this co-existence of idle and scarce resources.

The IER was established at the University of Warwick, United Kingdom in 1981, developing out of the former Manpower Research Group. The Institute has prepared annual assessments of Britain's economy and employment since 1978. In addition, it has produced a large number of studies of specific aspects of individual labour markets. The IER promotes advanced study and research on subjects such as labour market behaviour; macroeconomic factors affecting employment; the relationship between the labour market and the economy as a whole; demographic influences on the labour market; and international labour market comparisons.

The EPSG is a research/study group whose membership spans all the major European countries. The group focuses on problems of production, employment and technological change. The EPSG has been operating since 1978, actively encouraging members to correspond and meet on a regular basis for national and international conferences. The members bring a variety of disciplines to bear, depending on the topic covered, including economics, management and engineering.

DEREK BOSWORTH
DAVID F. HEATHFIELD

Part I
Capacity Measures

1 The CBI Industrial Trends Survey and Capacity Working

B. C. Rosewell

INTRODUCTION

This chapter describes the CBI Survey of Industrial Trends and how it is analysed and interpreted. The CBI conducts the Survey, and each month comments upon the results. We undertake occasional research work using the Survey, and we strongly welcome and encourage other research using our data. This chapter also outlines some considerations on capacity and capacity working from the Survey data.

THE CBI SURVEY

Each month CBI conducts a survey of around 1700 to 1800 firms in the manufacturing sector. The questionnaire is sent to a panel of firms who are not all CBI members, and most of the larger ones answer regularly each month; not all of the smaller ones do so. Coverage is approximately 56 per cent of manufacturing employment (in mid-1984). This breaks down as follows, using the most recent statistics available at the time of writing:

No. of employees	Average no. of firms responding	% of total employment in size band in 1979
Over 5000	48	66
500–4999	357	60
200–499	382	24
Under 200	855	6

Each month the questionnaire asks a very simple set of questions which require only the answer 'up/down/same' or 'above/below/normal'. It asks about total and export orders in relation to 'normal', the adequacy (or otherwise) of finished goods stocks, and about the direction of expected output and price changes over the next four months. Every three months a rather longer questionnaire is sent out, including the regular monthly questions, but also asking about the actual volume of output, about stocks, investment, capacity working, the constraints on output and investment and the reasons for investment. The questionnaires are included as Appendix A1.1.

Since the Survey's origin in 1958, questions have been added over the years, but very infrequently changed. The only major change has been to ask questions about output and order volumes (rather than values) since 1975. The reason for this apparent conservativeness has to do with the interpretation of tendency surveys. Questions are asked in the up/same/down format for two reasons. First, they are easy to answer and this helps considerably both in gaining participants and in ensuring that questionnaires are filled in at a high level within the firm. Secondly, it enables questions to be asked in the same context about expectations as well as actuality. This latter advantage has generated increasing interest in the Survey as expectations have become more important in modelling economic behaviour.

The disadvantage of such questions is that it requires a reasonable time series before they can be interpreted. This generates reluctance to change questions and break the series unless it is absolutely necessary, which was obviously the case with volume and value as inflation mounted during the 1970s. Even where it is clear that questions are being answered in different ways by different respondents, it may still be better to interpret the question and answers in this light rather than risk getting different answering practices (and unknown reliability) by changing it.

An example is the question about business optimism asked in the Quarterly Survey and which is used in the Central Statistics Office (CSO) composite leading indicator. The question asks:

Are you more or less optimistic than you were four months ago about the general business situation in your industry?

In a Survey on answering practices in 1982 (Ballance and Burton (1983)) it was established that about half the respondents answer with respect to levels of optimism rather than changes. In other words, of the respondents who are just as pessimistic as they were four months ago, about 50 per cent will tick the box marked 'less' and 50 per cent the box marked 'same'. However, changing the question would not only create a break in the series so that it would be impossible to interpret the results for some time, but probably also generate a different set of peculiarities in answering. So change is not undertaken lightly.

Having collected in all the questionnaires, which is done over a Survey period of about a fortnight, the next stage is to analyse the results. These are always published no more than a fortnight after the closing date: indeed the results of one Survey are sent out with the questionnaire for the next.

Sometimes the schedule is still tighter: for a short Monthly Enquiry the Survey may close on a Wednesday, have the computer run on Thursday, be written up and a Press Statement prepared on Friday, for publication in the Press on Monday. Up-to-date information is thus always available, but obviously all that is possible is less detailed analysis than we might sometimes like.

In computing the results of each Survey, every company is allocated to one of fifty individual industries, according to its main activity, drawn from the Standard Industrial Classification (SIC). Some large multi-product firms provide more than one response covering their different activities. A list of these is given in Appendix A1.2. Four employment size bands are also used. A weighting frame, supplied by the Business Statistics Office, is then applied to the results in each individual industry and size band cell. The weighting frame is necessary because the sample is not structured in any way. We make every effort to ensure a reasonably-sized population in each cell with continual activity in recruiting new participants. The weights are updated periodically, those currently used are for 1980.

For exports, no official weights are available. Instead the Survey is used to generate them. Companies are asked which of 10 bands their export value falls into, and average exports are computed for each cell, as a geometric mean. These are multiplied by the total number of enterprises in each cell (1980) to form the weighting frame. The main results are thus base weighted, while exports have a mix of base and current weighting.

INTERPRETATION

The CBI traditionally has commented on the so-called 'balance' statistic – i.e. the weighted percentage answering 'up' less the weighted percentage answering 'down' – using the time series of the balance on particular questions to gain an impression of the movement of the variable asked about. Positive balances imply upward movement in (say) output; larger positive balances than in the previous month imply a faster rate of increase than before. This method of interpretation has, in our experience, tracked well in most cases the actual statistics for the variable concerned provided by the CSO.

This of course implicitly involves transforming the balance statistic into a percentage rate of change for comparison with the official rate of change. Doing this suggests that we believe the distribution of responses to the questions follow a rectangular distribution.

Down	Same	Up

d_1 $\bar{x}$ d_2

d_1 and d_2 measure the boundaries of the indifference interval within which change in the variable is not perceived.

The rectangular distribution implies that if the proportion replying 'same' increases while leaving those replying 'up' and 'down' in the same relationship to each other x – the mean of the variable – will remain unchanged. This statistic has been used from the early work with tendency surveys and follows Theil (1966).

At first sight, such a distribution looks unlikely. It is more reasonable to suppose that answers are bunched round the mean, and follow a more nearly normal distribution, and this was the assumption made by Carlson and Parkin (1975) when they used Gallup poll data to generate a series for price expectations. It is indeed likely when questions refer to a macro variable such as the rate of inflation, which everybody is asked about. However, it should be remembered that the CBI Survey does not ask about an aggregate variable: it asks about the individual experiences of the responding firms, and then weights these together. In this case, it may well be that a rectangular distribution is more probable than a normal one. Some firms and industries will be doing better than the average, and some will be doing less well. Within an industry, however, perhaps a normal distribution will be the more likely, as firms within an industry may be more clustered around the mean. Investigation by Wren-Lewis (1985) suggests that a more normal distribution is better, and the CBI is doing further work on this problem.

For the present time, we shall continue to use the balance statistic, using it to track and predict output and other changes in variables.

Implicitly we are transforming the balance by a factor k to turn it into the equivalent of a percentage change. Figure 1.1 indicates how well the survey has predicted manufacturing output changes where $k = 0.1$. The CSO have usually used a factor of 0.125 here. While not a perfect fit, the changes predicted by the Survey have often been closer to the final figure than the provisional official statistic. In November 1984 we said that the Survey suggested that the index of manufacturing output was about 1 point too low. The following month it was revised up about 0.8, and in January another 0.5. Preliminary results suggest that using the trends balance in a regression to predict the level of manufacturing output over 1981 and 1982 would give a lower average error than using the provisional official statistic (Robinson (1985)).

Figure 1.1 Manufacturing output comparisons

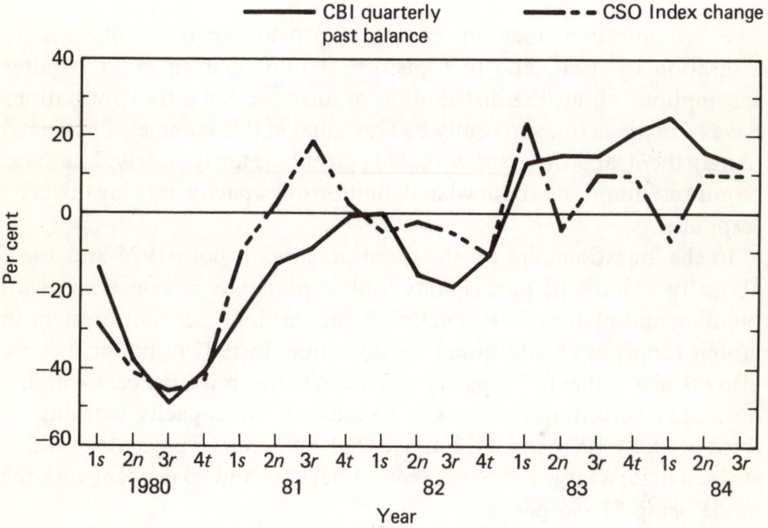

Quarterly data relates to January, April, July and October of each year.

(a) Capacity and Output

The Survey provides two ways of looking at capacity which may be more useful than the Wharton method of defining capacity from peak to peak, especially in a period in which it is not clear where local peaks exist.

Firstly the Survey asks a question:

Is your present level of output below capacity (i.e., are you working below a satisfactory full rate of operation)?

Secondly it asks about factors that are expected to constrain output over the next four months, and categorises these as follows:

Shortage of orders or sales
Skilled labour
Other labour
Plant capacity
Credit or finance
Materials or components.

The first question does not of course provide an index of capacity utilisation by itself, and to transform it into such an index requires assumptions about the distribution of answers. Such transformations have been made (most recently by Dewhurst in this volume). These tend to map the straightforward weighted percentage fairly closely. They also require assumptions about what definition of 'capacity' is being taken by respondents.

In the 'questionnaire on the questionnaire' in both 1976 and 1982, about two-thirds of participants took capacity to be concerned with building and plant: of the remaining one-third, 60 per cent brought in labour supply as an additional consideration. In 1982 respondents were also asked whether full capacity was taken to mean 100 per cent – and, if not, what percentage was taken to indicate full-capacity working. A third did take 100 per cent, but over half took it as a percentage which showed quite a large range between 71 per cent and 90 per cent with the mode being 81–85 per cent.

This varying behaviour by participants means that constructing an index of capacity and capacity utilisation is quite complicated, and will require strong simplifying assumptions. However, so long as participants have individually consistent definitions then changes in the percentage of respondents reporting excess capacity will certainly measure changes in the pressure of output on capacity. This can be checked by comparing the capacity-utilisation response with the percentage of respondents indicating that lack of capacity is an actual constraint on output. This is illustrated in Figure 1.2. It can be seen that they move closely together: as capacity utilisation improves, so too does

Figure 1.2 Survey data comparisons: capacity utilisation and shortages of plant capacity

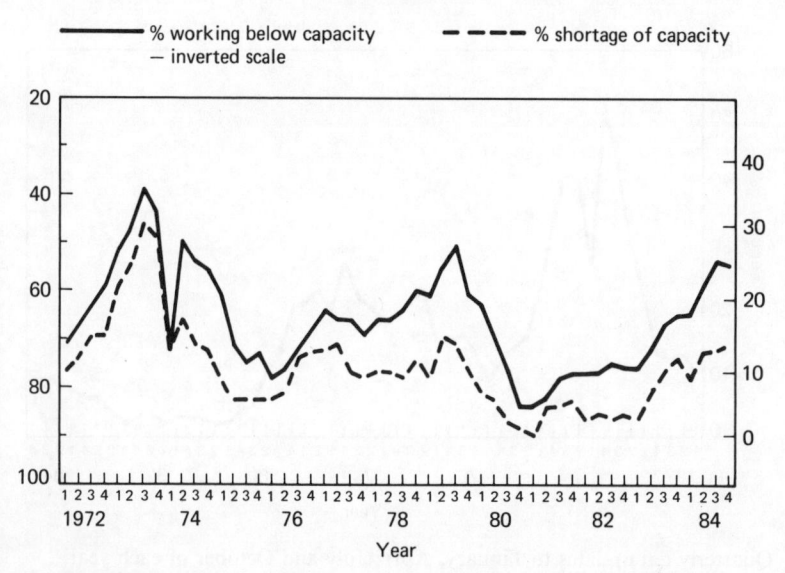

Quarterly data relates to January, April, July and October of each year.

the percentage of firms reporting capacity as a constraint. However, in 1977–8 and 1981–2 capacity utilisation began to improve, while the percentage of firms reporting capacity as a constraint remained fairly flat. This is in contrast to the 1972 recovery, when they moved strongly in line.

Skill shortages, shown in Figure 1.3 – which are another indicator of a lack of capacity in an area considered by some respondents in defining capacity – follow more closely the capacity-utilisation pattern until the most recent recovery, when skill shortages have been very slow to appear.

The capacity-utilisation question can also be used to throw some light on the difficult question of what has been happening to total capacity in manufacturing industry. In a period in which trend output was rising, local peaks could be used to identify capacity. In the last ten years, however, trend output has been downward, and in these circumstances it is not clear whether total capacity remained at its 1973 peak and how far – or when – scrapping of capital stock took place.

Statistics of the capital stock are of very little help here either. They

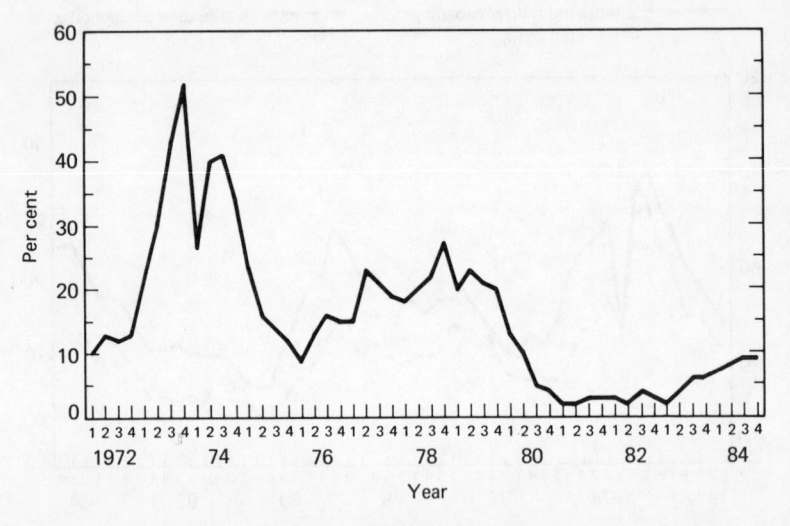

Figure 1.3 'Is shortage of skilled labour a factor likely to limit output over the next 4 months?' (Question 14)

Quarterly data relates to January, April, July and October of each year.

are derived from cumulated investment with associated estimates of rates of depreciation for different types of assets in different industries. These estimates are based on the technical rather than economic lives of the assets, and the capital stock will thus be over-estimated if economic conditions such as the oil price shocks or the depression of 1981–2 have accelerated depreciation and led to premature obsolescence of plant and buildings. Anecdotal evidence certainly suggests that such scrapping has occurred. Companies have closed, some large companies have slimmed down markedly, newspaper articles have chronicled the 'leaner' – if not fitter – state of British manufacturing industry.

If this is true and capacity has been scrapped in this way, then we would expect capacity utilisation to be improving while output remains flat, or to fall less sharply than output. Figure 1.4 shows how the balances on reported output compare with the percentage working below capacity between 1972 and 1984 and Figure 1.5 shows 1958–71. In Figure 1.5, the movements of the two series are aligned very closely with one another; in Figure 1.4, however, the relationship seems much less close.

The falls appear to be more closely matched than the rises – over the period 1981–4 capacity utilisation was steadily improving, and

Figure 1.4 Reported output volume and capacity utilisation in total manufacturing

— % balance – reported output   --- % working below capacity – inverted scale

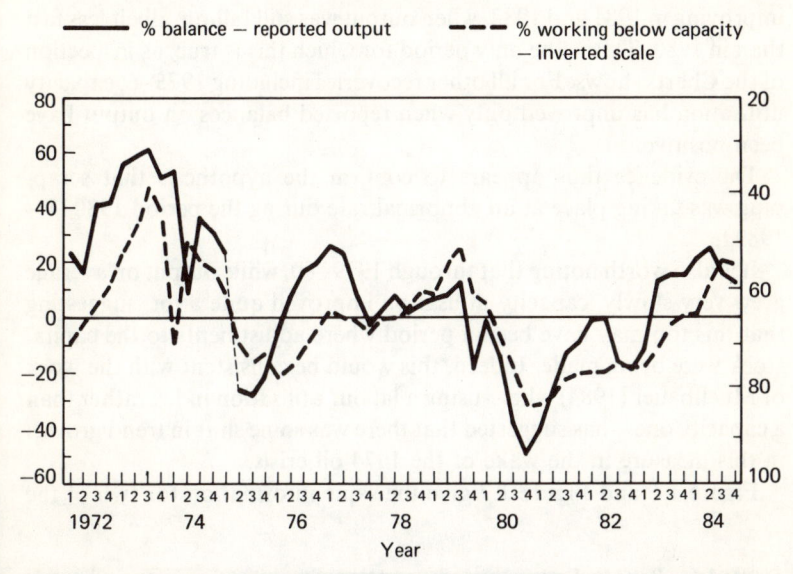

Figure 1.5 Reported value of output and capacity utilisation in total manufacturing (1958–71)

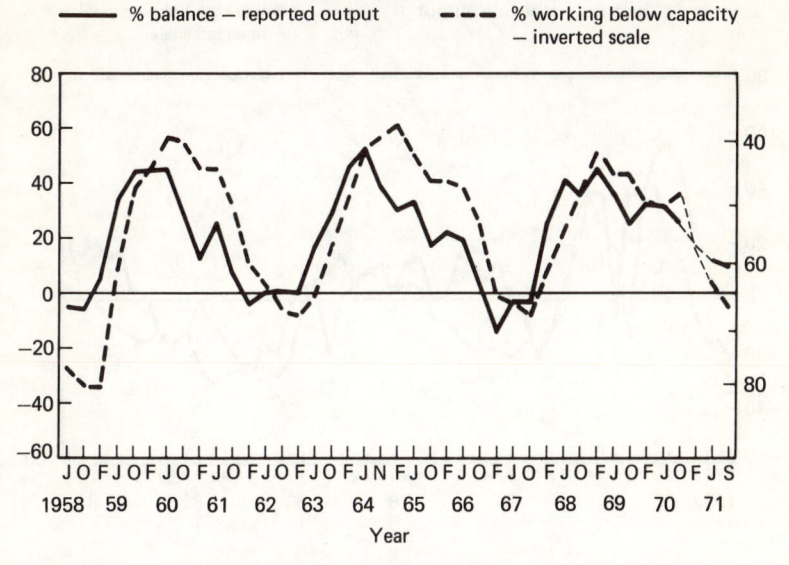

— % balance – reported output   --- % working below capacity – inverted scale

Quarterly data relates to January, April, July and October of each year.

improved more sharply once output began to rise in the first quarter of 1983 (i.e., the balances become positive). But utilisation was also improving in 1981 and 1982, when output was still falling, albeit less fast than in 1980. This is the only period for which this is true, as inspection of the Charts shows. For all other recoveries including 1975–6, capacity utilisation has improved only when reported balances on output have been positive.

The evidence thus appears to confirm the hypothesis that scrapping was taking place at an abnormal rate during the period 1980 IV–1983 I.

It is also worth noting that through 1979–80, while output on average grew very slowly, capacity utilisation improved quite a lot, suggesting that this too may have been a period where adjustments to the capital stock were being made. Indeed, this would be consistent with the work of Muellbauer (1984) who – using a labour utilisation index rather than a capacity one – has suggested that there was some shift in trend growth in this measure in the wake of the 1974 oil crisis.

Figure 1.6 and Figure 1.7 give the same information for two of the

Figure 1.6 Reported output volume and capacity utilisation in capital goods industries

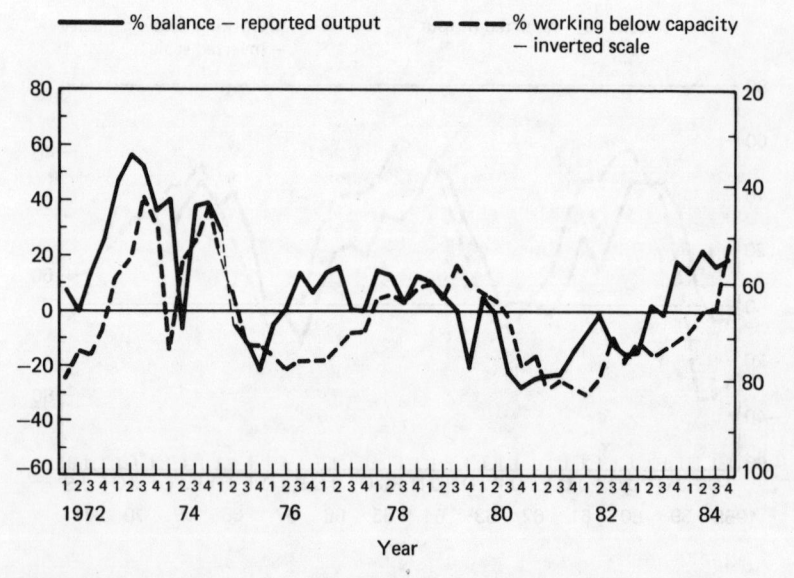

Quarterly data relates to January, April, July and October of each year.

Figure 1.7 Reported value of output and capacity utilisation in consumer goods industries

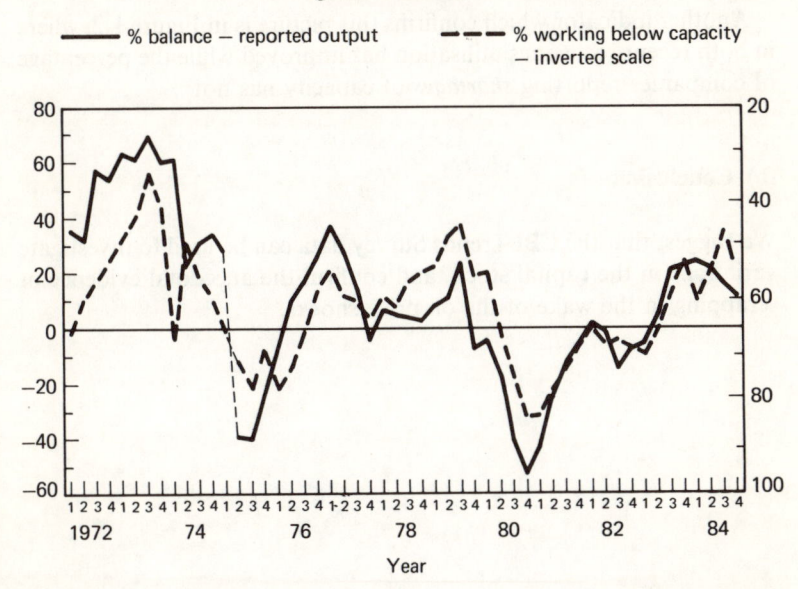

Quarterly data relates to January, April, July and October of each year.

sectors of manufacturing – that is, capital and consumer goods. Both show evidence of adjustment in the 1980–3 period, but on rather different time scales. The recovery in the capital goods sector started rather later and with output beginning to rise in 1983III, six months later than the consumer goods sector. The improvement in capacity utilisation only started in 1982II, compared with 1981I in consumer goods. In consumer goods, capacity utilisation began to improve as soon as the sharp 1980 fall in output had taken place and the decline became rather less marked. This suggests a fairly rapid adjustment. In the capital goods sector, on the other hand, the adjustment in capital stock did not begin to take place until four quarters after the output reduction had flattened out, suggesting rather slower adjustment. However, the 1976–7 period perhaps shows rather more adjustment of the capital stock in the capital goods sector than in consumer goods. Balances in this sector were certainly positive in this period, but at a rather small-level, yet capacity utilisation appears to be steadily improving throughout. In consumer goods this difference is less obvious, with capacity utilisation following output changes more closely.

Another indicator which confirms this picture is in Figure 1.2, where in both recent recoveries utilisation has improved while the percentage of companies reporting *shortages* of capacity has not.

(b) Conclusion

We suggest that the CBI Trends Survey data can be used to investigate variations in the capital stock, and confirm the anecdotal evidence of scrapping in the wake of the oil price shocks.

CBI Industrial Trends Survey   Number 95: January 1985

Please tick appropriate answers: If question not applicable, tick N/A

Please use space overleaf for any comments you would like to make on points not covered by your replies.

1. Are you more, or less, optimistic than you were four months ago about THE GENERAL BUSINESS SITUATION IN YOUR INDUSTRY

More	Same	Less
			11

2. Are you more, or less, optimistic about your EXPORT PROSPECTS for the next twelve months than you were four months ago

More	Same	Less	N/A
				12

3. Do you expect to authorise more or less capital expenditure in the next twelve months than you authorised in the past twelve months on:
   a. buildings
   b. plant & machinery

More	Same	Less	N/A
				13
				14

4. Is your present level of output below capacity (i.e., are you working below a satisfactory full rate of operation)

Yes	No	N/A
			15

5. **Excluding seasonal variations**, do you consider that in volume terms:
   a. Your present total order book is
   b. Your present export order book is
   (firms with no order book are requested to estimate the level of demand)

Above Normal	Normal	Below Normal	N/A
				16
				17

   c. Your present stocks of finished goods are

More than Adequate	Adequate	Less than Adequate	N/A
1	2	3	4	18

Excluding seasonal variations, what has been the trend over the PAST FOUR MONTHS, and what are the expected trends for the NEXT FOUR MONTHS, with regard to:

	Trend over PAST FOUR MONTHS				Expected trend over NEXT FOUR MONTHS			
	Up	Same	Down	N/A	Up	Same	Down	N/A

6. Numbers employed   19-20

7. Volume of total new orders   21-22
   of which: a. domestic orders   23-24
   b. export orders   25-26

8. Volume of output   27-28

9. Volume of: a. domestic deliveries   29-30
   b. export deliveries   31-32

10. Volume of stocks of: a. raw materials and brought in supplies   33-34
    b. work in progress   35-36
    c. finished goods   37-38

11. Average costs per unit of output   39-40

12. Average prices at which: a. domestic orders are booked   41-42
    b. export orders are booked   43-44

Industrial Trends Survey
January 1985

Confidential

Number 95

Confederation of British Industry
Industrial Trends Department
Centre Point
103 New Oxford Street
London WC1A 1DU

Telephone 01-379 7400

For office use only

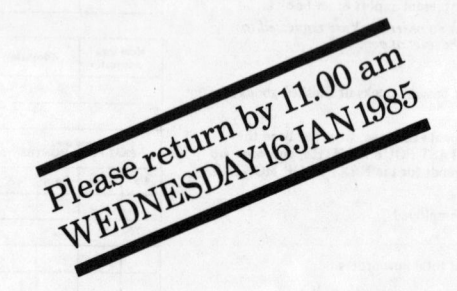

| | | 1 | 1-10 |

Please return by 11.00 am WEDNESDAY 16 JAN 1985

13. Approximately how many months' production is accounted for by your present order book or production schedule.

Less than 1	1-3	4-6	7-9	10-12	13-18	More than 18	N/A
1	2	3	4	5	6	7	8

45

14. What factors are likely to limit your OUTPUT over the next four months. *Please tick the most important factor or factors. If you tick more than one factor it would be helpful if you could rank them in order of importance*

Orders or Sales	Skilled Labour	Other Labour	Plant Capacity	Credit or Finance	Materials or Components	Other

46-52

15. What factors are likely to limit your ability to obtain EXPORT ORDERS over the next four months. *Please tick the most important factor or factors. If you tick more than one factor it would be helpful if you could rank them in order of importance*

Prices	Delivery Dates (compared with overseas competitors)	Credit or Finance	Quota & Import Licence Restrictions	Political or Economic Conditions Abroad	Other

53-58

16. a. In relation to expected demand over the next twelve months is your present fixed capacity:

More than adequate	adequate	less than adequate

59

b. What are the main reasons for any expected CAPITAL EXPENDITURE AUTHORISATIONS ON BUILDINGS, PLANT OR MACHINERY over the next twelve months. *If you tick more than one factor it would be helpful if you could rank them in order of importance.*

to expand capacity ☐ 60   other *(please specify)* ☐ 63
to increase efficiency ☐ 61   N/A ☐ 64
for replacement ☐ 62

c. What factors are likely to limit (wholly or partly) your capital expenditure authorisations over the next twelve months. *If you tick more than one factor it would be helpful if you could rank them in order of importance.*

Inadequate net return on proposed investment ☐ 65   Uncertainty about demand ☐ 69
Shortage of internal finance ☐ 66   Shortage of labour including Managerial and Technical Staff ☐ 70
Inability to raise external finance ☐ 67   Other *(please specify)* ☐ 71
Cost of finance ☐ 68   N/A ☐ 72

Please enter here the code number of the main manufacturing activity covered by this return (See Standard Industrial Classification circulated previously). ☐ 73-76

How many EMPLOYEES are covered by this return

(a) 0 – 199 ☐   (b) 200 – 499 ☐   (c) 500 – 4,999 ☐   (d) 5,000 and over ☐ 77

What is the annual ex-works value of your direct EXPORTS

Nil – £75th	£75th – £1m	£1m – £3m	£3m – £8m	£8m – £15m	£15m – £25m	£25m – £40m	£40m – £60m	£60m – £100m	£100m – £150m	Over £150m
0	1	2	3	4	5	6	7	8	9	10

78

Signature ....

Company ....
(Block Capitals)

Address ....

Note: If you wish your reply to remain anonymous, please detach this slip and return it under separate cover

Monthly Trends Enquiry
MAY 1985

Please return by 22 May 1985

Confederation of British Industry
Industrial Trends Department
Centre Point
103 New Oxford Street
London WC1A 1DU

Telephone 01-379 7400

For office use only

Please tick appropriate answers.
If question is not applicable, tick N/A

Excluding seasonal variations, do you consider that in volume terms:

(1) a. Your present total order book is
    b. Your present export order book is
    (firms with no order book are requested to estimate the level of demand)

	Above Normal	Normal	Below Normal	N/A
				11
				12

(2) Your present stocks of finished goods are

	More than Adequate	Adequate	Less than Adequate	N/A
				13

What, excluding seasonal variations, is the expected trend over the <u>next four months</u> with regard to:

(3) Volume of output
(4) Average prices at which domestic orders are booked.

	Up	Same	Down	N/A
				14
				15
	1	2	3	4

Please enter here the code number of the <u>main</u> manufacturing activity covered by this return (see Standard Industrial Classification previously circulated).   16-19

How many EMPLOYEES are covered by this return

(a) 0–199   (b) 200–499   (c) 500–4,999   (d) 5,000 and over   20

What is the annual ex-works value of your <u>direct</u> EXPORTS

Nil – £75th	£75th – £1m	£1m – £3m	£3m – £8m	£8m – £15m	£15m – £25m	£25m – £40m	£40m – £60m	£60m – £100m	£100m – £150m	Over £150m
0	1	2	3	4	5	6	7	8	9	10

21

Signature ....

Company ....
(Block Capitals)
Address ....

Note: If you wish your reply to remain anonymous, please detach this slip and return it under separate cover

A1.2 STANDARD INDUSTRIAL CLASSIFICATION

The classification used in the Survey is based on the 1980 Stanard Industrial Classification's Group and Activity Headings, published by HMSO.

Table 1	Total Manufacturing	– Tables 23 to 71
Table 2	Total Manufacturing (old definition)	– Tables 22, 24 to 71
Table 7	Capital goods industries	– Tables 35, 36, 37, 38, 39, 40, 41, 42, 43, 4, 45, 46, 47, 51, 52 and 53
Table 8	Intermediate goods industries	– Tables 22, 23, 24, 25, 26, 27, 28, 29, 31, 32, 33, 34, 56, 57, 60, 62, 64, 66, 67, 69 and 70
Table 9	Consumer goods industries	– Tables 30, 48, 49, 50, 54, 55, 58, 59, 61, 63, 65, 68 and 71
Table 10	Food, drink and tobacco	– Tables 54 and 55
Table 11	Chemicals	– Tables 28, 29, 30 and 31
Table 12	Metal manufacture	– Tables 24 and 25
Table 13	Engineering and allied industries	– Tables 32, 33, 34, 35, 36, 37, 38, 39, 40, 41, 42, 43, 44, 45, 46, 47, 48, 49, 50, 51, 52 and 53
Table 14	Textiles	– Tables 56, 57, 58, 59, 60, 61, 62 and 63
Table 15	Other manufacturing	– Tables 23, 26, 27, 64, 65, 66, 67, 68, 69, 70 and 71
Table 16	Mechanical engineering	– Tables 35, 36, 37, 38, 39, 40, 41, 42, 43 and 44
Table 17	Electrical and instrument engineering	– Tables 45, 46, 47, 48, 49 and 53
Table 18	Metal products	– Tables 32, 33 and 34
Table 19	Paper, printing and publishing	– Tables 66, 67 and 68
Table 20	All other manufacturing	– Tables 23, 26, 27, 64, 65, 69, 70 and 71
Table 21	Motor vehicles and other transport equipment	– Tables 50, 51 and 52
Table 22	Coal and petroleum products	– 1115, 120, 140 and 152
Table 23	Extraction of minerals and metalliferous ores	– 210, 231, 233 and 239
Table 24	Ferrous metals	– 221, 222 and 223
Table 25	Non-ferrous metals	– 224

A1.2 *(Contd.)*

Table	Description	Codes
Table 26	Building materials	241, 242, 243, 244, 245 and 246
Table 27	Glass and ceramics	247 and 248
Table 28	Industrial chemicals	2511, 2512, 2514, 2515, 2516, 2562, 2563, 2564, 2565, 2567 and 2569
Table 29	Agricultural chemicals	2568 and 2513
Table 30	Pharmaceuticals and consumer chemicals	255, 257, 258 and 259
Table 31	Man made fibres	260
Table 32	Foundries; and forging, pressing and stamping	311 and 312
Table 33	Metals goods n.e.s	313, 314, 3162, 3163, 3164, 3165, 3166, 3167 and 3169
Table 34	Hand tools and implements	3161
Table 35	Constructional steelwork	3204
Table 36	Heavy industrial plant	3205
Table 37	Agricultural machinery	321
Table 38	Metal working machine tools	3221
Table 39	Engineers' small tools	3222
Table 40	Industrial machinery	323, 324, 327, 3285 and 3286
Table 41	Contractors' plant	325
Table 42	Industrial engines, pumps and compressors	3281, 3283, 3287 and 3288
Table 43	Heating, ventilating and refrigerating equipment	3284
Table 44	Other mechanical engineering	326, 3289 and 329
Table 45	Office machinery and data processing equipment	330
Table 46	Electrical industrial goods	341, 342, 343, 3442, 347 and 348
Table 47	Electronic industrial goods	3441, 3443, 3444 and 3453
Table 48	Electrical consumer goods	346
Table 49	Electronic consumer goods	3452 and 3454
Table 50	Motor vehicles	351, 352 and 353
Table 51	Shipbuilding	361
Table 52	Aerospace and other vehicles	362, 363, 364 and 365

Table 53	Instrument engineering	—371, 372, 373 and 374
Table 54	Food	—411, 412, 413, 414, 415, 416, 418, 419, 420, 421, 422 and 423
Table 55	Drink and tobacco	—424, 426, 427, 428 and 429
Table 56	Wool textiles	—431
Table 57	Spinning and weaving	—432, 433 and 434
Table 58	Hosiery and knitwear	—436
Table 59	Textile consumer goods	—438, 4555 and 4557
Table 60	Other textiles	—435, 436, 439 and 4556
Table 61	Footwear	—451
Table 62	Leather and leather goods	—441 and 442
Table 63	Clothing and fur	—453 and 456
Table 64	Timber and wooden products other than furniture	—461, 462, 463, 464, 465 and 466
Table 65	Furniture, upholstery and bedding	—467
Table 66	Pulp, paper and board	—471
Table 67	Paper and board products	—472
Table 68	Printing and publishing	—475
Table 69	Rubber products	—481 and 482
Table 70	Plastics products	—483
Table 71	Other	—491, 492, 493, 494 and 495

References

BALLANCE, D. C. and BURTON, C. P. H. (1883) 'Answering Practices in the CBI Industrial Trends Survey', in 'Twenty-five years of "ups" and "downs"' (London: CBI).

CARLSON, J. A. and PARKIN, M. (1975) 'Inflation Expectations', *Economica* 42, pp. 123–380.

DEWHURST, J. H. Ll. (1981) *Capacity Utilisation and Below-capacity Working*, Chapter 3 below.

MUELLBAUER, J. (1984) 'Aggregate production functions and productivity measurements: a new look', CEPR discussion paper 34.

ROBINSON, G. N. (1985) 'The Use of Trends Survey Data in Measuring Manufacturing Output', CBI *Economic Situation Report* (March).

THEIL, H. (1966) *Applied Economic Forecasting* (Amsterdam: North Holland).

WREN-LEWIS, S. (1985) 'The Quantification of Survey Data Expectations', *National Institute of Economic and Social Research* (forthcoming).

2 Trend-Through-Peaks Methods of Estimating Capacity Utilisation
Richard Harris and Jim Taylor[1]

Information about the rate at which a nation's productive resources are being utilised is essential if policymakers take the view that one of their primary functions is to maintain a satisfactory level of capacity utilisation. Most economists and policymakers, for example, would argue that it is the government's responsibility to prevent both the over-utilisation of productive capacity (in order to avoid the emergence of inflationary pressure) and the under-utilisation of productive capacity (in order to avoid wasting scarce resources).

A necessary prerequisite to achieving a satisfactory level of capacity utilisation is the construction of a reasonably accurate measure of this variable – preferably for individual industries so that potential supply bottlenecks can be accurately identified. Two quite different approaches have been used. First, there is the survey method whereby firms are approached directly and asked to state their current level of capacity utilisation. This method has recently been adopted by the Fraser of Allander Institute at the University of Strathclyde in its quarterly *Scottish Business Survey*. Second, many attempts have been made to estimate capacity utilisation from time series data on output and related variables.[2] The latter methods sometimes rely on output data alone, such as the Wharton trend-through-peaks approach, whilst other methods use both output data and input data in order to estimate the limit on output imposed by the availability of factor supplies.[3]

The present chapter concentrates entirely on the methods that have been developed to estimate capacity utilisation from time series data on output and related variables. Specifically, we aim to describe and appraise various methods based on the trend-through-peaks approach. These range from the simple (but appealing) device of fitting straight lines to selected cyclical peaks in the output level (i.e., the Wharton method) to more complex techniques based upon fitting production functions to output data. The main object of the exercise is to discover whether approaches to estimating capacity utilisation based upon production function techniques offer any significant advantages over the use of the simpler Wharton trend-through-peaks method.

This chapter is in five sections. The first briefly discusses the concept of capacity output. Various methods of estimating capacity utilisation based upon the trend-through-peaks approach are then described. This is followed by a discussion of the methods employed to obtain a measure of the capital stock. Several estimated production functions for four United Kingdom industries are then presented and appraised. Finally, estimates of capacity utilisation based upon the methods discussed in the second section are compared.

CAPACITY OUTPUT

Fundamental to all methods of estimating capacity utilisation is the concept of 'capacity output'. Once capacity ouput has been estimated, capacity utilisation is then calculated by expressing *actual* output as a percentage of *capacity* output. But what exactly is capacity output?

In economic theory, capacity output is often defined as the level of output consistent with minimum long-run average costs. This definition differs from the *technical* concept of capacity output. The latter refers to the asymptotic limit of output which is determined by production techniques, the available stock of factors of production, and the maximum utilisation rate of each factor. Circumstances force us to take a more pragmatic view of capacity ouput in the present chapter. We assume here that an industry reaches its capacity level of output during those periods of time when output is at a cyclical peak. We further assume that an industry is producing on its production frontier at cyclical output peaks, and hence that peak output accurately reflects the *economic* capacity of the industry.

Since an industry is assumed to be operating on its production frontier at cyclical output peaks, it follows that spare productive capacity exists during interpeak periods. The existence of spare capacity means that firms are using fewer inputs than are available to them – either because the prices of these inputs are too high relative to the price of the output produced, or because the demand for output at existing prices is temporarily depressed. Firms are assumed to be producing at less than their capacity output during interpeak periods through *choice*. Spare capacity therefore exists because firms find it more profitable not to produce on their capacity ceiling. Yet this spare capacity is part of the industry's *economic* capacity as long as the industry anticipates that the spare capacity may be required in the foreseeable future in order to meet an increase in the demand for its output. It should also be noted that firms do not bear all the costs of carrying spare capacity themselves since workers may be laid off or may be working a shorter work week than they would prefer.

METHODS OF ESTIMATING UTILISATION

Three approaches to measuring capacity utilisation are discussed in this section. These three approaches are related in the sense that they all rely upon a trend-through-peaks procedure. We first consider the simplest of these, namely the Wharton method.

(a) The Wharton Method

The Wharton trend-through-peaks technique was devised by Klein (1960), who suggested that capacity output could be approximated by fitting straight lines to selected peak levels of output. Capacity utilisation is then calculated by expressing actual output as a percentage of estimated capacity output.

This device has the great attraction of simplicity and intuitive appeal. Its accuracy, however, is heavily dependent upon the validity of two assumptions. First, the selected output peaks are assumed to be of equal – or at least very similar – strength, and second capacity output is assumed to move along a linear time path between output peaks. The first assumption is probably the most critical, since an acceptable method of measuring the strength of individual peaks has not yet been discovered. Selecting output peaks therefore tends to rely heavily upon the judgement of the operator. This is clearly demonstrated in Figure 2.1, which shows the output peaks selected in the present study. The problem is highlighted by the difficulty of deciding whether a peak occurred in the 1979 mini-boom. Only in Food, Drink and Tobacco was the 1979 output peak above the output peak recorded in 1973. The choice for the other three industries is therefore between (i) extrapolating estimated capacity output from the 1973 boom through to 1982, and (ii) assuming that output reached its capacity level during the 1979 mini-boom. We have opted for the latter approach as far as the Wharton index is concerned. It is therefore possible that capacity output has been underestimated for these three industries since the output peak recorded in the 1979 mini-boom is likely to have been a relatively weak one for most manufacturing industries. This is supported by other evidence, such as the index of

Figure 2.1 Estimated capacity output: Wharton method and actual output (1956–82)

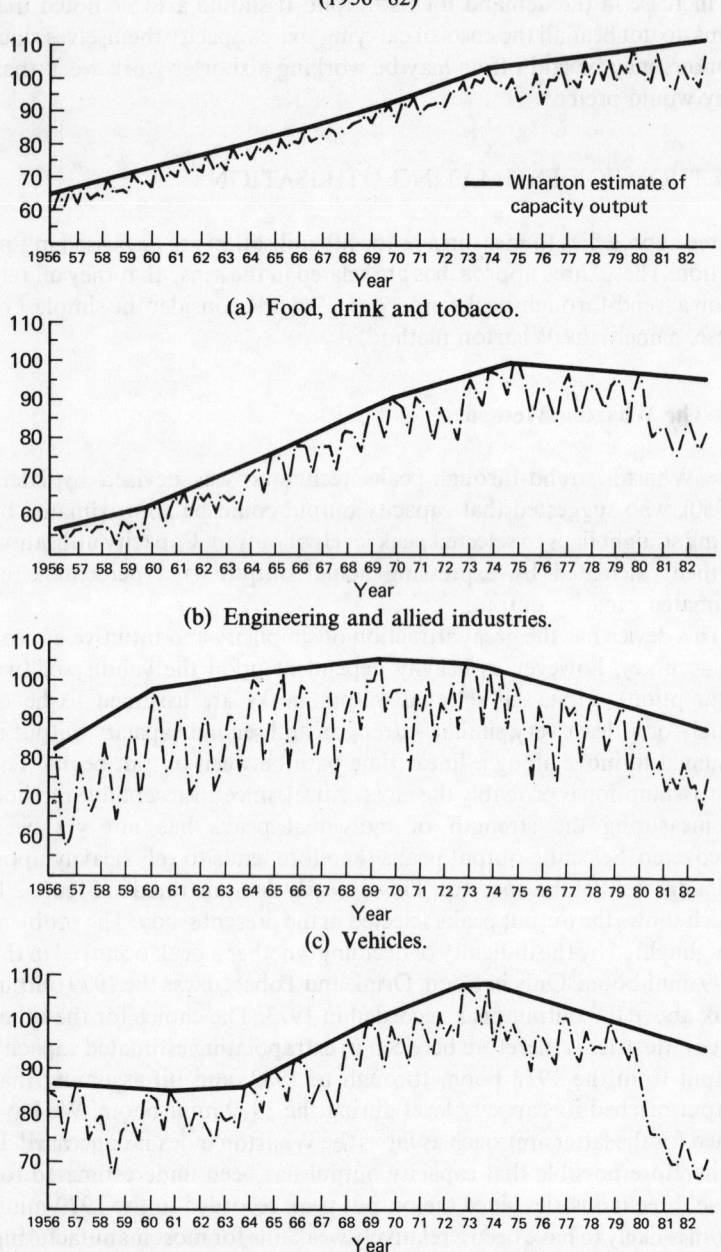

(a) Food, drink and tobacco.

(b) Engineering and allied industries.

(c) Vehicles.

(d) Textiles, leather and clothing

capacity utilisation provided by the Confederation of British Industry (CBI) and by the fact that the United Kingdom unemployment rate was about twice as high in 1979 as it was in 1973. The alternative procedure of extrapolating the linear trend fitted to the 1973 output peak was rejected since this would mean that estimates of capacity output for the 1974–82 period would then be based upon output trends established during the 1960s and early 1970s.

Selecting output peaks is clearly a hazardous procedure.

(b) The Capital Productivity Method

An obvious extension to the Wharton method is to estimate capacity output by utilising information not only about output but also about the relationship between output and available inputs. Since the amount of output that can be produced during any given period of time is constrained by the available stock of plant and machinery, estimates of capacity utilisation can be obtained by fitting straight lines to peaks in the output–capital stock ratio and then using the following formula:[4]

$$CU_t = \frac{Y_t/K_t}{(Y_t/K_t)^*} \times 100 \qquad (2.1)$$

where
CU_t = % capacity utilisation at t
Y_t/K_t = ratio of net output to capital stock at t
$(Y_t/K_t)^*$ = estimated full capacity levels of Y_t/K_t, obtained by interpolating between selected peak levels of Y_t/K_t.

The advantage of the capital productivity method over the Wharton method is that the estimates of capacity output are subject to a capital constraint. An obvious disadvantage is that it ignores any constraints on output resulting from the availability of non-capital inputs (such as labour). Moreover, it fails to allow for factor substitution between capital and labour inputs that may be occurring in the short term in response to relative shortages and surpluses, or in the long term in response to changes in relative factor prices. To meet unexpected increases in demand, for example, firms often resort to increases in overtime working, extra shifts and weekend work. More labour can therefore be employed to utilise existing capital more intensively – provided more labour is available at an acceptable wage level.

Since output may be constrained not simply by the availability of capital inputs at cyclical output peaks but also by the availability of other inputs – particularly labour – this suggests that estimates of capacity output should take capital and labour supplies into account simultaneously. Such an approach points towards a method based upon an acceptable production function.

(c) The Production Function Method

The production function approach to estimating capacity utilisation is based upon the notion that output is constrained by the availability of factor inputs and by currently available production technology. Treating output and inputs as if they were homogeneous, and assuming that output is produced with only two factors of production (capital and labour), the following function describes a general relationship between output and required inputs:

$$Y = F(K, L) \tag{2.2}$$

where:

Y, K and L = respectively net output, capital and labour.

The function F describes the technological relationship between output and these two inputs. Output is therefore constrained not only by available supplies of K and L, but also be currently available technology.

To estimate capacity output by the production function approach, it is first necessary to specify a particular functional form of equation (2.2) so that the parameters of the relationship can be estimated. We need to know the contribution of K and L (via the technology F) to the creation of output. Once these parameters have been estimated, capacity output itself can be estimated for the study period by substituting estimates of the available supplies of capital and labour into the production function.

Although a number of alternative functional forms are available for equation (2.2), we have restricted our investigation in the present chapter to the Cobb–Douglas and CES production functions. These are as follows (omitting time subscripts):

$$Y = A K_s^\alpha L_s^\beta \tag{2.3}$$

and

$$Y = [\alpha K_s^{\frac{\sigma-1}{\sigma}} + \beta L_s^{\frac{\sigma-1}{\sigma}}]^{\frac{v\sigma}{\sigma-1}} \tag{2.4}$$

where:

Y = net output
K_s = capital services used up in producing Y
L_s = labour services used up in producing Y
$A, \alpha, \beta, \sigma, v$ = parameters to be estimated.

Note that both the Cobb–Douglas and the CES production functions express output and inputs as *flows* during a specific time period. As Desai (1976) points out, the production function makes sense only if inputs are measured as flows. Moreover, no attempt is made to measure the influence of technical change on output growth by including an exponential time trend.[5] The existence of a close correlation between the capital stock series and an exponential time trend means that it is not possible to disentangle the influence of technical progress from that of the growth in the capital stock. The capital stock variable is therefore likely to incorporate both effects.

There are serious practical problems, however, in obtaining accurate quantitative estimates of K_s and L_s. It is often assumed that a proportional relationship exists between the available stock of a factor and the services extracted from that stock. But this assumption is unsatisfactory in time series estimates of production functions, since the utilisation rate of a firm's capital stock and the labour it employs may fluctuate markedly over time. Measurements of the stock of factor inputs cannot therefore be used as proxies for input flows if an accurate estimate of the relationship between output, capital and labour is to be obtained.

A more acceptable way of measuring input flows would be to use man hours as an estimate of the labour input and machine hours as an estimate of the capital input.[6] But data on machine hours are not available and there are problems with using man hours to estimate the labour services actually used up in production. First, the average work week is determined in part by contractual agreements between employers and workers. Second, employers may be reluctant to reduce the work week during periods of slack product demand if this is expected to harm worker morale. For both reasons, firms may find that they are under-utilising their employed workforce during recessions.[7] Man hours worked will therefore tend to over-estimate the input of labour when output demand is temporarily slack.

Attempts to overcome the problem that we do not have *direct* measures of capital and labour inputs have taken two routes. First, production functions have been estimated from a data set which has been selected so that the utilisation rate of capital and labour is approximately equal for all observations included in the sample. Both capital and labour will be close to full utilisation, for example, at peaks in the business cycle, and a production function can therefore be fitted simply to peak output levels (as suggested by Klein and Preston (1967)).[8] Non-peak observations are discarded. The capital and labour services used up in production at peak output levels are therefore assumed to be proportionately related to the respective capital and labour stocks owned or employed by the firm at these peaks. The production functions given by equations (2.3) and (2.4) above can therefore be rewritten as follows;

$$\bar{Y}_t = A\bar{K}_t^\alpha \bar{L}_t^\beta \qquad (2.5)$$

and

$$\bar{Y}_t = [\alpha \bar{K}_t^{\frac{\sigma-1}{\sigma}} + \beta \bar{L}_t^{\frac{\sigma-1}{\sigma}}]^{\frac{\nu\sigma}{\sigma-1}} \qquad (2.6)$$

where:

$\bar{Y}$, $\bar{K}$ and $\bar{L}$ signifies that the parameters of each equation describe the relationship between *peak* output and the corresponding peak values of capital and labour.

The primary disadvantage of estimating capacity output from a data set which is selected to include only output peaks is that a large proportion of available data is not being utilised. The logic underlying this approach is that the non-peak data should be discarded since neither the capital stock nor the man hours purchased by employers are accurate measures of the capital and labour services used up in production (except at output peaks).

There is, however, an alternative to discarding non-peak data from the sample of observations. This involves using the trend-through-peaks approach to obtain estimates of the capital and labour services used up in production for the entire time period. Straight lines are first fitted to the observed peaks in the output/capital stock and output/man hours ratios to provide estimates of peak capital productivity and peak labour productivity for interpeak periods. The actual capital and labour productivities are then expressed as a proportion of the estimated peak productivities:

$$k_t = \frac{Y_t/K_t}{(Y_t/K_t)^*} \quad \text{and} \quad l_t = \frac{Y_t/L_t}{(Y_t/L_t)^*} \qquad (2.7)$$

These estimates of the utilisation rate of capital and labour are then used to obtain estimates of the capital and labour services used up in production (omitting time sub-scripts):

$$K_s = kK \quad \text{and} \quad L_s = lL \qquad (2.8)$$

Equations (2.3) and (2.4) can now be estimated directly.

MEASURING THE CAPITAL STOCK

Estimates of the capital stock are needed for both the capital productivity method and the production function method of estimating capacity utilisation. It is therefore important to select an appropriate measure of the capital stock.

Two estimates of the capital stock, computed by the perpetual inventory method, are available from the CSO: the *net* capital stock and the *gross* capital stock. The net stock is simply the gross capital stock less capital consumption (i.e., economic depreciation plus retirements). The net stock is preferred to the gross stock since the latter does not allow for the decline in the productive capacity of capital as a result of depreciation (i.e., wear and tear as well as obsolescence). Estimating the net capital stock however requires accurate information on the depreciation pattern and retirement rate of capital assets, neither of which are directly available. This lack of direct information on capital consumption means that *ad hoc* procedures have to be used to obtain estimates of the net capital stock, the usual procedure being to assume that the capital stock renders services in equal amounts in each year of its estimated life.[9] The 'straight-line' method of estimating the rate at which depreciation removes vintage capital from the capital stock is questionable, however, since the time profile of depreciation is unlikely to have a uniform distribution. An alternative, and in our view more acceptable, procedure is to follow Denison's approach (1972, p. 102). One-quarter of the net capital stock (calculated by the straight-line method) is added to three-quarters of the gross capital stock. This procedure has the advantage that it assumes a slow rate of depreciation in the early years of a capital asset's life and a faster rate of depreciation as the capital asset approaches the end of its estimated life (see Figure 2.2).

The dearth of information about the rate at which the capital stock depreciates is not the only problem which has to be faced. Two further problems relate specifically to our study period. First, the rapidity of technical progress during the post-war years is likely to have led to a reduction in the service life of capital equipment. The actual service life is therefore likely to be lower than that assumed by the CSO in computing capital stock by the perpetual inventory method. Second, the sharp increase in fuel costs in the aftermath of the 1973 oil crisis is likely to have led to the premature scrapping of some capital stock. The capital stock estimates obtained by adding one-quarter of the net stock to three-quarters of the gross stock have therefore been amended as follows:

1. For investment undertaken after 1973 we assume that the average length-of-life estimates of the capital stock have been reduced to 75 per cent of those used by the CSO.[10]

Figure 2.2 Time pattern of capital stock: comparison of Denison and CSO estimates

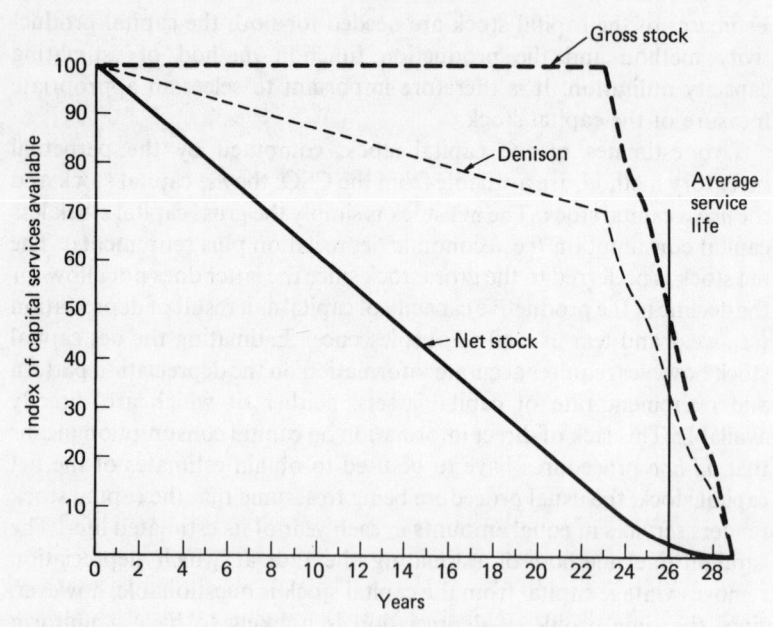

Source:
Note: Following the practice adopted by the CSO, the capital good is retired during the period 10 per cent either side of the average service life. This ensures a smoother rate of retirement and avoids the possibility of once for all significant decreases in the capital stock reflecting the retirement of assets bought during periods of very high investment (e.g., 1939–45).

2. Capital assets purchased before 1974 are assumed to have the average lives as specified by the CSO, except that the stock of these pre-1974 assets is assumed to be 20 per cent less than the CSO's value at the end of 1981.[11]

These two adjustments can be criticised on the grounds that they are arbitrary. Moreover, the required adjustments are likely to vary (perhaps substantially) between industries. Whilst these criticisms are potentially serious, we nevertheless believe that some adjustment has to be made to the official capital stock data if reliable estimates of capacity output are to be obtained.

Finally, a further adjustment needs to be made to take account of the increase in shift working in the industries during the post-war years. The average hours worked by machines has increased relative to the average hours worked by labour, not only because of a decline in the average work week but also because of the more widespread use of the shift system. In the vehicle industry, for example, only 13 per cent of workers were on a shift system in 1954 compared to 58 per cent in 1978. Estimates of the operating time of plant and machinery can be obtained from data on the percentage of workers in various types of shift system. These can then be applied to the capital stock estimates (see Appendix for details).

ESTIMATING CAPACITY OUTPUT USING THE PRODUCTION FUNCTION APPROACH

Once a suitable production function has been estimated for an industry, estimates of capacity output can be obtained by substituting the available capital and labour inputs into the estimated function. The first task, then, is to estimate an acceptable production function. A range of functions are estimated for each of four United Kingdom industry groups, since the choice of an appropriate production function is partly determined by the empirical validity of the selected function. Not only must the function fit the data well, but it must also be acceptable on theoretical grounds.

This section begins by presenting and evaluating a set of production functions estimated for each industry group. These are as follows:

1. Cobb–Douglas production function estimated from selected output peaks.
2. Cobb–Douglas production function estimated from the full data set.
3. CES production function estimated from selected output peaks.
4. CES production function estimated from the full data set.

The time period used for estimating these four production functions is 1954–82, and all were estimated from quarterly seasonally unadjusted data. An advantage of using seasonally unadjusted data is that no adjustments to the raw data are required (apart from the adjustments to the capital stock discussed in the previous section). A disadvantage is that estimated capacity output may exceed the output level that could be sustained for more than a short period of time. A quarterly output peak may be sustainable only because workers are willing to work long hours and with maximum effort for a few months in order to meet an unusually high level of demand.

The estimated production functions for each industry are given in Table 2.1. All functions were estimated directly using non-linear least squares (Hall and Hall (1980)). In all cases both the Cobb–Douglas and the CES fit the data closely. But the high values obtained for R^2

should not be taken too seriously since the sample size is very small for the equations using only peak output data, and since the equations using the entire data set have output on both sides of the equation (as a result of the way that capital and labour services are measured). A more reliable test of the estimated regression equations is to investigate the plausibility of the estimated parameters.

As far as the estimated Cobb–Douglas production functions are concerned, the estimates of α and β are more plausible when the full data set is used. This is certainly the case for Vehicles and for Textiles, Leather and Clothing. The fact that α and β sum to 2.16 and 2.38 for these two industries when peak data are used suggests that the true elasticities have not been accurately estimated. They are too high to be plausible. It should also be noted that the estimated equations for Textiles, Leather and Clothing are less reliable than those for the other three industries since the low D.W. statistic indicates that the estimated equations for this industry are misspecified. Estimates of capacity output for Textiles, Leather and Clothing obtained from the equations reported in Table 2.1 are therefore likely to be less reliable than for the other three industries.

Having estimated a production function for each industry, the next task is to use these functions for generating a capacity output series so that capacity utilisation can be estimated. To do this, it is first necessary to obtain estimates of the available supply of capital and labour inputs for the study period. These estimates of capital and labour supplies are then substituted into the estimated production functions in order to produce an estimate of capacity output. The method of estimating the capital stock available to each industry has already been described in detail in the previous section, and no further discussion is required here. The approach we have taken to estimate the labour available to each industry is very simple: straight lines have been fitted to the peaks in the time series of man hours worked. These fitted segments provide an estimate of the man hours that each industry could have called upon if output had been at its full capacity level.

ESTIMATES OF CAPACITY UTILISATION BASED ON THE WHARTON METHOD, THE CAPITAL PRODUCTIVITY METHOD AND THE PRODUCTION FUNCTION METHOD

Does it matter which method is used to estimate capacity utilisation? The estimates of capacity utilisation given in Figures 2.3 and 2.4 indicate that the estimates can vary substantially according to the method of capacity utilisation adopted.

Table 2.1 Estimated production functions for four United Kingdom industry groups

Industry and type of production function	α	β	σ	v	A	Seasonal Dummy	R^2	Log L	DW	df
Food, drink and tobacco										
(i) Peak-data:										
Cobb–Douglas	0.43 (42.4)	0.22 (2.9)			1.04		0.97	26.7		4
CES	0.59 (4.9)	0.43 (3.2)	1.59 (1.3)	0.82 (2.6)			0.98	27.1		3
(ii) All-data:										
Cobb–Douglas	0.43 (78.2)	0.20 (10.3)			1.02	−0.01 (81.8)	0.99	295.3	2.1	104
CES	0.70 (28.2)	0.28 (8.7)	0.68 (4.3)	0.57 (12.0)		−0.01 (2.5)	0.99	297.7	2.1	103
Engineering and allied industries										
(i) Peak-data:										
Cobb–Douglas	0.71 (45.1)	0.57 (5.5)			0.996		0.99	28.6		5
CES	0.56 (10.2)	0.45 (6.2)	0.41 (0.6)	1.00 (2.0)			0.99	28.8		4
(ii) All-data:										
Cobb–Douglas	0.71 (116.0)	0.29 (28.1)			1.00	0.01 (4.0)	0.99	307.1	2.1	102

Table 2.1 (Contd.)

Industry and type of production function	α	β	σ	v	A	Seasonal Dummy	R^2	Log L	DW	df
CES	0.71 (95.4)	0.29 (38.5)	0.80 (5.0)	0.97 (30.8)		0.01 (4.1)	0.99	307.8	2.2	101
Vehicles										
(i) Peak-data:										
Cobb–Douglas	0.79 (24.9)	1.37 (15.2)			0.998		0.99	24.2		3
CES	0.37 (16.5)	0.63 (28.2)	1.17 (2.5)	2.22 (10.5)			0.99	24.4		2
(ii) All-data:										
Cobb–Douglas	0.61 (26.1)	0.47 (12.6)			1.03	0.03 (3.4)	0.89	185.2	1.6	103
CES	0.54 (19.9)	0.45 (20.8)	0.76 (4.1)	1.05 (16.0)		0.03 (3.4)	0.89	186.9	1.7	102
Textiles, leather and clothing										
(i) Peak-data										
Cobb–Douglas	1.47 (4.7)	0.91 (2.7)			1.069		0.99	22.2		4
CES	0.74 (62.3)	0.29 (36.4)	2.83 (8.1)	2.00 (31.7)			0.99	40.0		3

(ii) All-data:

Cobb–Douglas	0.80 (86.7)	0.18 (40.8)		1.08	0.01 (2.7)	0.99	309.5	0.8	104
CES	0.90 (43.5)	0.16 (24.8)	3.76 (1.8)	1.05 (63.4)	0.01 (2.7)	0.99	319.1	0.8	103

Notes:
( ) = *t*-ratios.
Log L = log of the likelihood function.
df = degrees of freedom.
D.W. = Durbin–Watson statistic
Engineering and Allied Industries includes: engineering, shipbuilding and marine engineering, and metal goods not elsewhere specified.

Figure 2.3 shows the estimates of capacity utilisation obtained by the Wharton method, the capital productivity method and the production function method. The common thread running through these estimates is that all three were obtained by estimating capacity output from peak output data. In Harris and Taylor (1985), the same output peaks were used for all four methods so that a direct comparison could be made between estimates of capacity utilisation obtained from these three different approaches. In the present chapter, the peaks for the Wharton method were selected independently (see Figure 2.1). Unlike the other methods, the Wharton estimates included the output peak which occurred during the 1979 mini-boom. The alternative procedure of extrapolating the estimated peak output series from the 1973 peak through until 1982 was rejected (for obvious reasons).

It is clear from Figure 2.3 that the three methods of estimating capacity output based upon peak levels of output provide very similar estimates of capacity utilisation for Food, Drink and Tobacco for the entire study period. For the other three industries, however, several significant differences are worth noting. In both the Engineering and Vehicle industries, the three estimates follow very similar time paths until the mid-1970s, at which point some significant differences begin to appear. In the case of Textiles, Leather and Clothing, the Wharton estimates and the capital productivity estimates move together fairly closely during 1956–73 and again at the end of the period. Although the three estimates of capacity utilisation are thus very similar for much of the time period, marked differences occur towards the end of the study period in three of the four industries.

Two estimates of capacity utilisation are given for each industry in Figure 2.4, one based on peak output data and the other on the full data set. The CES production function is used in both cases. The most striking feature of these two estimates is that in three of the four industries (Engineering; Vehicles; Textiles, Leather and Clothing) the estimates obtained from the full data set are higher at the beginning of the time period and lower (substantially in the case of Textiles, Leather and Clothing) at the end of the time period. For Food, Drink and Tobacco, the estimates of capacity utilisation based on the full data set differ in only one respect from the estimates based on peak output data: they are higher by about 2 percentage points.

Figure 2.3 Estimated capacity utilisation rate using the CES production (peak-data) function, the Wharton method and the CES output–capital ratio (1956–82)

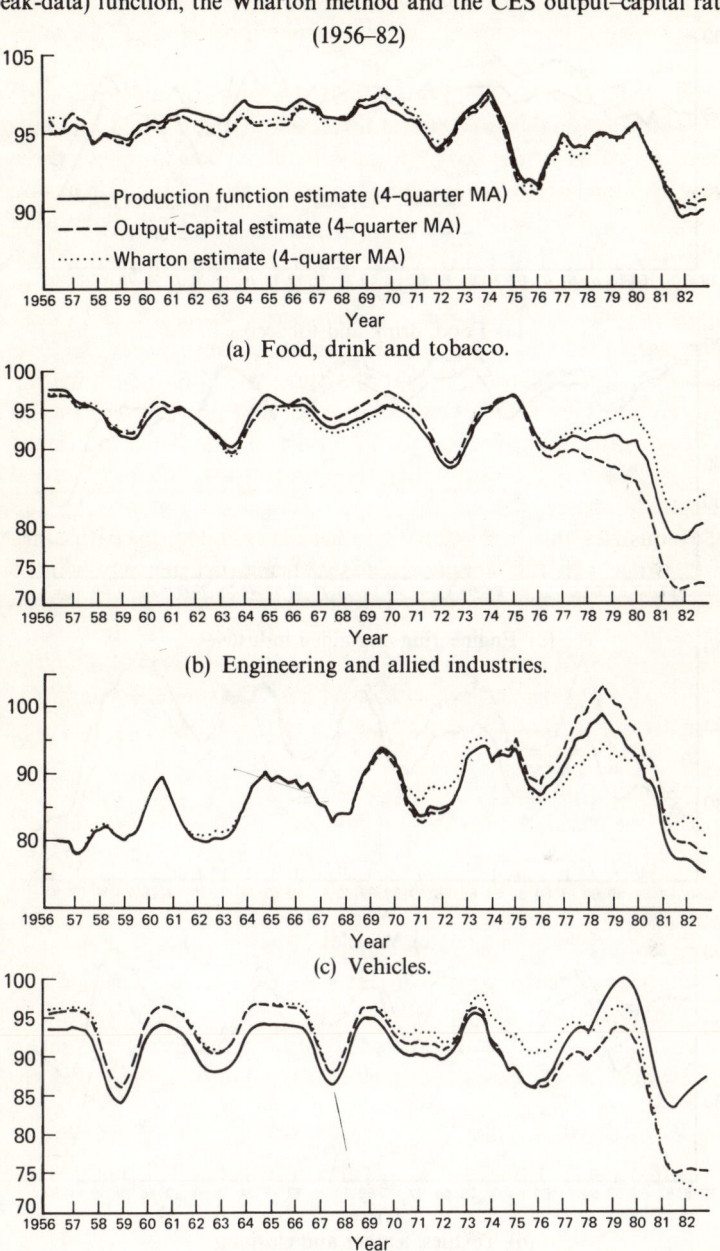

(a) Food, drink and tobacco.

(b) Engineering and allied industries.

(c) Vehicles.

(d) Textiles, leather and clothing.

Figure 2.4 Estimated capacity utilisation rate using the CES production function (1956–82)

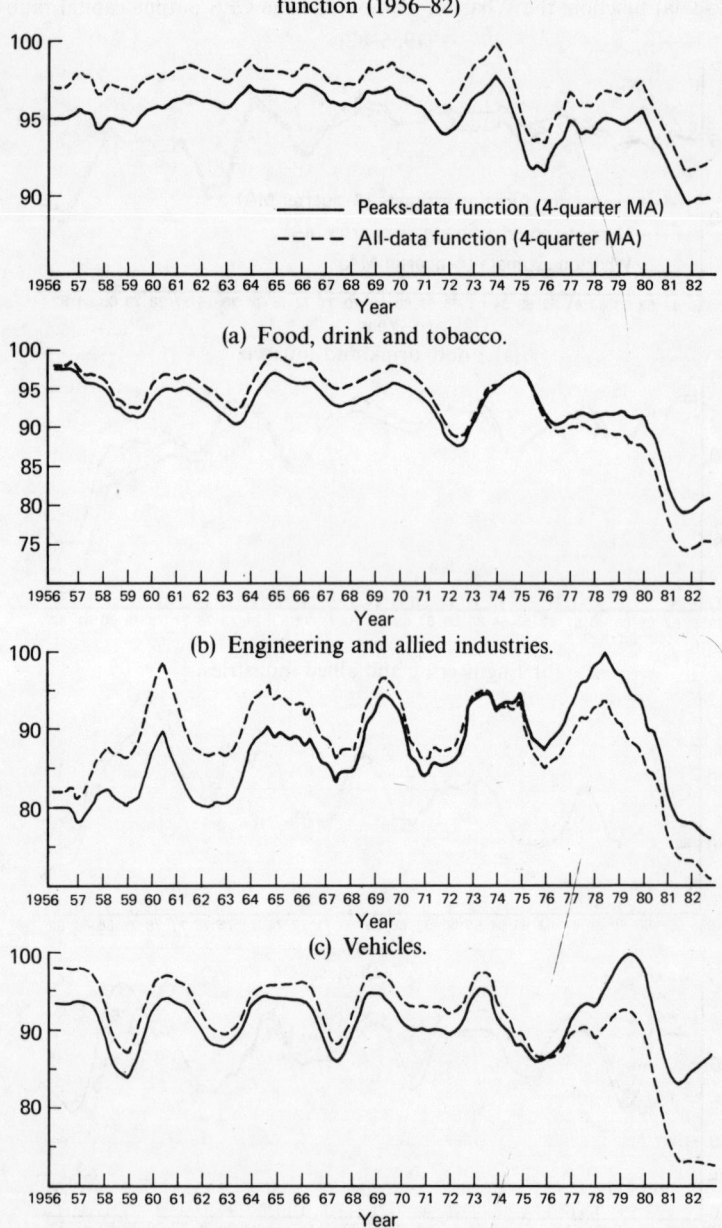

— Peaks-data function (4-quarter MA)
--- All-data function (4-quarter MA)

(a) Food, drink and tobacco.

(b) Engineering and allied industries.

(c) Vehicles.

(d) Textiles, leather and clothing.

CONCLUSION

This chapter has shown that there are several feasible alternative ways of estimating capacity utilisation based upon the trend-through-peaks approach. A central requirement of all these methods, however, is that the time series must be sufficiently long to provide an adequate number of peaks. Even when a sufficient number of peaks exist, there remains the thorny problem of selecting peaks of similar 'strength'. Since a method of measuring the strength of output peaks has not yet been devised (as far as we are aware), the selection of peak output levels is a 'hit and miss' affair. The criticism applies to all the methods of estimating capacity utilisation discussed in the present chapter.

We have argued that the simplest of the trend-through-peaks approaches (i.e., the Wharton method) is the least satisfactory, since estimates of capacity utilisation cannot be relied upon for the current time period if recent output peaks do not exist. The problem becomes particularly acute during periods of prolonged recession. This disadvantage of the Wharton approach, however, can be overcome (at least to some extent) if inputs are taken into account as well as outputs in the estimation of capacity output. More confidence can be placed in the estimates of capacity utilisation obtained from a standard production function – not only because it utilises information about capital and labour inputs but also because it rests on firmer theoretical foundations than the other two methods.

This does not mean, however, that the estimates of capacity utilisation provided by the production function approach can be relied upon with any great confidence. Indeed, there are various options available both in terms of the choice of production function and the data used to estimate the parameters of the chosen production function. Some of these choices – and the effect that these choices have on the estimates of capacity utilisation – have been considered in the present chapter. We do not at this stage feel sufficiently confident in any one of these approaches to make a firm recommendation to potential users. Our tentative view is that the production function method based on the full data set is likely to prove to be the most reliable.

Appendix

The trend increase in capital utilisation resulting from an increased incidence of shift working was calculated from data on the type of shift system used in manufacturing and the number of manual workers operating each system (see *Ministry of Labour Gazette* (April 1965), pp.148–55, and IFF (1978)). It was assumed that the stock of plant and machinery was apportioned out to its workers in a fixed manner. Thus, if x per cent of the workforce worked a three-shift system then they operated with x per cent of the stock of capital. Since operating a three-shift system results in plant and machinery being operated 24 hours a day, we assumed that x per cent of fixed assets were in operation for such a time period. Similar assumptions on hours of operation were made concerning the proportion of capital allocated to alternating day-and-night workers, double-day workers, and so on. Labour hours worked are based on *basic* and not actual hours, which is a simplification since data from the *New Earnings Survey* (NES) show that the average overtime hours worked by shift workers is often greater than those worked by non-shift workers. Basic hours were used because of insufficient information on hours worked for 1954 and 1964. Finally, the trend in utilisation was calculated for intervening years by interpolation and for years after 1978 by extrapolating the 1964–78 trend.

Notes

1. The authors are grateful to the ESRC for supporting the research reported in this chapter. They are also grateful to participants of the EPSG Conference on Capacity Utilisation held at the University of Warwick for helpful comments on an earlier draft of this paper.
2. See Paish (1962), Klein and Preston (1976), Pearce and Taylor (1968), Taylor, Winter and Pearce (1970) and Artus (1977).
3. See Christiano (1981) for a review of the various methods.
4. This formula is more accurately described as a measure of capital utilisation (rather than capacity utilisation). An alternative approach based on the output/capital ratio is used by Panić (1978).
5. Initially, we attempted to measure technical change by including an exponential time trend, but the parameter was statistically insignificant and often had a negative sign.
6. An alternative is to use electricity consumption to approximate the capital services used up in production, but electricity is not the only fuel used by plant and machinery and the mix of fuels used is likely to have changed over time. (See Bosworth, 1979.)
7. See Taylor (1974, 1979).
8. Output levels were defined as capacity levels of output only if an output peak coincided with a peak in both the labour hours series and the output–capital stock series (as in Harris and Taylor, 1985).
9. An alternative method is to use the 'double-declining' approach, which substracts a constant proportion of the *remaining* capital stock each year.
10. See Griffen (1976) for a discussion of the estimated service lives of capital equipment.
11. The reduction in asset values between 1974 and 1982 is assumed to have occurred exponentially (using a double-declining rate of depreciation). This ensures a smooth pattern of retirements with the most severe depreciation occurring in the immediate aftermath of the 1973–4 oil crisis. No allowance has been made for the second oil crisis in 1979–80.

References

ARTUS, J. R. (1977) 'Measure of potential output in manufacturing for eight industrial countries', 1955–78, *IMF Staff Papers* 24 (March), pp.1–35.

BOSWORTH, D. L. (1979) 'Capital stock, capital services and the use of fuel consumption proxies: an appraisal' in Patterson, K. D. and Schott, K. (eds) *The Measurement of Capital* (London: Macmillan).

CHRISTIANO, L. J. (1981) 'A survey of measures of capacity utilization', *IMF Staff Papers* 28 (March), pp. 144–98.

DENISON, E. F. (1972) 'Final comments', *Survey of Current Businesses* 52, pp. 95–110.

DESAI, M. (1976) *Applied Econometrics* (Deddington: Philip Allan).

GRIFFEN, T. (1976) 'The stock of fixed assets in the UK: how to make the best use of statistics', *Economic Trends* 276 (October) (London: CSO).

HALL, B. H. and HALL, R. E. (1980) *Time Series Processor, Version 3.5, User's Manual* (Stanford: Stanford University Press).

HARRIS, R. and TAYLOR, J. (1985) 'The Measurement of Capacity Utilization' *Applied Economics* 17 (October), pp. 849–66.

HEATHFIELD, D. F. (1972) 'The measurement of capital usage using electricity consumption data for the UK', *Journal of the Royal Statistical Society* (Series A) 135, pp. 208–20.

IFF (1978) *Shiftworking in Manufacturing Industry: Great Britain* (London: IFF Research Ltd).

KLEIN, L. R. (1960) 'Some theoretical issues in the measurement of capacity', *Econometrica* 28 (April), pp. 272–86.

────── and PRESTON, R. S. (1967) 'Some new results in the measurement of capacity utilisation', *American Economic Review* 57, pp. 34–58.

NES (New Earnings Survey) Department of Employment (London: HMSO).

PAISH, F. W. (1962) 'Output, inflation and growth', in *Studies in an Inflationary Economy* (London: Macmillan).

PANIĆ, M. (1978) *Capacity Utilization in UK Manufacturing Industry* (London: NEDO).

PEARCE, D. W. and TAYLOR, J. (1968) 'Spare capacity: what margin is needed?', *Lloyds Bank Review* (July), pp. 1–11.

TAYLOR, J. (1974) *Unemployment and Wage Inflation* (London: Longman).

────── (1979) 'The theory and measurement of labour hoarding: a comment'. *Scottish Journal of Political Economy* 26, pp. 191–201.

────── WINTER, D. and PEARCE, D. W. (1970) 'A 19-industry quarterly series of capacity utilization in the United Kingdom, 1948–1968', *Oxford Bulletin* 32 (May), pp. 113–32.

3 Capacity Utilisation and Below-Capacity Working

J. H. Ll. Dewhurst

INTRODUCTION

This chapter is concerned with the construction of indices of capacity utilisation from data collected from surveys of firms. In particular, we are concerned with the responses to questions asking whether firms are operating at full capacity. This type of data is collected in various countries and for the empirical part of this chapter we use two sources – data collected by the Confederation of British Industry (CBI) for manufacturing industry in Scotland and data published by the Institut National de la Statistique et des Etudes Economiques (INSEE) for French industry. A more thorough description of this type of data is contained in Christiano (1981).

The methodology presented in this chapter is concerned with transforming one series relating to capacity utilisation to another which measures capacity utilisation as an index. The index may then be compared directly with other index measures such as those that may be constructed by the Wharton method. The problem of defining what is meant by 'capacity utilisation' is thus not directly germane to the argument presented here. For the purposes of this chapter, 'full capacity' and 'capacity utilisation' are taken to be whatever the respondents to the survey in question assume them to mean. The problem of what is meant by the respondents is not dealt with in this chapter, although it is clearly an important issue.

The transformation suggested in this chapter is not new. Similar ideas may be found in Enzler (1968) and Ruist and Söderstrom (1975). Indeed there is no difference between the theoretical results derived in this chapter and those of Ruist and Söderstrom, although the derivations are slightly different.

Throughout this chapter we shall assume three critical items. First that all firms respond to the question posed with the same understanding.

This is a sweeping assumption that has at least three important aspects – (i) that all firms understand the question as referring to a particular time period, (ii) that all firms understand the question as referring to the utilisation of a particular set of resources (although Ruist and Söderstrom argue that this is likely to be true for the Swedish data they analyse, it is unlikely to be so for the CBI data used in this chapter – see Price (1983)) and (iii) that all firms stating they are not working below full capacity are indeed operating at 100 per cent of their possible output (this again appears unwarranted for the CBI data – see Ballance and Burton (1983)).

Second we shall assume that the published data on the percentage of firms operating below full capacity is not a simple percentage, but a weighted percentage where firms are weighted by size, which we measure by full capacity output. Although the data series we use are weighted percentages the weights used are not full capacity output (though the differences may be relatively small). The CBI data, for instance, is weighted in proportion to net output.

Finally we assume that the respondents to the survey constitute a representative sample of the population from which they are drawn. This would allow us to calculate potential output given our index and a series for actual output.

THE THEORETICAL MODEL

In this section we develop a formal model that links a series of the weighted percentage of firms working below full capacity (W) and an index of capacity utilisation (U).

We start by assuming that the capacity utilisation rate of the jth firm in the industry is a random variable r_j, and seek to define a plausible distribution for this variable. It should be noted at the outset that any such distribution will not necessarily be time invariant. However, for the purposes of the exposition of the theoretical model – which is essentially static – no explicit mention of any time parameter will be made.

We suppose that there is a finite probability that the jth firm is working at full capacity denoted by k_j.
Thus

$$k_j = P[r_j = 100]$$

We further assume that a firm cannot operate at a level in excess of full capacity (so that $r_j \leq 100$) or have a negative capacity utilisation rate (implying $r_j \geq 0$). For intermediate values of r_j we assume that there exists a density function $f_j(r:z_j)$ that defines a probability distribution of r_j over the range [0, 100] where z_j is a vector of unknown parameters of the function.

Thus we may write:

$$P[r_j < 0] = 0$$

$$P[0 \leq r_j < a] = \int_0^a f_j(r; z_j) dr \qquad 0 \leq a < 100$$

$$P[r_j = 100] = k_j$$

$$P[r_j > 100] = 0$$

If this is to be a proper probability distribution, then:

$$P[-\infty \leq r_j \leq \infty] = 1$$

$$\Rightarrow \lim_{a \to 100} \int_0^a f_j(r; z_j) dr + k_j = 1$$

or

$$\lim_{a \to 100} \int_0^a f_j(r; z_j) dr = 1 - k_j \qquad (3.1)$$

Note that we could equivalently consider a probability density function defined for $r_j \geq 0$, $g_j(r; y_j)$ and let

$$k_j = \int_{100}^{\infty} g_j(r; y_j) dr$$

Suppose there are N firms in the industry.

Let the size (full capacity output) of the jth firm be x_j.

The actual output of the jth firm is $\frac{1}{100} \cdot r_j \cdot x_j$.

The expected output of the jth firm is given by

$$E[r_j | x = x_j] \cdot x_j/100$$

and the expected output of the industry

$$\sum_{j=1}^{N} E[r_j | x = x_j] \cdot x_j/100.$$

Therefore the expected industrial capacity utilisation rate

$$E[u] = \frac{\sum_{j=1}^{N} E[r_j | x = x_j] x_j}{\sum_{j=1}^{N} x_j}. \tag{3.2}$$

Consider the survey data:
P [Firm j responds below full capacity]
$= P[r_j < 100 | x = x_j]$

$$\therefore E[W] = \frac{100 \sum_{j=1}^{N} P[r_j < 100 | x = x_j] \cdot x_j}{\sum_{j=1}^{N} x_j} \tag{3.3}$$

$$= \frac{100 \sum_{j=1}^{N} (1-k_j) \cdot x_j}{\sum_{j=1}^{N} x_j}$$

Let

$$\sum_{j=1}^{N} x_j = X$$

Then

$$E[U] = \frac{1}{X} \cdot \sum_{j=1}^{N} E[r_j | x = x_j] \cdot x_j$$

$$= \frac{1}{X} \sum_{j=1}^{N} \left[\lim_{a \to 100} \int_0^a r \cdot f_j(r; z_j) dr + 100 k_j \right] \cdot x_j$$

$$= \left[\frac{1}{X} \sum_{j=1}^{N} \left[\lim_{a \to 100} \int_0^a r \cdot f_j(r; z_j) dr \cdot x_j \right] + 100 \sum_{j=1}^{N} k_j \cdot x_j \right]$$

$$= \frac{1}{X} \sum_{j=1}^{N} x_j \cdot \lim_{a \to 100} \int_0^a r \cdot f_j(r; z_j) dr + (100 - E[W])$$

Thus assuming that the expected values of the capacity utilisation index and of W are close to their actual values, we may write.

$$U = \frac{1}{X} \sum_{j=1}^{N} x_j \lim_{a \to 100} \int_0^a r \cdot f_j(r; z_j) dr + (100 - W) \tag{3.4}$$

We note that the first term on the right-hand side of equation (3.4) relates to the weighted average level of capacity utilisation in firms which are working below full capacity. The second term is the weighted percentage of firms which are working at full capacity. As the first term may be taken to be strictly positive, the index of capacity utilisation will thus always be greater than the weighted percentage of firms working at full capacity.

Without additional assumptions or information it is impossible to proceed further. To use this model in an empirical exercise we shall need to simplify the theory. In this chapter, we chose to do this by means of the following assumption.

$$f_j(r; z_j) = f(r; z) \qquad \text{for all } j$$

This assumption states that the distribution of r_j is identical across firms. In particular it must follow from this that the rate of capacity utilisation of a firm is independent of the size of the firm.

$$U = \frac{1}{X} \lim_{a \to 100} \int_0^a r \cdot f(r; z) dr \cdot \sum_{j=1}^{N} x_j + (100 - W)$$

$$= (100 - W) + \lim_{a \to 100} \int_0^a r \cdot f(r; z) dr \qquad (3.5)$$

Further

$$W = \frac{100 \cdot \sum_{j=1}^{N} (1-k) \cdot x_j}{\sum_{j=1}^{N} x_j}$$

$$= 100 \cdot (1-k)$$

But

$$k = 1 - \lim_{a \to 100} \int_0^a f(r; z) dr$$

$$\lim_{a \to 100} \int_0^a f(r; z) dr = W/100 \qquad (3.6)$$

Therefore given the weighted percentage of firms working below capacity we may construct a capacity utilisation index from equation (3.5) subject to the constraint given by equation (3.6).

EMPIRICAL EXERCISE: 1

In this section of the chapter we use the methodology outlined in the previous section to construct an index of capacity utilisation from a series giving the weighted percentage of firms reporting to be working at less than full capacity. The particular series that we have used is that published by the CBI for the Scottish manufacturing sector. This series runs from February 1967 to July 1984. From 1967 until 1971 the CBI Industrial Trends Survey – from which our data is taken – was conducted three times a year (excepting for a cancellation of the planned February 1971 Survey due to the postal strike). Since 1971, the survey has been held quarterly. This change in frequency should be borne in mind when looking at the seasonal fluctuations in Figure 3.2.

One further point about the series should be mentioned. In April 1975 the question that the respondents were required to answer was altered slightly to its present form

Is your present level of output below capacity (i.e., are you working below a satisfactory full rate of operation)?

The published series contains two figures for April 1975 and the ratio of these two figures was used to scale all the figures prior to April 1975, in order to obtain a more consistent series.

Restating the results of the previous section, we have

$$U = (100 - W) + \lim_{a \to 100} \int_0^a r.f(r;z)dr \qquad (3.5)$$

and

$$\lim_{a \to 100} \int_0^a f(r;z)dr = W/100 \qquad (3.6)$$

It is clear that in order to calculate a value for U given a value for W we shall need to specify the function f. The choice of any particular function must to a large extent be arbitrary. The choice made here (to use a generalised χ^2 distribution) was influenced by several considerations. First, it appeared desirable that if possible we should adopt a one-parameter distribution, for *a priori* information about anything other than plausible shapes for f was extremely scarce. If we adopt a one-parameter distribution, then we may solve equation (3.6) for z (which is now our single parameter of the distribution) and then substitute that value into equation (3.5) in order to obtain U. Second, certain possible distributions were rejected because of the implausibility of the limiting value of U as W tended to 100. Finally, the constructed indices of capacity utilisation given in Dewhurst, Forbes and Parrillo (1983) were taken as an indication of the likely range of values for any index of capacity utilisation. The χ^2 distribution appeared to satisfy most – if not all – of our *a priori* requirements.

Thus
$$f(r;z) = \frac{(r/2)^{z/2-1} \cdot \exp(-r/2)}{2 \cdot \Gamma(z/2)}$$

where:
$$\Gamma(p) = \int_0^\infty x^{p-1} \cdot \exp(-x) dx$$

and $z \geq 1$ is the degrees of freedom parameter of the distribution which need not in this case be an integer.

Therefore for any value of W we were able to calculate z from

$$\int_0^{100} \frac{(r/2)^{z/2-1} \cdot \exp(-r/2)}{2 \cdot \Gamma(z/2)} dr = W/100$$

and thence we could derive a value nor U from

$$U = (100 - W) + \int_0^{100} \frac{(r/2)^{z/2} \cdot \exp(-r/2)}{\Gamma(z/2)} dr.$$

In this we were greatly aided by Algorithm AS32 for the incomplete gamma integral (Bhattacharjee, 1970).

A plot of U against W is shown in Figure 3.1. It can be seen that the

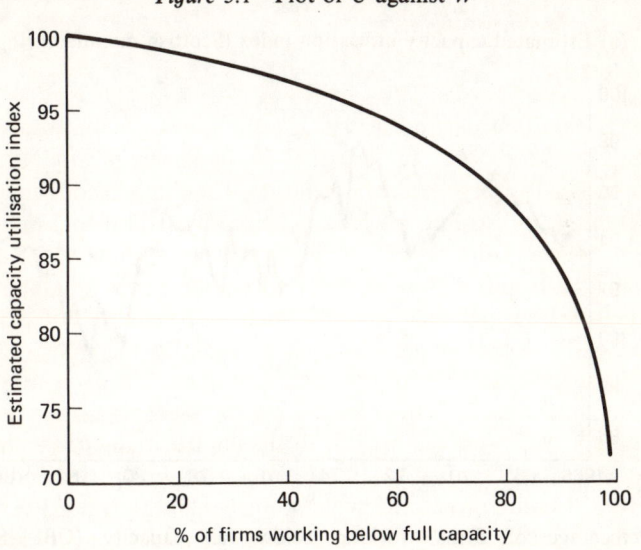

Figure 3.1   Plot of U against W

effective range of U is between 71.5 (when $W = 99$) and 99.96 (when $W = 1$). Using this model, 77 per cent of firms would have to be working below full capacity before the index of capacity utilisation fell below 90. Applying the model to the CBI data, we obtain a capacity utilisation index for Scottish manufacturing. The CBI series and the capacity utilisation index are shown in Figure 3.2. The index exhibits clear cyclical behaviour and a gradual downward trend. The range of values achieved

Figure 3.2 Capacity utilisation: Scottish manufacturing

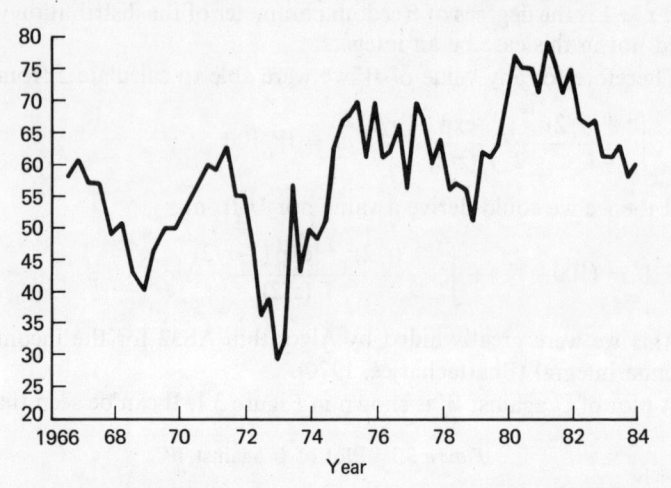

(a) Estimated capacity utilisation index (Scottish manufacturing).

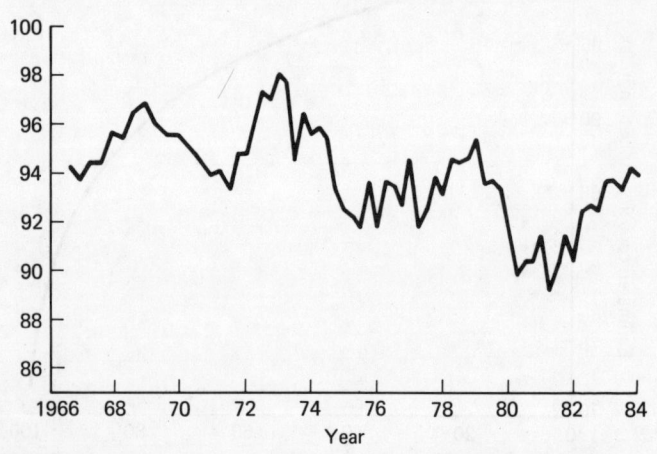

(b) Percentage of firms working below full capacity (CBI, Scottish manufacturing).

is 89.19 (in October 1981) to 98.07 (in July 1973). Since October 1981 the capacity utilisation level appears to have climbed back to the higher levels experienced in the late 1970s.

In the years for which they overlap, the pattern of the index is very similar to that exhibited by the Wharton School index given in Dewhurst, Forbes and Parillo.

A final word of caution is perhaps appropriate. The assumption of a common distribution for r for all firms is likely to be violated in an industrial grouping as varied as Scottish manufacturing. Slightly more reliance might be placed on an index that was based on disaggregated data. It is hoped to pursue this point in further research.

EMPIRICAL EXERCISE: 2

One of the main reservations that one must have about an empirical exercise such as that described in the previous section of this chapter is that there is no objective method of ascertaining whether the transformation leads to an accurate index of utilisation. Comparison with other measures – although perhaps indicating plausibility – suffers from the defect that it is not an absolute test and that the other indices may well measure different conceptions of capacity utilisation. In this section, we present some evidence which goes some way to providing a better test of the transformation.

The INSEE publish for the French economy a series giving the percentage of firms which claim to be meeting "bottlenecks" in their production process which would prevent them increasing output in response to an increase in demand for their product. For the purposes of this study, we equate that percentage with the percentage of firms working at full capacity. As the INSEE questionnaire subsequently asks for information on the category of 'bottleneck' (capital equipment, labour, raw materials), it seems likely that firms would answer the first question with a wider perspective than considering capital stock as the sole determinant of full capacity output. If we denote this series by F_1, then in the notation of above we may write

$$W = (100 - F_1)$$

In the same survey, firms are also asked to estimate by what percentage they could increase their output without an increase in their inputs (in stock terms) given an increase in the demand for their products. The weighted average of responses is published. Denoting this series by F_2, we may write

$$U = \left(\frac{100}{100 + F_2}\right) 100$$

The series F_1 and F_2 are shown in Figure 3.3. Again there is a slight problem of seasonality. The data we use runs from March 1968 until June 1980. From the beginning of the sample period until June 1978, the survey was held three times a year (in March, June and November). From October 1978 the figures are given for four months each year (in October, January, March and June).

Applying our transformation to the first series, we may obtain an estimated value for capacity utilisation which we may then compare with the 'actual' series generated by the second of the published series. The estimated index and the 'actual' index are shown in Figure 3.4.

The correspondence between the two indices is striking, and much closer than we had expected. Having said that, inspection of Figure 3.4 would seem to indicate that the estimated series is initially slightly more volatile than the 'actual' series and latterly underestimates the 'actual' series, although by only 1–2 per cent. It is clear from the data that a dramatic shift occurred in 1974–5. If this were due to the oil price rise, then it is at least conceivable that the appreciation of capacity utilisation might alter as a result. This might explain the second of the points noted

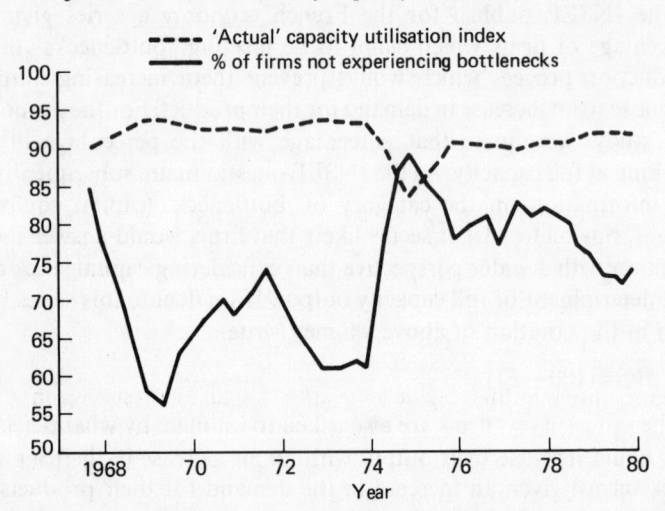

Figure 3.3 French industry capacity utilisation (INSEE)

Figure 3.4 French industry: 'estimated' and 'actual' capacity utilisation index

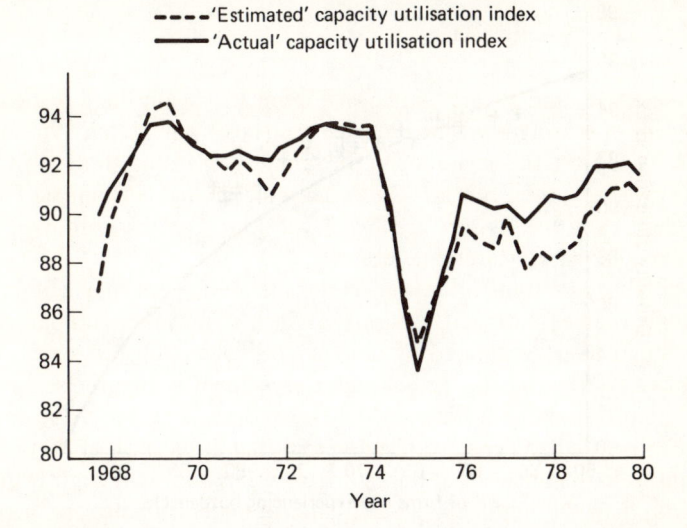

above. However there might well be other explanations of the shift in the data, of which we are not aware.

In Figure 3.5, we show a scatter diagram of the published data and superimposed on that the transformation curve of Figure 3.1. Although our estimated curve does pass through the data points, it does not appear to be the 'line of best fit'. In particular, the data suggests a smaller response in U to changes in W for values of W below about 82 per cent, and a much higher response for values above that level than our transformation allows for. In the light of this, further research is being undertaken with this data, using a more general model which allows for the relaxation of some of the drastic assumptions of the second section of this chapter.

Although we would not wish to claim that the results of this section are a vindication of using our transformation on the Scottish data, it is reassuring that the transformation does appear to fit the published French data reasonably well. It might be, however, that any model designed along the lines above with equally plausible assumptions would fit just as well (if not better). The method might thus be robust to the choice of particular model within fairly wide limits. Again we would like to test these assertions at a later date.

Figure 3.5 French industry: published data on capacity utilisation

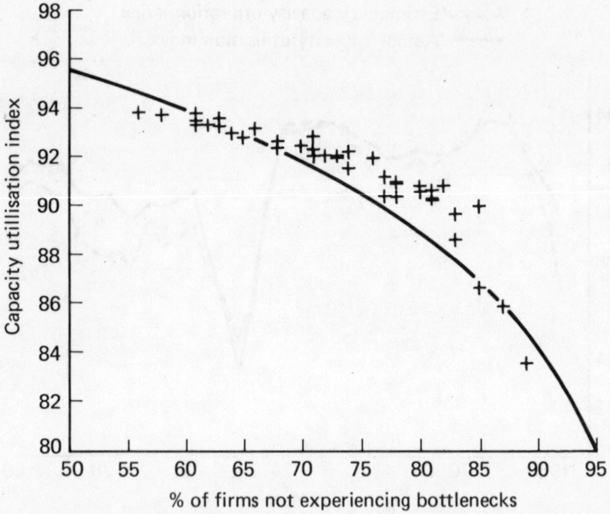

CONCLUSION

There is no doubt that the results presented in this chapter are based on some rather arbitrary and sweeping assumptions. However the results indicate that it is perfectly feasible to construct a plausible index of capacity utilisation from the survey data. Moreover, other measures of capacity utilisation such as the Wharton index or indices based on time trend regressions (see Christiano or Dewhurst, Forbes and Parrillo for a description of these methods) are not above criticism. The Wharton School method relies heavily on the researcher's ability to identify 'peaks' correctly, and the regression methods are based on extremely naive models that are unlikely to hold exactly in practice. Given the ease of constructing an index from the CBI data as is done in this chapter, we would suggest that the method contained in this chapter is as attractive as other methods.

As a final point it is worth mentioning that although the relationship derived here between the Survey series and our index of capacity utilisation is monotonic, it is not linear. The use of the CBI series as a proxy for capacity utilisation in, for example, econometric models of the United Kingdom, would thus introduce a specification error. This may not be too severe normally as a linear approximation of the curve shown in Figure 3.1 would be reasonable for the variation shown in the CBI series over any three to four-year period. However, if one wished to study the medium or long term rather than the short term, then there would seem to be a case for using a conversion of the CBI data into an index along the lines suggested in this chapter. This case would be strongest for a period of study that included both 1973 and 1981.

References

BALLANCE, D. C., and BURTON, C. P. H. (1983) 'Answering practices in the CBI Industrial Trends Survey' in 'Twenty-five years of "ups" and "downs"' (London: CBI).

BHATTACHARJEE, G. P. (1970) 'AS32 The incomplete gamma function', *Applied Statistics* 19 (3), p. 285.

CHRISTIANO, L. J. (1981) 'A survey of measures of capacity utilisation', IMF *Staff Papers* 28, p. 144.

DEWHURST, J. H. Ll., FORBES, D. and PARILLO, S. (1983) 'Capacity utilisation indices for Scottish manufacturing industry: 1951–1980', Department of Economics, University of Dundee, Working Paper 22.

ENZLER, J. J. (1968) 'The federal reserve board manufacturing capacity index: comparisons with other sources of capacity information', *American Statistical Association, Proceedings of the Business and Economics Section*, p. 35.

PRICE, R. (1983) 'The CBI Industrial Trends Survey – an insight into answering practices' in 'Twenty-five years of "ups" and "downs"' (London: CBI).

RUIST, E. and SÖDERSTRÖM, H. T. (1975) 'Measuring capacity utilisation and excess demand', *European Economic Review* 6, p. 369.

4 Alternative Aggregate Measures of Capacity Utilisation Based on a MACE Production Function

John Helliwell, Peter Sturm and Gérard Salou[1]

INTRODUCTION

The concepts of potential output and capacity utilisation are important both in economic policy discussions and econometric model building. Concerning the former, the evaluation of a given policy stance and the accompanying budget position will to no small degree depend on – among other important factors – the assumed degree of capacity utilisation in the economy scrutinised. In macroeconomic models, the degree of capacity utilisation is likely to enter various important behavioural relationships – in particular price, import and export equations, but possibly also the various factor demand functions (e.g., investment and employment equations). In contrast to this crucial role of the concept of capacity utilisation in applied economics and policy analysis is the lack of a uniform definition of the important variable underlying it: potential output. The purpose of this chapter is not to analyse the reasons for the lack of uniformity with respect to potential output definitions and measurement or to attempt reducing the existing variety in this realm. Rather, this chapter reports on some preliminary results of ongoing research with a particular type of aggregate production function (MACE) and presents some alternative measures of potential output and capacity utilisation which can be derived from the MACE framework.

The chapter is organised as follows: the first section gives a summary description of the MACE function with references to its precise definition and measurement results. The next section defines four alternative measures of potential output which can be derived from the

MACE production function, enumerates the aspects in which they differ and presents their empirical estimates. The last section discusses the empirical relevance of the various measures, and reports on their comparative performance in various behavioural equations of macro models in the seven major OECD countries.

THE MACE PRODUCTION FUNCTION

'MACE' is an acronym (from MACro Energy) for medium-term macroeconomic models featuring a particular design of an economy's supply side and its interaction with the remainder of the economy – in particular the price formation process and the determination of foreign trade flows. The MACE framework was first developed for the Canadian economy by Helliwell *et al.* (1984a). The Canadian MACE model has since been developed further (see Helliwell *et al.*, 1984b for the latest version) and has been successfully used for the purpose of policy analysis and cliometric exercises, e.g. to explain the relationship between the apparent slowdown in productivity growth and inter-factor substitution (see Helliwell, 1984c). More recently the MACE framework has been applied to the seven largest OECD economies, and efforts are presently under way to integrate MACE supply blocks into the OECD's INTERLINK model (see Helliwell *et al.*, 1984d).

The structure of (and logic behind) the MACE framework has been comprehensively described and discussed in the sources referenced above. In the present context, it will suffice to give a concise overview over the three-factor nested aggregate production function which is at the core of the MACE framework. The outer function (FO (...)) combines total labour input and a capital–energy bundle ($KEBSV$) to define gross output ($QBSV$). Labour input is the product of total employment (ETB), and a labour efficiency index (PI) assuming that technical progress is Harrod neutral and disembodied:

$$QBSV = FO\,(KEBSV; ETB \times PI) \qquad (4.1)$$

The functional form chosen for FO (...) in past applications of the MACE framework has been either Cobb–Douglas or CES with constant returns to scale imposed. For those countries for which the growth of technical progress (and thus the labour efficiency index) has slowed down significantly over the observation period (early 1960s to early 1980s) the labour efficiency index PI grows at a declining rate, asymptotically approaching the (stable) growth rate observed in the United States. In the case of the United States, there is no strong evidence that the growth of labour efficiency has declined over the observation period when duly adjusting observed productivity growth for interfactor substitution and low average rates of capacity utilisation in the wake of the two oil price shocks. Actual (i.e., observed) and cyclically adjusted (i.e., modelled) labour efficiency indices in the MACE model are depicted in Figure 4.1.[2]

Changes in the capital–energy bundle ($KEBSV$) are defined by an inner CES function ($FI(...)$) which combines gross investment (IBV) and concommittant energy inputs. The capital–energy ratio for gross investment in each period is chosen so as to minimise joint capital/energy costs for this investment under the assumption that the relative price of these two factors ($PENB/UCC$) will remain stable in the future. In addition it is assumed that a given percentage ($R1$) of the capital stock in place (KBV) can be 'retrofitted' so as to adjust its capital–energy ratio to the current cost minimising optimum. The resulting recursive formula for the capital–energy bundle is:

$$KEBSV = KEBSV(-1) \times (1 - R1 - RSCBR) + FI(KBV(-1) \times R1 + IBV); PENB/UCC) \qquad (4.2)$$

where $FI(...)$ represents the inner CES function and $RSCBR$ is the scrapping or depreciation rate applied to fixed capital – depending on whether the gross or net capital stock is used.

Distribution parameters and scale factors for factor inputs for the inner and outer functions were estimated from observed input and output quantities, under the assumption that on average factor input ratios are cost-minimising subject to observed factor price ratios. The elasticity of substitution between capital and energy ($SIGMA$) and the retrofitting parameter ($R1$) of the inner function were estimated by joint grid search, choosing the parameter pairs which maximised the likelihood functions of the regression of actual energy demand on synthetic energy demand computed from the model for alternative pairs of $SIGMA$ and $R1$ and actual factor prices. The elasticity of substitution of the outer function was estimated by regressing the average product of labour on its real wage, and Harrod neutral technical progress was determined by regressing the growth of each country's measured labour efficiency index[3] on the ratio of the United States labour efficiency index over that of the country's efficiency index. A complete listing of

Figure 4.1 MACE model: labour efficiency index

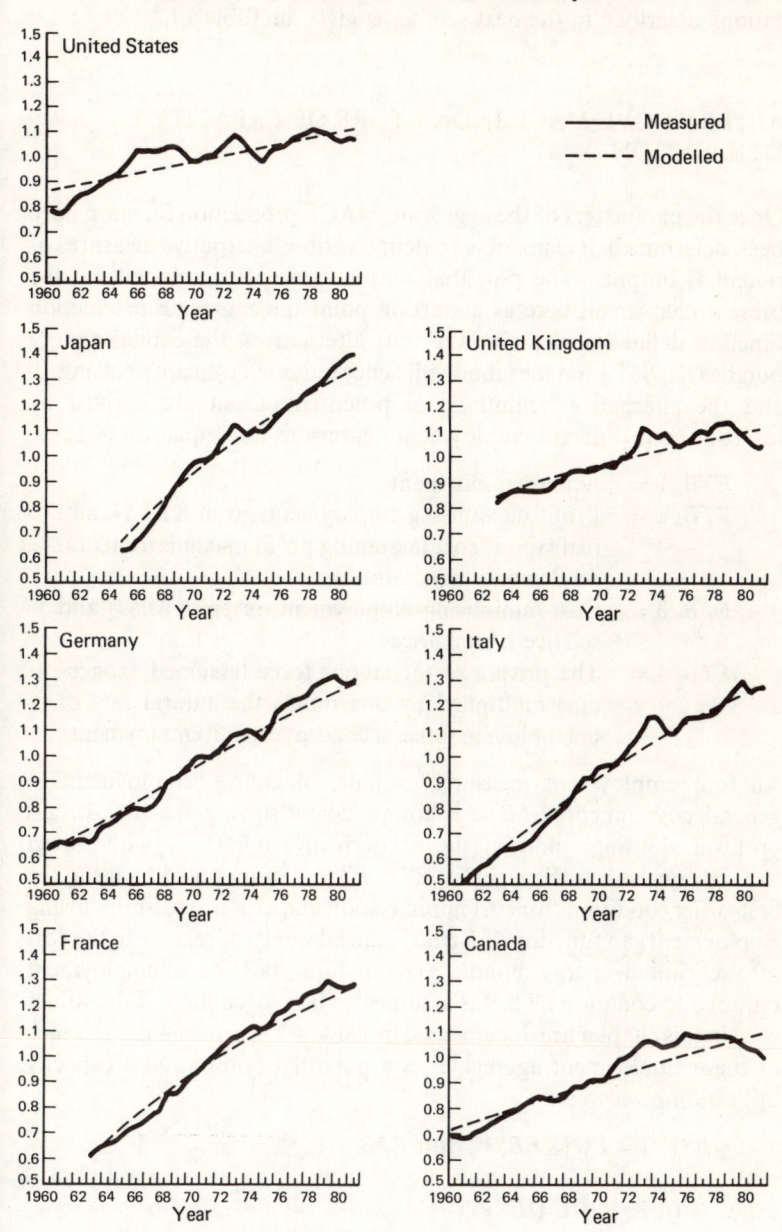

Source: Helliwell *et al.* (1984e).

parameters for the MACE production function used in the computations described in the next section is given in Table 4.1.[4]

ALTERNATIVE MACE INDICATORS OF CAPACITY UTILISATION

Once the parameters of the aggregate MACE production function have been determined, it is possible to define various alternative measures of potential output.[5] The potential output concepts developed for the present chapter all take as a starting point the aggregate production function defined above. For the four alternatives, the capital–energy bundle ($KEBSV$) and the labour efficiency index (PI) remain unchanged, and the alternative definitions of potential output are derived by inserting four different employment aggregates into equation (4.1):

ETB. 1 = Actual employment
ETB. 2 = Profit-maximising employment, given $KEBSV$ and real labour cost (assuming profit maximisation and no demand constraint)
ETB. 3 = Cost-minimising employment, given $KEBSV$ and relative factor prices
ETB. 4 = The private sector labour force (assumed exogenous) multiplied by one minus the natural rate of unemployment (i.e., a concept of 'full' employment).

All four employment measures exclude, of course, employment in general government. *ETB.* 2 is computed by solving the (first-order) profit-maximising condition (the first derivative of FO (...) with respect to ETB equals the real wage) for *ETB*. *ETB.* 3 is computed by using the first-order conditions for cost minimisation and express cost-minimising employment as a function of $KEBSV$ and labour costs relative to the cost of the capital–energy bundle. The natural rate of unemployment required to compute *ETB.* 4 is assumed to be exogenous and the values used in this chapter are documented in Table 4.2. Corresponding to each of these employment aggregates is a potential output and a capacity utilisation measure:

$$QBSV.i = FO(KEBSV; PI \times ETB.i)$$

$$CU.i = QBV/QBSV.i$$

$i = 1, 2, 3, 4$

where QBV is the actual gross output observed, $QBSV.i$ is the ith

Table 4.1 Parameter values of the aggregate production structure[a]

	Outer CES function				Inner CES function				
	Elasticity of substitution	Scale parameters		Catch-up coefficient	Elasticity of substitution	Retrofitting parameter	Scale parameters		
		Labour	capital–energy bundle				Energy		Capital
Country	TAU	B	C		SIGMA	R1	b		c
United States	1.01	0.710	0.35	n.a.	0.5	0.7	0.87		0.003
Japan	0.7	0.001	0.31	0.054	0.8	0.9	0.77		0.109
Germany	0.99	0.597	0.34	0.031	0.5	0.5	0.82		0.005
France	0.8	0.048	0.38	0.053	0.8	0.3	0.86		0.053
United Kingdom	0.6	0.002	0.65	0.137	0.3	0.1	0.78		7.E−5
Italy	0.8	0.019	0.25	0.047	0.5	0.6	0.77		0.005
Canada	1.01	0.708	0.35	0.036	0.9	0.1	0.89		0.065

Notes:
[a] See Appendix for a discussion of how these parameter estimates were derived.
n.a. Not applicable.

Table 4.2 Natural rates of unemployment (%)

	USA	Jap	Ger	Fra	UK	Ita	Can
1960	5.1	1.3	1.0	2.0	1.7	4.2	4.1
61	5.2	1.3	1.0	2.1	1.9	4.4	4.3
62	5.2	1.3	1.0	2.1	2.1	4.5	4.4
63	5.2	1.3	1.0	2.2	2.3	4.7	4.6
64	5.3	1.3	1.0	2.2	2.5	4.9	4.8
65	5.3	1.3	1.0	2.3	2.7	5.1	5.0
66	5.3	1.3	1.0	2.4	2.9	5.2	5.1
67	5.3	1.3	1.0	2.4	3.1	5.4	5.3
68	5.4	1.3	1.0	2.5	3.3	5.6	5.5
69	5.4	1.4	1.0	2.5	3.5	5.7	5.6
70	5.4	1.4	1.0	2.6	3.7	5.9	5.8
71	5.5	1.4	1.0	2.6	3.9	6.1	6.0
72	5.5	1.4	1.0	2.7	4.2	6.3	6.2
73	5.5	1.5	1.2	3.0	4.4	6.4	6.3
74	5.6	1.6	1.6	3.5	4.6	6.6	6.5
75	5.6	1.7	1.9	4.0	4.8	6.8	6.7
76	5.6	1.8	2.2	4.4	5.0	6.9	6.8
77	5.6	1.9	2.5	4.9	5.2	7.1	7.0
78	5.7	2.0	2.8	5.3	5.4	7.3	7.2
79	5.7	2.1	3.1	5.8	5.6	7.5	7.4
80	5.7	2.2	3.4	6.2	5.7	7.6	7.5
81	5.7	2.3	3.7	6.7	5.9	7.8	7.7
82	5.8	2.4	4.1	7.2	6.1	8.0	7.9

Source: Estimates based on values for standardised unemployment rates (OECD, 1984, Annex Table R12).

potential output measure and $CU.i$ is the ith rate of capacity utilisation.

A basic assumption characterising all MACE models is that *both* capital and labour are quasi-fixed inputs which are only gradually adjusted to desired levels (with different speeds of adjustment, of course). At any given point of time both the capital stock and employment are thus fixed, and changes in the rate of output are brought about by varying the utilisation rate of the fixed factors. This utilisation rate corresponds to $CU.1$, defined above. It is a short-term concept, applicable over the period for which neither labour nor capital inputs can be varied significantly. Our empirical results suggest that this utilisation rate varies quite systematically with demand pressure, cost (or profit) conditions, and actual relative to desired inventory levels (see Figure 4.2 and Table 4.3 taken from Helliwell *et al.*, 1984e).

Figure 4.2 MACE model: intensity of factor utilisation

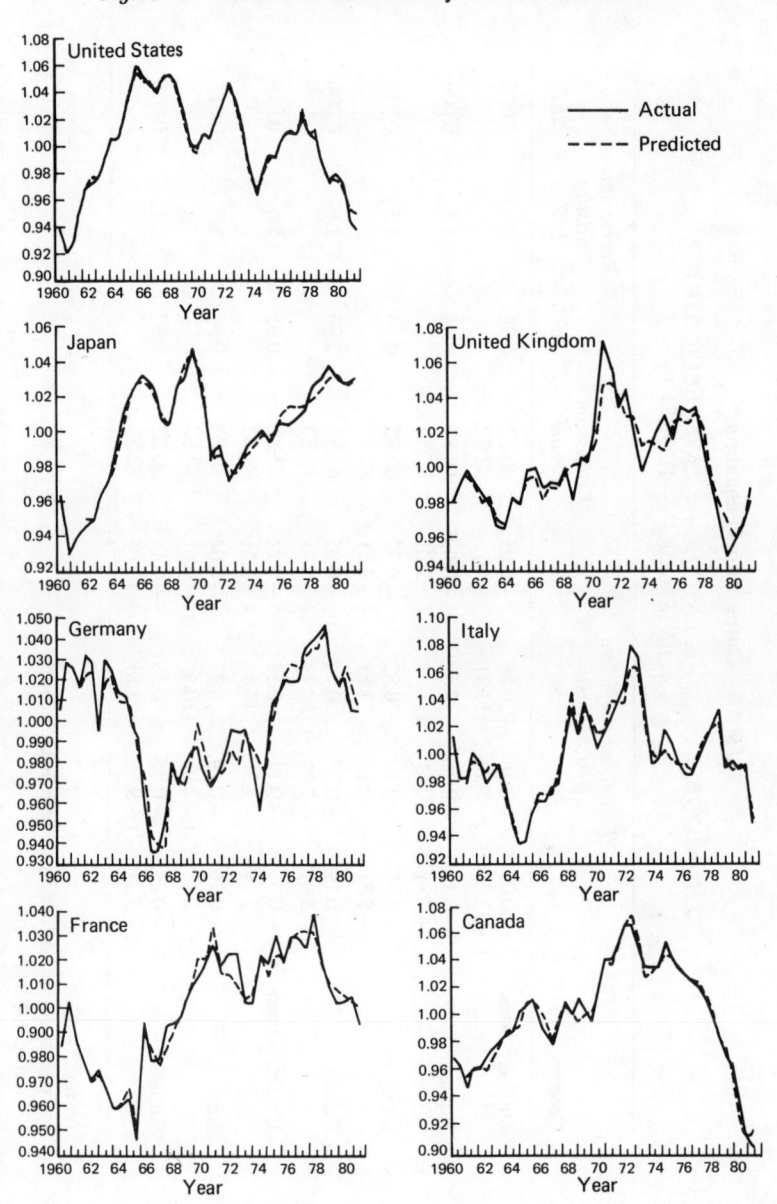

Table 4.3 Output supply equations[a]

$$LN(QBV/QBSV) = a_0 + a_1 LN(CQB) + a_2 LN(SALEV/QBSV) + a_3 LN(STOCKV(-1)/QBSV) + u$$

Country	a_0	a_1	a_2	a_3	Estimation Period	R^2	DW	SEE
United States	−0.09 (−23.2)	−0.36 (−9.6)	0.86 (11.1)	−0.05 (b)	60.S2 82.S2	0.98	1.8	0.006
Japan	−0.14 (−2.8)	−0.26 (−10.6)	0.59 (17.3)	−0.09 (−2.2)	66.S2 82.S2	0.96	1.8	0.009
Germany	−0.58 (−5.8)	−0.1 (b)	0.82 (7.8)	−0.37 (−4.5)	60.S2 82.S2	0.93	1.5	0.011
France	−0.19 (−5.0)	−0.27 (−7.0)	0.74 (10.1)	−0.05 (−2.8)	63.S2 82.S2	0.96	1.6	0.006
United Kingdom	−0.31 (−2.1)	−0.11 (−1.3)	0.58 (3.5)	−0.21 (−1.5)	63.S2 82.S2	0.85	1.6	0.014
Italy	−0.16 (−2.1)	−0.19 (−2.9)	0.77 (10.4)	−0.04 (−0.6)	60.S2 82.S2	0.94	1.5	0.012
Canada	−0.27 (−5.3)	−0.35 (−9.8)	0.59 (18.8)	−0.11 (−2.6)	60.S2 82.S2	0.97	1.7	0.008

Notes:
[a] Estimation technique: two stage least squares.
[b] Coefficient imposed.

Given sufficient time, profit-maximising entrepreneurs will bring actual employment in line with optimal (i.e., profit-maximising) employment, given the capital stock and the real (product) wage. This leads to the second potential output ($QBSV.\,2$) and the corresponding capacity utilisation ($CU.\,2$) measures defined above.[6] Alternatively, 'optimal' employment can be defined as the labour input at which total unit costs are minimised, which leads to the third concept of potential output ($QBSV.\,3$).

Even after entrepreneurs have adjusted employment so that the nominal wage equals the marginal value product of labour, the unemployment rate may deviate from the 'natural' rate (e.g., because the real wage is too high to attain full employment). It is thus possible to calculate what potential output and the associated capacity utilisation rate would be if the real wage adjusted to levels consistent with full employment. This is what the fourth capacity utilisation measure ($CU.\,4$) tries to answer: it represents the ratio of actual over potential output, the latter being computed for a given capital stock and employment equal to the private sector labour force minus natural unemployment. The input quantity and price assumptions underlying the four potential output and capacity utilisation measures are summarised in Table 4.4, and the actual measures of capacity utilisation are juxtaposed with an 'official' reference measure ($REFCU$) in Table 4.5.

Capacity utilisation measures $CU.\,2$, $CU.\,3$ and $CU.\,4$ may appear artificial in that of the two quasi-fixed inputs only one – employment – is

Table 4.4 Assumptions underlying alternative potential output measures

Potential Output	Factor Quantities		Factor Costs			Output Price
	Capital	Employment	Capital	Energy	Labour	
$QBSV.\,1$	Actual	Actual	n.a.	n.a.	n.a.	n.a.
$QBSV.\,2$	Actual	Profit-maximising	n.a.	n.a.	Actual	Actual
$QBSV.\,3$	Actual	Cost-minimising	Actual	Actual	Actual	n.a.
$QBSV.\,4$	Actual	Full	n.a.	n.a.	Flexible (a)	Flexible (a)

Notes:
(a) Assuming profit-maximising behaviour and flexible real wages leading to full employment.
n.a. Means variable does not enter the calculation of the potential output measure concerned.

Table 4.5 Alternative measures of capacity utilisation

	UNITED STATES					JAPAN				
	CU1 USA	CU2 USA	CU3 USA	CU4 USA	REFCU[a] USA	CU1 JAPAN	CU2 JAPAN	CU3 JAPAN	CU4 JAPAN	REFCU[a] JAPAN
1960	0.931	0.835	1.010	0.928	1.019					1.013
61	0.939	0.846	1.017	0.928	0.972					1.048
62	0.971	0.911	1.071	0.968	0.983					1.016
63	0.984	0.936	1.091	0.980	0.983					1.008
64	1.005	0.998	1.131	1.006	0.980					1.047
65	1.029	1.049	1.172	1.036	1.002	0.947	0.875	1.069	0.948	0.956
66	1.057	1.133	1.214	1.070	1.024	0.943	0.813	1.078	0.944	0.939
67	1.044	1.091	1.173	1.057	0.992	0.957	0.797	1.111	0.958	0.993
68	1.052	1.135	1.186	1.067	1.017	0.984	0.830	1.131	0.985	1.002
69	1.036	1.140	1.172	1.052	1.045	1.021	0.856	1.128	1.023	1.028
70	1.000	1.059	1.103	1.004	0.971	1.031	0.879	1.086	1.032	1.048
71	1.007	1.041	1.090	1.003	0.949	1.006	0.889	1.085	1.007	0.987
72	1.027	1.087	1.125	1.026	1.010	1.029	0.922	1.078	1.029	0.986
73	1.041	1.124	1.166	1.047	1.064	1.037	0.950	0.986	1.039	1.114
74	0.997	1.004	1.084	0.996	1.030	0.990	0.873	1.000	0.991	1.041
75	0.973	0.896	0.985	0.951	0.913	0.975	0.925	1.046	0.973	0.901
76	0.992	0.944	1.030	0.975	0.985	0.993	0.974	1.070	0.991	0.971
77	1.009	0.982	1.068	0.998	1.017	0.997	1.006	1.086	0.996	0.983
78	1.014	0.997	1.086	1.011	1.051	1.005	1.004	1.069	1.003	1.006
79	1.008	0.975	1.079	1.006	1.072	1.010	1.007	1.107	1.009	1.034
80	0.981	0.903	1.036	0.969	1.009	1.028	1.030	1.141	1.030	1.037
81	0.977	0.862	1.024	0.962	1.012	1.035	1.078	1.152	1.035	1.005
82	0.941	0.813	0.979	0.911	0.908	1.029	1.069		1.029	0.968

	GERMANY					FRANCE				
	CU1 GER	CU2 GER	CU3 GER	CU4 GER	REFCU[a] GER	CU1 FRA	CU2 FRA	CU3 FRA	CU4 FRA	REFCU[a] FRA
1960	1.011	0.949	1.302	1.011	1.013					1.001
61	0.987	0.933	1.243	0.990	1.016					1.005
62	0.974	0.917	1.186	0.977	0.997					1.005
63	0.955	0.864	1.125	0.958	0.983	0.993	0.976	1.052	1.000	1.004
64	0.975	0.893	1.137	0.978	1.034	0.982	0.956	1.052	0.991	1.023
65	0.983	0.924	1.145	0.986	1.050	0.972	0.922	1.044	0.980	0.996
66	0.972	0.899	1.118	0.975	1.013	0.963	0.888	1.029	0.971	1.012
67	0.950	0.817	1.060	0.945	0.935	0.961	0.865	1.022	0.966	0.986
68	0.991	0.882	1.115	0.989	0.968	0.970	0.900	1.073	0.973	0.966
69	1.005	0.933	1.130	1.007	1.012	0.978	0.911	1.093	0.980	1.016
70	1.022	1.042	1.132	1.025	1.024	0.994	0.929	1.102	0.995	1.001
71	1.006	1.002	1.094	1.008	0.995	1.002	0.959	1.113	1.002	0.976
72	1.013	1.026	1.096	1.014	0.997	1.015	0.962	1.122	1.015	1.001
73	1.026	1.078	1.119	1.028	1.049	1.023	0.989	1.132	1.026	1.048
74	1.015	1.060	1.097	1.011	1.015	1.023	1.031	1.106	1.029	1.038
75	0.986	0.970	1.047	0.969	0.937	1.003	1.010	1.075	1.002	0.923
76	1.027	1.043	1.101	1.012	0.995	1.020	1.060	1.087	1.020	0.994
77	1.029	1.055	1.101	1.018	1.006	1.025	1.075	1.092	1.026	0.999
78	1.030	1.032	1.088	1.023	1.010	1.031	1.075	1.100	1.032	1.007
79	1.037	1.013	1.078	1.036	1.049	1.033	1.080	1.099	1.032	1.046
80	1.025	0.995	1.049	1.027	1.037	1.015	1.044	1.077	1.015	1.026
81	1.004	0.936	1.007	0.997	1.006	1.003	1.016	1.062	0.998	0.993
82	0.984	0.854	0.975	0.963	0.964	1.000	1.001	1.052	0.993	0.971

Table 4.5 (Contd.)

| | UNITED KINGDOM ||||| ITALY |||||
	CU1 UKM	CU2 UKM	CU3 UKM	CU4 UKM	REFCU[a] UKM	CU1 ITA	CU2 ITA	CU3 ITA	CU4 ITA	REFCU[a] ITA
1960						0.998	0.799	1.311		1.021
61						0.993	0.749	1.268		1.045
62						0.988	0.741	1.246		1.058
63	0.985	0.944	1.144	0.986	1.035	0.991	0.808	1.241	0.950	1.065
64	0.994	0.961	1.165	1.002	1.002	0.963	0.789	1.181	0.948	0.990
65	0.981	0.940	1.158	0.992	0.976	0.936	0.703	1.143	0.954	0.967
66	0.966	0.917	1.127	0.977	0.980	0.963	0.738	1.175	0.921	1.011
67	0.981	0.923	1.128	0.989	1.018	0.972	0.770	1.201	0.913	1.027
68	0.999	0.939	1.135	1.008	1.016	0.997	0.815	1.225	0.935	1.030
69	0.990	0.928	1.110	1.001	1.000	1.025	0.835	1.214	0.949	1.012
70	0.995	0.949	1.103	1.006	0.980	1.032	0.942	1.205	0.971	1.012
71	0.994	0.910	1.070	1.001	1.013	1.011	0.949	1.159	1.000	1.019
72	1.012	0.946	1.077	1.001	1.026	1.033	0.995	1.157	1.012	0.977
73	1.066	1.057	1.117	1.020	1.008	1.067	1.176	1.182	0.991	0.976
74	1.040	1.056	1.065	1.086	0.975	1.054	1.132	1.104	1.005	1.038
75	1.008	1.018	1.031	1.060	0.979	0.995	1.000	1.052	1.040	1.047
76	1.017	0.973	1.014	1.018	1.050	1.015	1.045	1.073	1.042	0.922
77	1.023	0.925	0.996	1.016	1.019	0.991	0.959	1.040	0.981	1.011
78	1.034	0.932	1.004	1.021	0.950	0.993	0.973	1.057	0.994	1.002
79	1.020	0.914	0.983	1.036	0.973	1.018	0.973	1.073	0.968	0.995
80	0.978	0.867	0.928	1.028	1.013	1.012	0.894	1.065	0.971	1.041
81	0.954	0.803	0.883	0.972	1.035	0.993	0.905	1.033	0.993	1.076
82	0.974	0.812	0.900	0.921	1.072	0.972	0.755	0.982	0.989	1.033
				0.926	0.995				0.964	0.976
					0.954				0.938	
					0.965					

CANADA

	CU1 CAN	CU2 CAN	CU3 CAN	CU4 CAN	REFCU[a] CAN
1960	0.966	1.001	1.091	0.944	0.998
61	0.954	0.967	1.063	0.933	0.976
62	0.968	0.967	1.073	0.956	0.981
63	0.979	0.969	1.079	0.972	0.980
64	0.937	0.967	1.085	0.989	1.009
65	1.006	1.018	1.101	1.015	1.017
66	1.004	0.986	1.091	1.019	1.014
67	0.982	0.978	1.075	0.994	0.992
68	1.003	0.999	1.102	1.011	1.007
69	1.007	1.042	1.113	1.017	1.021
70	0.999	1.020	1.080	1.000	0.967
71	1.031	1.093	1.108	1.029	0.963
72	1.046	1.124	1.130	1.046	0.989
73	1.067	1.133	1.174	1.074	1.050
74	1.044	1.049	1.133	1.055	1.040
75	1.035	1.046	1.093	1.033	0.950
76	1.048	1.104	1.139	1.045	0.985
77	1.032	1.079	1.105	1.022	0.986
78	1.023	1.031	1.064	1.012	1.003
79	1.007	0.936	1.037	1.006	1.058
80	0.978	0.849	0.983	0.978	1.031
81	0.950	0.820	0.944	0.952	1.029
82	0.905	0.734	0.857	0.880	0.920

Note:

[a] *REFCU* represents an official measure of capacity utilisation presented here for comparison with the alternative MACE-based measures.

For Germany, France, and Italy *REFCU* is the result of an industry survey. For the United States and Canada *REFCU* is based on a synthetic measure of potential output. For Japan and the United Kingdom *REFCU* is based on a potential output defined as the phase average trend of actual output.

adjusted to its optimal level, while the other—capital—is assumed to remain fixed. It seems more plausible that in practice entrepreneurs would adjust both quasi-fixed input quantities simultaneously to achieve a desired input mix. Such a behavioural hypothesis requires, however, an additional assumption about the optimum level of output, since under the assumptions of profit-maximisation, constant returns to scale and fixed input and output prices the optimum level of output is either zero or indeterminate. All applications of MACE models therefore contain an output expectations equation. Once expected output is determined, a corresponding desired capital stock as well as the optimal employment level can be computed on the basis of relative input prices. The optimal capital stock (and corresponding energy requirement) combined with the matching optimal employment level can be used to compute yet another capacity utilisation measure—one for which capital, labour and energy inputs are fully adjusted to optimal levels and subject to given output expectations and given relative input prices.[7] Of course, this potential output measure will be equal to expected output adjusted for anticipated increases in labour efficiency. Since this output measure is based on expectations rather than on technical capacity to produce using existing factor stocks, it would be inappropriate to consider it at par with the potential output measures defined before. This does not, however, exclude the possibility that such an expected output concept may play an important role in a dynamic macro model.

INTERPRETATION AND COMPARISON OF RESULTS

The first capacity utilisation indicator ($CU.1$) measures the intensity with which actually employed factors are used, and thus shows available room for short-term increases in output, without increases in capital, energy and employment. In the MACE framework, this variable is used as the dependent variable in the output equation (see Table 4.3). It shows a clearly discernable cyclical pattern with quite different cyclical positions among the major seven OECD countries in the early 1980s. Comparing it with the second measure ($CU.2$) conveys information on whether actual employment exceeds or falls short of optimum employment. In the latter case, one can expect employment and output to increase in subsequent periods. For 1982 the figures for the United States and Canada imply a large future employment increase which has since materialised. Employment increases have been modest, however, in the United Kingdom for which 1982 figures likewise suggest imminent

Figure 4.3 **MACE model: real labour cost gap**

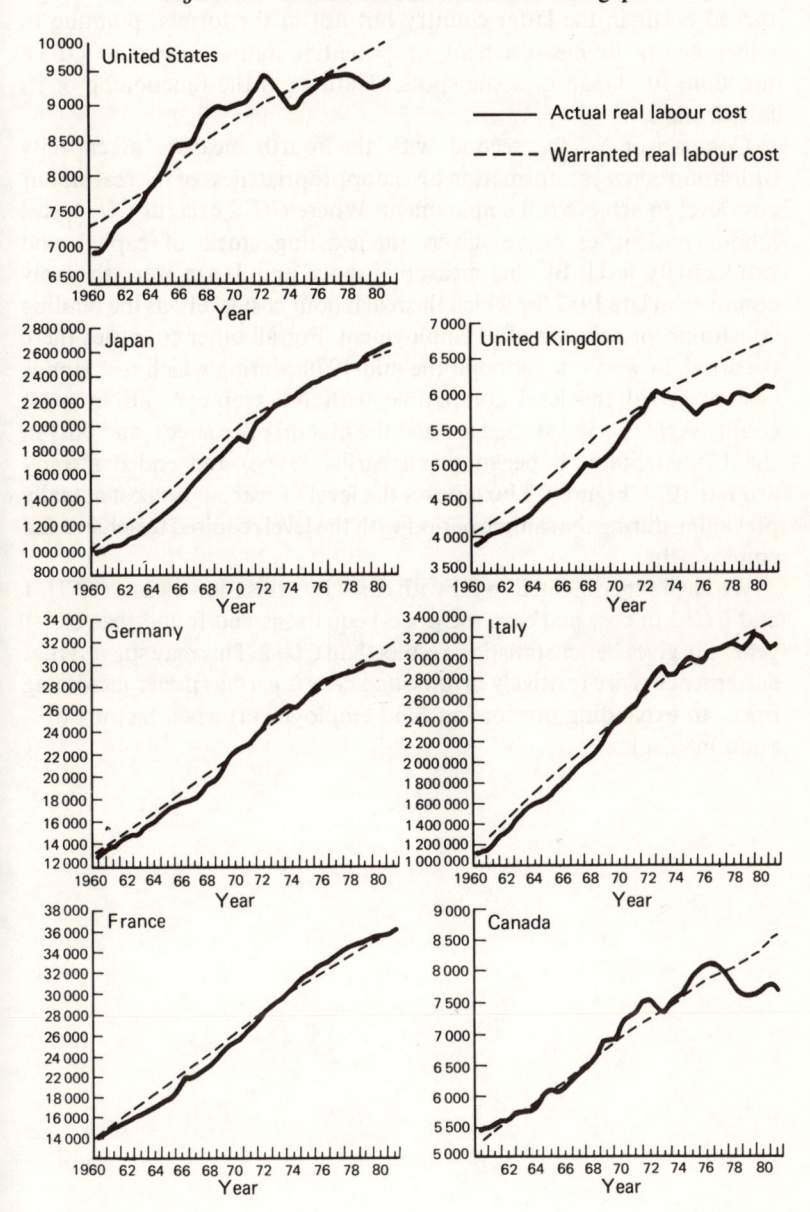

employment expansion. For Japan and France, the 1982 figures suggest subsequent reductions in employment (i.e., $CU.1$ $CU.2$) which did indeed occur in the latter country but not in the former, pointing to either errors in measurement of potential output (e.g., the $QBSV$ function) for Japan or some special features in the functioning of its labour market.

Comparison of the second with the fourth measure of capacity utilisation conveys information on the appropriateness of the real labour cost level to achieve full employment: Where $CU.2$ exceeds $CU.4$, real labour cost is excessive, given the existing stock of capital and productivity level. By this measure France and Japan were the only countries in late 1982 for which the real labour cost level was the binding constraint for achieving full employment. For all other countries there occurred, however, a period in the mid-1970s during which real labour cost exceeded the level compatible with full employment. In most countries this period started around the first oil price shock, and only in the United States it began much earlier (1966) and ended already around 1974. Figure 4.3 juxtaposes the level of real labour cost actually prevailing during the sample period with the level required to achieve full employment.

We have experimented so far with capacity utilisation measures $CU.1$ and $CU.2$ in cost mark-up (or price-) equations and found that $CU.1$ generally gives better statistical results than $CU.2$. This may suggest that entrepreneurs are relatively myopic and *ceteris paribus* prefer increasing prices to expanding production (and employment) when factor utilisation intensifies.

Appendix

THE PRODUCTION STRUCTURE: SPECIFICATION AND PARAMETER DERIVATION

The production structure is based on a nested double CES production function, combining capital, labour and energy to define gross output.

(a) The Inner CES Function

The inner function which combines energy and capital in a vintage bundle has the form

$$KEBSV = KEBSV(-1).(1 - R1 - RSCRB) + [IBV + R1.KBV(-1)].$$
$$[b + c.(c.UCC/(b.PENB))^{s-1}]^{s/(s-1)} \quad (A4.1)$$

where:

$KEBSV$	=	vintage capital–energy bundle
$R1$	=	retrofitting parameter
$RSCRB$	=	scrapping rate
IBV	=	gross fixed investment
b, c	=	scale parameters in the inner CES function
UCC	=	capital cost variable
$PENB$	=	energy price index (for final users)
s	=	elasticity of substitution between energy and capital.

In this equation the business gross fixed capital stock (KBV), business gross fixed investment (IBV), the price index of energy used by business ($PENB$) and the scrapping rate ($RSCRB$) are variables available from official statistics.

The user cost of capital UCC is computed as

$$UCC = PIB.(RSCRB + RHOR).$$
$$(1 - RITC - RTYB.PVDEP)/(1 - RTYB) \quad (A4.2)$$

where PIB is the (observed) business gross fixed investment deflator and $RHOR$ (the 'real supply price of capital') was defined as a constant, with a value such that on average total factor earnings exhaust total output over the sample period. $RITC$ is the rate of investment tax credit, $RTYB$ is the effective (marginal) tax rate on business income and $PVDEP$ is the unit present value of tax depreciation allowances.

Assuming that the capital–energy ratio (EK) is optimal (subject to prevailing relative prices $PENB/UCC$) on average over the sample period implies that

$$c/b = (\text{MEAN}(EK)/\text{MEAN}[(UCC/PENB)^s])^{1/s} \quad (A4.3)$$

which allows direct computation of c/b from observed variables for any given value of s, the elasticity of substitution between capital and energy. Normalising $KEBSV$ such that MEAN($KEBSV$) = MEAN(KBV) allows b to be computed

as
$$b = 1/(1 + (c/b)^s \operatorname{MEAN}((PENB/UCC)^{1-s}) \quad (A4.4)$$

The elasticity of substitution (s) and the retrofitting parameter ($R1$) are determined by estimating the energy demand function

$$\ln(ENBV) = a_1 \ln(EBSV) + u \quad (A4.5)$$

where u represents the stochastic error term and $EBSV$ is the vintage energy requirement needed to operate the capital stock KBV subject to prevailing relative energy prices ($PENB/UCC$), defined as

$$EBSV = EBSV(-1).(1 - R1 - RSCRB)$$
$$+ (IBV + R1.KBV(-1)).((c.UCC)/(b.PENB))^s \quad (A4.6)$$

To obtain a starting value, $EBSV$ is set equal to $ENBV$ at the beginning of the sample period, on the assumption that no large and surprising changes in energy prices have occurred over the preceding few years.

The parameter pair (s, $R1$) which maximised the likelihood function of regression (A4.5) was chosen as the preferred parameter combination.

This completes the estimation of all the relevant parameters of the inner CES function.

(b) The outer CES Function

The outer function, which bundles labour and the capital–energy aggregate into gross output, has the form

$$QBSV = (B.(PI.ETB)^{-r} + C.KEBSV^{-r})^{-1/r} \quad (A4.7)$$

where:

$QBSV$	= potential output (at normal rates of factor utilisation)
B, C	= scale factors in the outer CES function
PI	= labour efficiency index
ETB	= total employment, business
r	= substitution parameter in the outer CES function, with $1/(1+r)$ = elasticity of substitution (TAU)
$KEBSV$	= vintage capital–energy bundle (see above).

Cost-minimising behaviour by producers implies that on average

$$KEBSV/ETB = ((WSSE/PI)/CKE)^{1/(1+r)} \quad (A4.8)$$

where $WSSE$ is observed labour cost per man year and CKE is the cost of the capital–energy bundle computed from the dual cost function to the inner CES function

$$CKE = (b^s.UCC^{1-s} + c^s.PENB^{1-s})^{1/(1-s)} \quad (A4.9)$$

The parameter TAU ($= 1/(1+r)$) was determined from the regression

$$\ln(QBV/(ETB.PI)) = a_0 + TAU.\ln(WSSE/(PQB.PI)) + u \quad (A4.10)$$

where PQB is the deflator for gross output ($QBSV$) at factor cost. Equation (A4.10) requires PI to be known, while in turn the determination of PI requires knowledge of TAU (see below). PI and TAU were therefore determined by an iterative procedure, starting with an assumed value of $TAU = 1$.

Equation (A4.7) can be inverted and solved for the labour–efficiency bundle

$$B.PI^{-r} = (QBSV^{-r} - C.KEBSV^{-r})/ETB^{-r} \qquad (A4.11)$$

Assuming that on average the observed input ratios are cost-minimising (subject to observed relative factor prices) allows the parameter C to be determined as follows:

$$C = \text{MEAN}(PKQ)/(\text{MEAN}(NKS) + \text{MEAN}(PKK)) \qquad (A4.12)$$

where:

$\text{MEAN}(PKQ) = \text{MEAN}((CKE/WSSE).(QBV/ETB)^{-r})$
$\text{MEAN}(NKS) = \text{MEAN}((ETB/KEBSV)^{(1+r)})$
$\text{MEAN}(PKK) = \text{MEAN}((CKE/(WSSE.ETB).(KEBSV/ETB)^{-r})$.

A labour–efficiency bundle can now be computed as:

$$B^{-1/r}.PIM = ((QBV^{-r} - C.KEBSV^{-r})/ETB^{-r})^{-1/r} \qquad (A4.13)$$

where PIM is the observed labour–efficiency index which includes cyclical variations and is obtained by substituting actual output (QBV) for potential output ($QBSV$) in the inverted production function (A4.11).

This bundle was used as the dependent variable for the various tests of the time invariance of the rate of technical progress and the testing of the embodiment and catch-up hypotheses. Parameter B can be determined from this bundle by normalising the calculated labour efficiency index such that

$$PI_{1971.S1} = 1.0$$

and imposing the constraint that MEAN ($QBSV$) equals MEAN (QBV) over the sample period.

This completes the determination of the parameters for the outer CES function.

The values of the structural production function parameters for the inner and outer CES function thus derived are reported in Table 4.1 in the text.

Notes

1. Opinions expressed in this chapter are those of the authors, and do not necessarily represent those of the OECD.
2. The procedures and results for the constancy tests of labour efficiency growth are reported in detail in Helliwell *et al.* (1984e).
3. The measured labour efficiency index is obtained by dividing actual output by a weighted average of factor input quantities, the weighting scheme corresponding to the nested CES production structure.
4. For a detailed description of estimation procedures for these parameters, see the technical Appendix to this chapter.
5. In fact, the various potential output concepts defined are not unique to a MACE production function, and could be applied to other aggregate production functions as well. It would indeed be interesting to determine how sensitive alternative potential output measures are to both changes in MACE function parameters and altogether different aggregate production functions.
6. Conceptually, it would be possible to calculate an alternative potential output measure in which employment is held constant and the capital stock is adjusted to the level at which the user cost of the capital–energy bundle equals its marginal value product, given the level of employment. It is questionable, however, whether such a concept is of any empirical relevance, and these calculations were not carried out.
7. Needless to say, this capacity utilisation measure would be homogeneous of degree zero in input and output prices as long as the price level (or its rate of change) has no impact on the formation of output expectations.

References

HELLIWELL, J. F., McRAE, R. N., BOOTHE, P., HANSSON, A., MARGOLICK, M., PADMORE, T., PLOURDE, A. and PLUMMER, R. (1984a) 'Energy and the National Economy: An Overview of the MACE Model', in Scott, A. D. (ed.) *Progress in Natural Resource Economics* (Oxford: Oxford University Press).

———MACGREGOR, M. E. and PADMORE, T. (1984b) 'Economic Growth and Productivity in Canada, 1955–1990', *discussion paper* 84–30, (Vancouver: University of British Columbia).

———(1984c) 'Stagflation and Productivity Decline in Canada 1974–82', *Canadian Journal of Economics* 17, pp. 191–216.

———STURM, P. and SALOU, G. (1984d) 'International Comparison of the Sources of Productivity Slowdown 1973–1982', *working paper* 1465 (New York: National Bureau of Economic Research).

———STURM, P. and SALOU, G. (1984e) 'A Revised INTERLINK Supply Block: Model Specification and Empirical Results', typescript (Paris: OECD).

OECD (1984) *Economic Outlook* 36, p. 177.

5 Capacity Utilisation in a Vintage Model of United Kingdom Manufacturing

J. Ansar, A. Ingham, H. Leon, M. Toker and A. Ulph[1]

INTRODUCTION

'Capacity utilisation', 'capital utilisation' (or whatever) is a decision by a firm to operate at different levels of activity. Questions about utilisation thus become questions about how firms or industries operate. This was recognised by Winston and McCoy (1974), who considered optimal idleness in a model in which the cost of labour varied over the 24 hours of a day. These changes in wage rates produced a rhythm which will be reflected in when machines are used. In their model, machines are homogeneous and output and labour combine through a neo-classical production function to determine the output level. So in order to produce a given output per day it is possible to vary the capital–labour ratio across the day whilst installing sufficient machines to generate the desired output overall.

This chapter considers a different approach in terms of technical structure, but retains the approach of examining the optimal decisions of firms. Our primary concern is with the demand for energy by manufacturing industry in the United Kingdom, but as we model this by considering the optimal decisions made by firms in manufacturing industry we obtain a statement about the capital that industry uses. Previous work on the demand for energy, for example Berndt and Wood (1975) and Griffin and Gregory (1976) have produced conflicting conclusions on such a fundamental property of the nature of the production function as whether capital and energy are complements or substitutes. The Berndt–Wood study – which finds that energy and capital are complements – was a time series study, and broadly all time series studies since have confirmed complementarity. To contrast with this, cross-sectional studies – of which Griffin–Gregory is one – have concluded that capital and energy are substitutes. The conventional wisdom to explain this is that time series studies for a single country reflects short-term substitution possibilities, whilst the cross-sectional studies across countries will reflect more long-term possibilities. Whilst capital and energy are substitutable in the long run, they are thus not in the short run. Clearly if one wishes to study energy as an input into the productive process, one has to do so within a model which has a temporal structure of production which is determined by the data.

Our reasons for considering a model in which production is not represented by a smooth concave aggregative neoclassical production function are not purely empirical, however. In that model, firms are able to vary the mix of factors in each period. We wish to take account of the fact that capital is durable, and at the time it is installed has particular energy, materials and labour requirements. More flexibility exists at the design stage than during operation, and thus the response of industry and the economy will be less immediate than in the neoclassical case. The model we are here talking about is the vintage model of production, an excellent discussion of which is contained in Salter (1966). An application of this model to the responsiveness of the economy is contained in Ingham, Weiserbs and Melese (1982).

In this chapter we are not concerned directly with energy, but the capital use decisions of firms. However, we do wish to focus on the question as to how unexpected energy price changes have affected the production decisions of manufacturing industry, and in particular how much capital it may use and its nature in terms of the *ex ante* design of machines installed.

The chapter proceeds as follows. Our next section discusses the vintage model, and what we might choose to mean by capacity utilisation within it, the next section describes some empirical estimation that we have done to discover the vintage structure of manufacturing industry in the United Kingdom between 1955 and 1983. After that the fourth Section describes the vintages used and the quasi-rents on machines used using a simulation model with coefficients derived from our estimation. This allows us to construct a utilisation index using arguments contained in the second Section. Finally we discuss further work which is in progress. At this stage, we would like to issue an important warning. Our work is very much at an intermediate stage, and we recognise that much remains to be done before it can be regarded as satisfactory. Our purpose in presenting this now is to give some indication as to an alternative methodology, and how it might be implemented.

CAPACITY UTILISATION IN A VINTAGE MODEL

As the vintage model of production is by now well known and adequately referred to elsewhere, we describe it only briefly to determine notation – and, in particular, to discuss what could be meant by 'capacity utilisation' in such a structure, and how it could be measured. We shall proceed by setting down the assumptions on firms' behaviour and on the technical constraints that they face. The model we use is a supply side one in that we consider the actions of firms only so that the demand for output and the price at which it is sold are considered exogenous.[1] The structure of industry is also something that will be taken as outside this model, and whilst the degree of competition is important in explaining utilisation, we shall consider this in a somewhat indirect way.

Firms will be assumed to be expected profit-maximisers in all aspects of the firm's operations. This will be a crucial fact to remember. The most general structure of technology that we wish to consider is the putty-semi-putty vintage model, discussed by Fuss (1977) amongst others. We shall generally deal with the putty clay restricted version of this, and so will give specific detail only for that case. However, it will be useful to refer to the more general case, which we hope to investigate in the future. So in order to keep this discussion simple, and diagrammatic, we shall limit the discussion of the putty-semi-putty model to the case of two factors – energy and labour.

In the two-factor putty-semi-putty model, decisions about the use of the two factors and substitution between them is given by the *ex post* isoquant for unit output level given in Figure 5.1.

BB represents the choices that can be made at the production stage in a machine of type b (say). These choices – and hence the location and shape of the isoquant BB – depend on choices made at the design or *ex ante* stage.

Choices about design and operation will be made at each stage – *ex ante* and *ex post* corresponding to cost-minimisation. So point C will be the chosen design of technique for vintage v if $\omega(v)$, $\beta(v)$ (fully defined later) are the present value expected prices. However, at time t if the factor prices are $w(t)$, $b(t)$ then point D will be the operation decision of the firm, which will be different from the design requirements at C. This could be the case at time $t = v$, as $\omega(v)/\beta(v)$ is not necessarily equal to $w(v)/b(v)$, so that new machines are operated differently to their design.

The putty-semi-putty model is the most general model that we could consider. This means that it is the most difficult to estimate as we need to unravel two sets of isoquants from the data. We shall now discuss a more realistic model which is more readily estimated.

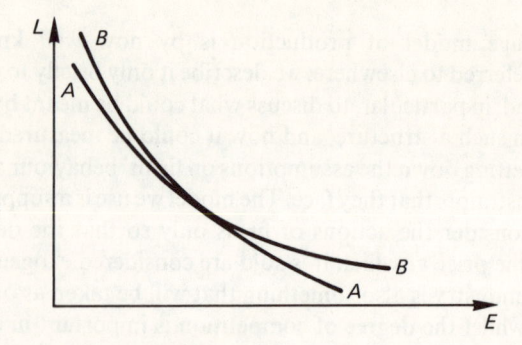

Figure 5.1 Ex post and ex ante isoquant: unit output level

The model that we have produced estimates for is the putty-clay version in which the *ex post* isoquant is taken to be the Leontief fixed coefficient one in which no substitution between factors is allowed. Furthermore we also limit ourselves to considering a Cobb–Douglas isoquant for the *ex ante* substitution possibilities. Whilst the latter assumption is important for empirical implementation, they do not limit the applicability of the method.

The firm has two decisions. First what should its investment plan be – how many new machines should be installed and what their design in terms of the future requirements of the other factors per machine will be. Second, how much it should produce and which machines – of all those available from previous investment decisions, all with potentially different factor requirement coefficients – should be used. Profit-maximisation or cost-minimisation is used to solve both problems. We do not, however, explain the investment or output decision, both of which would require modelling the demand side.

A machine is defined so that when first installed it produces one unit of output.

A machine installed at time t embodies $\kappa(t)$ units of capital and requires $\lambda(t)$ units of labour and $\varepsilon(t)$ units of energy.[3] The *ex ante* production function allows any choice of κ, λ, ε as long as they satisfy the unit isoquant.

$$A^t \kappa^{\alpha_1} \lambda^{\alpha_2} \varepsilon^{\alpha_3} = 1.$$

They are chosen to minimise expected cost. Let $U(t)$ be the set of future time periods in which a machine installed at time t is used, and let d_t^ς be the discount factor appropriate to time period ς, looking forward from

Figure 5.2

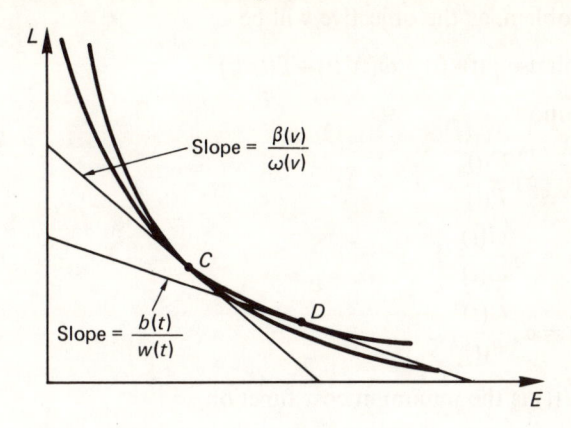

period t

$$d_t^s = \prod_{i=0}^{s-1}\left(\frac{1}{1+r_{t+i}}\right)$$

where:
r is the interest rate relevant to the firm
$p(t)$ is the price of a unit of capital at time t
$w(t)$ is the price of a unit of labour service at time t
$b(t)$ is the price of a unit of energy at time t.

The superscript e denotes a future expected value. The firm then chooses $\kappa(t), \lambda(t), \varepsilon(t)$ to minimise

$$p(t)K(t) + \sum_{S \in U(t)} d_t^s(w(s)\lambda(t) + b(s)\varepsilon(t))$$

subject to the isoquant previously given

$$A^t \kappa(t)^{\alpha_1} \lambda(t)^{\alpha_2} \varepsilon(t)^{\alpha_3} = 1$$

If we define present value expected prices

$$\omega(t) = \sum_{S \in U(t)} d_t^s w^e(s)$$

and

$$\beta(t) = \sum_{S \in U(t)} d_t^s b^e(s)$$

then the problem becomes a straightforward Cobb–Douglas minimisation problem, as the objective will be

minimise $p(t)\kappa(t) + \omega(t)\lambda(t) + \beta(t)\varepsilon(t)$

with solution

$$\kappa(t) = \alpha_1 \frac{C(t)}{P(t)}$$

$$\lambda(t) = \alpha_2 \frac{C(t)}{\omega(t)}$$

$$\varepsilon(t) = \alpha_3 \frac{C(t)}{\beta(t)}$$

where $C(t)$ is the minimum cost function

$$C(t) = A^{-t}(\alpha_1)^{-\alpha_1}(\alpha_2)^{-\alpha_2}(\alpha_3)^{-\alpha_3} p(t)^{\alpha_1} \omega(t)^{\alpha_2} \beta(t)^{\alpha_3}$$

Consider now a machine installed at time v. At time t we can calculate its variable operating cost. We can do this either in terms of the operating costs of a machine or of a unit of capital. We shall do it in terms of the latter.

$l(v)$ = no. of workers required per unit of capital of

$$\text{vintage } v = \frac{\lambda(v)}{\kappa(v)}$$

$e(v)$ = energy required per unit of capital of vintage $v = \dfrac{\varepsilon(v)}{\kappa(v)}$

The variable cost of operating capital of vintage v at time t is therefore

$$VC_t(v) = l(v)w(t) + e(v)b(t).$$

It is now possible to answer the question of which machines which are available will be used to produce a given level of output. This is done using Figures 5.2 and 5.3 which are well known from Salter (1966). Vintages are sorted in order of increasing variable cost.[4] Those with lesser cost will be used in priority to those with greater cost. Now calculate the output obtainable from each vintage. This is

$$Y_t(v) = \frac{\bar{K}(v)}{\kappa(v)} \delta^{t-v}$$

where:
$\bar{K}(v)$ is the quality of investment at time v, which we take to be

Figure 5.3

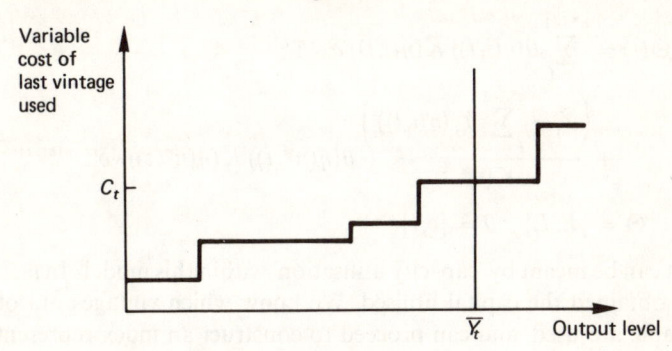

exogenously given and δ is a depreciation and/or technical progress factor.

Now let (v,t) be the rank of the vth vintage at time t in terms of increasing variable cost. Calculate $n^*(t)$ to be the marginal vintage at time t, if a predetermined level of output $\overline{Y}_t$ is produced, i.e.:

$$\sum_{i=1}^{n^*-1} Y_t(\eta(i,t)) < \overline{Y} < \sum_{i=1}^{n^*+1} Y_t(\eta(i,t))$$

so that vintage n^* may be only partially utilised
where:

$$\eta(n(v,t),t) = v$$

so that vintage $n^*(t)$ must be used in order to produce Y_t and is the most expensive vintage used. Note that it may be necessary that the marginal vintage n^* is not fully used. However, all other vintages will be fully used and must be if costs are to be minimised and profits maximised. The process can be illustrated with Figure 5.3.

Here the marginal vintage has variable cost C_t and is the fourth vintage in variable cost terms. This marginal vintage is not fully used.

All the information about the firms' two decisions is now available, and we are able to answer the two motivating questions about factor demands and the utilisation of available capacity.

Total factor demands will be

$$\Theta(t) = \sum_{i=1}^{n^*-1} \theta(\eta(i,t)) \, \bar{K}(\eta(i,t)) \, \delta^{t-\eta(i,t)}$$
$$+ \frac{\left(\bar{Y}_t - \sum_{i=1}^{n^*-1} Y_t(\eta(i,t))\right)}{Y_t(n^*,t)} \theta(\eta(n^*,t)) \, \bar{K}(\eta(n^*,t)) w \delta^{t-\eta(n^*,t)}$$

$$\Theta = \{E, L\} \quad \theta = \{e, l\}.$$

What can be meant by 'capacity utilisation' within this model? In fact, we have obtained the capital utilised. We know which vintages out of all available are used, and can proceed to construct an index representing this. In terms of the capacity utilisation function of Johansen (1972), however, we have a capacity utilisation function equal to 1 everywhere in a region G and 0 everywhere not in G except for the marginal vintage.[5] And to move away from this property we need to relax the putty-clay structure to a putty-semi-putty structure which we discuss on p. 105 below.

What do we mean by 'available capital'? An answer to this really requires knowledge of when capital is scrapped and when it is idle. This would require quite detailed information on firms' expectations of investment and production in the future, which we do not have, as well as price expectations. We therefore define available capital to be the set of profitable vintages. A vintage will be profitable if the price of output resulting from using one unit of capital of that vintage exceeds the variable cost of operating that unit of capital. In fact, the marginal vintage is defined as the most expensive vintage in terms of variable cost for which variable cost does not exceed price. This would then determine output produced using Figure 5.3 in a slightly different way (see Figure 5.4).

At price $\bar{p}$, the first four vintages cover their costs and will all be fully utilised, producing output Y_t. This price exceeds the variable cost on the marginal vintage c_t, yielding a quasi-rent on capital of $(\bar{p} - c_t)$. In a perfectly competitive market this quasi-rent would be zero. But we do not impose any assumptions of competition, and so the quasi-rent can be positive, zero or negative. The set of available capital will be the set of vintages which have quasi-rents greater or equal to zero. So we are able to calculate two sets – one of profitable vintages or available capital and another of vintages used to produce the observed output or used capital. One set will be a sub-set of the other. The order of inclusion may be either way, and will correspond to under- or over-utilisation. Constructing an

Figure 5.4

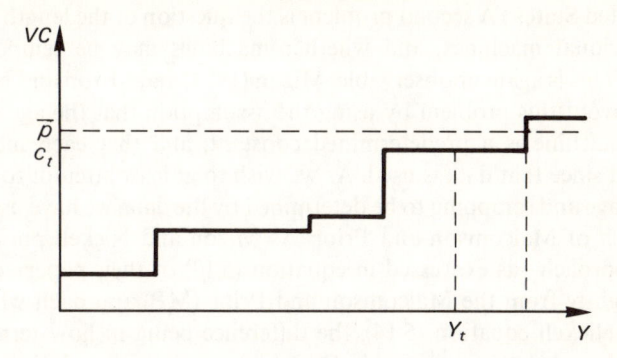

Note: $i = 1$, $A = 1$, $\beta = 1$; $i = 2$, $A = 2$, $\beta = 0.95$; $i = 3$, $A = 2$, $\beta = 1$.

index now becomes an aggregation problem, as each vintage has different operating requirements. The homogeneity of output can be used to avoid this problem. Our utilisation index is then the ratio of actual output to potential output if all available capital were used. It should be said that this index is produced merely as an indicator of utilisation, and that different indices may be required for different purposes. As we have full information about vintages which may be used and are not and so on, this enables questions about manufacturing decisions to be answered directly. Our task is now to obtain estimates for the parameters of the putty-clay model, and we report on this in the next Section.

ESTIMATING A PUTTY-CLAY MODEL

We now have the task of obtaining estimates so that the nature and usage of capital stock in manufacturing can be calculated. The putty-clay restriction is extremely convenient here in that a methodology for estimating the parameters exists. This is the approach of Malcomson and Prior (1979).

Vintage models have been estimated by Hausman (1973), Mizon (1974), Malcomson and Prior (1979) and Mizon and Nickell (1983), using regressions on currently observed variables and a variety of model specification and assumptions which allow this to be done. The problem to be solved is how to avoid having to have observations on the individual vintages which are generally unavailable. (Although sometimes they are for a micro study which allows different procedures and specifications to be used – Fuss (1977) did this for electricity generation in the United States.) A second problem is the question of the length of life of individual machines, and whether machines may be temporarily retired. This is again unobservable. Mizon (1974) and Mizon and Nickell (1983) avoid this problem by using the assumption that the age of the oldest machine is a predetermined constant, and that each machine installed since that date is used. As we wish to at least attempt to allow both usage and scrapping to be determined by the data, we have used the approach of Malcomson and Prior. As Mizon and Nickell point out, their approach – as expressed in equation (5.13) of their paper – differs only slightly from the Malcomson and Prior (MP) approach which is Mizon–Nickell equation (5.14); the difference being in how terms are collected, and the *ex ante* Cobb–Douglas assumption used.

We now describe the application of the Malcomson–Prior model of vintage production to a four factor model.[6] This requires minor generalisation which is of a complex rather than deep nature. Complexity is introduced because the *ex ante* choice of technique is described by three independent variables rather than a single one which can conveniently be chosen to be the output per machine ratio. Fortunately, the generalisation produces regression equations which are exactly analogous in form.

The MP model is extremely ingenious in starting from a vintage model and producing equations which allow all of the parameters to be identified without having any data on the individual vintage input and output characteristics. This is done by deriving from the necessary (and sufficient) conditions for intertemporal profit-maximisation an expression for the quasi-rent of a machine, and then using this to obtain an equation in the change in output which depends only on how total factor inputs change (data on which is available), provided that the quasi-rent can be approximated in a way which requires that changes occur in a slow rather than fast way. This enables some of the parameters to be estimated, but unfortunately not those of the *ex ante* production function. These are obtained by considering the contemporary cost function for a vintage – that is, the cost of operating a vintage at the date at which it is first installed. For particular expectations it can be shown that the length of life of equipment depends only on the rate of return from holding a machine, and that this implies that the contemporary cost will be the same for all periods for which these are the same. As the contemporary cost function depends on the parameters of the *ex ante* production function, this relation allows them to be estimated. However, it is unfortunate that such key technical parameters as the *ex ante* production coefficients should depend on the particular form that expectations take.

The MP model may be written in the following way, with obvious notation, and using the MP notations wherever available.

$$y(t) = \int_{v \in V(t)} u(v) e^{-d(t-v)} m(v) dv \quad (5.1)$$

where $u(v)$ – the designed output per machine – is obtained from the *ex ante* relationship

$$Y(v) = A e^{gv} K(v)^\alpha L(v)^\beta E(v)^\gamma M(v)^\eta$$

where:

$$\alpha + \beta + \gamma + \eta = 1.$$

This latter restriction is used to obtain the per machine relationship.

$$\frac{Y(v)}{K(v)} = u(v) = A e^{gv} \lambda(v)^\beta \varepsilon(v)^\gamma \mu(v)^\eta.$$

For this *ex ante* relationship the cost function for each vintage v, at time t, $c(v, t)$ depends on $\lambda(v), \beta(v), \mu(v)$ rather than just λ (or as MP write, u). For the moment replace $c(u, v, t)$ by $c(v, t)$, whilst remembering that

$$c(v, t) = w(t) e^{\psi_1(t-v)} \lambda(v) + b(t) e^{\psi_2(t-v)} \varepsilon(v) + d(t) e^{\psi_3(t-v)} \mu(v)$$

$$= c(\lambda, \varepsilon, \mu, v, t)$$

The present value of net revenue remains the same in form

$$J = \int_0^\infty \beta(t) \left(p(t) y(t) - \int_{v \in v(t)} c(v, t) m(v) dv - q(t) m(t) \right) dt \quad (5.2)$$

and the maximisation of (5.2) subject to (5.1) gives the new necessary conditions

$$(y) \quad \beta(t) \left(p(t) + \frac{\partial p(t)}{\partial y(t)} y(t) \right) - \phi(t) = 0 \quad (5.3)$$

$$(m) \quad -\beta(t) q(t) + \int_{\theta \in u(t)} (\phi(\theta) u(t) e^{-\delta(\theta - t)} - \beta(\theta) c(t, \theta)) d\theta = 0 \quad (5.4)$$

$$\begin{cases} (\lambda) & \int_{\theta \in u(t)} \left(\phi(\theta)e^{-\delta(\theta-t)}\beta\frac{u(t)}{\lambda(t)} - \beta(\theta)\frac{\partial c(t,\theta)}{\partial \lambda(t)} \right)d\theta = 0 \\ (\varepsilon) & \int_{\theta \in u(t)} \left(\phi(\theta)e^{-\delta(\theta-t)}\gamma\frac{u(t)}{\varepsilon(t)} - \beta(\theta)\frac{\partial \theta(t,\theta)}{\partial \varepsilon(t)} \right)d\theta = 0 \\ (\mu) & \int_{\theta \in u(t)} \left(\phi(\theta)e^{-\delta(\theta-t)}\eta\frac{u(t)}{\mu(t)} - \beta(\theta)\frac{\partial c(t,\theta)}{\partial \mu(t)} \right)d\theta = 0 \end{cases} \quad (5.5)$$

$$(L)\ \phi(t+L(t)u(t)e^{-\delta L(t)} - \beta(t+L(t))c(t,t+L(t)) = 0 \quad (5.6)$$

These conditions are the same excepting that (2.5) in the MP paper is replaced by the set (5.5).

Equations (5.3)–(5.6) can be given standard economic interpretation. (5.3) says that $\phi(t)$ discounted using $\beta(t)$ should equal marginal revenue.

This gives the dynamic multiplier ϕ the interpretation of a marginal cost. (5.4) are dynamic conditions saying that the marginal products with respect to the three variable factors – labour, energy and materials – at the design stage should equal the appropriate factor price ratio. (5.6) says that the quasi-rent on the marginal unit of capital should equal zero.

This set can be used to derive a condition which enables the derivatives in MP to proceed as before.

From the new cost function it is seen that

$$\frac{\partial c(v,t)}{\partial \lambda(v)} = w(t)e^{\psi_1(t-v)} \quad \frac{\partial c(v,t)}{\partial \varepsilon(v)} = b(t)e^{\psi_2(t-v)}$$

$$\frac{\partial c(v,t)}{\partial \mu(v)} = d(t)e^{\psi_3(t-v)}$$

So that using this in equations (5) gives

$$(\beta + \gamma + \eta) \int_{\theta \in u(t)} \phi(\theta)e^{-\delta(\theta-t)}u(t)d\theta = \int_{\theta \in u(t)} \beta(\theta)c(t,\theta)d\theta$$

and then using this in (4) gives

$$\beta(t)q(t) = \left[\frac{i}{\beta+\gamma+\eta} \right] \int_{\theta \in u(t)} \beta(\theta)c(t,\theta)\,d\theta$$

or

$$\int_{\theta \in u(t)} c(t,\theta) \frac{\beta(\theta)}{\beta(t)} d\theta = \left[\frac{\beta+\gamma+\eta}{\alpha}\right] q(t)$$

which is the exactly analogous statement that the discounted operating cost over the life of a machine is equal to a constant fraction

$$\left[\frac{\beta+\gamma+\eta}{\alpha}\right]$$

of its original capital cost. An analogous expression to (4) in the MP paper can also be obtained. Rewrite (4) as

$$q(t) = \int_{\theta \in u(t)} \left[\frac{\phi(\theta)u(t)e^{-\delta(\theta-t)}}{\beta(t)}\right] d\theta - \int_{\theta \in u(t)} \frac{\beta(\theta)}{\beta(t)} c(t,\theta) d\theta$$

or

$$q(t) = \alpha \int_{\theta \in u(t)} \frac{\phi(\theta)u(t)}{\beta(t)} e^{-\delta(\theta-t)} d\theta$$

so

$$\frac{q(t)}{u(t)e^{\delta t}} = \alpha \int_{\theta \in u(t)} \phi(\theta) e^{-\delta \theta} d\theta$$

Now we can express the quasi-rent on a machine at the time of its installation as

$$p(t)u(t) - (1+\mu)c(t,t) = (1+\mu)\left[\left[\frac{\dot{\beta}(t)}{\beta(t)} + \frac{\dot{q}(t)}{q(t)} - \delta - \frac{\dot{u}(t)}{u(t)}\right] + \frac{1}{q(t)}\left[\frac{1-\alpha}{\alpha}\right]\left[-\frac{\dot{u}(t)}{u(t)} - \delta\right]\right]$$

Now

$$u(t) = A e^{gt} \lambda(t)^\beta \varepsilon(t)^\gamma \mu(t)^\eta$$

and

$$c(t,t) = w(t)\lambda(t) + b(t)\varepsilon(t) + d(t)\mu(t).$$

This gives us the equation which when expressed in a discrete analogue is able to be estimated, as it involves observable variables only.

This expression depends on parameters of the *ex ante* production function, depreciation or learning by doing parameters and current price variables – the interest rate and price of new machines. Because of this, it is possible to justify the aggregation procedure, and to use it in a regression equation. One proceeds by calculating for the discrete analogue to the continuous model used up to now the change in the payment to capital by installing and scrapping the optimal quantity and design of machines at time t from what would occur if no change in capital stock occurred between one period and the next. This change depends only on output and factor prices and total output and factor use. It is equal to the quasi-rent on new machines with two extra terms – one the quasi-rents to machines not used at time t-1 but used at time t, the other being quasi-rents on machines need at time t-1 but not at t. Neglecting these terms and normalising the consequent error term, one obtains an estimable equation:

$$y(t) = b_0 + b_1 y(t-1) + b_2 \frac{1}{p(t)} ((w(t)N(t) + b(t)E(t) \\ + g(t)M(t)) + r(t)q(t)m(t) - [q(t+1) - q(t)]m(t)) \\ + b_3 \frac{w(t)}{p(t)} N(t-1) + b_4 \frac{F(t)}{p(t)} E(t-1) + b_5 \frac{g(t)}{p(t)} m(t-1) \\ + b_6 \frac{q(t)}{p(t)} m(t) + \xi(t) \tag{5.7}$$

This enables the parameters $\mu, \delta, \psi_2, \psi_3, \psi_4$ to be estimated – i.e., the mark-up and decay parameters on all factors. Unfortunately the parameters of the *ex ante* production function cannot be separately identified from the rate of technological progress, and a separate exercise has to be carried out to identify these.

We have data on all variables except materials used, although the Great Britain rather than United Kingdom data on hours worked means that we have to make the assumption that we can use the former series. Until we can obtain data on material purchase (or are able to construct a satisfactory series), we are restricted to estimating a KLE model, and this is what we have done.

Equation (5.7) was modified in two other ways before estimation. We split the composite term on cost $-w(t)N(t) + b(t)E(t) + g(t)M(t) + r(t)q(t)m(t) - [q(t+1) - q(t)]m(t)$ – into its component parts, so that a test on equality of parameter estimates could be carried out. Secondly we followed MP in recognising that purchases of equipment is not the same as bringing new plant into operation, and we have allowed for this by eight quarter lags on $m(t)$ with coefficients giving the distribution of new installation according to date of expenditure on new equipment. This gives an equation to be estimated:

$$y(t) = b_0 + b_1 y(t-1) + b_2 \sum_{i=0}^{8} \gamma_i \frac{m(t-i)r(t-i)q(t-i)}{p(t)}$$

$$- b_2' \sum_{i=0}^{8} \gamma_i' \frac{(q(t+1)-i)-q(t-i))}{p(t)} m(t-i)$$

$$+ b_3 \frac{w(t)N(t)}{p(t)} + b_3' \frac{w(t)N(t-1)}{p(t)} + b_4 \frac{b(t)E(t)}{p(t)}$$

$$+ b_4' \frac{b(t)E(t-1)}{p(t)} + b_5 \frac{1}{p(t)} \sum_{i=0}^{8} \rho_i q(t-i)m(t-i)$$

$$+ S_1 + S_2 + S_3 + \xi(t) \tag{5.8}$$

where:
b_1, b_3', b_4' are defined by
$b_1 = \delta$
$b_3' = -(1+\mu)(1+\psi_2)$
$b_4' = -(1+\mu)(1+\psi_3)$

and the theoretical restrictions,
$b_2 = b_2' = b_3 = b_4 = 1 + \mu$
$\gamma_i = \gamma_i'$

Estimates of the coefficients are presented in Table 5.1 for the interest rate definition of the Treasury Bill rate plus 5 per cent. Instrumental variables estimation was carried out as the input decisions are likely to be simultaneous. The estimates and statistics that we obtain for *OLS* and *IV* indicate that input variables are endogenous, so that a complete factor demand system is necessary.

There are several checks that can be made to check that the model represented by equation (5.8) is consistent with the data. One set is given by goodness of fit and residual statistics. All four regressions would seem satisfactory on this count. A second check is the sets of restrictions and the third the economic plausibility of the results. In terms of residual characteristics the most satisfactory equation uses an interest rate given by the Treasury Bill rate and estimated by instrumental variables. For this regression

$$1 - \delta = 0.13 \quad (1+\mu)(1+\psi_2) = 0.33 \quad (1+\mu)(1+\psi_3) = 0.027$$

Whilst this gives a plausible depreciation rate $1 - \delta$ and the negative sign

Table 5.1 Estimates for equation [3.8], using instrumental variables

Coefficient	Estimate	t-statistic
b_0	−20.8	
b_1	0.87	
$b_2\gamma_i$		
$i = 0$	0.033	0.63
1	−0.096	−1.51
2	−0.025	−0.44
3	0.024	0.40
4	0.010	0.15
5	−0.102	−1.30
6	0.114	1.66
7	−0.009	−0.16
8	−0.013	−0.27
$b'_2\gamma'_i$		
$i = 0$	5.32	1.02
1	−2.18	−0.38
2	−3.36	−0.63
3	4.63	0.89
4	−4.09	−0.65
5	−8.76	−1.27
6	−0.92	−0.16
7	−0.55	−0.11
8	2.10	0.38
b_3	−0.19	−0.04
b'_3	0.33	1.40
b_4	0.053	1.66
b'_4	−0.026	−1.32
$b_5\rho_i$		
1	0.848	0.748
2	−0.255	−0.232
3	−0.551	−0.465
4	−0.481	−0.379
5	1.053	0.786
6	−0.286	−0.243
7	−0.559	−0.438
8	0.618	0.521
S_1	2.23	0.55
S_2	6.71	1.28
S_3	7.51	1.44
D.W. = 2.15		

for $(1+\mu)(1+\psi_2)$ could be explained by quite strong learning by doing, it is very hard to accept the two sets of coefficient restrictions.

The second stage estimates the coefficients of the *ex ante* production function. This equation is derived as follows. Suppose that the expectations that firms have about future factor prices depend only on the length of time into the future that the expectation is for, and the original factor price, so that we have a series of factor price expectation equations such as the following

$$\frac{w(t+i)}{p(t+i)} = \frac{w(t)}{p(t)} F(i)$$

where:
w/p is the real wage at periods $t, t+i$ (expected for the latter period)

and also that the expected discounted cost of a unit of factor service over the life of a machine is the product of the cost of a unit of factor service at the time of installation and a function of the expected life of the machine. Inserting this expectational model into the necessary condition for profit-maximisation by firms, we obtain an expression for the quasi-rent on new machines at the time of installation. For the equation we estimated at the previous stage, we had already obtained an expression which depended on parameters of the *ex ante* production function and the difference between the firms' discount rate and the implicit rate of return on holding machines as an asset. For the periods in which this difference is the same, the planned length of life of equipment installed in those two periods will also be the same, and furthermore the ratio of the value of output to the minimum operating cost (including capital cost) if a machine at the time of installation is also constant. So we obtain an equation

$$\frac{e^{gt}q(t)}{p(t)^{\alpha_1}w(t)^{\alpha_2}b(t)^{\alpha_3}} = \frac{e^{g(t+i)}q(t+i)}{p(t+i)^{\alpha_1}w(t+i)^{\alpha_2}b(t+i)^{\alpha_3}}$$

for periods $t, t+i$ such that

$$r(t) - \frac{\dot{p}(t)}{p(t)} = r(t+i) - \frac{\dot{p}(t+i)}{p(t+i)}$$

This is a regression in $\alpha_1, \alpha_2, \alpha_3$ which were unidentifiable in the previous regression equation.

Of course, one would never expect the expression above to hold exactly, and because the length of life must be in units of quarters, we group together observations by imposing a partition on the values of

$r(t) - \dot{p}(t)/p(t) = z(t)$ and imposing the same length of life on machines installed in all periods in the same partition. A partition is created by grouping together all time periods, s, for which

$$n + \frac{m}{10} - \frac{1}{2} < z(t) \leqslant n + \frac{m}{10} + \frac{1}{2} \text{ for all integers of } n, m;$$

we then ran the regression

$$\ln \frac{q(t)}{q(t+i)} = gi + \alpha_1 \ln \frac{p(t)}{p(t+i)} + \alpha_2 \ln \frac{w(t)}{w(t+i)}$$
$$+ \alpha_3 \ln \frac{b(t)}{b(t+i)}$$

This gives us results presented in Table 5.2.

Again labour poses a serious challenge to the specification used. Despite expressing the regression equation in a variety of ways, it turns out to be not possible – so far, at least – to obtain either a significant or positive exponent for labour. The problem arises from the strong correlation between all the price series which would make it difficult to pick up the correlation between output price and wage rate independently of the correlation with fuel prices and capital price. Wage rates show slightly lower correlations than the other variables, although all correlations are above 0.95. Attempts to reduce the problem of common trends by considering a regression of the form, using the fact that $\alpha_1 + \alpha_2 + \alpha_3 = 1$.

$$\ln \frac{q(t)}{q(t+i)} \frac{w(t+i)}{w(t)} = gi + \alpha_1 \ln \frac{p(t)}{p(t+i)} \frac{w(t+i)}{w(t)}$$
$$+ \alpha_3 \ln \frac{b(t)}{b(t+i)} \frac{w(t+i)}{w(t)}$$

have not produced any more acceptable result.

However apart from labour the results are rather good. Overall goodness of fit and residual statistics are acceptable, and the assumption of *ex ante* constant returns to scale is accepted.

The ratio α_4/α_3 which could be interpreted as a ratio of factor shares or marginal products, is approximately 4. Other rationalisations of the poor results in the context of the labour services are that it is not clear that we have the correct labour usage (or labour price series), and it may well be that because of the correlations all the value added is being attributed to

Table 5.2 Regression results

(a) Equation

$$\ln\frac{q(t)}{q(t+i)} = gi + \alpha_1 \ln\frac{p(t)}{p(t+i)} + \alpha_2 \ln\frac{w(t)}{w(t+i)} + \alpha_3 \ln\frac{b(t)}{b(t+i)}$$

Coefficient	Estimate	t-statistic
g	0.0003	0.753
α_1	0.824	8.31
α_2	−0.073	−0.81
α_3	0.204	6.51
	$R^2 = 0.998$	
	$D.W. = 1.95$	

(b) Equation

$$\ln\frac{q(t)}{q(t+i)}\frac{w(t+i)}{w(t)} = gi + \alpha_1 \ln\frac{p(t)}{p(t+i)}\frac{w(t+i)}{w(t)} + \alpha_3 \ln\frac{b(t)}{b(t+i)}\frac{w(t+i)}{w(t)}$$

Coefficient	Estimate	t-statistic
g	0.001	3.56
α_1	0.90	9.25
α_3	0.14	10.1
	$R^2 = 0.965$	
	$D.W. = 1.77$	

capital so that we should see the results as corresponding to a capital–energy aggregate model.

This indicates that we might wish to use these results in two ways. First to use evidence on the breakdown of value added between capital and labour to attribute part of the estimated capital exponent to labour, and second to consider a capital–energy input model alone.

CALCULATING THE VINTAGES USED AND QUASI-RENTS

To calculate the vintages used in each period, we merely replicate the decision made by the firm at each period as described on p. 82–86 above, now that we know the coefficients of the *ex ante* production function, the depreciation rate and rate of technical progress. We have indicated that we do not fully believe the coefficient estimates that we have obtained. Any further work is therefore going to be illustrative, and so we take advantage of this in modifying the coefficients and structure for computational simplicity.

The first consideration comes from the quantity of data that is available. We have 90 quarterly observations on all the series that we need. The number of observations that we can actually use to investigate the operating decisions of manufacturing industry is much less than this. Observations at the beginning of the sample are lost in building up the capital stock from past decisions and observations at the end are lost to expectation formation. At this stage, the problem of expectation formation is avoided by assuming that firms form correct expectations about future prices. This is, of course, extreme and undesirable for this sample as it means that oil price increases in the middle and late 1970s were correctly anticipated. As it is unlikely that they were correctly anticipated, the actual capital stock installed will not have adjusted to the new relative prices as quickly as we are obtaining data. The sample period is split into three sub-periods of length 30. Machines are assumed to be used for no more than 30 periods. The first 30 periods thus go in building up the capital stock and the last 30 periods go to constructing the price expectations for the new machines constructed and used in the last of the middle group of periods. For each of the middle 30 periods we are able to decide which of the available vintages of capital to use, and which type of new vintage to construct. Period 31 corresponds to 1967 Quarter 3 and period 61 corresponds to 1975 Quarter 1 which is the period for which our calculations refer.

The next problem is the coefficients to be used. In this illustrative exercise, we use the estimated coefficient for energy and divide the estimated capital coefficient into a part corresponding to capital *per se* and a part corresponding to labour. We do this using the coefficient that MP obtained in their capital–labour study. This gives us the coefficients $\alpha_1 = 0.24, \alpha_2 = 0.56, \alpha_3 = 0.20$ As a check on the reasonableness of these coefficients a study by Beanstock, Dalziel and Warburton (1984) gives coefficients $\alpha_1 = 0.43, \alpha_2 = 0.39, \alpha_3 = 0.27$ (see Ingham, 1984). We will thus be attributing more productivity to labour and less to capital and energy than that study. The other coefficients to be decided upon are the depreciation term δ and the efficiency term A. We have estimated δ on p. 94 and found it to be 0.87. This is too low, as it makes very recent vintages very unproductive, so we have used two different depreciation terms $\delta = 0.95$ and $\delta = 1.0$, with corresponding depreciation rates of 0.05 and 0. In the latter case, machines do not depreciate at all and this has a striking consequence on the vintages used. The efficiency parameter A is not estimated. We could do this in a maximum likelihood way following the procedure described in the next Section. However, we will need to ensure that the observed output level can be obtained from the number of vintages included in the capital stock at each period. This will also depend on the depreciation rate. As a very first attempt we have chosen $A = 1$ to go with $\beta = 1$ and $A = 2$ to go with $\delta = 0.95$. This probably gives rather too short a run of vintages used, but the changes necessary to maintain consistency with an expected length of life of 30 quarters are probably small.

The calculations required are done by a FORTRAN program which calculates the design coefficients of each vintage, calculates the current variable cost per unit of output of each vintage, sorts these into increasing order, calculates the marginal vintage and reports which vintages are used, the total factor demands and output, and the variable cost on the marginal vintage. The difference between the marginal vintage variable cost and the output price will be a measure of the quasi-rents on capital. Out of the total surplus will come profits, capital payments and tax payments, and of course we should discuss whether this should be included in variable cost or not. The presence of a surplus will indicate that there are machines available which cover their operating costs and which are not used, and the lower the difference between the quasi-rent and output price the greater the quantity of profitable machines that will be used and this is one of the capacity utilisation indices proposed on pp. 86–87.

Table 5.3 presents the sorting calculation for the first five periods (Quarters 67_3–68_3). They are ranked in increasing variable cost per unit of output, and the period in which they were first installed is indicated alongside this variable cost.

The ordering of vintages appears to be driven by the expected prices at the period of installation which determines the coefficients (rather than current prices), as the ranking presented here is the same in all five periods; however, there are some surprises – such as the profitability of vintages 1–10 compared with 10–28. From this ranking, we calculate the output from each vintage and from vintages in order of increasing cost until we come to the marginal vintage at which the observed output level is reached. The results of this exercise are presented in Table 5.4.

Table 5.4 gives in order of columns, the current time period, the number of the marginal vintage used (MV), the number of vintages used

Table 5.3 Sorting calculations (first 5 periods) $A = 1, \beta = 1$

	Period								
	1		2		3		4		5
Vintage no	MVC	Vintage no	MVC	Vintage no	MVC	Vintage no	MVC	Vintage no	MVC
1	4.4221	32	4.2422	33	4.3285	34	4.4262	35	4.413
2	4.4345	1	4.2511	32	4.3656	33	4.4510	34	4.446
3	4.4404	2	4.2629	1	4.3752	32	4.4890	33	4.471
31	4.4458	3	4.2687	2	4.3873	1	4.4981	32	4.509
4	4.4470	31	4.2724	3	4.3932	2	4.5107	1	4.518
6	4.4556	4	4.2749	31	4.3966	3	4.5167	2	4.531
5	4.4563	6	4.2831	4	4.3996	31	4.5209	3	4.537
7	4.4609	5	4.2838	6	4.4081	4	4.5233	31	4.541
8	4.4651	7	4.2882	5	4.4088	6	4.5320	4	4.543
9	4.4732	8	4.2921	7	4.4133	5	4.5328	6	4.552
10	4.4801	9	4.2999	8	4.4173	7	4.5374	5	4.553
30	4.4832	10	4.3065	9	4.4253	8	4.5416	7	4.557
11	4.4946	30	4.3084	10	4.4321	9	4.5498	8	4.562
20	4.5086	11	4.3204	30	4.4337	10	4.5568	9	4.570
18	4.5171	20	4.3334	11	4.4463	30	4.5591	10	4.577
12	4.5172	18	4.3417	20	4.4596	11	4.5715	30	4.579
19	4.5183	12	4.3420	18	4.4681	20	4.5853	11	4.592
21	4.5184	19	4.3427	12	4.4686	18	4.5941	20	4.606
17	4.5212	21	4.3428	19	4.4692	12	4.5944	18	4.614
16	4.5212	17	4.3456	21	4.4693	19	4.5952	12	4.615
29	4.5223	16	4.3457	17	4.4723	21	4.5953	19	4.615
14	4.5274	29	4.3460	16	4.4723	17	4.5983	21	4.616
15	4.5281	14	4.3518	29	4.4725	16	4.5984	17	4.619

13	4.5310	15	4.3524	14	4.4786	29	4.5989	16	4.619
22	4.5375	13	4.3553	15	4.4792	14	4.6047	29	4.619
28	4.5510	22	4.3611	13	4.4822	15	4.6054	14	4.625
23	4.5641	28	4.3736	22	4.4880	13	4.6085	15	4.626
24	4.5730	23	4.3865	28	4.5009	22	4.6147	13	4.629
27	4.5753	24	4.3950	23	4.5142	28	4.6280	22	4.635
26	4.5793	27	4.3971	24	4.5229	23	4.6416	28	4.648
25	4.5821	26	4.4010	27	4.5250	24	4.6506	23	4.662
		25	4.4037	26	4.5290	27	4.6529	24	4.671
				25	4.5319	26	4.6569	27	4.672
						25	4.6598	26	4.677
								25	4.680

Table 5.4 Marginal vintages used and their variable cost $A = 1$, $\beta = 1$

TIME	MV	£VS	VC	LD	ED
31	18	15	4.52	0.0141	7.28
32	18	15	4.34	0.0098	4.79
33	20	16	4.45	0.0158	7.86
34	20	17	4.59	0.0113	5.25
35	11	17	4.59	0.0104	6.11
36	30	17	4.54	0.0134	6.55
37	30	18	4.42	0.0099	4.31
38	10	18	4.57	0.0125	5.99
39	9	18	4.69	0.0140	6.65
40	8	18	4.54	0.0151	7.32
41	7	18	4.43	0.0146	7.41
42	7	19	4.67	0.0108	4.76
43	5	19	4.91	0.0121	5.45
44	6	19	4.95	0.0130	6.12
45	4	19	5.40	0.0088	5.51
46	31	19	5.70	0.0129	6.38
47	3	19	5.96	0.0122	6.26
48	2	20	5.78	0.0085	3.47
49	1	19	5.68	0.0086	5.62
50	2	21	5.83	0.0079	3.16
51	1	21	5.81	0.0076	4.81
52	1	22	5.37	0.0077	4.92
53	1	23	4.98	0.0078	5.08
54	32	23	5.47	0.0085	5.93
55	32	24	6.18	0.0067	4.34
56	33	23	6.95	0.0085	6.06
58	34	25	8.24	0.0063	4.26
59	35	25	8.59	0.0073	5.02
60	37	24	9.36	0.0069	5.21
61	38	24	10.26	0.0071	5.36

(£VS), the variable cost on the marginal vintage (VC), total labour demand (LD) and total energy demand (ED). Quite surprising fluctuations occur in labour and energy demand as the vintages used change. The number of vintages used over time generally increases. There is a case of a vintage being laid off and brought back – for example vintage 2 is used in Quarter 48 and 50 but not Quarter 49. Vintage 34 is idle in Quarter 57, but used in Quarter 58. These are the only examples of this, however. Plots of the ratio of marginal variable cost to price (VR_i) and

Figures 5.5–5.7 show the ratios of forecast to actual factor demands LR_i and ER_i.

Corresponding calculations for $A = 2$, $\beta = 0.95$ are presented in Tables 5.5 and 5.6. In this case, the depreciation effect dominates the relative price effect so that one always uses the most recent vintages. The production decision then becomes how many vintages to use – either to remain profitable or to produce the decided output.

Figure 5.5 Ratio of marginal variable cost to price (VR_i)

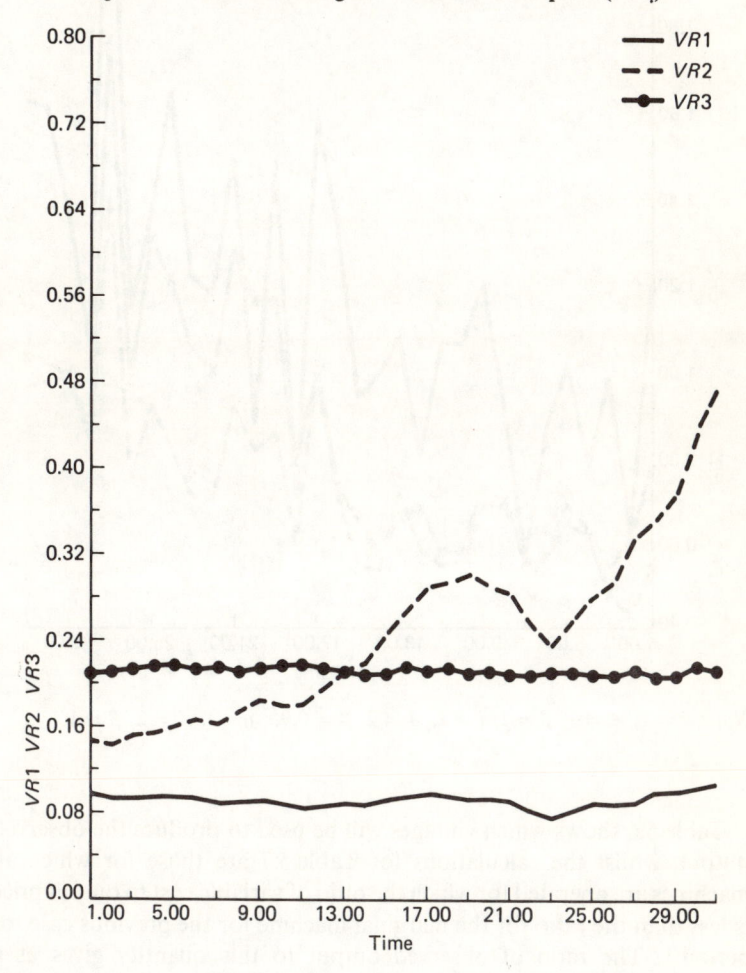

Note: $i = 1$, $A = 1$, $\beta = 1$; $i = 2$, $A = 2$, $\beta = 0.95$; $i = 3$, $A = 2$, $\beta = 1$.

Figure 5.6 Energy demand

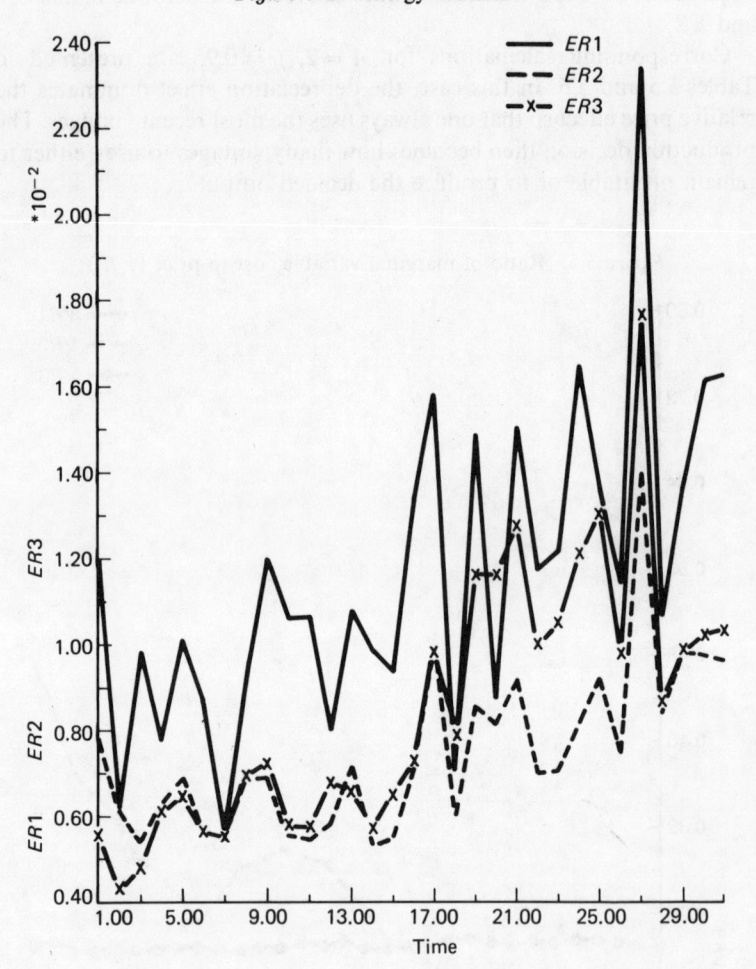

Note: $i = 1$, $A = 1$, $\beta = 1$; $i = 2$, $A = 2$, $\beta = 0.95$; $i = 3$, $A = 2$, $\beta = 1$.

Table 5.6 shows which vintages will be used to produce the observed output, whilst the calculations for Table 5.7 are those for which all machines are operated for which the ratio of variable cost to output price is less than the ratio for the marginal machine for the previous case for period 1. The ratio of observed output to this quantity gives us a utilisation index. The index of capacity utilisation $CU = Y/M$ where M is

Figure 5.7 Labour demand

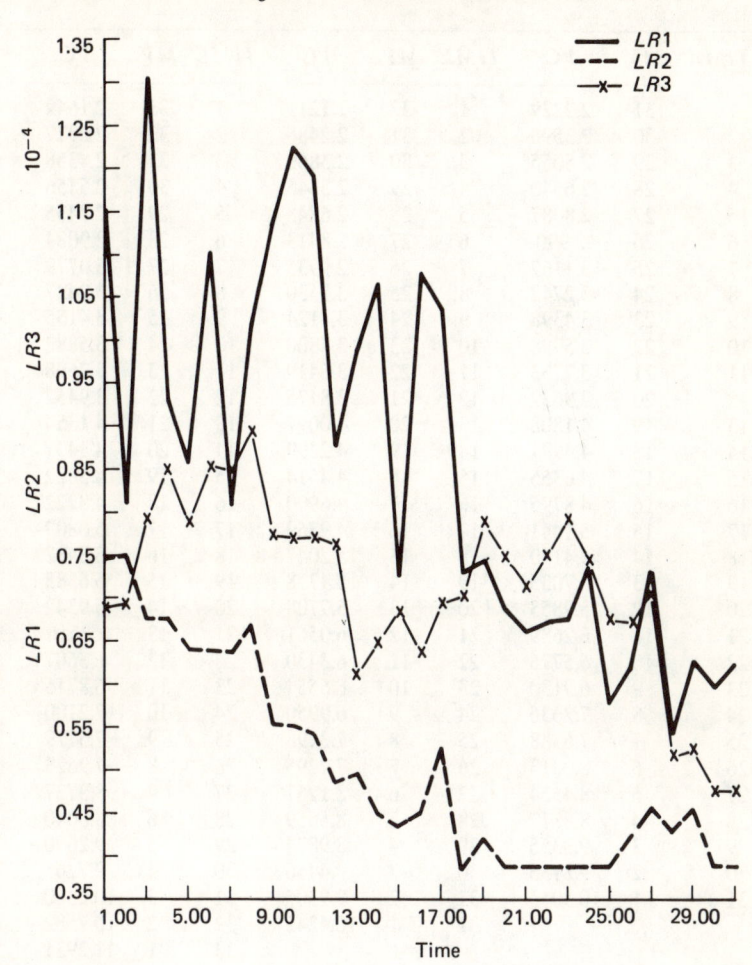

the output when all profitable machines are operated. This is shown in Figure 5.8.

FURTHER WORK AND THE NEED FOR A PUTTY-SEMI-PUTTY MODEL

The calculations in the previous section can only be thought of as illustrative, for two reasons. The coefficients were estimated outside of

Table 5.5 Sorting calculations (first 3 periods) $A = 2, \beta = 0.95$

TIME	MV	VC	TIME	MV	VC	TIME	MV	VC
1	31	2.2229	1	32	2.1211	1	33	2.1642
2	30	2.3596	2	31	2.2486	2	32	2.2977
3	29	2.5055	3	30	2.3869	3	31	2.4358
4	28	2.6540	4	29	2.5345	4	30	2.5856
5	27	2.8087	5	28	2.6848	5	29	2.7455
6	26	2.990	6	27	2.8413	6	28	2.9084
7	25	3.1167	7	26	2.9935	7	27	3.0779
8	24	3.2742	8	25	3.1530	8	26	3.2427
9	23	3.4398	9	24	3.3124	9	25	3.4155
10	22	3.5998	10	23	3.4800	10	24	3.5882
11	21	3.7733	11	22	3.6419	11	23	3.7698
12	20	3.9632	12	21	3.8175	12	22	3.9452
13	19	4.1808	13	20	4.0097	13	21	4.1354
14	18	4.3997	14	19	4.2299	14	20	4.3437
15	17	4.6355	15	18	4.4514	15	19	4.5822
16	16	4.8795	16	17	4.6900	16	18	4.8222
17	15	5.1441	17	16	4.9369	17	17	5.0807
18	14	5.4140	18	15	5.2047	18	16	5.3482
19	13	5.7035	19	14	5.4778	19	15	5.6383
20	12	5.9853	20	13	5.7708	20	14	5.9342
21	11	6.2689	21	12	6.0561	21	13	62516
22	10	6.5775	22	11	6.3430	22	12	6.5607
23	9	6.9130	23	10	6.6554	23	11	6.8715
24	8	7.2636	24	9	6.9950	24	10	7.2100
25	7	7.6388	25	8	7.3498	25	9	7.5779
26	6	8.0313	26	7	7.7295	26	8	7.9623
27	5	8.4554	27	6	8.1267	27	7	8.3737
28	4	8.8817	28	5	8.5559	28	6	8.8040
29	3	9.3355	29	4	8.9874	29	5	9.2690
30	2	9.8135	30	3	9.4466	30	4	9.7365
31	1	10.3013	31	2	9.9305	31	3	10.2340
			32	1	10.4242	32	2	10.7582
						33	1	11.2931

the model used, in that the regressions were for derived equations whereas the calculations on vintages used (and their characteristics) involved the model structure directly, and there is no reason as to why the total predicted factor demands should approximate the observed total factor demands – which, in fact, they don't. This will contribute to the discrepancy between output price and the variable cost on the marginal vintage. The second problem was that the coefficients A and β were in fact

Table 5.6 Marginal vintages used and their variable cost $A = 2$ $B = 0.95$

TIME	MV	£VS	VC	LD	ED
31	23	9	6.913046	0.009144	4.714374
32	23	10	6.655398	0.009144	4.714374
33	24	10	7.209975	0.008172	4.287346
34	24	11	7.436790	0.008172	4.287346
35	25	11	7.863508	0.007755	4.138991
36	26	11	8.198487	0.007833	4247461
37	26	12	8.038403	0.007833	4.247461
38	27	12	8.755121	0.008227	4.524348
39	28	12	9.461619	0.006833	3.819893
40	28	13	9.203817	0.006833	3.819893
41	29	13	9.456498	0.006656	3.780548
42	30	13	10.502990	0.005994	3.457894
43	31	13	11.634871	0.006144	3.613773
44	32	13	12.342167	0.005471	3.282563
45	33	13	14.201300	0.005270	3.228008
46	34	13	15.799422	0.005416	3.389032
47	35	13	17.390715	0.006190	3.961216
48	36	13	17.754428	0.004499	2.938645
49	37	13	18.452488	0.004865	3.234489
50	36	15	17.928540	0.004499	2.938645
51	36	16	17.869890	0.004499	2.938645
52	36	17	16.493849	0.004499	2.938645
53	36	18	15.296033	0.004499	2.938645
54	36	19	16.883804	0.004499	2.938645
55	36	20	19.013358	0.004499	2.938645
56	37	20	20.656243	0.004865	3.234489
57	39	19	25.530325	0.005262	3.604633
58	38	21	28.552478	0.004959	3.347020
59	39	21	31.546120	0.005262	3.604633
60	41	20	38.728458	0.004471	3.145798
61	42	20	45.061399	0.004442	3.164877
TIME	MV	£VS	VC	LD	ED

guessed, so as to keep the predicted length of life within bounds for the data span and expectational model used.

In fact the parameter A cannot be estimated using the MP methodology, but the calculations in the last section suggest a way of doing this which can be extended to all the parameters of the model. For a given value of A we calculate predicted factor demands for labour and energy, $\hat{L}_t$ and $\hat{E}_t$ and consequently the prediction errors $(\tilde{L}_t - \hat{L}_t)$ and $(\tilde{E}_t - \hat{E}_t)$ where ~ denotes observed values. We can thus obtain the conditional

Table 5.7 Marginal vintage details and total output produced when mark-up held constant $A = 1$, $B = 1$

TIME	MV	£VS	VC	LD	ED	Y
31	2	31	9.813542	0.008424	3.337782	198.244863
32	2	32	9.930482	0.008424	3.337782	199.793686
33	3	32	10.233985	0.009591	3.835044	198.373958
34	4	32	10.537043	0.010297	4.152282	196.776949
35	5	32	10.606787	0.009564	3.886712	195.553277
36	6	32	10.504245	0.010385	4.254530	196.144495
37	6	33	10.787957	0.010385	4.254530	196.016791
38	8	32	10.625821	0.010971	4.582279	192.102068
39	9	32	10.928667	0.009479	3.996912	190.919921
40	9	33	11.157014	0.009479	3.996912	193.581667
41	9	34	11.464079	0.009479	3.996912	194.219968
42	11	33	11.544901	0.009379	4.043117	190.500871
43	13	32	11.634871	0.007476	3.296684	187.141876
44	14	32	11.715273	0.007940	3.543109	187.424155
45	16	31	12.148598	0.008315	3.801219	183.617757
46	17	31	12.840001	0.007576	3.501140	181.567445
47	19	30	12.747030	0.008178	3.874126	177.349871
48	19	31	13.012547	0.008178	3.874126	178.152407
49	20	31	12.818881	0.009098	4.369418	175.017425
50	21	31	13.147842	0.008590	4.190973	171.150361
51	22	31	13.178365	0.008165	4.055676	167.322788
52	21	33	13.420834	0.008590	4.190973	169.592796
53	20	35	13.775079	0.009098	4.369418	170.979715
54	23	33	13.884508	0.008572	4.339975	162.652365
55	26	31	14.187522	0.007755	4.138991	154.571673
56	27	31	14.629163	0.007833	4.247461	152.743697
57	28	31	16.198995	0.008227	4.524348	150.811707
58	31	29	16.818198	0.005994	3.457894	142.805231
59	32	29	17.525603	0.006144	3.613773	141.472671
60	33	29	19.298585	0.005471	3.282563	141.462665
61	35	28	20.006937	0.005416	3.389032	137.918911
TIME	MV	£VS	VC	LD	ED	Y

likelihood $L((\tilde{L}_t - \hat{L}_t), (\tilde{E}_t - \hat{E}_t))$ which is a function–in this case–of A alone, so that a conditional maximum likelihood estimator would be arg max $L(A)$. As suggested on p. 99, it would be sensible to perform this maximisation over A and β and a grid search to find A, β which maximise

$$L((\tilde{L}_t - \hat{L}_t(A, \beta), (\tilde{E}_t - \hat{E}_t(A, \beta)))$$

can relatively easily be done.

Figure 5.8 Index of capacity utilisation

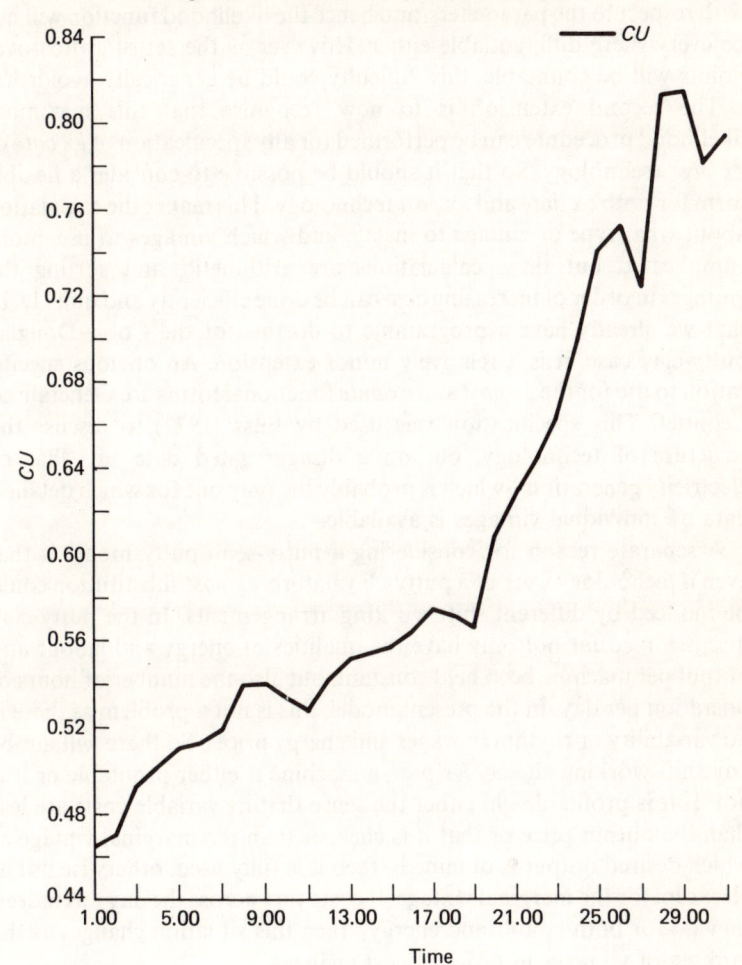

This is extendable in two ways. First to search over all parameters $(\alpha_1, \alpha_2, \alpha_3, \beta, A)$. This extends the computational size of the problem, but not its difficulty. A difficulty does exist in that it is not possible to calculate the partial derivatives of the likelihood function with respect to the parameters, which would allow more efficient optimisation algorithms to be used, as changing the parameters will potentially change the vintages used. At a switch-over point when a vintage drops out and is replaced by another, the total factor demands will not be differentiable with respect to the parameters, and hence the likelihood function will not be everywhere differentiable either. However as the set of switch-over points will be countable, this difficulty could be generically avoided.

The second extension is to now recognise that this maximum likelihood procedure can be performed for any specification of *ex ante* or *ex post* technology. So that it should be possible to consider a flexible form for both *ex ante* and *ex post* technology. This makes the calculation about what type of vintage to install, and which vintages to use, more complicated but these calculations are arithmetic, and sorting the vintages in order of increasing cost can be done efficiently and quickly. In that we already have a programme to do this for the Cobb–Douglas putty-clay case, it is a relatively minor extension. An obvious specification to use for the *ex post* and *ex ante* functional forms are Generalised Leontief. This specification was used by Fuss (1977) to discuss the structure of technology, but on a disaggregated data set – that of electricity generation – which is probably the only one for which detailed data on individual vintages is available.

A separate reason for considering a putty-semi-putty model is that even if technology were of a putty-clay nature, *ex post* substitution could be induced by different shift working arrangements. In the putty-clay discussion so far not only have the qualities of energy and labour and output per machine been held constant, but also the number of hours of operation per day. In the present model, this is not a problem as there is no variability or rhythm in wages and energy prices. So there will not be any shift working choice. *Ex post*, a machine is either profitable or it is not. If it is profitable – in either the sense that its variable costs are less than the output price or that it is cheaper than the marginal vintage at which desired output is obtained – then it is fully used, otherwise not at all except for the marginal vintage. If costs vary across the day – as indeed they do for both labour and energy – then this situation changes as the ranking of vintages in order of cost changes.

Now define units for labour and energy so that a unit costs the same at each moment throughout the day. On a vintage with a putty-clay structure the relationship between output, inputs and the amount of time operated will change from the linear relationships in Figure 5.11 to the non-linear relationships in Figure 5.12.

The slopes will depend on the *ex ante* choice of design, the variability of costs throughout the days, and the basic price/wage levels. Now consider two vintages (I, II), I having a higher labour to energy requirement than II. From Figure 5.13, we can see that vintage I will be

Figure 5.9 Deflated wage index

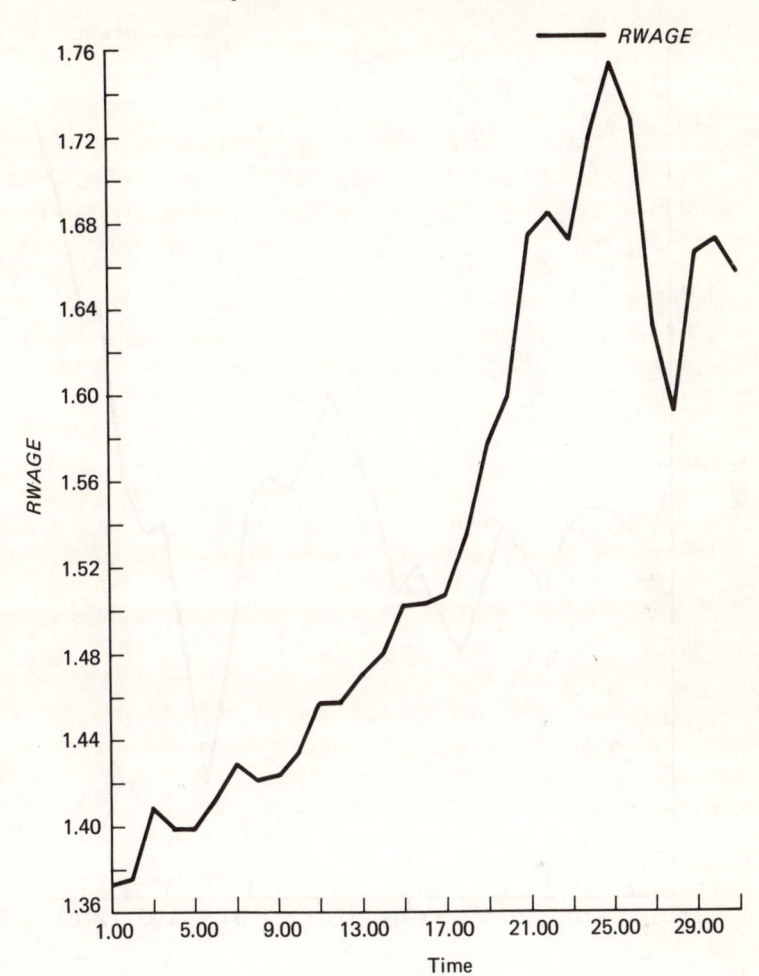

used for more hours of the day than vintage II. However, this could reverse if the wage rate/energy/price ratio changes sufficiently that Figure 5.13 becomes the position in Figure 5.14.

If firms operate for as long as variable costs are covered, then the same output will be produced, but from the two vintages being used for different amounts of time and thus from different quantities of inputs.

Figure 5.10 Real energy price index

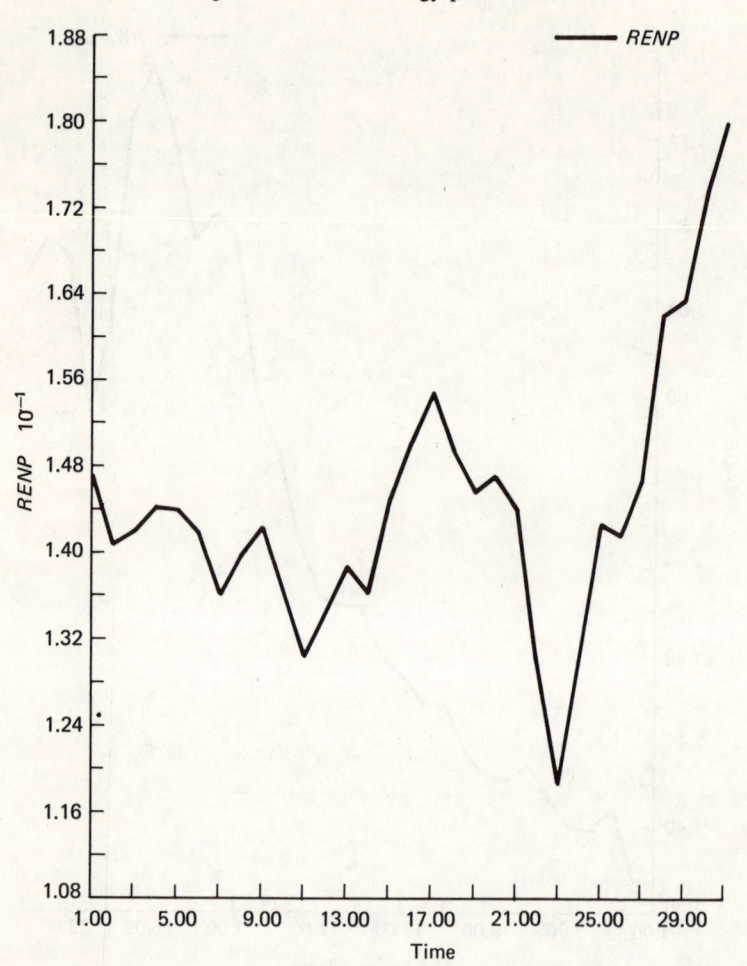

Note: This is calculated as a weighted average of the individual energy prices, with weights the proportion of those components in the total energy consumption.

There will thus be apparent *ex post* substitution. In this case, the degree of *ex post* substitution reflects the changes in capacity use that have taken place due to the shift in factor prices. However, the situation becomes difficult if true *ex post* substitution possibilities exist, as it becomes

Figure 5.11

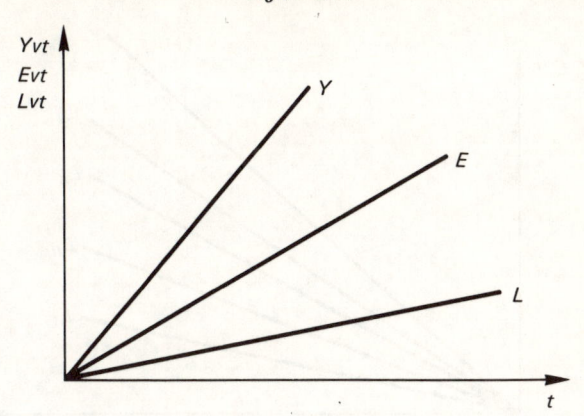

Figure 5.12

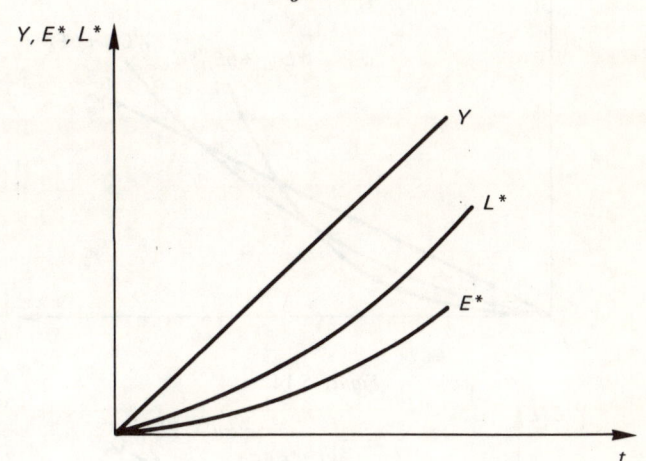

necessary to separate out substitution from changes in capacity use. So when factor prices change, the firm will adjust the factor usage on each vintage as well as the number of hours each will be used. Nor will this be done in a necessarily monotonic way – that is, machines currently on overtime use may be replaced by machines not on overtime use.

What would then be meant by capital or capacity usage? Well, we would have estimates of the designed expected minimum cost structure

UK Manufacturing

Figure 5.13

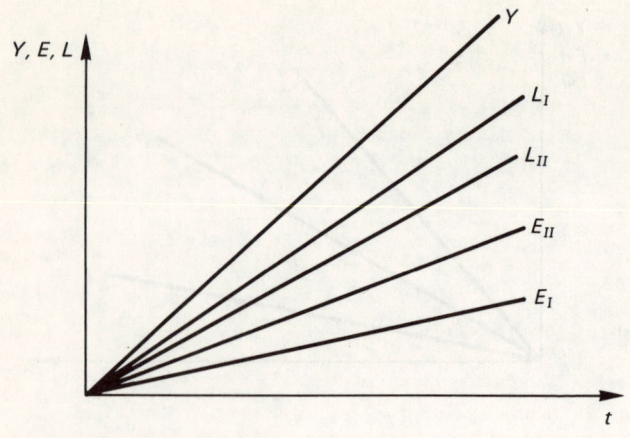

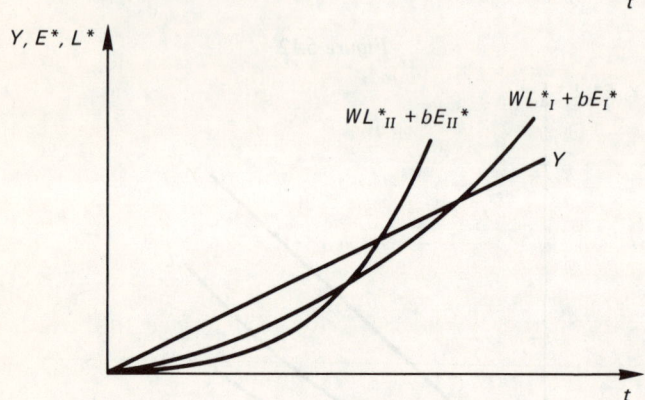

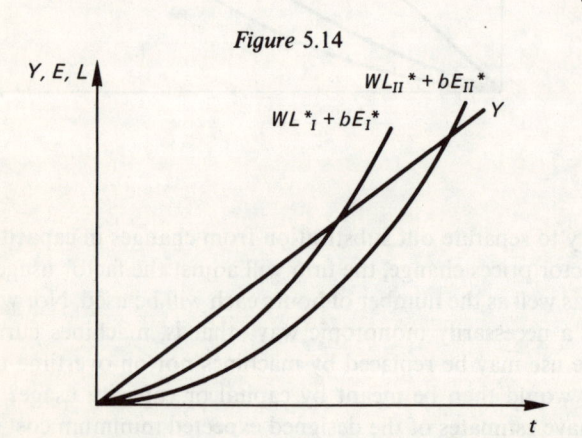

Figure 5.14

of production. Together with the estimates of the actually used structure of machines used, this gives a picture of how actual capital used differs from intended capital used. However, we now meet the aggregation problem head on.

An index requires us to add up machines of differing characteristics. A retreat to either the marginal vintage or the homogeneity of output can be made. But this is a strong assumption also.

Notes

1. The work is financed by a grant from the Department of Energy for a study on Demand for Energy by United Kingdom Manufacturing. We are grateful for their support. They should not be held responsible or seen as agreeing with the methods and views contained in this chapter.
2. These are measured respectively by the Manufacturing Index of Industrial Production and the Price of Home Sales Index.
3. At a later stage we hope to include a materials input variable. Of course the list of inputs could be expanded in a natural way.
4. This will be variable cost per unit of output produced, which is

$$\frac{CV_t(v)}{\kappa(v)} \cdot \delta^{t-v}$$

5. G is defined by Johansen (1972), p. 35. It is the set of currently used input coefficients, or the utilisation region.
6. Ideally we would like to use a four-factor KLEM analysis throughout. As mentioned later data limitations restrict the estimation to KLE at present.

References

BEENSTOCK, M., DALZIEL, A. and WARBURTON, P. (1984) 'Aggregate Investment and Output in the UK', *Recherches Economiques de Louvain* 50.

BERNDT, E. and WOOD, D. (1975) 'Technology, Prices and the Derived Demand for Energy', *Review of Economics and Statistics* 57.

FUSS, M. (1977) 'The Structure of Technology Over Time', *Econometrica*, 45.

GRIFFIN, J. and GREGORY, P. (1976) 'An Intercountry Translog Model of Energy Substitution Responses', *American Economic Review* 66.

HAUSMAN, J. (1973) 'Theoretical and empirical aspects of vintage capital models', Ph.D. thesis, Oxford University, unpublished.

INGHAM, A. (1984) 'Comment on Aggregate Investment and Output in the UK', *Recherches Economiques de Louvain* 50.

────── WEISERBS, D. and MELESE, F. (1982) 'Unemployment Equilibria in a Small Resource Importing Economy with a Vintage Production Structure', in Eichorn, W. *et al.* (eds) *Economic Theory of Natural Resources* (Wurzburg: Physica Verlag).

JOHANSEN, L. (1972) *Production Functions* (Amsterdam: North-Holland).
MALCOMSON, J. and PRIOR, M. (1979) 'The Estimation of a Vintage Model of Production for UK Manufacturing', *Review of Economic Studies* 46.
MIZON, G. E. (1974) 'The estimation of non-linear econometric equations: an application to the specification and estimation of an aggregate putty clay relation for the UK' *Review of Economic Studies*, XLI.
────── and NICKELL, S. T. (1983) 'Vintage models of UK manufacturing industry', *Scandinavian Journal of Economics* 85.
SALTER, W. (1966) *Productivity and Technical Change* (Cambridge: Cambridge University Press).
WINSTON, G. and McCOY, T. (1974) 'Investment and the Optimal Idleness of Capital', *Review of Economic Studies* XLI (3).

Part II
Labour

6 The Dough, the Doughnut and the Hole: Unemployment, Labour Utilisation and Labour Market Accounting

Chris de Neubourg

It is the aim of this chapter to develop labour market accounts that allow investigation of trends and fluctuations in the magnitude and composition of the stock of labour resources, their determinants and the international differences within them. The accounts attempt to provide a better coverage of the (under-)utilisation of labour resources than is given by traditional labour force and unemployment data. This work is motivated by the wish to refine the treatment of under-utilisation and to gain insight into the elements and determinants of different forms of labour slack.

A balanced and accurate picture of actual labour conditions has to be based on a broad range of indicators of labour market activity: Shiskin's (1976) recommendation to measure 'the doughnut and the hole' can safely be extended towards the careful study of 'the dough, the doughnut and the hole'.

The labour market accounts, as outlined below, elaborate the ideas of Maddison (1980) and the German 'Institut für Arbeitsmarkt- und Berufsforschung' (IAB) (Mertens and Klauderü, 1980), and emphasise not only a systematic treatment of the demographic definition of labour resources, but extend the coverage of the accounts towards utilisation measured in man hours (worked and lost). Since changes in and the manipulation of time schedules have become more frequent over the last few decades, this extension is highly relevant, and yields significant differences in terms of international policy practice.

Labour market accounts can serve several purposes. Depending on their detail and character, they can provide a statistical and analytical tool for many kinds of analyses. In making progress in this area of research, decisions have to be taken concerning the width and the depth of the accounts in order to avoid the risk of gathering data in so much detail that the ambition kills the legitimate efforts (de Neubourg, 1983). Given the state of the art, it is wise to confine a first approach to stock data, and direct the analysis to investigations that may sustain macroeconomic policy. Other researchers choose to emphasise flow data intended to illuminate more selective policy issues (Lindley, 1983; Reyher and Bach, 1980; Mordasini, 1983).

In order to get a clear picture of the requirements that labour market accounts should meet, a thorough study and critique of the traditional concepts 'employment, unemployment and labour force', and several proposed alternatives is necessary. Critical evaluations of the reliability and the usefulness of the concepts are not new, and many amendments and alternatives to them are suggested in the literature. The larger part of them focusses on the inadequacy of the measurements, especially where the under-utilisation of labour resources is concerned. Such critical analysis is not only interesting by itself, but at the same time provides useful standards for the design of a new analytic framework. The traditional concepts, their shortcomings and the important alternatives, are extensively discussed in the first Section of this chapter.

This chapter deals only with issues directly linked with the construction and the empirical application of labour market accounts: specifically the utilisation accounts.

The discussion and construction of these analytical instruments however, are fundamental, but initial activities.

THE UTILISATION OF LABOUR RESOURCES: CONCEPTS AND MEASUREMENT

Since Keynes, both economists and their audience have become used (and attached) to the unemployment rate as a measure of under-utilisation of available manpower, as doctors are used to their thermometer: they rely on it as the main diagnostic apparatus, and they judge the success of their remedial treatment in terms of its benefit. There are some good reasons for this persistent confidence. The rate of unemployment is straightforward and easy to understand. On the other hand, it is surprising that scientists who – under different circumstances – use the most ingenious and sophisticated methods to study the problems at hand, are satisfied with a single number to describe the state of the labour market. This Section discusses the advantages and disadvantages of the unemployment rate, and related measures of labour capacity utilisation. More specifically, it investigates the possibilities for refining labour market analysis.

As explained in the Introduction, the basic concern is to outline a reliable picture of the extent to which an economy uses its available labour resources, both cyclically and in the economic growth process. This Section emphasises traditional concepts and measurements and various alternative approaches. The statistical, analytical and diagnostic characteristics of each will be discussed. As far as feasible, the proposed concepts are illustrated empirically with data for the United States.

In the second Section, a system of national labour market accounts will be developed and applied to two countries: the Netherlands and the United States. Further research will extent the empirical discussion towards the eight countries.

(a) Unemployment, Employment and Labour Force: Concepts and Definitions

The International Labour Office (ILO) has recommended definitions of unemployment, employment and labour force which have been endorsed by all the countries studied here, and therefore provide major guidelines for the present chapter.

The recommended definitions are reproduced in detail in Appendix A6.1 and can be summarised as follows:

1. *Employment*
   The sum of all persons above a specified age who, during a specified brief survey period, were at work (for some time) or with a job but not at work (because of temporary absence due to illness, holiday, etc.) regardless their status (employee, on own account, unpaid family worker).
2. *Unemployment*
   The sum of all persons above a specified age who, during a specified brief period, were without a job, seeking work for pay or profit and were available for employment, regardless of whether they had previously been employed or not.
3. *Labour force*
   The sum of all employed and unemployed persons.

One should remark that, although the definitions are fairly precise and clear, there are some 'grey areas', mainly concerning working age and the length of reference period. Differences between countries, resulting from different interpretations of these definitions are not our major concern in this chapter (for an extensive discussion see Sorrentino, 1978).

Figures for various countries presented in this Section have been – so far as reasonably possible – corrected for differences in definitions.

Unemployment statistics – and especially the unemployment rate (unemployment divided by labour force) – are frequently-used indicators of labour slack in Western economies, particularly in the political arena. So often and centrally brought before the spotlight, it is not surprising to recognise that many economists and statisticians think that the picture becomes over-exposed and that a more critical appraisal should take place. This becomes even more imperative when governments (or government agencies) calculate the number of unemployed on other (national) criteria which are influenced by political considerations. In France, Germany, the Netherlands and the United Kingdom, the regularly quoted official unemployment figures refer to registered unemployment. Fortunately, labour force sample surveys or household sample surveys are also available for these countries: an international comparative unemployment rate can be produced using these data (see Table 6.3 and Sorrentino, 1978).

(b) Shortcomings of the Traditional Concepts

The intensity of criticism against published unemployment rates (and thus, by definition, employment and labour force) seems to bear a cyclical character. A slackening economy, especially when the downswing shows some persistence, inspires closer inspection of the figures. The main objections put forward in recent decades can be summarised under three headings:

1. the concepts are not measured properly and are subject to technical shortcomings;
2. the concepts do not measure what they ought to measure;
3. secular changes and demographic developments have affected the meaning and significance of the measures.

The arguments lead to divergent conclusions concerning the degree of over-estimation or under-estimation of labour slack in official unemployment rates, depending on the purpose of the analysis. The most significant critical comments will be discussed in the rest of this Section.

Some major trends can be observed. In the early 1950s, most authors worried about the accuracy of measurement and about how full employment (or the target rate of unemployment) should be defined.[1] In most industrialised countries the late 1960s were characterised by a 'tight' labour market. Economists were then discussing whether the unemployment rate accurately reflected the tightness of the market, often in the light of less satisfying estimates of the Phillips curve. Today, more than ever, the philosophy and the conceptual framework are under attack.[2]

Now several economists and statisticians believe, on the one hand, that the unemployment rate masks important historical changes with extensive economic and social consequences, and therefore distorts our understanding of ongoing developments. On the other hand, the unemployment rate is said to be an increasingly unreliable cyclical indicator because of major changes in economic and social policy that either cushion the rate or overestimate it, depending on the authors' points of view.

Measurement Errors and Technical Shortcomings

There are significant differences in coverage between official unemployment counts, calculated from survey data (Canada, Japan, Sweden, United States) and those in the countries where the official count is based on registration data. The technical and statistical comments of the critics on the former type are rather mild and are more of a warning nature, referring to changes in the size of the sample, methods of sampling and interpretation of the significance of intertemporal changes both for the aggregate unemployment and for detailed break-downs (Lebergott, 1954; Moore, 1973; Tella, 1965; Flaim, 1979). Conceptual and definitional changes in the Current Population Survey in the United States were, for example, introduced in January 1967 in response to recommendations of the Gordon Committee (see Stein, 1967). These definitional, computational and survey changes, together with minor additions to the questionnaire in 1970, are believed to offset each other: their impact on aggregate unemployment in the United States is estimated not larger than one-tenth of a percentage point (Flaim, 1979: 0.18). In general, most authors agree that the unemployment rate is one of the most carefully prepared statistical series in the United States (Lebergott, 1954, p. 390).

Discussion of the official unemployment rate in France, Germany, the Netherlands and the United Kingdom – where registration figures are the official indicator – is much more critical. The figures not only largely depend on the eligibility criteria for unemployment compensation benefits, but are also open to direct (and indirect) political manipulation. Policymakers may change definitions and shift certain groups in and out of the labour force easily, altering eligibility criteria, and thus directly influencing unemployment figures. On the other hand, registration figures are more frequently available and provide a more reliable basis for regionally disaggregated estimates. Survey definitions can also be manipulated for political reasons, although less easily than registration data. Their availability may also be suppressed or delayed. Under the active impetus of the European Statistical Offices (Eurostat), the EEC countries have introduced regular two-yearly labour force sample surveys which provide the basic data to calculate unemployment and labour force estimates.

To illustrate the differences between survey and registration data, Table 6.1 compares unemployment rates calculated from these sources for four countries.

From Table 6.1 it can be seen that the direction of the difference between the official (registration) figures and the unemployment rate estimated from Labour Force Sample Survey data is not the same in all countries. In the Netherlands and the United Kingdom, the registration figures tend to be smaller than the LFSS estimates, whereas in Germany and France the reverse is usually true. This is due to differences in legislation and registration practices (Sorrentino, 1978; Moy and Sorrentino, 1981). The difference varies over time, while registration and survey figures tend to converge in more recent years. However, Table 6.1 provides only an aggregate view. This implies that the stock of unemployed defined by the survey and that defined by registration are not necessarily the same. It is likely that two underlying distortions offset each other, resulting in aggregate figures that look similar. On the one hand registration defines a number of persons as unemployed while they are not actually available for work and actively looking for a job (two basic requirements, stemming from the ILO recommendations and used in Canada, Japan, Sweden and the United States). On the other hand, there are people actively seeking work and actually available for the market, who are not counted as unemployed because they do not fit eligibility requirements for registration or unemployment compensation benefit, but who ought to be defined as unemployed according to the internationally accepted definitions. In consequence of these offsetting

Table 6.1 Comparison of registration and survey unemployment rates (1959–80)

	France Registered (1)	LFSS (2)	Germany Registered (3)	LFSS (4)	Netherlands Registered (5)	LFSS (6)	United Kingdom Registered (7)	LFSS (8)
1959	1.3	1.7	2.6	2.0	1.5	n.a.	2.0	2.7
60	1.3	1.5	1.3	1.1	0.9	n.a.	1.5	2.1
61	1.1	1.4	0.8	0.6	0.6	n.a.	1.4	1.9
62	1.2	1.3	0.7	0.6	0.6	n.a.	1.9	2.6
63	1.4	1.2	0.8	0.4	0.7	n.a.	2.3	3.2
64	1.1	1.3	0.8	0.4	0.6	n.a.	1.6	2.4
65	1.4	1.4	0.7	0.3	0.7	n.a.	1.4	2.0
66	1.4	1.7	0.7	0.3	1.0	n.a.	1.4	2.1
67	1.8	1.8	2.1	1.3	2.0	n.a.	2.2	3.2
68	2.1	2.3	1.5	1.1	1.8	n.a.	2.4	3.2
69	1.7	2.2	0.9	0.6	1.3	n.a.	2.4	3.0
70	2.4	2.4	0.7	0.5	1.1	n.a.	2.5	3.1
71	2.7	2.6	0.8	0.6	1.6	n.a.	3.4	3.8
72	2.8	2.7	1.1	0.7	2.8	n.a.	3.7	4.2
73	2.7	2.6	1.2	0.7	2.8	3.1	2.6	3.1
74	2.8	2.8	2.6	1.6	3.5	3.7	2.6	3.1
75	4.2	4.1	4.7	3.3	5.0	5.1	4.1	4.5
76	4.6	4.5	4.6	3.4	5.3	5.2	5.6	5.9
77	4.9	4.8	4.5	3.4	5.1	5.0	6.0	6.2
78	5.3	5.2	4.3	3.3	5.0	5.1[a]	6.0	6.1
79	6.1	6.0	3.8	2.9	5.0	5.3[a]	5.6	5.5
80	6.4	6.3	3.8	2.9	5.8	6.1[a]	7.3	6.9
81	7.5	7.3	5.5	4.0	9.1	9.1	10.2	10.5
82	8.4	8.2	7.5	5.8	12.6	11.1	11.9	11.7

Notes:
n.a. Not available.

Sources:
Columns (1)–(5), (7), (8) 1959: Sorrentino (1978).
1960–73: *Handbook of Labor Statistics* (1980).
1974–80: Moy and Sorrentino (1982), pp. 3–13.
Column (6): *Sociale Maandstatistiek* (1980), p. 18.
Column (7): *Annual Abstract of Statistics,* various issues.
Column (8): Great Britain only. Preliminary figures based on new British unemployment data.

distortions, the composition of the stock of unemployed persons may differ widely according to the computation method. This is important if figures are used to decide on policy measures.

Although the greater openness of registration data to political manipulation must be acknowledged, the major critique of this type of unemployment rate estimates refers to the impact of legislative and institutional regulations and the consequential incomparability of figures between countries. The influence of changes in laws and institutions is extensively discussed below.

Employment and Unemployment Concepts do not Measure What They Ought to Measure

Although there are internationally-accepted ILO recommendations defining employment and unemployment, there is no consensus among economists and policymakers on what employment and unemployment ought to measure. According to the ILO definitions, a quantitative estimate of the labour slack in an economy at a certain point of time should be expected. As, however, the unemployment rate is used to justify (or rationalise) very divergent policies, it is not surprising to find the rate under attack from different points of view.

This led the United States Department of Labor to introduce seven different concepts and estimates of the unemployment rate, each one appropriate to a particular philosophy and political faith about what exactly the rate should reflect (Shiskin, 1976).

Economic Hardship Some economists feel that unemployment is overestimated by traditional standards because they are convinced that it should measure economic hardship. They want to use the figures to express the hardship experienced by job seekers. The definitions of 'hardship' itself, however, vary greatly between different analysts (Shiskin, 1976). Some view economic hardship in terms of subsistence, and according to their views the traditional estimates overestimate the 'real' economic hardship. They suggest a need to limit the count to, for example, male household heads (with unemployment rates of 2 per cent in 1973 and 5.5 per cent in 1975 in the United States compared with aggregate unemployment rates being up 4.9 per cent and 8.5 per cent respectively – see Marie and Badnarzik, 1976; Friedman, 1975). Others (e.g., Perry, 1970) want to weight the unemployed by relative wages by age–sex group, in order to measure more accurately what they could contribute to production if employed, and what they themselves lose by being unemployed.

Levitan and Taggart (1973), on the other hand, argue that it is preferable to measure 'the number of persons who experience difficulties in competing for gainful employment paying an adequate wage'. For that purpose, they construct a 'subemployment' measure – an index of employment and earnings inadequacy. It is clear that in that light unemployment is an under-estimate of economic hardship.

The remarks concerning economic hardship are interesting in the context of welfare issues, but the published statistics are not specifically designed to measure economic hardship (Shiskin, 1976) and economic hardship is irrelevant to the basic purpose, which is to measure the (cyclical) performance of the economy in real (not in money) terms (Cain, 1979). Moreover, the countries under study have a developed social system that, through compensation benefits, relieves the financial burden of unemployment. This is not to say that unemployment may not be an important figure when studying poverty and the distribution of welfare. It seems, however, difficult to define economic hardship adequately.

To conclude, 'economic hardship' is of secondary interest from a macroeconomic point of view, which emphasises the rate of utilisation of available labour resources.

A second group of critics, who think that the concepts of unemployment and employment do not measure what they ought to measure, are arguing that important aspects of labour slack are omitted by definition. In contrast to the former group, they are convinced that the primary concern of the data should be to measure the (cyclical) performance of the economy. Their critical remarks are more specifically addressed to cyclically determined flows into and out of the registered labour force. As the unemployment rate basically consists of two counts – the number of unemployed and the number of people in the labour force – it is important that the latter should be insensitive to cyclical fluctuations and secular changes, in order to allow the rate to reflect these fluctuations and developments adequately. This, however, is hardly the case. Two major reasons are responsible: first, both employers and workers react to the relative tightness of the market – the former by labour hoarding and dishoarding and the latter through discouragement and encouragment; second, increasing government intervention counter-cyclically influences the volume of labour force by diverting people to various social security benefit categories.

Discouragement The discouragement effect of the cyclical downswing certainly is a phenomenon that has often been discussed. It points to the relationship between cyclical variations in economic activity and in labour force participation. The hypothesis holds that when economic activity declines, workers become discouraged and leave the labour force (or fail to enter it). As the period of economic slack grows larger, pressure on 'additional' workers to enter the labour force builds up, and this is assumed partially to offset the discouragement effect (Strand and Dernburg, 1964). Whatever the net effect is empirically, it throws doubt on the reliability of the unemployment rate as a cyclical indicator. In fact, when discouragement occurs, the unemployment rate systematically underestimates the 'real' rate of job seekers to the labour force (see, for example, Killingsworth, 1963; Leon, 1981). Almost every economist agrees that people respond to changes in wages, prices and the probability of getting a job. Whatever that response is, there is no reason why it should be limited to persons already in the reported labour force. If, in other words, the labour force participation is elastic – reacting to changes in aggregate economic activity – the unemployment rate (with a varying labour force in the denominator) partially depends on the changes in economic activity and is, therefore, a misleading indicator of these changes. In this broader dimension, labour force status is no longer a dichotomous (in or out) but rather a continuous variable (Mincer, 1973; Green, 1977).

The potential expansion and contraction of the labour force can be illustrated empirically, showing that a sixth of the persons not in the labour force during the last quarter of 1975 worked at some time during the preceding 12 months; about 700 000 workers were squeezed out because of the slack in the economy (data regarding the United States). Over the same period in 1975, 4.3 million persons (out of 59 million not in the labour force) reported that they wanted jobs but did not look for them for a variety of reasons; another 1 million because of discouragement over job prospects. During the first nine months of the recovery dating from March 1975, labour force growth, on the other hand, was substantial – 1.2 million, compared with the median path of virtually no growth in prior recessions (Shiskin, 1976).

This introduces the problem of measuring the discouraged (added) worker effect (sometimes called the number of 'hidden unemployed'). The subject matter of 'wanting to work but not seeking a job' is fairly intangible and so 'we pass to the wilderness of estimates' (Lebergott, 1954, p. 397). Two main kinds of solutions are found – either we use data stemming from questionnaires in the household surveys, or we trust econometric estimates. In 1967, the United States Bureau of Labor Statistics (BLS) introduced a question in the Current Population Survey allowing to estimate the number of potential workers who are not looking for work because they think jobs are not available. Table 6.2 gives quarterly estimates of the number of 'discouraged workers'. From Table 6.2 it can be observed that they show close relationship to the unemployment rate. As for econometric results, various authors

Table 6.2 Estimates of 'discouraged workers' from BLS survey data and the unemployment rate: United States, quarterly data (1967–81)

Quarter	Discouraged workers × 1000	Unemployment rate	Quarter	Discouraged workers × 1000	Unemployment rate
1967 I	755	3.7	1974 I	649	5.0
II	667	3.9	II	641	5.1
III	764	3.9	III	625	5.6
IV	737	3.9	IV	825	6.6
68 I	697	3.7	75 I	1064	8.1
II	696	3.6	II	1123	8.8
III	660	3.6	III	1171	8.4
IV	610	3.4	IV	973	8.3
69 I	606	3.4	76 I	964	7.7
II	574	3.5	II	922	7.6
III	543	3.6	III	782	7.7
IV	580	3.6	IV	994	7.7
70 I	595	4.2	77 I	942	7.5
II	616	4.8	II	1062	7.2
III	669	5.2	III	1067	6.9
IV	717	5.8	IV	990	6.6
71 I	744	6.0	78 I	906	6.3
II	737	5.9	II	842	6.0
III	799	6.0	III	850	5.9
IV	772	5.9	IV	787	5.9
72 I	828	5.9	79 I	713	5.8
II	806	5.7	II	814	5.7
III	716	5.5	III	729	5.7
IV	719	5.3	IV	766	5.9
73 I	615	5.0	80 I	949	6.2
II	775	4.9	II	921	7.3
III	665	4.8	III	961	7.5
IV	686	4.8	IV	1055	7.5
			81 I	1115	7.4
			II	1018	7.4
			III	1050	7.2
			IV	1201	8.4

Source: Employment and Earnings (January issues).

attempted to obtain reliable figures for the United States (Tella, 1964, 1965; Strand and Dernburg, 1964; Simler and Tella, 1968; Butler and Demopoulos, 1972; Bowen and Finegan, 1969). A striking feature of the econometric approach is the substantial difference in the results: for 1960 they varied from 380 000 (Bowen and Finegan) to 780 000 (Tella) to 1.2 million (Strand and Dernburg). Moreover, Gastwirth (1973) indicated that some of the models can yield negative estimates, and that the estimates are far more variable than the BLS survey data. He also showed that some of the models are extremely sensitive to small changes in the value of a parameter. Both Mincer (1973) and Gastwirth (1973) discuss the differences between the BLS and the econometric estimates. They explain the differences by the characteristics of models (especially the capacity concept of full employment beneath statistical features) by an unrealistic estimate of the rate of increase in labour force participation by so-called 'secondary' workers and by the fact that survey data do not distinguish between cyclical and non-cyclical discouragement. Both authors tend to rely on the more conservative BLS data rather than on econometric estimates, but Mincer emphasises the importance of entries and re-entries into (rather than withdrawals from) the labour force. He concludes that there is only a small proportion of discouraged workers among those currently wanting a job (but not seeking), and that apparently discouragement is quite a temporary status and consequently difficult to measure (Mincer, 1973).

From the above review it should be clear that the registered labour force – defined as the sum of employed and unemployed – is not the exact count of all the persons within a population who react to changes within the labour market. When the economy is growing rapidly, workers are not only recruited from the 'official reserve', known as labour force, nor do they all find their way back to that official reserve when economic activity is slackening. This affects the adequacy of the unemployment rate as a cyclical indicator.

Labour Hoarding There is a second behavioural reason why the rate of unemployment does not reflect what is actually happening on the labour market in cyclical ups and downs. This reason is related to the behaviour of employers and to the fact that unemployment is measured in persons rather than in hours. Early in the downturns of the business cycle employers prefer to reduce hours of work rather than laying off workers. Taylor (1976) explains that this reluctance to dismiss workers (labour hoarding) will be important 'until forecasts about the likely course and duration of the recession are more certain'. There are several sound reasons for a slow and prolonged relation of employment levels to changes in output, including legal and institutional constraints (contractual agreements), technical constraints (indivisibilities in the production process), and economic constraints (such as the costs of hiring and firing workers and retraining costs). When, however, the cyclical downswing lasts for some time, employers are usually forced to dismiss a part of their employees, resulting in a rise in unemployment. These adjustment mechanisms are very important. In March 1932, 63 per cent of the manufacturing employees were on part-time work (Barret, 1932) while Bancroft (1962) estimates the man hours lost by involuntary part-time workers (short time) at 36.6 per cent of the man hours lost by the unemployed in July 1961 (both figures for the United States). It is, however, clear that traditional unemployment and labour force statistics, which count persons regardless of the actual and the usual hours of work, do not reflect these important movements.

Table 6.3 gives an estimate of the hours lost due to unemployment and due to involuntary part-time work (for economic reasons), their ratio and their annual percentage changes for 1967–81.

Labour force time lost as a percentage of the available labour force time is systematically higher than the corresponding unemployment rate. This difference is for the largest part attributable to the fact that labour force time lost incorporates time lost by involuntary part-time workers. Column 6 illustrates that the time lost by this category of labour slack was a fairly stable percentage of total labour force time lost (20 per cent): deviations in specific years were due to stronger oscillations in the share of time lost due to unemployment. A comparison between columns 7 and 8 leads to the conclusion that strong oscillations in the absolute amounts of time lost occur both in unemployment and in involuntary part-time work, though yearly percentage changes are generally larger in time lost due to unemployment.

Disguised Unemployment One should remark that involuntary part-time workers belong to the employed population and are counted as such, although they are in fact partially unemployed. There is another category of workers who are in the same position and who are often referred to as 'disguised unemployed', in the sense used by Robinson (1937, pp. 82–101). (Sometimes 'disguised unemployment' is used as a synonym for 'discouraged workers'; see, for example, Tella, 1965.) The term refers to the condition in which a member of the labour force is at work, but is so ineffectually used that he or she contributes little to the value of the national product (Dunlop, 1950). Unlike the involuntary

Table 6.3 Labour force time lost due to unemployment and involuntary part-time work: United States (1967–81)

	(1) Labor force time lost as per cent of available labor force time[a]	(2) Unemployment rate	(3) Aggregate hours lost by the unemployed (× 1000)	(4) Aggregate hours lost by persons on part-time for economic reasons (× 1000)	(5) Labor force time lost Columns (3)+(4) (× 1000)	(6) Aggregate hours lost by persons on part-time for economic reasons as per cent of labor force time lost (Columns (4)/(5))	(7) Annual percentage change of aggregate hours lost by the unemployed (t+1)−t/t	(8) Annual percentage change of aggregate hours lost by persons on part-time for economic reasons (t+1)−t/t
1967	4.2	3.8	98 145	34 824	132 969	26.2		
68	4.0	3.6	92 329	32 899	125 228	26.3	−5.9	−5.5
69	3.9	3.5	92 727	34 130	126 857	27.0	0.4	3.7
70	5.3	4.9	135 826	39 332	175 158	22.5	46.5	15.2
71	6.4	5.9	166 880	43 870	210 750	20.8	22.9	11.5
72	6.0	5.6	160 830	43 558	204 388	21.3	−3.6	−0.7
73	5.2	4.9	141 950	41 565	183 514	22.6	−11.7	−4.6
74	6.1	5.6	168 540	47 971	216 511	22.2	18.7	15.4
75	9.1	8.5	267 019	60 343	327 362	18.4	58.4	25.8
76	8.3	7.2	246 293	57 702	303 995	19.0	−7.8	−4.4
77	7.6	7.0	230 026	53 656	283 682	18.9	−6.7	−7.0
78	6.5	6.0	201 418	55 191	256 609	21.5	−12.4	2.9

79	6.3	5.8	198 873	55 648	254 521	21.9	−1.3	0.8
80	7.9	7.1	254 261	65 317	319 578	20.4	27.9	17.4
81	8.6		275 904	73 598	349 500	21.1	8.5	12.7

Note:
[a] Aggregate hours lost by the unemployed and persons on part-time for economic reasons as per cent of potentially available labour force hours.

Sources:
Column (1) 1967–79: *Handbook of Labour Statistics* (1980), p. 61.
1980, 1981: *Employment and Earnings* (January 1981, 1982).
Columns (3), (4): See Appendix A6.2.

part-time workers, these persons do not suffer from partial unemployment and should not be treated as such. As long as they are paid there is an employer who judges it more productive to let them work rather than to dismiss them, and therefore they should be regarded as employed (the criterion of 'contributing to the value of the national product' is too vague to be operational). There is, however, a problem when non-paid members of the labour force (other than salary or wage earners), such as self-employed people and unpaid family workers who work at least 15 hours a week are concerned. There may be a good deal of 'underemployment' (disguised unemployment) among them at a certain moment in history, constituting an available labour reserve for employment in industry. This reserve may also be very important to the secular process of economic growth (see, for example dualist theories of Japanese economic growth and Knox, 1979), but it remains very difficult to quantify the number involved, except for *post hoc* inferences from long-run statistics. In general, one cannot criticise traditional unemployment statistics for excluding these categories (although the Thirteenth International Conference of Labour Statisticians, ILO in Geneva (1982), devoted a large part of its discussions to measuring underemployment – ILO, 1982).

Legislation and Government Policy   A third kind of critique, suggesting that the concepts of unemployment and labour force do not (no longer) measure what they ought to measure, relates to the impact of legislation and government policy on the figures. Again the measurement of labour slack and the (cyclical) performance of the economy is regarded as the main task. And again there is no consensus among the authors on whether legislation and government policy exert either an upward or a downward bias on the unemployment rate. Maddison is among the authors who articulate the latter conviction. He states that 'the rise in unemployment has been lower than could legitimately have been expected, partly because governments have tried to mitigate the social impact of their cautious macro-economic policies by diverting labour slack into channels other than overt unemployment' (Maddison, 1980, p. 176). He cites the example of Germany where this policy is pursued most vigorously. The German authorities encouraged people to withdraw from the labour force by schemes to promote early retirement or to retain young people in education and training; they also encouraged work sharing by paying unemployment insurance for those working short time (Maddison, 1980). Another example is invalidity insurance in the Netherlands. Installed in 1967, the number of beneficiaries is now 600 000: a vast part of the former are regarded as 'hidden unemployed' (van den Bosch and Petersen, 1981; Bax, 1982; Aarts et al., 1982). For France, Granier and Maddison (1982) calculated that the unemployment rate would have been 2 per cent higher (in 1980) if the effect of the reduction in hours worked (due to illness, personal reasons, industrial conflicts, etc.) had been taken into account.

They argue that the existence of social security schemes has a similar reduction of effective working time as side-effect. For the United States, Hedges (1977) calculated the impact of absence from work attributable to illness or injury and to personal or civic reasons and found that the average worker lost three weeks out of 52 for these reasons. Another issue, frequently investigated in the United States, concerns the effect of training programmes. Enrolment in employment and training programmes can be expected to reduce the unemployment rate because the participants in most programmes are classified as 'employed' in the Current Population Survey (Flaim, 1979, p. 22). Estimates are not easy to make, but all point in the same direction: the unemployment rate is reduced by 0.15 percentage point (for 1971 – R. Smith, 1973), by 0.3 per cent (for 1971 – Small, 1972), by 0.4 per cent (in 1976 – Cohen, 1969) or by 0.3 per cent (in 1976 – Tella, 1976), depending on the method and the assumptions of the estimation. Sorrentino (1978) finally points to the extreme differences between the countries she investigated in efforts made to reduce unemployment by other means than creating employment, in other words, by stimulating people to withdraw from the registered labour force (defined as the sum of employed and unemployed). She especially envisages Sweden and Japan where the (adjusted) unemployment rate is very low compared with other countries, but where the number of persons involved in various (re)training and retirement programmes is very high (Sorrentino, 1978, pp. 29–33; for Sweden see especially Table 9, p. 33). Finally, in those countries in which official unemployment rates are based on registration data, there exists the possibility of cushioning unemployment by altering the eligibility criteria (see Harris, 1976, pp. 95–106, for an overview of the practices in the EEC).

There are, however, offsetting effects of legislation and especially of social security laws. Flaim (1979, p. 20) distinguishes in an excellent survey of the United States literature three major sources of potential upward bias in the unemployment rate for the United States: (i) the extension of the unemployment insurance programme may have increased both the duration and frequency of unemployment; (ii) the job seeking requirements currently associated with certain welfare programmes have caused many persons to look for work (or to report that they have been looking for work) who otherwise would not have done so; (iii) the imposition or raising of minimum wages will cause an increase in unemployment. He concludes, however, that the actual effect on the rate is extremely difficult to estimate. The first source is generally acknowledged to have caused a small upward bias 'perhaps on the order of 0.2 to 0.4 percentage point' (Flaim, 1979, p. 20). As for the second source, he criticises the high estimates of Clarkson and Meiners (1977), and quotes others as more realistic estimates (0.3 per cent in 1977). The impact of minimum wages is widely discussed, but reliable estimates are extremely difficult to make because of interacting effects like changes in the demographic composition of the labour force (Flaim, 1979, p. 22).

From the above review it becomes clear that legislation and government action have an impact on the labour market and on the estimates of unemployment and the labour force. It is difficult to quantify the effects, but this does not mean that the assumed effects are unimportant or negligible. We should rather be cautious in interpreting the published unemployment rates because there are sound reasons to believe that they do not really measure what we expect them to measure. It is, in this context, important to develop a system of labour market accounts, using multiple ratios in order to widen our views as much as possible and to make as much of the mechanisms mentioned above visible.

The Impact of Secular Changes and Demographic Development

Two major changes in the post-war period are assumed to have influenced the unemployment count and its interpretation. The first concerns the gradual reduction in hours worked per employee per year; the second consists of shifts in the demographic composition of the labour force.

Changes in Annual Hours Worked per Employee Table 6.4 shows that average annual hours worked per employee in 1970 (in the United States) amounted to only 57 per cent of these for 1870, thus illustrating the substantial drop in labour input per employee over the last century. This downward trend was even more pronounced during the post-war decades in the European countries (except France). The average reduction in annual hours worked per employee during the 1970s greatly exceeded previous decade averages (except for Canada where annual hours worked changed less during the 1970s than in the 1950s or 1960s and for Germany and the United Kingdom where reduction progressed at the same (high) rate throughout the post-war period).

Table 6.4 Hours worked per employee per year (1870–81) (1870 = 100)

	1870[a]	1870 = 100	1950	60	70	73	78	81 1870 = 100	1981[a]
Canada	2964	100	66.4	63.3	60.9	60.3	58.5	58.4	1730
France	2495	100	67.5	67.3	64.1	61.9	58.6	57.7	1701
Germany	2941	100	78.7	70.8	64.8	62.1	58.9	57.1	1681
Japan	2945	100	77.7	83.2	76.5	75.1	72.7	72.7	2140
Netherlands	2964	100	74.5	73.4	64.4	61.6	56.4	57.0	1689[b]
Sweden	2945	100	66.2	61.9	56.4	53.3	49.6	49.3	1451[c]
United Kingdom	2984	100	65.6	64.1	58.1	56.6	53.6	50.4	1503
United States	2964	100	63.0	60.6	57.6	56.9	54.7	53.4	1582

Notes:
[a] Absolute figures.
[b] 1980.
[c] 1979.

Sources:
France, Germany, Japan, Netherlands, United Kingdom, United States: Maddison (1983).
Canada, Sweden and 1970 figure for all countries: Maddison (1982).

Without discussing the components of the reduction in detail, we can see that two underlying developments are important in this respect: a simple reduction of the contractual working time per day and per year (due to more and to longer holidays and absence attributable to illness; personal reasons, etc.) and a substantial increase in the number of voluntary part-time workers. Surprisingly, the weekly contractual working time for full-time workers remained stable after the introduction of the 40-hour work week.

Both developments are important if one wants to study real labour slack in an economy. Although aggregate employment (measured in number of persons) has steadily increased since 1945, the utilisation of labour capacity measured in total hours worked decreased in the same period, leaving an increasing part of the labour resources unused. Both the effect of the trend reduction in actual hours worked and the effect of a downward accentuation in cyclical downswings are not reflected in the unemployment count; Granier and Maddison (1982, p. 22) calculated the official unemployment rate accounted for about 71 per cent of the real labour slack measured in hours in 1980 in France.

Since manipulation of the working time is an important instrument for employers to react to cyclical changes (overtime and short time – see what has been said above about labour hoarding), the consideration of hours worked (rather than persons employed and unemployed) is also important when indicators of cyclical performance are requested. Maddison (1980, pp. 185–6) found for Germany and the United Kingdom that reduction of net overtime was an important element of labour slack during the 1973–5 recession. For Germany, the IAB has noted a perverse cyclical movement in sickness absence; the phenomenon is also noticed in France (Maddison, 1980) illustrating that workers may also react to cyclical developments by changing time worked.

In addition to changes in working time due to the mechanisms described above, the growing proportion of voluntary part-time workers has also produced a net reduction of average annual hours worked per person. This phenomenon became specially important during the 1970s, as is illustrated in Table 6.5 for the United States. The share of part-time workers in total employment in the United States increased from 8.4 per cent in 1955 and has leveled off at 14.4 per cent since 1975. Table 6.6 displays changes in the share of part-time employment as a percentage of

Table 6.5 Voluntary part-time employed as a percentage of total employed: United States (1955–81)

1955	8.4	1964	11.1	1973	14.0
56	9.3	65	11.2	74	14.0
57	9.6	66	11.7	75	14.3
58	9.8	67	12.4	76	14.3
59	10.1	68	12.8	77	14.4
60	10.3	69	13.3	78	14.4
61	10.7	70	13.7	79	14.3
62	10.6	71	13.9	80	14.4
63	10.7	72	14.0	81	14.3

Sources:
1955–8: *Annual Report on the Labour Force* (1955–8 issues).
1959–65: *Employment and Earnings* (1960–6 issues).
1963–79: *Handbook of Labor Statistics* (1980).
1980–1: *Employment and Earnings* (1980, 1981).
The 1955–62 values have been adjusted to the new age limits (16 and older) by subtracting 0.5 per cent (calculated from the overlapping period) from these values.

Table 6.6 Voluntary part-time employed as a percentage of total employed by sex (1973–9)

	Germany Male	Germany Female	France Male	France Female	Netherlands Male	Netherlands Female	United Kingdom Male	United Kingdom Female	United States Male	United States Female
1973	1.0	20.0	1.4	11.2	1.1	15.5	1.8	38.3	8.0	26.3
75	1.1	20.8	2.1	14.0	1.5	18.6	2.2	40.9	8.9	27.3
77	1.1	24.4	2.3	15.2	1.5	19.0	2.1	40.4	9.1	27.0
79	0.9	24.2	2.0	15.2	1.8	23.2	1.3	37.7	8.6	26.3

Sources:
European countries calculated from *Labour Force Sample Surveys* (1979–81).
United States: *Handbook of Labour Statistics* (1981).

total employment between 1973 and 1979 according to sex for France, Germany, the Netherlands, the United Kingdom and the United States. It shows that the percentage share of part-time workers is particularly high for female workers and (except for the United States) extremely low for males.

It can also be seen that the share of part-time employment kept growing during the 1970s for France, Germany and especially for the Netherlands. In the United Kingdom and United States, part-time employment was already very popular and stagnated after 1973 on a higher level than the other countries attained in 1979.

It is clear that by measuring the labour force in persons, the distinction between full- and part-time work is blurred. As the share of part-time workers is growing significantly, and as work-sharing is increasingly considered as an important instrument for counter-cyclical economic policy[3] measurements of the labour force, employment and unemployment in persons reflect only partly the trends and cycles in the utilisation of labour resources.[4] This affects the adequacy of a full employment target (or unemployment target rate) set in persons rather than in hours. Increased work-sharing then lowers the unemployment rate without ameliorating the under-utilisation of labour resources – i.e., more people have a job but for less hours a week than would be the case without work-sharing. Consequently the number of unemployed declines, while the total sum of hours worked or lost due to non-utilisation remains unchanged. Unemployment is redistributed and becomes hidden beneath the appearance of figures measured in persons. Owing to this, the strength of the unemployment rate as an indicator of (cyclical) performance is seriously affected.

Demographic Composition of the Labour Force and Patterns of Activity Rates The composition of the labour force is subject to considerable changes in course of time due to large differences in the size of the cohorts entering the labour force and to sex-specific participation rate changes. Both developments will be discussed in some detail, because they are often said to exercise an upward pressure on the unemployment rate, transforming the latter into an inflated – and, therefore, unreliable – (cyclical) indicator of economic performance and labour market tightness.

Intertemporal changes in fertility result in large differences in the size of the cohorts entering the population of working age. This, in turn, causes changes in the size and the composition of the (potential) labour force. Over the past 20 years, the maturing of the post-1945 'baby boom' made these shifts highly visible. As can be seen from Table 6.7, all industrial countries studied here have been subject to significant changes in the size of the birth cohort entering the population of working age, though the timing of the changes differs among them.

Evidently, not every person enters into the labour force at the age of 16. Prolonged stays in full-time education dampen the impact from year to year. Moreover, the number of people entering the population of working age is partly offset by a number of persons leaving the population due to death or emigration. The latter stayed relatively stable throughout the period; therefore the size of the birth cohort entering the population of working age, together with the participation rates, are the most important determinants of the size of the labour force.

In 1962 the birth cohort entering the population or working age was significantly higher than in any of the previous years in most of the countries under study – except for Germany (where the 1962-cohort was one of the smallest in the period 1950–82) and in the Netherlands and Sweden (where the upward jump was registered respectively one and three years earlier). Before the early 1960s, the size of birth cohorts entering the labour force was more or less stable, with a downward trend in France, Germany and the United Kingdom, and an upward trend in the Netherlands, Sweden and the United States. During the following decades the size remained stable at a high level in France and at a low level in Japan. The magnitude of the cohorts between 1960 and 1980 in the Netherlands, Sweden and the United Kingdom diminished slightly until 1974 and then rose at a steady rate. In Germany, the birth cohort entering the population of working age grew after 1960, but not as fast as in the other countries. In the United States, to conclude, the size of the cohort increased continuously, with a second jump in 1968 and a top in 1976 when the birth cohort entering the population of working age was twice as large as the corresponding cohort in 1950.

Table 6.7 Size of the birth cohort entering the population of working age (1950–81) (1950 = 100)

	France	Germany	Japan	Netherlands	Sweden	United Kingdom	United States
1950	100	100[a]	100	100	100[a]	100[b]	100
51	96	101	103[a]	101	102	102[b]	99
52	95	102	101[a]	101	107[a]	103[b]	99
53	93	109	97[a]	105	109[a]	109[b]	104
54	93	117	89[a]	106	113[a]	109[b]	106
55	92	118	102	109	118[a]	105[b]	108
56	84	108	111[a]	106	116	99	114
57	80	87	114[a]	111	121	106	122
58	89	92	109[a]	121	138	116	139
59	96	91	113[a]	126	152	122	131
60	97	67	92	118	161	120	130
61	99	80	85[a]	166	162	122	129
62	131	87[a]	132[a]	159	161	156	175
63	140	94	139[a]	149	156	142	165
64	141	99	141[a]	143	154	132	165
65	141	99	127	139	148[a]	127	164
66	141	97	117	138	141	122	168
67	136	98	110	141	135	120	173
68	137	97	103	139	135	121	180
69	134	100	97[a]	140	136[a]	121	184
70	135	100	96	141	131	120	189
71	135	105[a]	91	143	134	124	192
72	135	109	88	145	135	128	199

Table 6.7 (Contd.)

	Canada	France	Germany	Japan	Netherlands	Sweden	United Kingdom	United States
73		136	111	91	147	134	132	199
74		135	117	93	151	131	134	199
75		138	121	91	149	131	136	198
76		137[a]	124	90	155	128	141[a]	201
77		140	125	91	155	131	144	197
78		138[a]	130	94	157	135	147	194
79		142	132	96	159	142	150	191
80		143	130	102	156	154	150	
81			131	83	153	154		

Notes:

[a] Estimated by means of interpolation—e.g., an unknown cohort of 15 years old in 1961 can be estimated by averaging those 14 years of age in 1960 and those aged 16 in 1962.
[b] Estimated by means of extrapolation, with the help of (a) the 15–19 year age group of this period and (b) an estimated death and net emigration rate.

Sources: See Appendix A6.3.

Large birth cohorts and constant or rising participation rates for young people, result in an increase in the youth labour force. The unemployment rate for these age groups is on average higher than for other age groups. The very fact that the share of young people in the labour force increased is assumed to exert an upward pressure on the aggregate unemployment rate, exaggerating – according to some authors – the under-utilisation of manpower.

Various studies have tried to adjust the aggregate unemployment rate for the type of compositional change mentioned above.[5] Such adjustments are not simple, mainly because it is difficult to disentangle the separate underlying effects. The problem can best be illustrated by the equation which is usually applied, expressing the change in the aggregate unemployment rate between two years:

$$U^t = U^b + \sum_i (w_i^b \Delta u_i + u_i^b \Delta w_i + \Delta u_i \Delta w_i) \tag{6.1}$$

where:

U^b and U^t = overall unemployment rates in the base year (b) and some other year (t)
w_i = labour force proportion of the ith age group;
u_i = unemployment rate for the ith age group;
Δ = the change between periods b and t.

Equation (6.1) decomposes the change in aggregate unemployment rate between the two years in three components:

$\sum w_i^b \Delta u_i$ = the 'pure cyclical effect' = the change in the aggregate rate that would have occurred had the structure remained unchanged and unemployment rates applicable to each age group changed as they actually did

$\sum u_i^b \Delta w_i$ = the 'direct compositional effect' = the change in U that would have occurred if labour force participation had changed when the age group specific unemployment rates had remained unchanged

$\sum \Delta u_i \Delta w_i$ = the 'interaction term'.

The interaction term reflects the two main cross-effects – namely the 'crowding effect' and the 'discouraged worker effect' – both pointing out the close interrelation between the age proportions in the labour force and the age specific unemployment rates. The former effect refers to the fact that a larger cohort of young workers implies a consequent rise in the youth unemployment rate, unless the number of entry level jobs expands sufficiently. Wachter (1976) stated that young entrants mainly compete with their peers rather than with all the other (older) people on the labour market; this explains why large groups of new entrants relative to a stable number of jobs for which they can apply, cause an upward shift in the unemployment rate for the affected age groups.[6] The 'discouraged worker effect' indicates that high unemployment rates for specific age groups cause 'some' discouragement among the members of these age groups. There is neither a technical solution which permits disentanglement of these effects nor a theoretically correct way to handle the interaction term. Moreover, the interaction term can be large relative to the other terms of equation (6.1) (one-half or more the size of the 'direct' composition effect), leading to serious differences in the quantitative estimates of the direct compositional effect presented thus far in the literature.

The empirical difficulty in adjusting an unemployment rate for compositional changes is paralleled by the analytical obscurity of the arguments in favour of the adjustment. Since the arguments are similar when changes in labour force participation rates are considered, we first discuss these changes more generally.

During the past three decades, a dramatic increase in labour force participation rates for women, a slower but steady decline for men and an erratic pattern for teenagers constitute another major shift in the composition of the labour force.[7] Since 1950, the proportion of women engaged in or seeking market work rose from about one-third to more than one-half in the 1980s (in the United States). Noticeable differences occurred in the timing of the changes for the different groups. In the 1950s, the jump in the participation rate for women aged 45-9 was considerable; after 1960 large increases occurred among women under age 45.

Among them, the increase was most prominent for married women. Currently, about 65 per cent of women in the 20-45 age group and half of the married women, belong to the labour force (all figures for United States). Although the participation rate for men remains substantially above the female rate, a steady overall decline can be observed, mainly attributable to a sharp decline in the older age groups and a milder decline among men younger than 20. The changes in the participation rates for teenagers show, both for males and for females, an erratic picture.[8] From Table 6.8 it can be seen that although labour force participation trends by sex are generally the same in the eight countries under study, differences amongst them occur both in participation rates themselves and in the rates of change over time. Male participation declined between 1960 and 1980 in all countries; in France, Germany and the Netherlands, the decline is most pronounced. Canada, Japan and the United Kingdom show a somewhat different picture: the male participation rate declined in the early 1960s but remained more or less stable afterwards. Remarkable are the relatively low participation rates for men in 1980 in France, Germany, the Netherlands (1975) and Sweden.

Female participation rates show an opposite trend to that for males in most of the countries. Female labour force participation rates rose dramatically between 1960 and 1980 in all countries except in France, Germany and Japan. Japan even shows a strong downward movement between 1960 and 1975. In 1980, female participation rates exceeded 50 per cent in Canada, Sweden (nearly 60 per cent) and the United States, Germany and the Netherlands show respectively low (38.2 per cent in 1980) and extremely low (32.3 per cent in 1975) female participation percentage, with France, Japan and the United Kingdom in an intermediate position.

It can be noted from Table 6.8 that the changes during the 1970s were more dramatic than had been the case previously. Since women have tended to have a higher unemployment propensity than men, various authors have 'corrected' unemployment rates for changes in sex composition in a way analogous to the correction made for birth cohort changes.[9] The same basic formula and criticism as forwarded above apply to these adjustments – i.e., significant technical problems appear when different effects have to be disentangled. Are these 'corrections' really necessary and theoretically defensible?

Three arguments are usually put forward to justify an age and/or sex adjustment of the aggregate unemployment rate:

1. Movements in the aggregate unemployment rate attributable to the age and sex composition should generally be given less importance both from an analytical and a policymaking view.

    Female and young workers are assumed to have a lower attachment to the labour force and can be defined as 'secondary' workers. Unemployment among them is therefore analytically different in meaning and politically less significant than unemployment among 'primary' workers.
2. A simple definition of the full employment target as the non-inflationary unemployment rate requires measuring the rate free from compositional effects.
3. Knowledge of the influence of compositional changes upon the

Table 6.8 Labour force participation rates approximating United States Concepts[a] (1960–80)

	Canada	France	Germany	Japan	Netherlands[b]	Sweden	United Kingdom	United States
Male:								
1960	82.2	84.3	82.7	84.2	92.8	n.a.	86.0	83.3
1965	79.4	81.5	80.8	81.1	89.7	80.7	83.5	80.7
1970	77.8	74.6[c]	78.8	81.5	86.8	77.2	79.8	79.7
1975	78.4	73.2	72.0	81.0	82.1	77.0	81.2	77.9
1980	78.3	n.a.	70.2[d]	79.6	n.a.	75.0	78.0[d]	77.4
Female:								
1960	30.2	43.0	41.2	52.7	26.3	n.a.	38.7	37.7
1965	33.9	40.6	40.0	48.8	29.1	45.6	40.7	39.3
1970	38.3	40.0[c]	38.6	49.3	30.5	49.0	41.1	43.3
1975	44.4	42.5	37.4	44.8	32.3	55.2	46.6	46.3
1980	50.3	n.a.	38.2[d]	46.6	n.a.	59.7	47.6[d]	51.6

[a] Data relate to the civilian labour force of working age as per cent of the civilian population of working age. Working age = 15 and over in France, Sweden, United States; = 15 and over in Canada, the Netherlands, Germany and Japan; = 15 and over before 1973 and 16 and over after 1973 in the United Kingdom.
[b] Figures as published by Maddison (1982).
[c] Break in the comparability because of revised revisions.
[d] Preliminary estimates.

Sources: Sorrentino (1978); Moy and Sorrentino (1982).

unemployment rate can enable a better insight into the working of the labour market and into how the rate might be affected by future changes.

The first argument is invalid for several reasons. The major secular change that occurred in the post-war decades concerns the significant and accelerated entry of certain demographic groups (mainly women) into the labour force. This implies a long-term shift from non-market to market activities by women, but also a shift of economic activities – especially of family-substituting activities (e.g., child care) – from the non-market to the market sector of the economy.[10] These changes reflect secular developments in role perceptions by sex (increasing emancipation) and role definition (induced by declining fertility and the increasing number of non-married or economically independent women) and alter, in turn, the labour force attachment of new entrants. The argument of Cain (1979) and others that so-called secondary workers have a lower attachment than primary (older male) workers is therefore dubious. The very fact that more female and young workers enter the labour force illustrates their changing attitudes towards paid labour. It is unreasonable to assume that these groups attach less importance to their jobs than other workers. Defining unemployment amongst them as less significant is, therefore, an arbitrary decision. Nor can the fact that women (or the young) belong to a high unemployment group, be interpreted as a result of the assumed differential attachment since their relatively high susceptibility to unemployment is imposed by the market; they apparently hold jobs which are relatively sensitive to cyclical movements. This can easily be understood if we consider two hypothetical economies with a 100 per cent male labour force and the other with a 50 per cent male labour force. Suppose a recession causes 10 per cent unemployment in both countries. Unemployment incidence by sex in the first country is easy to forecast, but what determines the sex composition of unemployment in the latter? The two variables which are relevant in this case are the distribution of men and women over different occupations and the cyclical sensitivity of each occupation. If occupations are disproportionally distributed by sex, and if women are over-represented in cyclically sensitive economic activities, this will produce an uneven incidence of unemployment by sex. This means that women are not more prone to unemployment because of their sex, but because of their jobs. If these jobs were held by men – because of a lack of female participation in the first country – these men would become equally unemployed. The story is, however, more complicated, because new entrants have so far been ignored. Suppose the same situation with 10 per cent unemployment, but with a simultaneous 10 per cent increase in the labour force. In the first economy all entrants are male, in the second 50 per cent are female. What happens? Unemployment rises and again the sex incidence in the former case does not cause any problem. The sex composition of unemployment in the second country, however, depends not only on the variables that were important previously, but also on the respective absorption rates for male and female new entrants. This, in turn, may be influenced by the substitutability of men and women. If the newly-entering men, for example, drive out the women already employed, then an overall increase of the aggregate unemployment rate with a decreasing unemployment rate for men may result. This actually happened in the United States where the overall unemployment rate was higher in 1979 (5.8) than in 1960 (5.5), even though the jobless rate for males 20 years old and over had dropped significantly (from 4.7 per cent in 1960 to 4.1 per cent in 1979). The example illustrates that the first argument to adjust the aggregate unemployment rate for demographic shifts in the labour force is based on a questionable assumption concerning the strength of labour force attachment by different demographic groups. It ignores the fact that generally unemployment is not a chosen status, but rather one that is imposed by the market; the composition of unemployment is, therefore, theoretically irrelevant for its aggregate volume.

The second argument in favour of a (demographic) adjustment of the aggregate unemployment rate – the definition of a non-inflationary unemployment rate requires a compositional neutral rate – is related to the observation that the same unemployment rate not always reflect a similar degree of market tightness. This observation is often made when the full employment target is set by means of the Phillips curve.

At a given time a reduction of unemployment below a 2 per cent threshold may risk stimulating inflation while under other circumstances or in another country a reduction of a much higher rate may have the same effect. This is primarily due to the heterogenity of the labour force and the existence of non-competing groups on the market. Sex and age categories, though certainly very important are however not the only sources of heterogenity, and it seems rather arbitrary to 'correct' the unemployment rate in this respect only for these distortions. Antos, Mellow and Triplett (1979) add two other arguments why this correction is at least only partially meaningful. They argue that one cannot determine the non-inflationary unemployment rate solely from analyses of labour market effects, since inflation also depends on a number of factors in addition to the wage-cost pressures - including pressures on capacity, external slacks and expectations. Second, they point out that other changes in the labour market are equally important, such as unemployment insurance and minimum wages. Given the partiality of the proposed corrections in the light of what has been said, the second argument is not strong enough to justify a change in definition of the unemployment rate.

The third argument, finally, is important but does not require a redefinition of the unemployment rate. Better insight into the functioning of the labour market and into the likely effects of future compositional changes is obtained more thoroughly when multiple ratios are studied within a system of labour market accounts. This system would leave the traditional unemployment indicator unaltered and map the underlying movements and developments - including the effects of compositional changes stemming from different origins - as accurately as possible.

Concluding Remarks

The traditional unemployment measure and the related concepts of 'employment' and 'labour force' have been criticised for both measurement and conceptual reasons. We reached the following conclusions:

1. Registration data, used to calculate official unemployment rates, depend too directly on current social security practices to guarantee a reliable estimate of the number of unemployed.
2. The discouraged (added) worker effect affects the size of the labour force; consequently cyclical movements in the unemployment rate (with a cyclically varying 'labour force' in the denominator) are no longer the sole product of variations in the share of unemployed in the labour force; this diminishes the reliability of the unemployment rate as a cyclical indicator.
3. Labour hoarding and dishoarding are not reflected in the unemployment rate since the latter is expressed in persons: a cyclical bias of the unemployment rate results.
4. Differences in the impact of legislation and government policy upon the labour force and the number of unemployed introduce problems of intertemporal and international comparability.
5. Significant changes in the real number of hours worked and in the share of part-time workers are masked when labour force and (un)employment are measured in persons, and therefore the unemployment rate underestimates real labour slack.

Three other reasons for criticising the unemployment rate found in the literature are said to be insufficient to justify a redefinition of the traditional concepts. They relate to the emphasis that should be given to economic hardship rather than to under-utilised labour resources, to the omission of disguised unemployment from the traditional counts and to the impact of the age and sex composition of the labour force upon the interpretation of the unemployment rate.

However, it is clear from the discussion that 'labour force, employment and unemployment' are used to analyse a broad diversity of labour market issues, and that each study imposes its requirements on the presentation of the basic data. Measurements to highlight the impact of cyclical movements on the labour market should be of a different nature than those required to discuss the necessity and the viability of social security policy. Since, however, only the traditional counts are currently available and easily accessible, investigations of widely divergent nature and purposes use only these figures. Efforts should therefore be made to organise the data in a way that allows relatively easy calculation of various counts and ratios related to the nature of the questions which have to be answered.

On the other hand, even when discussing the same subject, the simple counts of employment and unemployment are poor instruments to study ongoing developments on the labour market, as the unemployment rate is a poor instrument to judge the cyclical situation of an economy. Rather than to rely on one indicator, a set of ratios and counts is required in order to obtain a trustworthy picture of the labour market.

Both a method for organising data in a way that can easily be handled and a set of indicators to be used in labour market analysis in general and utilisation analysis in particular, are offered in the labour market accounts which are developed in the next Section. In order to get a clear picture of the requirements that newly developed accounts should meet, a study and critique of several proposed alternatives to the traditional concepts is useful. Together with the critical appraisal of the traditional concepts discussed here, the conclusions provide useful standards to design a new system.

(c) Suggested Adjustments to Traditional Concepts

Critical review of the traditional concepts 'employment, unemployment and labour force' has led various authors to suggest adjustments, particularly to unemployment and the unemployment rate. Two broad categories of amendement can be distinguished: first those that aim to improve the unemployment rate as a cyclical indicator of labour utilisation, and second those that emphasise other aspects of unemployment, such as the economic hardship experienced by job seekers or job losers. The discussion here is confined to those adjustments which retain the basic unit (persons) used in the traditional concept and which do not extend their observation range beyond the registered labour force (the sum of employed and unemployed). Alternatives and supplements to the traditional concepts that use man hours as the unit of measurement and base their estimates of labour slack on a demographic definition of total available labour resources are reviewed later.

Adjustments to the Unemployment Rate as a Cyclical Indicator

Time-weighted Unemployment Rate According to the ILO definitions, only those persons who did not work at all during the survey week and were looking for work are counted as unemployed; all persons who worked one hour or more for pay or profit are counted as employed. This dichotomy in the definition introduces a downward bias in the unemployment rate since it classifies those who usually work full-time but worked short time during the survey period because of slack work, lay-offs or other economic reasons, as employed (while they are, in fact, partially unemployed). On the other hand, offsetting this is the 'overestimation' of the unemployment rate due to the fact that not all the unemployed are looking for full-time jobs, though each unemployed person receives equal weight in the unemployment count regardless of the fact whether he or she is looking for a full-time or for a part-time job. To allow for these offsetting phenomena, Shiskin (1976) developed a 'time-weighted unemployment rate', which corrected both numerator and denominator of the unemployment rate for these phenomena.[11]

The rate then estimates total full-time job seekers plus half-time part-time job seekers plus half-total on part-time for economic reasons as a percentage of the civilian labour force less part-time labour force.

The time-weighted unemployment rate (U-6 in Shiskin's and BLS terminology) shows empirically the same movements as the 'unadjusted' traditional unemployment rate, but is situated on a somewhat higher level (± 1.5 per cent higher in the United States – Shiskin, 1976). Although the rationale behind the adjusted rate as a correction for part-time unemployment is reasonable, it suffers from the characteristics of a 'halfway' solution: on the one hand the numbers are expressed in persons, but no longer reducible to natural individuals, while on the other hand it does not grasp all the consequences of making allowances for the time dimension (such as overtime, labour hoarding, reductions in the time effectively worked). This is to say that the adjusted unemployment rate on the one hand loses its easy interpretability as 'all persons affected by unemployment' while, on the other, it does not gain enough in content to express fully the time dimension of unused labour resources.

The Unemployment Rate Adjusted for Discouragement On p. 127 above the discouraged worker effect and its consequential under-estimate of the unemployment rate is discussed. Econometric estimates of the number of discouraged workers were said to be too unstable to be used for a robust correction of the unemployment rate for this effect. In 1967, a question was added to the United States Current Population Survey, which allows an estimate of the number of discouraged workers. Various authors have proposed to use these data to adjust the unemployment rate.[12] The 'unemployment rate adjusted for discouragement' is then defined as the (time-weighted) unemployment plus discouraged workers as a percentage of the civilian labour force plus discouraged workers (U-7 in Shiskin's terminology – Shiskin, 1976).

The adjusted rate moves parallel with the unemployment rate. Its value is logically higher than that of the traditional rate since it adds the same number to the numerator (the number of unemployed) and to the denominator (the labour force). Discouragement may be an important phenomenon significantly contributing to the volume of the labour slack at a certain moment, and fluctuating cyclically; an indicator that includes the discouraged unemployed can therefore be of great analytical value. It is, however, difficult to measure the number of discouraged persons since it depends on the motives of people who cease to look for a job. Moreover, trying to get more insight into the latent unused labour resources, the correction should include more aspects than discouragement from job search, since investigations showed that the discouraged are but a small portion of those people whose 'entry and quit' behaviour is affected by the current labour market conditions (Mincer, 1973). The 'unemployment rate adjusted for discouragement' is therefore a useful – though limited – concept, but loses substantially because of (inevitable) inaccurate measurement.

Compositionally Neutral Unemployment Rate As previously demonstrated, the composition of the labour force changed dramatically after World War II. Shifts in the age and sex composition were caused by demographic fluctuations and by changes in the labour market participation rates for several groups. Since some of these groups – in particular, younger people and female workers – are relatively over-represented in sectors of the labour market where the unemployment incidence is higher, some authors advocate a downward correction of the unemployment rate in order to construct a 'compositional neutral unemployment rate'.[13] The adjustment is normally made on the basis of the arithmetic given by equation (6.1). We argued, however, that the use of the equation involves significant technical problems. Moreover, the theoretical reasons for this type of adjustment are said to be insufficient to justify amendments of the traditional concepts.

Full-time Equivalent Unemployment Rates As was the case for the weighted unemployment rate, the full-time equivalent unemployment rate takes the full-time and part-time character of jobs – both those held by workers and those wanted by job seekers – into account. The principle is simple: members of the labour force are weighted according to whether they hold or seek full-time or part-time jobs. The weights, however, no longer represent an arbitrary fraction but are the hours actually worked on an average by full- and part-time employees holding non-agricultural wage and salary jobs in the respective years. In 1974, for example, the weights were 42.2 (hours) for full-time job seekers and 18.4 (hours) for part-time job seekers (United States figures, given by Gilroy, 1975). The adjusted number of employed in full-time equivalent units then consists of the product of the official employment figure and average weekly hours of all those at work divided by the full-time work week.[14]

This hypothetical jobless rate can further be adjusted for involuntary part-time work, analogous to the weighted unemployment rate discussed previously. The weight of involuntary part-time workers is, however, no longer arbitrarily set on one-half (see definitions above); in the full-time equivalent rate – the total weekly hours lost by persons working part-time for economic reasons are first imputed and subsequently divided by the weekly hours actually worked by full-time workers. In 1974, this resulted in an additional 1 458 000 'unemployed persons' in full-time equivalent units (United States figures, Gilroy, 1975).

The number of individuals defined as discouraged workers by means of survey results (see definitions above), can also be expressed in full-time equivalent units. Each of the age–sex groups is then divided into a full- and a part-time category equal in proportion to those of the unemployed persons in the same group, multiplied by the actual hours worked by their employed peers. The sum of these counts is divided in turn by their respective (per sex) full-time weekly hours. The total number of discouraged workers in full-time equivalent units can subsequently be added to the weighted unemployment rate in full-time equivalent units in order to construct the 'unemployment rate adjusted for involuntary part-time workers and for discouragement expressed in full-time equivalent units'.[15]

The adjusted unemployment rates expressed in full-time equivalents have the same analytical characteristics as their counterparts expressed in persons. They provide fairly reasonable corrections but do not grasp the full consequences of introducing the time dimension, nor do they provide more reliable estimates of discouragement effects. On the other hand, they are no longer reducible to natural persons and therefore lose in comprehensibility compared to the traditional unemployment rate.

Index of Unemployment Severity The index of unemployment severity, developed by G. H. Moore (1973) and further refined by Gilroy (1975), combines two principal dimensions to the measurement of unemployment – namely the number of unemployed and the average length of time they have been looking for work. The severity of unemployment estimates the number of days each worker would have been jobless if average unemployment during the year – measured as the product of the average yearly unemployment rate and the mean duration in days – were distributed among all persons in the labour force. The index of unemployment severity is then expressed as annual changes respective to a certain base year. It appears that the severity index fluctuates more dramatically over the business cycle and lags behind the unemployment rate (Gilroy, 1975).

The index is a useful analytical barometer of changes in the job market. It is less affected by the changing age–sex composition of the labour force, mainly because the relatively high portions of young people and women in recent years is partly offset by the fact that these groups have shorter spells of unemployment.[16] This is, however, no more than a historical coincidence in the United States, which may turn out to be non-existent in other countries or in different time periods. Analytically, the index is a poor measure of the extent to which labour resources are used; it seems to be only relevant as a highly sensitive cyclical indicator which reflects changes in the burden of unemployment. Analogous to the previous indicator, the index of unemployment severity can be expressed in full-time equivalent units, making allowance for the different weight of job seekers looking for full-time and part-time work.[17]

Adjustment to the Unemployment Rate for Other Purposes

The unemployment rate may serve various other purposes in addition to its use as an indicator of the cyclical performance of an economy. If, for example, the purpose is the analysis of the economic and psychological hardship experienced by job seekers, the scope of the measure may be limited to those who are considered to be suffering most severely. One might thus want only to count either those persons unemployed for longer periods, or those who lose their jobs, or unemployed heads of households or the unemployed who are looking for a full-time job. Behind these choices of category lie hidden assumptions about the attachment of different categories of workers to the labour force, and about the social impact of unemployment among different groups.

Shiskin (1976) suggests four possible indicators, identified by the symbols U-1 through U-4 (in addition to the traditional unemployment rate U-5, the weighted unemployment rate U-6 and the unemployment rate adjusted for discouragement U-7):

U-1 = Persons unemployed 15 weeks or longer as a per cent of civilian labour force.
U-2 = Job losers as per cent of civilian labour force.
U-3 = Unemployed household heads as per cent of household head labour force.
U-4 = Unemployed full-time job seekers as per cent of full-time labour (including those employed part-time for economic reasons).

Shiskin demonstrates that each of them is cyclically sensitive, and by its movements can give an indication of the cyclical performance.

The adjusted unemployment estimates represent a range of value judgements on the hardship experienced by unemployed from a very narrow to a very broad view. None of them, however, can be said to represent a thorough estimate of all the dimensions of labour slack, mainly because of their inability to make allowance for variability in hours (as they are all measured in persons) and because they are limited to the registered labour force and do not cover all the individuals who react on labour market developments, nor the total available labour resources in an economy.

(d) Measurements in Man Hours

In the discussion of the traditional concepts, several arguments were advanced in favour of measures of unemployment, unused labour resources or labour slack in terms of man hours rather than persons. We can broadly summarise these under five headings:

1. Although average contractual weekly hours of full-time workers have not changed to a significant extent, average yearly contractual hours of full-time workers have decreased significantly in the post-1945 decades due to more and longer holidays and authorised absences from work.

2. The proportion of part-time workers has risen.
3. Average hours effectively worked have fallen because of a significant rise in absence due to illness, injury, personal and civic reasons. Absence for these reasons may fluctuate according to the cyclical situation.
4. Overtime and short-time work for economic reasons are commonly used instruments to absorb fluctuations in economic activity.
5. The development of the welfare state stimulates substitution of household activities by market work, thus transferring activities from the non-market to the market sector and increasing the individual time effectively available for market work.

Although these arguments are convincing and manipulation of the working time is more and more seen as a useful instrument for labour market policy, few estimates of labour slack measured in hours are found. This has to be attributed to the fact that working time – both as a relevant variable and as a policy instrument – was only recently discovered. Consequently, statistical data are rather poor in this domain.

The most important and elaborate estimate for labour slack using man hours as a unit of measurement is 'labour force time lost'. The measure was developed by G. Bancroft (1962) and reintroduced again by Gilroy (1975). It estimates the extent to which the nation's labour force is utilised at a point in time by the ratio 'total man hours worked by the employed to hours potentially available to the labour force'. If there is no unemployment or part-time employment for economic reasons, the ratio is 100, the difference between the actual ratio and 100 is a measure of unutilised manpower–labour force time lost.

The United States Bureau of Labor Statistics has published data on labour force time lost since 1962 (data are available since 1955). Total hours provided by the economy are the sum of the total hours worked by those persons at work and the hours imputed to those persons with a job but not at work. Total hours lost by the economy are estimated by adding the hours lost by unemployed workers (persons seeking full- and part-time work are treated differently) and those hours lost by persons working part-time for economic reasons. Total man hours potentially available to the economy are the sum of total hours provided and total hours lost. The calculation implies the choice of a standard for the full-time work week imputed to those seeking full-time work and those persons who are unemployed part-time for economic reasons, since it is not known how long exactly they would have worked. The standard chosen by BLS is 37.5 hours. This choice is rather arbitrary (midway between the 40 hours standard and the 35 hours cut-off point, which distinguishes full-time from part-time workers). A case could also be made for choosing either the 40 hours standard or the average hours worked by full-time workers (e.g., 43.2 hours a week in 1974). Unemployed people seeking part-time jobs are assumed to have lost those hours actually worked by their employed peers. Note, therefore, that total hours provided by the economy and hours lost by unemployed seeking part-time work, are calculated by means of a variable standard.

Figure 6.1 expresses the measure of labour force time lost and the traditional unemployment rate (1959–81). The movements of the series are very close together; the difference between them is cyclically insensitive[18] and narrowing in 1963 (due to better measurements – see Gilroy, 1975).

Although the per cent of labour force time lost and the unemployment rate are reasonably similar in cyclical sensitivity, the former is a

Figure 6.1 United States: labour force time lost and unemployment rate (1959–81)

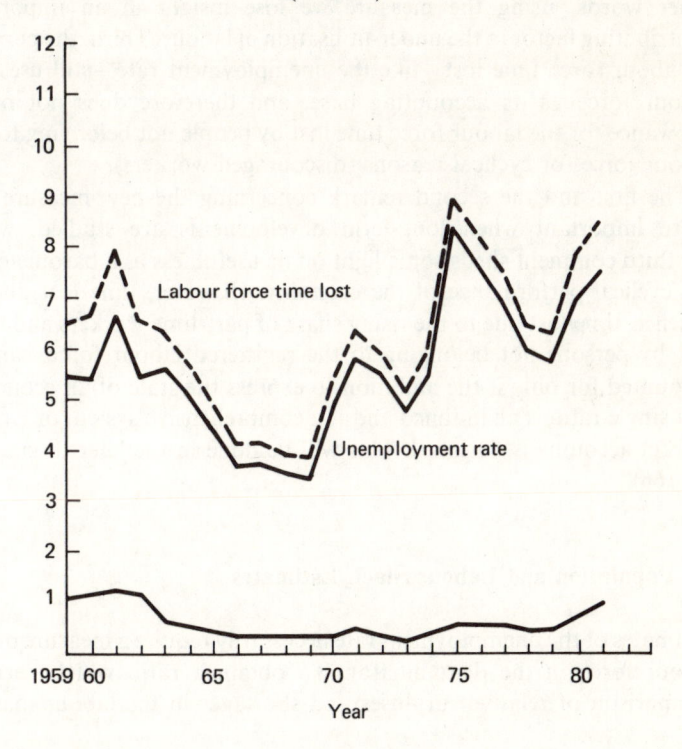

conceptually more explicit and comprehensive measure of labour force utilisation, since it partly takes the manipulation of the working time into consideration. One should note, for example, that especially early in a cyclical downswing, the number of unemployed may rise, while other employees are still 'over-utilised' by working overtime; this effect is reflected in the labour force time lost.

However, the per cent of labour force time lost has other drawbacks of which the choice of the 'standard hours' criterion is only a minor one. Labour force time lost by absence due to illness, injury, personal and civic reasons, industrial disputes, holidays and bad weather, is not counted as lost but as 'provided' by the economy. Although the economy provides those hours, and the persons normally filling these hours are not looking for another job, one cannot argue that during these hours the labour force is used. Moreover, changes in the amount of hours lost for these reasons, may affect total demand for labour. Second, if more persons work part-time, the labour force time lost is affected both in its numerator and denominator, while it may also be interpreted as an under-utilisation of the potentially available labour force time. In other words, using the measure we lose insight in an important contributing factor to the under-utilisation of labour. Third, the per cent of labour force time lost – like the unemployment rate – still uses the labour force as its accounting base, and therefore does not make allowance for the labour force time lost by people not belonging to the labour force for cyclical reasons (discouraged workers).

The first and the second remark concerning the new measure are more important when long-term developments are studied, while the third comment sheds some light on its usefulness as a barometer of the cyclical performance of the economy. However, time lost due to absence, time lost due to the rising share of part-time workers and time lost by persons not belonging to the registered labour force, can be accounted for only if the ambition to express the state of an economy in a single ratio is abandoned and if a comprehensive system of labour market accounts is designed. This will be done in the later discussion (p. 166).

(e) Population and Labour Slack Estimates

Estimates of the unemployment rate necessarily require a measure of the labour force in the denominator. To obtain a ratio which permits comparison of relative surpluses and shortages in the labour market over time it is assumed that the population at working age – which offers labour services to the economy – is adequately measured by the registered labour force. More specifically, the difference between the sum of the individuals offering labour and the volume of the registered labour force should not be influenced by economic changes, such as cyclical fluctuations or economic growth. Two reasons were given above for believing that this assumption is unrealistic.

First, the size of the labour force varies cyclically due to the discouragement (additional worker) effect. This implies that the unemployment rate is no longer an accurate estimate of the impact of cyclical movements on the labour market. Second, persistent (and significant) changes in labour force participation rates occur, induced by long-term economic and social changes. A second element of uncertainty is thus introduced, since new entrants or re-entrants become increasingly important and enlarge the gap between the real and the registered labour force (Sorrentino, 1978). This implies that the number of people reacting to changes in the labour market (or to economic changes in general) is significantly higher than the registered labour force. Attachment to the labour force, measured by some kind of active 'working' or 'seeking' behaviour, is a very poor criterion to define the labour market relevant population. This is confirmed by empirical research. Gastwirth, for example (1973, p. 23) concludes that 'the results of the "Work Experience Report" also indicate a growing attachment to the labour force of many so-called secondary workers'. Mincer (1973) reports that by far the larger part of new job holders (entrants and re-entrants) comes from outside the official labour reserve (even if discouraged workers are included in the latter) and that the available labour reserve is, therefore, much larger than the official estimate.

These two arguments led to the introduction of another accounting base, which is less affected by distortions over time. The readily available solution is to choose 'the population at working age', although it is easy to imagine the problems introduced by this choice (see below). Because the number unemployed is but a tiny fraction of the entire population at working age, the resulting measure of economic performance is usually defined as the 'employment–population ratio'. The ratio is introduced by Moore (1973) and its use is advocated by Shiskin (1976), Steinberg (1976) and Leon (1981).

To illustrate why this indicator is preferred by a number of authors to an adjustment of the traditional unemployment rate, two observations made in the earlier discussion should be kept in mind. First, correcting the unemployment count in order to account for the discouragement effect cannot be done accurately – i.e., the labour force count cannot be adjusted, making its measurement independent from the cyclical situation. Second, annual changes in the registered labour force are far more erratic than annual changes in the population at working age. This points to the fact that the labour force by itself is co-determined by long-term economic and social-changes, and by cyclical fluctuations.

The employment–population ratio essentially answers the question 'what proportion of the working age population is employed?'. The two numbers needed for its calculation are the total non-institutional working age population and (civilian) employment (in persons). For the United States the measure fluctuates between 54 per cent and 60 per cent in the period 1950–80. Figure 6.2 shows the time path of the ratio by certain age–sex groups for the United States. Simple eyeballing demonstrates that the ratio is suited to study trends and amplitude differences between various groups, but that it seems less cyclically sensitive compared to the unemployment rate. Before, discussing its advantages and disadvantages, however, let us have a closer look at its statistical and analytical features.

Statistically, employment is a firmer and more objective concept than unemployment, since the former is easier to define and to measure. An individual is classified as employed if he or she has been working at least one hour for wage or profit during the survey week: in measuring unemployment, uncertainty may arise such as in the determination of whether jobless persons are actively seeking work or whether they are currently available for work.[19] Additionally, employment is less subject to measurement and sampling errors, while seasonal adjustment is more accurate.[20]

The major analytical strength of the employment–population ratio is that it is undisturbed by shifts of workers in and out the labour force. Its steady time path in the post-war period, however, suggests that it might be less useful as a measure of the cyclical performance of the economy. A closer examination of its properties compared to those of other indicators is therefore needed.

Comparing the employment–population ratio for both sexes 16 years and over in Figure 6.2 and the simple count of employment (as a percentage of the population older than 15), it can be seen that the latter is strongly dominated by the long-term growth trend: it is clear that the employment–population ratio is superior in this context, since it relates changes in the level of employment to changes in the population. Evaluation of the job growth is, therefore, easier. The participation rate (the labour force as a percentage of the population older than 15)

Figure 6.2 United States: employment–population ratio by age, sex and unemployment rate (1959–80)

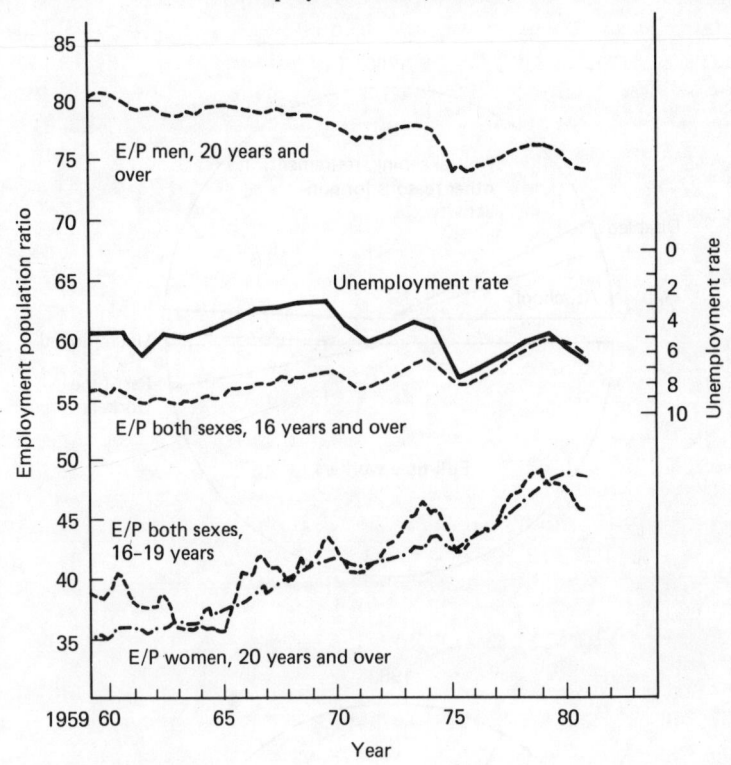

[Figure 6.2: Line graph showing E/P men, 20 years and over; Unemployment rate; E/P both sexes, 16 years and over; E/P both sexes, 16–19 years; E/P women, 20 years and over, from 1959 to 1980. Left axis: Employment population ratio (35–85). Right axis: Unemployment rate (0–10, inverse).]

(a) Major shifts.
(b) Percentage changes.

demonstrates no cyclical pattern, although it functions well as an indicator of secular trends. The employment–population ratio is, nevertheless, analytically superior because the labour force concept underlying the participation rate is difficult to interpret. When the unemployment rate is drawn at an inverse scale, which more or less matches the range of observation of the employment–population ratio (both sexes, 16 years and older), it can be seen from Figure 6.2 that the movements of both rates are consistent with each other. They generally correspond to changes in aggregate demand (Green, 1977) but are not consistent in the timing of peaks and troughs: the employment–population ratio lags about four months.[21]

Figure 6.3 The Netherlands: deployment of persons 15 and older

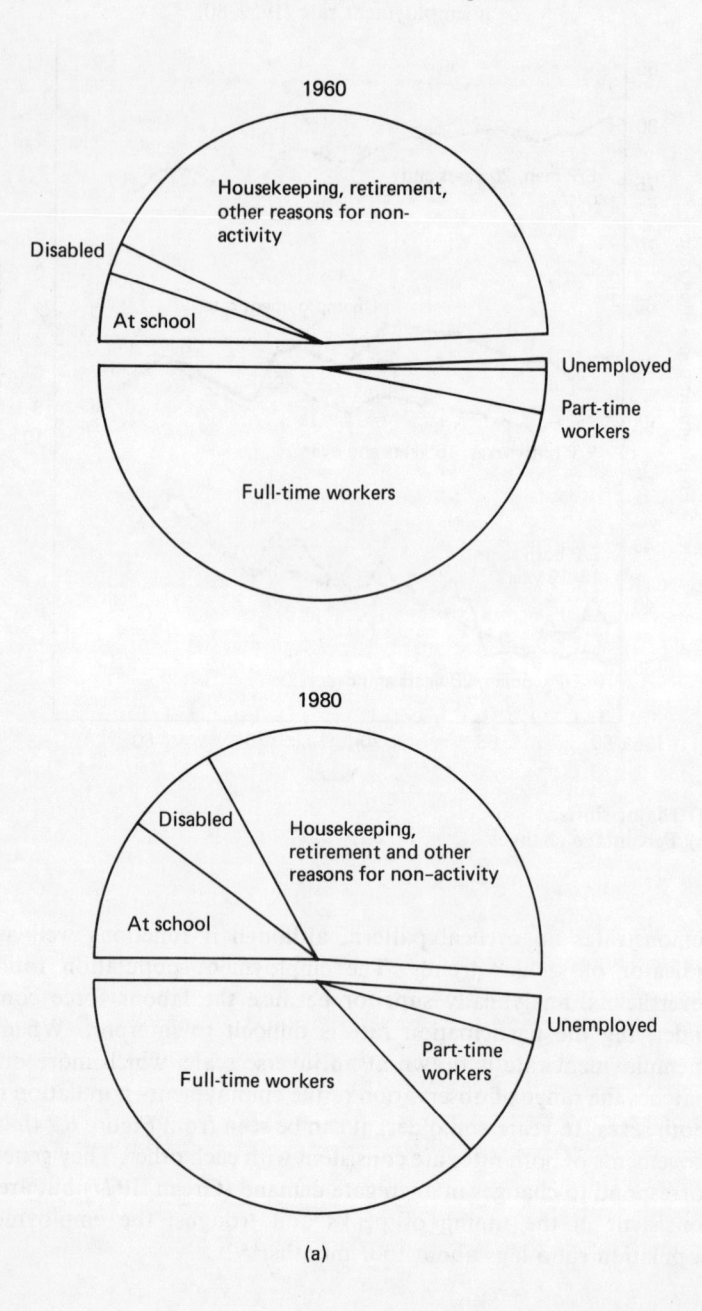

(a)

Figure 6.3(b)

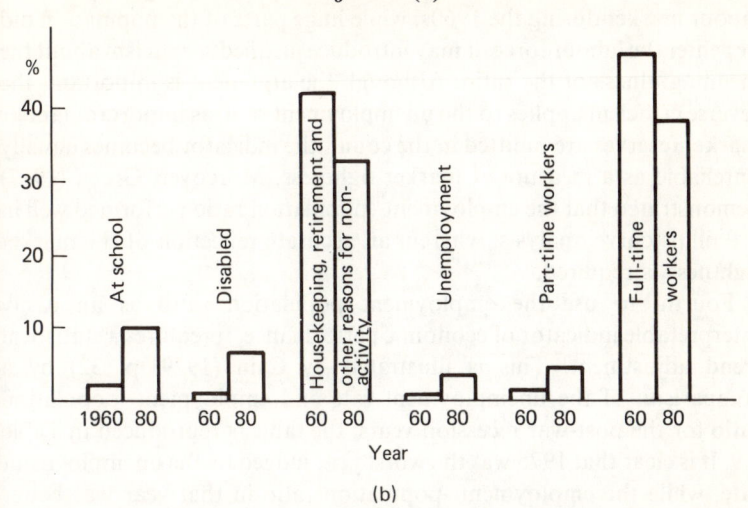

[Bar chart with y-axis in % (0 to 40+), x-axis showing Year pairs 1960/80, 60/80, 60/80, 60/80, 60/80, 60/80. Categories: At school, Disabled, Housekeeping, retirement and other reasons for non-activity, Unemployment, Part-time workers, Full-time workers.]

(b)

Shiskin (1976) concludes that, judged by the standards of the National Bureau for Economic Research, the unemployment rate and the employment–population ratio are more or less of the same quality. As a 'measure of performance' the employment–population ratio is certainly superior. The latter may therefore be considered as a reliable alternative to the former.

This does not, however, mean that the employment–population ratio is free of disadvantages. Five major points of criticism may be formulated. First, the employment–population ratio is less suitable as an indicator of the economic hardship imposed by unemployment. Unemployment is more unambiguous as an indicator of the disutility experienced by unemployed persons (Cain, 1979; Shiskin, 1976). Since, however, we argued that measuring economic hardship is not a major aim of indicators of economic performance, this drawback is not very serious.

Second, the employment–population ratio is counted in persons and the same remarks as made above concerning the importance of the time dimension of labour slack apply here, too. In the light of the growing significance of part-time work and of under-utilisation of labour resources due to involuntary short-time work, this disadvantage cannot be ignored.

Third, is it realistic to use the entire population as a base in the denominator of the ratio since a vast part of the population is not interested in market work at all? Remembering the tightness of the labour market during the 1960s, while huge parts of the population did not enter the labour force, it may introduce justified scepticism about the meaningfulness of the ratio. Although the argument is important, the reverse criticism applies to the unemployment rate; as important labour market reserves are omitted in the count, the indicator becomes equally unreliable as a measure of market tightness. Moreover, Green (1977) demonstrated that the employment–population ratio performed well in a Phillips curve analysis, wherein an accurate reflection of the market tightness is required.

Fourth, to use the employment–population ratio as an easily interpretable indicator of economic performance, it requires a statistical trend adjustment. This is illustrated by Cain (1979, p. 32) by a comparison of the unemployment rate and employment–population ratio for the post-war recession years: the table is reproduced in Table 6.9. It is clear that 1975 was the worst year judged by the unemployment rate, while the employment–population ratio in that year was better than in the other years (except in 1970). Measuring the change in the employment–population ratio relative to the preceding year, a more consistent ordering of the recession years results. Cain is certainly right when he states that the employment–population ratio misses the easy interpretability of the unemployment count. However, calculating yearly changes is not complicated, while the 'new' ratio reveals more information than the unemployment rate. In fact, the higher employment–ratio for 1975, combined with a very high unemployment rate, indicates that important differences in the volume of labour supply

Table 6.9 Unemployment rate, employment–population ratio and yearly changes in the employment–population ratio: United States (post-1945 recession years)

Year	Unemployment rate	Employment–population ratio (E/P)	$(E/P)_t - (E/P)_{t-1}$
1949	5.9	54.6	−1.2
54	5.5	53.8	−1.5
58	6.8	54.2	−1.5
61	6.7	54.2	− .7
70	4.9	56.1	− .4
75	8.5	55.3	−1.7

Source: Cain (1979), p. 32.

have appeared; this information is not given by the unemployment rate alone.

The most important drawback of the employment–population ratio signalled by various authors, however, is the fact that it is the product of offsetting movements in certain age–sex groups (see also Figure 6.2). This is not insuperable by itself, but it introduces conceptual ambiguity in providing an indication of the performance of the economy with respect to the goal of full employment. This means that a decrease of the employment–population ratio cannot simply be interpreted as a decrease of the performance of the economy, since changes in the employment–population ratio may be caused by increased schooling and protracted retirement. 'Another way of making this point is to recognise that E/P would rise, other things being equal, if high school and college attendance declined, if pension plans were curtailed, and if welfare payment, disability and old-age benefits, and scholarships were reduced' (Cain, 1979, p. 33). Although these comments are relevant, they also apply to the unemployment rate. This rate is equally an amalgam of underlying contrasting trends, principally between men and women, but also among different age and marital status groups. Moreover, it only seems easier to determine a target value for economic policy defined in terms of the unemployment rate.[22]

One important difference between the employment–population ratio and the unemployment rate, however, remains unchallenged – namely that changes in the former are far more difficult to interpret as either positive or negative developments, when no other data are given. Cain concludes: 'This theoretical shortcoming, along with the mixed empirical aspects of the E/P statistic, is too great a price to pay for its superiority as an objective measurement' (Cain, 1979, p. 33). Although the subsequent rejection of the employment–population ratio has to be understood in the light of Cain's historical defence of the unemployment rate, his point of view is somewhat myopic. This is particularly true when it is recognised that the interpretation of the unemployment rate is likewise not unproblematic, especially in the light of the significant demographic and compositional changes depicted above.

We do agree with Cain that the unemployment rate is more valuable in economic analysis than some of its critics want us to believe. We fail, however, to understand why the analysis of economic performance – whether long-term or cyclical – should be limited to the interpretation of a single number. A banker understands that yearly profits do not tell the whole story about the economic performance of enterprises and he (or she) will study entire accounts (and often a lot more) before allowing a loan. Analogously, a policymaker or a professional economist should not base his (or her) judgement about the performance of a national labour market on a single number. We agree with Shiskin (1976) who states that the employment–population ratio and the unemployment rate, like other economic indicators, should be used in conjunction with a broad range of indicators of labour market activity currently available, in order to develop a balanced and accurate picture of actual labour conditions. He also warns against the use of one single number without any breakdowns. We advocate to extend Shiskin's recommendation to measure 'the doughnut *and* the hole' towards the careful study of 'the dough, the doughnut and the hole'. In order to ameliorate our insight into the significant developments on the labour market and exploit the possibilities provided by the modern statistical apparatus, labour market analysis should be based on a comprehensive though detailed system of labour market accounts, as a satellite of the traditional national accounts. Single counts and ratios like the unemployment rate, the employment–population rate, the participation rate, the labour force time lost, etc. can then be interpreted as elements in a broader picture. Broken down into relevant categories and related to each other, they can then play the role they deserve in economic analysis and policy design.

A SYSTEM OF LABOUR MARKET ACCOUNTS

The first part of this chapter reviewed criticisms of the concept and measurement of unemployment as an estimate of the under-utilisation of labour resources, advanced sceptical remarks on the predominant unemployment fetishism in labour market analysis and discussed adjustments and alternatives to the unemployment rate put forward in the literature. Both the critical remarks and the rationales behind the proposed alternatives can be summarised as four requirements that superior measures of the utilisation of labour resources should meet:

1. The employment recruitment base should be better defined than is done by the traditional labour force count, since the 'labour market population' is usually larger than the registered labour force (see arguments and adjustments above related to the discouragement effect).
2. The data should be counted in persons and in hours, since average yearly hours worked per employee changes drastically over time due

to cyclical manipulations of the hours actually worked, to shifts from full- to part-time schedules and to longer and more frequent holidays and absences (see arguments and adjustments above related to labour hoarding, overtime and short time, time weighted rates, full-time equivalent rates and labour force time lost).
3. The figures should be given with enough detail to highlight prevailing compositional shifts in age and sex.
4. The data should be organised in a way that allows one to monitor the impact of social and economic policy upon the utilisation of labour resources.

In this part of the chapter a system of labour market accounts will be developed and applied to the post-1945 developments in the Netherlands and the United States. Other systems and proposals for similar accounts found in the literature will also be discussed.

(a) Range, Details and Organisation of Labour Market Accounts

Orientation

Prompted by high unemployment rates during the 1970s, labour market policies have been intensified and diversified in many countries.[23] The design and the evaluation of these policy measures urge the labour market statistician and analyst to provide an adequate basis for monitoring, forecasting or simulation. A system of labour market account should therefore be policy-oriented in the sense that it should provide a minimal set of observations that may illuminate the impact and effectiveness of specific policy measures. However, given the state of the art and the fact that many statistical and conceptual problems still have to be solved, a firmer articulation of the kind of policies the accounts intend to cover is needed. Although recently much attention was given to so-called 'structural labour market policy' – intended to ensure a better match of qualifications of demand and supply in many respects – the major concern of economic (labour market) policy is the dramatic under-utilisation of labour resources in quantitative terms. In our view, the development of a labour market account should follow this priority, and accept a primary orientation towards labour utilisation accounts and macroeconomic types of policy in general. This is, however, not a very restrictive constraint if the major areas of political measures are summarised. Labour market policy directed towards an amelioration of the utilisation of labour resources may use several different types of instruments, including unemployment benefit and other social security programmes, measures to preserve existing – or to create new jobs (in the private and in the public sector, and including wage policy), and measures that manipulate the supply of labour – e.g., retirement programmes, work-sharing, creation of part-time jobs, migration policy. We explicitly exclude policy measures intended to stimulate geographical and/or functional mobility, because the monitoring of those types of policy requires a specific nature and organisation of data (see later, when we discuss other accounting frameworks in the literature).

Range

The span of analysis of labour market accounts should stretch beyond the traditional labour force count. Two empirical observations can be given to justify this requirement. In the first place it can be labour force participation rates are varying over time and between countries. Participation rates rise in many countries, indicating that the registered labour force of today may be a significant underestimate of the participating population of next year. Moreover, as illustrated in Table 6.8, trends in the participation rates are highly different for men and women. This indicates that the sex (and age) composition of the labour force is subject to voluminous changes over time. The only way to overcome this difficulty is to adopt a demographic framework for the accounts.

The second reason to investigate the (changes in the) utilisation of the *entire population* – rather than the registered labour force – is found in the cyclical 'enter and quit' behaviour of the population at working age. As extensively discussed above, a notable part of the population that does not belong to the registered labour force reacts to cyclical movements. Since both estimates from surveys and those from econometric equations are unreliable, the only way to deal with this part of the 'labour market relevant population' is by not excluding it *a priori* from the analysis and to start with a demographic concept of labour supply rather than with a behavioural definition of the labour force (either one works, or one actively looks for a job).

Labour market accounts have to be framed with both persons and hours as *units of measurement*. Traditional analyses have tended to deal only in terms of the number of persons. However, working hours became increasingly important since a significant drop in the average *actual* hours worked per person per year (as opposed to average weekly working hours) has to be noted in recent decades. In addition to the data discussed above, this is illustrated in Table 6.10. From the Table it can be seen that the average actual hours worked per person in employment has declined, especially during the 1970s, though the timing differs between the countries. In France and Japan, the decline was most prominent between 1970 and 1975; the decline in the Netherlands was particularly pronounced throughout the whole period while Sweden, the United Kingdom and the United States have known a drop of the average actual hours worked in more specific periods.

Moreover, manipulation of working time and measures that stimulate work-sharing become an important element in the policy debate.[24] It is believed that it is possible to divide the same amount of employment, in work hours, between a larger number of people by reducing the average number of hours worked per person in employment.[25] The viability and the effectiveness of this kind of policy can be analysed only when data on labour utilisation are given in terms of hours. Finally, measurement of labour utilisation in hours is needed to sustain the modern productivity

Table 6.10 Average actual hours worked per person in employment 1960–81 (average annual growth rates, in percentages)

	1960–70	70–3	73–6	76–9	79–81
Canada	n.a.	n.a.	n.a.	n.a.	n.a.
France	−0.5	−1.0	−1.1	−0.8	n.a.
Germany	n.a.	n.a.	n.a.	n.a.	n.a.
Japan	−0.8	−1.8	−1.6	0.3	−0.3
Netherlands	−1.4	−2.0	−1.7	−2.1	n.a.
Sweden	−0.9	−1.7	−0.7	−1.6	−0.7
United Kingdom	−0.1	−0.3	−1.1	−0.9	n.a.
United States	−0.5	−0.2	−1.1	−0.2	−0.6

Sources:
France 1973–80 : Granier (1982).
    1960–73 : Maddison and Granier (1980).
Japan : *Yearbook of Labour Statistics* referring to employees in enterprises with 30 or more employees.
Netherlands: Calculated from data supplied by the 'Economisch Instituut voor het Midden- en Kleinbedrijf', referring to employed persons in the private enterprise sector excluding agriculture and fishing.
Sweden: *Swedish National Accounts.*
United Kingdom: Maddison (1980).
United States: *United States National Accounts* (data referring to employees only).

analysis where the output per work hour is increasingly used as the yardstick of productivity.

So far, the discussion of the range of ideal labour market accounts is confined to the supply side of the market; accounts, however, should enclose other labour market relevant data. Obviously, figures on total output, the number of jobs, vacancies, productivity and the capital stock are important, though not all of them are readily available or easily accessible.

Detail

As stipulated above, labour market accounts should provide data in enough detail to monitor developments on the market and the impact of policy. From the discussion on the measurement of the under-utilisation of labour it becomes clear that the following sub-divisions are relevant in this respect:

1. Total population sub-divided into at least three age categories: < 15, > 15 and 15 > 65.
2. Net migration.
3. Population > 15 and/or population 15 > 65 sub-divided according to active and non-active status in traditional sense.
4. Population > 64 distinguished by active category and retired category.
5. Non-active population sub-divided towards reason for non-activity.
6. Labour force sub-divided into three categories: employed, with a job but not at work, and unemployed.
7. Employed and unemployed population by full-time or part-time status.

The actual elaboration of these requirements is further displayed and discussed below (p. 175).

A decision has also to be taken on the levels of disaggregation for which the data are gathered and presented. Although many relevant disaggregations can be thought of, the availability and accessibility of data make disaggregation towards sex, age groups and marital status groups the only feasible options. For certain benchmark years (e.g., Census years) further sub-division towards (for example) level and type of educational attainment may be possible.

Transparency

It is important that labour market utilisation accounts should be easy to read and to interpret. This will stimulate their uses in analyses and policy design. An important gain in comprehensibility is made when the numbers in the tables are consistent and avoid overlapping: numbers should thus consistently add up to to actual totals (in the last instance to 'total population'). This holds even if it means that rounding errors are inevitable or estimates have to be made on the basis of clearly specified assumptions. Apprehension is also raised when traditional and alternative ratios of utilisation can easily be calculated.

Static or Dynamic

As we stated that labour market accounts should primarily be oriented towards labour utilisation analysis and the study of macroeconomic types of policy, preference should be given to the processing of stock data. This type of data is also relatively easily accessible in a digestible form (as opposed to flow data). The latter type is usually not available for longer time spans in most of the European countries; moreover, its reliability is questionable. This is not to say that the analysis of flow data would be irrelevant, or that the system of labour market accounts as presented below cannot be dynamised. This possibility will be discussed later.

(b) Labour Market Accounting Frameworks in the Literature

Labour Utilisation Accounts

Maddison (1980) has given a major impulse to the development of the labour utilisation accounts. He proposes a comprehensive approach in official statistics in order to overcome the under-estimate of unemployment by official figures of the registered unemployed that neglect other dimensions of labour slack 'such as reversal of previous migration flows or declines in labour force participation or in working hours' (p. 175). His accounting framework distinguishes two separate accounts: the 'monitoring account' and the 'use of potential account'. The former builds up an estimate of total hours worked (H) in the economy from the following components:

P = population of working age (15–64)
a = activity rate – i.e., the ratio labour force to population of working age
u = unemployment rate
$1-u$ = employment rate
d = average number of days worked per year per employee
h = average number of hours worked per day per employee.
$H = P.a(1-u)d.h.$ (6.2)

To calculate the average number of hours actually worker per year per employee, Maddison takes the following items into account:

1. Free Sundays and Saturdays per year.
2. Public holidays and days of vacation.
3. Time lost through incapacity, bad weather, industrial disputes and for personal reasons.
4. Basic hours of full-time workers.
5. Basic hours of part-time workers.
6. Overtime and short time.

Flow Accounts

The analysis of stocks (and net changes in them) offers but a partial picture of labour market developments. The employment rate, for example, may be the same in two years, hiding the fact that only 30 per cent of the unemployed are the same in the two years and ignoring the movement of the other 70 per cent in and out the yearly stock of registered unemployed. In order to describe the prevailing processes on the labour market, information about the actual flows on the market is needed. Labour market flow accounts are set up to organise this information on flows in a systematic and comprehensive way. Their aims are to clarify how many persons leave an 'activity state' to enter another within a defined period: activity states refer to different labour market statuses such as unemployed, employed, retired, following full-time education, etc.

Labour market flow accounts are usually built up from demographic counts while the key concept and unit of measurement is the 'change of status'. Figure 6.4 sketches the basic outline of any labour market flow account for one period. Empirically each cell in the matrix should be filled with two figures: the number of individuals belonging to a certain category in the beginning of the period and entering another status

Figure 6.4 Simplified outline for labour market flow accounts

		Status at time $t+1$				
		Employed $t+1$	Non–active population $(t+1)$	Unemployed $(t+1)$	Emigration	Deaths	Population at time t
Status at time t	Employed t						
	Non–active population t						
	Unemployed t						
	Immigration						
	Births						
	Population at time $t+1$						

category and the volume of the opposite flows (flows can evidently be zero). Labour market flow accounts are especially developed by the IAB (Institut für Arbeitsmarkt- und Berufsforschung) for Germany (Reyher and Bach, 1980).[26]

The information provided by labour market flow accounts is particularly useful to study the 'enter, quit and search' behaviour of individuals. In this respect, the data are suited for microeconomic analyses of the labour market as suggested in the search theory formulated by Holt (1971) and Phelps (1970).[27]

Although empirical investigations on the basis of flow data yield interesting results – especially with respect to theoretical questions – these data and analyses are less suited to study the utilisation of labour resources. They give priority to the analysis of the mechanisms and the movements *in* the labour market. The bottleneck in this field, however, is still the absence of reliable empirical data for most of the countries, while the purpose of the studies is rather ambitious.

(c) **Labour Market Utilisation Accounts: an Outline**

According to the requirements formulated above (p. 166) the total population should be chosen as the basis for labour market utilisation accounts. It has been stressed that the accounting framework pictures the deployment of population over various activity categories: Figure 6.5 sketches the actual categories chosen in this publication. It can be seen from Figure 6.5 that attention is given to the transparency and consistency of the system in the sense that the numbers in the categories add up to meaningful sub-totals which, in turn, finally constitute the total population.

The detail in the outline can better be judged from column 1 in Figure 6.6. It stresses that the total population is sub-divided into three age categories (younger than 15, between 15 and 64 and older than 65). The total population at working age (aged 15 > 65) consists of two groups: the non-active population and the labour force. The members of the non-active population are grouped according to the observed reason for non-activity, whereas the labour force is sub-divided into two categories 'employed' and 'unemployed'. In the former, a distinction can be made according to whether the persons are actually at work or not; those with a job but not at work are grouped by reason of the absence from their jobs. Both employed and unemployed are sub-divided into full-time and part-time categories, while the employment status is specified for the employed. Finally, seven additional sub-divisions are introduced on the right-hand side of the scheme so that the ratios discussed above can easily be calculated from the basic table. They sub-divide total population according to their domestic or migratory status, the population older than 15 into an active and a non-active category, the civilian labour force according to nationality, the part-time employees according to whether they work voluntarily or involuntarily part-time and finally the total unemployed according to the duration of unemployment, to their status in the household and to whether they are new entrants of job-losers.

The empirical applicability of this accounting framework for a country is discussed in the next paragraph: three preliminary remarks can, however, be made already. First, Figure 6.6 gives an ideal framework, which certainly has to be modified according to the availability of the data for each country. Second, problems can be foreseen for persons who have a double status, such as students with a job or workers with more than one job. Third, the system cannot deal with hidden employment.

Beneath the accounting framework with persons as the unit of measurement, Figure 6.6 also provides a systematic treatment of the utilisation of labour resources in terms of hours. The framework in hours is mainly given for the same sub-divisions as specified for the framework in persons. The yearly hours available for work in an

Figure 6.5 Deployment of total population

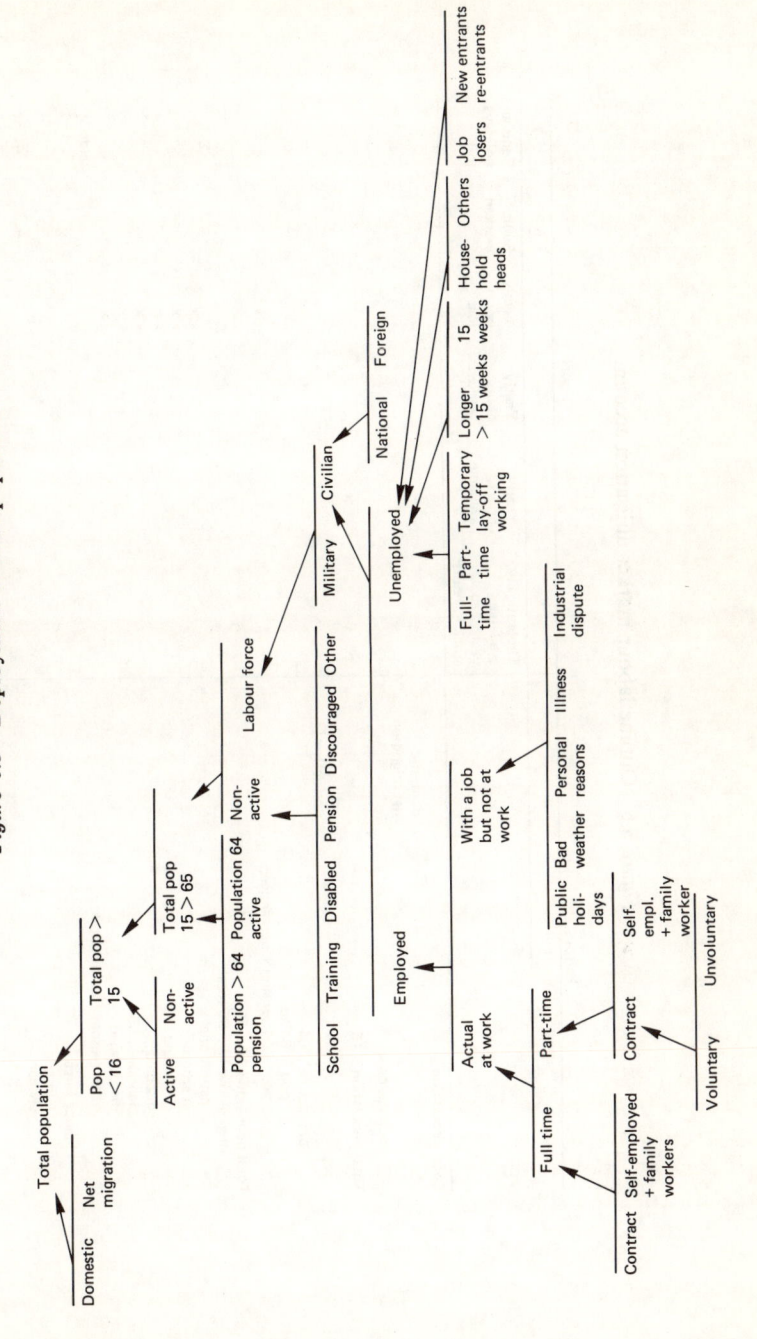

Figure 6.6 Outline labour market utilisation account

Persons	Hours					
1	2	3	4	5	6	7
	Theoretically available yearly labour stock in hours[a]	Yearly hours available[b]	Yearly hours worked[c]	Yearly hours lost[d]	Sums worked	Sums and holidays lost

Total population
   domestic
   net migration
  population < 16
Total population > 15   active   0
                      non-active

Rows (with column marks):

- population < 16
- Total population > 15 — col 2: 0
- population > 64 — col 3: ×
  - pop > 64 active — col 4: ×; col 6: Σ
  - pop > 64 pension + non-active — col 5: ×; col 7: Σ
- Total population 16 > 65 — col 2: 0
- non-active 15 > 65 total — col 3: ×; col 7: Σ
  - institutional — col 5: ×
  - at school — col 5: ×
  - in training — col 5: ×
  - disabled — col 5: ×
  - pension < 65 — col 5: ×
  - discouraged — col 5: ×
  - other reasons for non-activity — col 5: ×
- labour force — col 4: ×
  - military — col 6: Σ; col 7: saldo
  - civilian   foreign / national — col 6: Σ; col 7: Σ

```
                                                      Σ        Σ        Σ
                              Σ Σ      Σ Σ        × × × × ×       × × ×

                                           × × ×

                                  × ×          × × ×
```

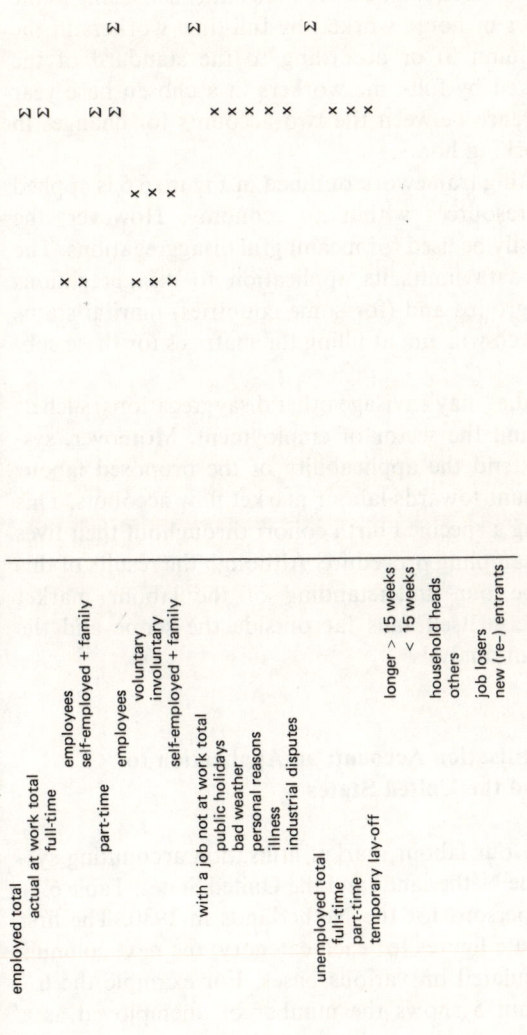

employed total
  actual at work total
    full-time
      employees
      self-employed + family
    part-time
      employees
        voluntary
        involuntary
      self-employed + family
  with a job not at work total
    public holidays
    bad weather
    personal reasons
    illness
    industrial disputes

unemployed total
  full-time
    longer > 15 weeks
    < 15 weeks
  part-time
  temporary lay-off
  household heads
  others
  job losers
  new (re-) entrants

Notes:

a = Product hours worked by full-time workers in base year and persons.
b = Product hours worked by full-time workers in observation year and persons.
c = Product hours worked by full-time workers in observation year and persons.
d = Product hours worked by corresponding population category in observation year and persons.

(a) **Deployment of labour force time.**
(b) **Deployment of labour force time as percentage of total time available.**

economy are the sum of the total yearly hours worked and the total yearly hours lost (respectively columns 4 and 5 in Figure 6.6; columns 6 and 7 indicate how the hours are summed over both categories). The yearly hours available for work can be calculated either according to the standard of the number of hours worked by full-time workers in the observation years (column 3) or according to the standard of the number of hours worked by full-time workers in a chosen base year (column 2). The difference between the two accounts for changes in contractual weekly working hours.

Basically the accounting framework outlined in Figure 6.6 is applied to aggregate labour resources within an economy. However, the framework can also easily be used for meaningful disaggregations. The actual availability of data limits its application to disaggregations according to sex, age groups and (for some countries) marital status groups. Ongoing research will aim at filling the matrices for these subgroups.

Future empirical studies may envisage other disaggregations, such as the educational level and the sector of employment. Moreover, systematic surveys can extend the applicability of the proposed labour market utilisation account towards labour market flow accounts. This can be done by studying a specified birth cohort throughout their lives by means of a rotated sampling procedure. Although the results of this analysis would enlarge our understanding of the labour market substantially, the exercise itself falls far outside the scope and the possibility of the present analysis.

(d) Labour Market Utilisation Account: an Application to the Netherlands and the United States

Tables 6.11–6.16 apply our labour market utilisation accounting system outlined above to the Netherlands and the United States. Table 6.11 shows the account in persons for the Netherlands in 1980. The first column gives the absolute figures for each category, the next columns shows percentages calculated on various bases. For example the 6.7 figure on line 34 column 5 shows the number of unemployed as a percentage of total labour force, i.e. the unemployment rate.

The figure (45) in line 20 column 3 is the number of employed as a percentage of total population 15 and older, hence it is the employment–population ratio. A similar table for the United States (Table 6.12) shows a 7.0 per cent unemployment rate at line 32 column 5; the employment–population ratio is displayed at line 32 column 5 (57.6 per cent).

Although Tables 6.11 and 6.12 provide only aggregate data for 1980, some interesting observations can be made:

1. The age structure of the population differs in the Netherlands from that in the United States. There are more young people and fewer old people in the United States than in the Netherlands.
2. There is a significant difference in the ratio of active to non-active population. In the Netherlands more than half (50 per cent) of the population aged 15 and over was inactive in 1980. In the United States the corresponding ratio was only 36.8 per cent in the same year.
3. A striking difference can be seen in the share of disabled persons in the population and in the non-active population. In the United States they accounted for 3 per cent of the total population and for 8.2 per cent of the non-active population. In the Netherlands these percentages were respectively 6.6 and 13 per cent.
4. More people older than 15 attend school in the Netherlands (9.9 per cent) than in the United States (4.5 per cent).
5. The employment–population ratio is significantly higher in the Unites States than in the Netherlands (57.6 per cent v. 45 per cent), but civilian employment accounts for approximately 91 per cent of total labour force in both countries.
6. The average number of persons with a job but not at work (yearly averages) amounted to 15.2 per cent of the labour force in the Netherlands. In the United States, this average was only 5.4 per cent, indicating that Dutch workers have more holidays, more paid leave and more sickness absence.
7. The number of part-time workers differs between the countries. These workers account for 17.5 per cent of total employment in the United States (including 4.3 per cent who are on part-time involuntarily) and for 15.2 per cent in the Netherlands.
8. In the United States, 13 per cent of the population aged 65 and over was economically active in 1980; in the Netherlands only 2.4 per cent.

As indicated above, labour market utilisation accounts should also be calculated with hours as the unit of measurement. The results for 1980 are shown in Tables 6.13 and 6.14 for the Netherlands and in Tables 6.15 and 6.16 for the United States. Tables 6.13 and 6.15 give the accounts in hours as outlined in Figure 6.6. The taxonomy of the data in these tables, however, does not permit the same easy computation or percentages and ratios as in Tables 6.11 and 6.12. The same data are therefore organised

Table 6.11 The Netherlands: labour market utilisation account in persons (1980)

	(× 1000)	Percentages					
1. Total population	14209	100					
2. National population	13689						
3. Foreign population	520						
4. Population <15	3134	22					
5. Population ≥15	11075						
6. Population >64	1642	12					
7. Population >64 active	39						
8. Population >64 non active	1603						
9. Population 15–64	9433	66					
10. Non-active population ≥15	5611		50.7		100		
11. At school	1094				19.5		
12. Disabled (WAO)	524				9.3		
13. Disabled (other)	205				3.7		
14. Other reasons	3788				67.5		
15. Active population ≥15	5464		49.3		100		
16. Military	106				1.9		
17. Civilian labour force	5358						
18. National	n.a.						
19. Foreign	n.a.						
20. Employed	4994		45.1		91.4	100	
21. Actual at work	4002					73.2	100
22. Full-time	3242						80.1
23. Employees	2689			29.3			49.2
24. Self-employed + family workers	553						10.1
25. Part time	760			6.9			13.9
26. Employees	721						13.2
27. Self employed + family workers	39						0.7
28. With a job but not at work	992					18.2	19.9
29. Public holidays	145						2.7
30. Bad weather	18						0.3
31. Paid leave	405						7.4
32. Illness	42						7.8
33. Industrial disputes	0						0.0
34. Unemployed	364		3.3		6.7		

Sources: See Appendix A6.4.

Table 6.11 (Contd.)

		(× 1000)	Percentages						
1.	Total population	14209							100
2.	National population	13689							96
3.	Foreign population	520							4
4.	Population < 15	3134							
5.	Population ≥ 15	11075							
6.	Population > 64	1642						100	
7.	Population > 64 active	39						15	
8.	Population > 64 non active	1603						85	
9.	Population 15–64	9433							
10.	Non-active population ≥ 15	5611							
11.	At school	1094							
12.	Disabled (WAO)	524							
13.	Disabled (other)	205							
14.	Other reasons	3788							
15.	Active population ≥ 15	5464							
16.	Military	106							
17.	Civilian labour force	5358							
18.	National	n.a.							100
19.	Foreign	n.a.							2.4
									97.6
20.	Employed	4994	100						
21.	Actual at work	4002	64.9						
22.	Full-time	3242		100					
23.	Employees	2689	53.8	81					
24.	Self-employed + family workers	553	11.1	19					
25.	Part time	760			100				
26.	Employees	721	14.4		67.2				
27.	Self employed + family workers	39	0.8		13.8				
28.	With a job but not at work	992				100			
29.	Public holidays	145	2.9			18			
30.	Bad weather	18	0.4			1			
31.	Paid leave	405	8.1				100		
32.	Illness	424	8.5				95		
33.	Industrial disputes	0	0.0				5		
								100	
								14.6	
								1.8	
								40.8	
								42.7	
								0.0	
34.	Unemployed	364							

Sources: See Appendix A6.4.

Table 6.12 United States: labour market utilisation account in persons (1980)

		(× 1000)	Percentages								
1.	Total population	223 239	100								
2.	domestic	222 779									
3.	net migration	460									
4.	Population < 16	54 293	24.3								
5.	Population > 15	168 946	75.7	100							
6.	population > 64	23 300	10.4								
7.	> 64 active	3 031									
8.	> 64 non-active	20 269									
9.	Population > 15 non-active	62 125		36.8	100						
10.	institutional	2 700				4.3					
11.	at school	7 621				12.3					
12.	housekeeping	29 880				48.1					
13.	disabled	5 115				8.2					
14.	retired	10 738				17.3					
15.	discouraged	970				1.6					
16.	other reasons for non-active	5 100				8.2					
17.	Population > 15 labour force	106 821		63.2	100						
18.	military	2 102			1.2							
19.	civilian	104 719										
20.	Employed	97 270		57.6			100				
21.	actual at work	91 486					91.1				
22.	full-time	74 430			54.2			85.6			
23.	part-time	17 056									
24.	voluntary	12 842				44.1					
25.	involuntary	4 214				10.1					
26.	with a job not at work	5 785			3.4				5.4		
27.	vacation	3 268				1.9					
28.	bad weather	153				0.1					
29.	illness	1 404				0.8					
30.	industrial disputes	104				0.1					
31.	all other	856				0.5					
32.	Unemployed	7 448			4.4			7.0			
33.	full-time	6 108				3.6			5.7		
34.	part-time	1 341				0.8			1.3		

With further breakdown columns showing: 100; 69.7, 16.0; 12.0, 3.9; 3.1, 0.1, 1.3, 0.1, 0.8.

Sources: See Appendix A6.5.

Table 6.12 (Contd.)

	(×1000)	Percentages					
1. Total population	223 239	100					
2. domestic	222 779	99.8					
3. net migration	460	0.2					
4. Population < 16	54 293						
5. Population > 15	168 946						
6. population > 64	23 300	100					
7. > 64 active	3 031	13.8					
8. > 64 non-active	20 269		100				
9. Population > 15 non-active	62 125		13				
10. institutional	2 700		87				
11. at school	7 621						
12. housekeeping	29 880						
13. disabled	5 115						
14. retired	10 738						
15. discouraged	970						
16. other reasons for non-active	5 100						
17. Population > 15 labour force	106 821						100
18. military	2 102						2
19. civilian	104 719						98
20. Employed	97 270	100					
21. actual at work	91 486	94.1	100				
22. full-time	74 430		76.5	100			
23. part-time	17 056		17.5	81.4			
24. voluntary	12 842		13.2	18.6			
25. involuntary	4 214		4.3				
26. with a job not at work	5 785	5.9		100			
27. vacation	3 268		3.4	75.3			
28. bad weather	153		0.2	24.7			
29. illness	1 404		1.4		100		
30. industrial disputes	104		0.1		56.5		
31. all other	856		0.9		2.6		
32. Unemployed	7 448				24.3	100	
33. full-time	6 108				1.8	82	
34. part-time	1 341				14.8	18	

Sources: See Appendix A6.5.

Table 6.13 The Netherlands: labour market utilisation account in hours (1980a)

	Theoretically available yearly labour stock in hours[a]	Yearly hours available[b]	Yearly hours worked[c]	Yearly hours lost[d]	Sums and saldi hours worked	Sums and saldi hours lost
1. Total population						
2. domestic						
3. net migration						
4. population < 15						
5. Total population > 15	2547	1938			655	1283
6. population > 64		287			6	281
7. pop. > 64 active			6			
8. pop. > 64 pension + non-active				281		
9. Total population 15 > 65						982
10. non-active 15						
11. at school				191		
12. disabled (WAO)				92		
13. disabled (other)				36		
14. other reasons for non-activity				663		
15. labour force					655	301
16. military			19		19	
17. civilian						
18. foreign						
19. national						
20. employed total						
21. actual at work total					636	

22.	full-time				568
23.		employees		441	
24.		self employed + family		127	
25.	part-time				68	64
26.		employees		64	62
27.		self employed + family		4	2
28.	with a job not at work total				173
29.	public holidays				25
30.	bad weather				3
31.	paid leave				71
32.	illness				74
33.	industrial dispute				
34.	unemployed total			64	64

Notes:

[a] Product hours worked by full-time workers in base year and persons.
[b] Product hours worked by full-time workers in observation year and persons.
[c] Product hours worked by corresponding population category in observation year and persons.
[d] Product hours worked by full-time workers in observation year and persons.

Sources: See Appendix A6.4.

Table 6.14 The Netherlands: labour market utilisation account in hours (1980b)

		(× 10⁶)	Percentages
1. Population ≥ 15:	Theoretically available yearly labour stock in hrs	2547	100
2.	Yearly hours available	1938	76
3.	Yearly hours worked	655	26
			49
4.	Yearly hours lost	1283	100 33.8
			66.2
5. Population ≥ 64:	Yearly hours available	287	
6.	Yearly hours worked	6	
7.	Yearly hours lost	281	100
8. Non-act. pop. ≥ 15: Yearly hours lost		982	100 50.7
9. Yearly hours lost by: those at school		191	9.9 14.9 19.5
10.	disabled (WAO)	92	4.7 7.2 9.4
11.	disabled (other)	36	1.9 2.8 3.7
12.	with other reasons for non-activity	663	34.2 51.7 67.5
13. Active pop. ≥ 15: Yearly hours available		956	
14. Yearly hours worked		655	
15. Yearly hours worked by: military		19	1
16.	civilian labour force	636	32.8
17.	full-timers	568	29.3
18.	employed f.t.	441	22.8
19.	self-employed f.t.	127	6.6
20.	part-timers	68	3.5
21.	employed p.t.	64	3.3
22.	self-employed p.t.	4	0.2
23. Active pop. ≥ 15: Yearly hours lost		301	15.5 23.5
24. Yearly hours lost by: part-timers		64	3.3 5.0
25.	employed p.t. (actual at work)	62	3.2
26.	self-employed p.t.	2	0.1
27.	those with a job but not at work	173	8.9 13.5
28.	public holidays	25	1.3 4.8
29.	bad weather	3	0.2 0.2
30.	paid leave	71	3.7
31.	illness	74	3.8
32.	industrial disputes	0	0.0
33.	the unemployed	64	3.3 5.0

			1.9
			0.2
			5.5
			5.8
			0.0

Sources: See Appendix A64.

Table 6.14 (Contd.)

		(× 10⁶)	Percentages
1.	Population ⩾ 15: Theoretically available yearly labour stock in hrs	2547	
2.	Yearly hours available	1938	
3.	Yearly hours worked	655	
4.	Yearly hours lost	1283	
5.	Population ⩾ 64: Yearly hours available	287	
6.	Yearly hours worked	6	
7.	Yearly hours lost	281	
8.	Non-act. pop. ⩾ 15: Yearly hours lost	982	
9.	Yearly hours lost by: those at school	191	
10.	disabled (WAO)	92	
11.	disabled (other)	36	
12.	with other reasons for non-activity	663	
13.	Active pop. ⩾ 15: Yearly hours available	956 100 100	
14.	Yearly hours worked	655 68.5	
15.	Yearly hours worked by: military	19 2.0	
16.	civilian labour		
	force	636 66.5 100 100	
17.	full-timers	568 59.4 2.9	
18.	employed f.t.	441 46.1 97.1 100	
19.	self-employed f.t.	127 13.3 86.7	
20.	part-timers	68 7.1 10.4 100	
21.	employed p.t.	64 6.7 67.3	
22.	self-employed p.t.	4 0.4 19.4	
			9.8
			0.6
23.	Active pop. ⩾ 15: Yearly hours lost	301 31.5 100	
24.	Yearly hours lost by: part-timers	64 6.7 21.3 100	
	(actual at work)		
25.	employed p.t.	62 6.5 20.6	
26.	self-employed p.t.	2 0.2 0.7	
27.	those with a job but		
	not at work	173 18.1 57.5 100	
28.	public holidays	25 2.6 8.3 14.5	
29.	bad weather	3 0.3 1.0 1.7	
30.	paid leave	71 7.4 23.6 41.0	
31.	illness	74 7.7 24.6 42.8	
32.	industrial disputes	0 0.0 0.0 0.0	
33.	the unemployed	64 6.7 21.3 100 96.9	
			3.1

Sources: See Appendix A6.4.

188

Table 6.15 United States: labour market utilisation account in hours (1980a)

	Hours × 10⁹					
	Theoretically available yearly labour stock in hours[a]	Yearly hours available[b]	Yearly hours worked[c]	Yearly hours lost[d]	Sums and saldi hours worked	Sums and saldi hours lost
1. Total population						
2. domestic						
3. net migration						
4. population < 16						
5. Total population > 15	403.8	388.4			188.0	200.4
6. population > 64						
7. population > 64 active						
8. population > 64 non-active						
9. non-active > 15 total						142.8
10. institutional				6.2		
11. at school				17.5		
12. housekeeping				68.7		
13. disabled				11.8		
14. retired				24.7		
15. discouraged				2.2		
16. other reasons for non-activity				11.7		
17. labour force						
18. military			4.8		4.8	
19. civilian						
20. employed total					183.2	27.1
21. actual at work total						

22.	full-time		165.8	5.3
23.	part-time		17.4	21.8
24.		voluntary	12.6	
25.		involuntary	4.8	
26.	with a job not at work total			13.3
27.	vacation			7.5
28.	bad weather			0.4
29.	illness			3.2
30.	industrial disputes			0.2
31.	all others			2.0
32.	unemployed total			17.1
33.	full-time			14.0
34.	part-time			3.1

Notes:

[a] = Product hours worked by full-time workers in base year (1960) and persons.

[b] = Product hours worked by full-time workers in observation year and persons.

[c] = Product hours worked by corresponding population category in observation year and persons.

[d] = Product hours worked by full-time workers in observation year and persons.

Sources: See Appendix A6.5.

Table 6.16 United States: labour market utilisation account in hours (1980b)

		($\times 10^9$)							Percentages						
1.	Population > 15 theoretically available	403.8	100												
2.	yearly hours available	388.4	96.2	100											
3.	yearly hours worked	188.0	46.6	48.4											
4.	yearly hours lost	200.4	49.6	51.6											
5.	Population >15 non-active	142.8			100	100	100	100	100						100
6.	institutional	6.2							1.6	4.5					4.3
7.	at school	17.5							4.5						12.3
8.	housekeeping	68.7							17.7						48.1
9.	disabled	11.8							3.0						8.3
10.	retired	24.7							6.4						17.3
11.	discouraged	2.2							0.6						1.5
12.	other reasons for non-active	11.7							3.0						8.2
13.	Population >15 active labour yearly available	245.6						36.8							
14.	total worked	188.0					100								
15.	military worked	4.8				1.2									
16.	civilian worked	183.2				47.2									
17.	full-time	165.8				42.7									
18.	part-time	17.4				4.5									
19.	voluntary	12.6			3.2										
20.	involuntary	4.8			1.2										
21.	Population > 15 labour force total lost	57.5						14.8			28.7				
22.	at work full-time	5.3						1.4			2.6				
23.	part-time	21.8						5.6			10.9				
24.	with a job not at work	13.3						3.4			6.6				
25.	vacation	7.5							1.9						3.7
26.	bad weather	0.4							0.1						0.2
27.	illness	3.2							0.8						1.6
28.	industrial disputes	0.2							0.1						0.1
29.	all other	2.0							0.5						1.0
30.	unemployed	17.1						4.4			8.5				
31.	full-time	14.0							3.6						7.0
32.	part time	3.1							0.8						1.5

Sources: See Appendix A6.5.

Table 6.16 (Contd.)

		($\times 10^9$)	Percentages						
1.	Population > 15 theoretically available	403.8							
2.	yearly hours available	388.4							
3.	yearly hours worked	188.0							
4.	yearly hours lost	200.4							
5.	Population > 15 non-active lost	142.8							
6.	institutional	6.2							
7.	at school	17.5							
8.	housekeeping	68.7							
9.	disabled	11.8							
10.	retired	24.7							
11.	discouraged	2.2							
12.	other reasons for non-active	11.7							
13.	Population > 15 active labour yearly available	245.6	100						
14.	total worked	188.0	76.5	100					
15.	military worked	4.8		2.6					
16.	civilian worked	183.2	74.6	97.4	100				
17.	full-time	165.8	67.5		88.2				
18.	part-time	17.4	7.1		9.3	100			
19.	voluntary	12.6				72.4			
20.	involuntary	4.8				27.6			
21.	Population > 15 labour force total lost	57.5	23.4	100					
22.	at work full-time	5.3	2.2	9.2					
23.	part-time	21.8	8.9	37.9					
24.	with a job not at work	13.3	5.4	23.1	100				
25.	vacation	7.5	3.1	13.0	56.4				
26.	bad weather	0.4	0.2	0.7	3.0				
27.	illness	3.2	1.3	5.6	24.1				
28.	industrial disputes	0.2	0.1	0.3	1.5				
29.	all other	2.0	0.8	3.5	15.0				
30.	unemployed	17.1	7.0	29.7		100			
31.	full-time	14.0	5.7	24.3		81.9			
32.	part time	3.1	1.3	5.4		18.1			

Sources: See Appendix A6.5.

in a different way in Table 6.14 for the Netherlands and Table 6.15 for the United States (figures for 1980). Again, a comparison between the countries can be made. Roughly, the same observations hold as for the account in terms of persons. Column 6 in both tables is of special importance when describing time worked and time lost by the economically active population (labour force). In the Netherlands 31.5 per cent of labour force time was lost or unused in 1980. Of the labour force time lost or unused 57.5 per cent (column 8 in Table 6.14) was lost by to persons with a job but not at work in the Netherlands while in the United States this category accounted for only 23.1 per cent of labour force time lost or unused (column 9, Table 6.16). The unused time of part-time workers was responsible for 21.3 of total labour force time lost or unused in the Netherlands; in the United States this amounted to 37.9 per cent. The labour force time lost due to unemployment was larger in the United States than in the Netherlands (29.7 per cent in the United States v. 21.3 per cent in the Netherlands).

Tables 6.14 and 6.16 provide insight in addition to the accounts in persons (Tables 6.11 and 6.12). In the second column, the effect of a downward trend in the normal working time for full-time workers is made visible. The 'theoretically available yearly labour stock in hours' is calculated as the product of the total population aged 15 and over and the normal working time for full-time workers in a base year (here 1960 in both tables). It can be seen that the yearly hours available (computed as the product of the population aged 15 and over and the normal working time for full-time workers in 1980) amount to only 76 per cent of the theoretically available labour stock in the Netherlands and to 96.2 per cent in the United States. This indicates that there has been a significant decline in the contractual working time for full-time workers in the Netherlands. It can be seen – comparing Tables 6.11 and 6.14 and Tables 6.12 and 6.16 – that the share of part-time employment is less measured in hours (10.4 per cent in the Netherlands and 9.3 per cent in the United States) than measured in persons (15.2 per cent and 18.6 per cent respectively).

Evidently more differences and similarities between the countries and the accounts expressed in persons and in hours could be stressed. Our purpose is, however, to illustrate only that labour market utilisation accounts are useful instruments to study international differences on the labour market. Moreover, measurements in hours are shown to be complementary to measurements in persons, especially when manipulation of the working time becomes an important policy practise.

Labour market utilisation accounts are also useful tools in the

Chris de Neubourg 193

Figure 6.7 The Netherlands: in deployment of labour force time (1960—80)

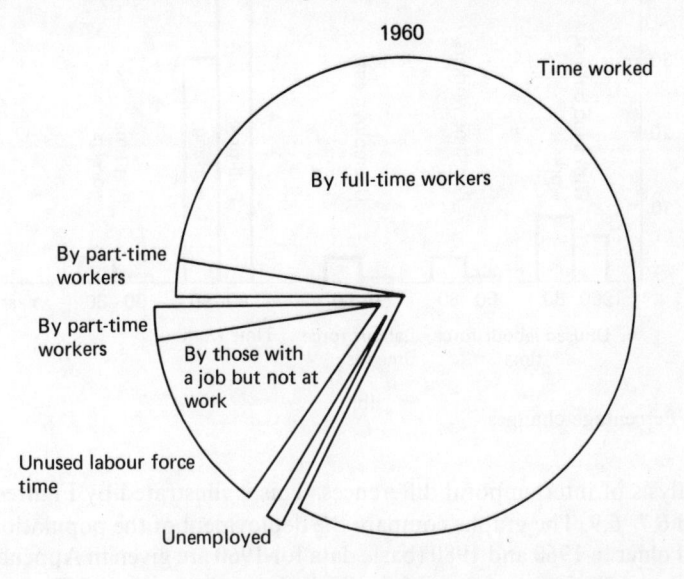

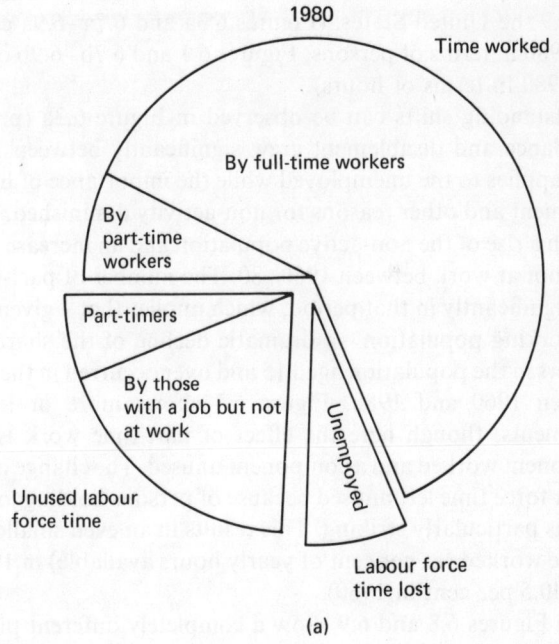

1960

- Time worked
- By full-time workers
- By part-time workers
- By part-time workers
- By those with a job but not at work
- Unused labour force time
- Unemployed

1980

- Time worked
- By full-time workers
- By part-time workers
- Part-timers
- By those with a job but not at work
- Unused labour force time
- Unemployed
- Labour force time lost

(a)

(a) Major shifts.

194   The Dough, the Doughnut and the Hole

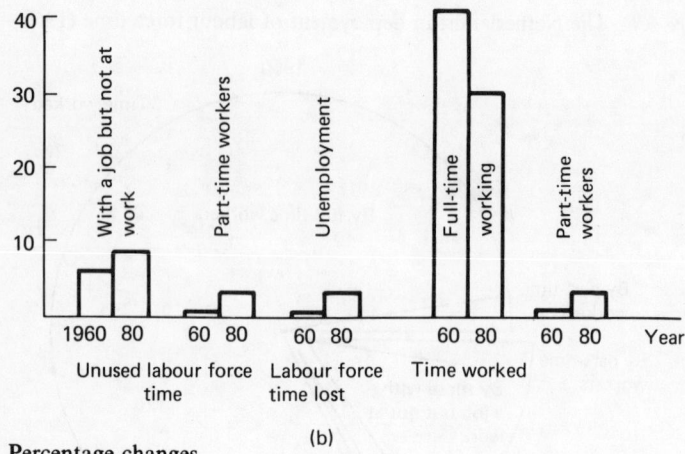

[Bar chart showing percentage changes between 1960 and 1980 across five categories: "With a job but not at work" and "Part-time workers" (Unused labour force time); "Unemployment" (Labour force time lost); "Full-time working" and "Part-time workers" (Time worked).]

(b) Percentage changes.

analysis of intertemporal differences. This is illustrated by Figures 6.3 and 6.7–6.9. The graphs compare the deployment of the population 15 and older in 1960 and 1980 (basic data for 1960 are given in Appendices A4 and A5). Figures 6.3 and 6.7 refer to the Netherlands and Figures 6.8 and 6.9 the United States. (Figures 6.3a and 6.7a–6.9a compare 1960 and 1980 in terms of persons; Figures 6.1 and 6.7b–6.9b compare 1960 and 1980 in terms of hours).

Outstanding shifts can be observed in Figure 6.3a (p. 000); school attendance and disablement grew significantly between 1960–80; the same applies to the unemployed while the importance of housekeeping, retirement and other reasons for non-activity diminished. This resulted in both a rise of the non-active population and an increase of the labour force not at work between 1960–80. The number of part-time workers rose significantly in that period, which implies that – given the decreasing working population – a dramatic decline of the share of full-time workers in the population aged 15 and over occurred in the Netherlands between 1960 and 1980. Figure 6.7 shows more or less the same movements, though here the effect of part-time work is split into a component worked and a component unused. The change in the share of labour force time left unused because of persons holding jobs but not at work is particularly striking. This results in an even smaller percentage of time worked (as per cent of yearly hours available) in 1980 (33.8 per cent; 40.5 per cent in 1960).

The Figures 6.8 and 6.9 show a completely different picture for the United States. In that country, the working population as a percentage

Chris de Neubourg 195

Figure 6.8 United States: deployment of persons 15 and older

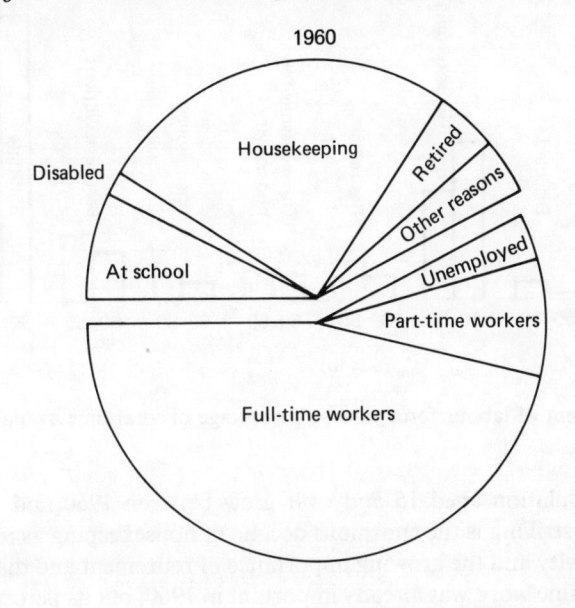

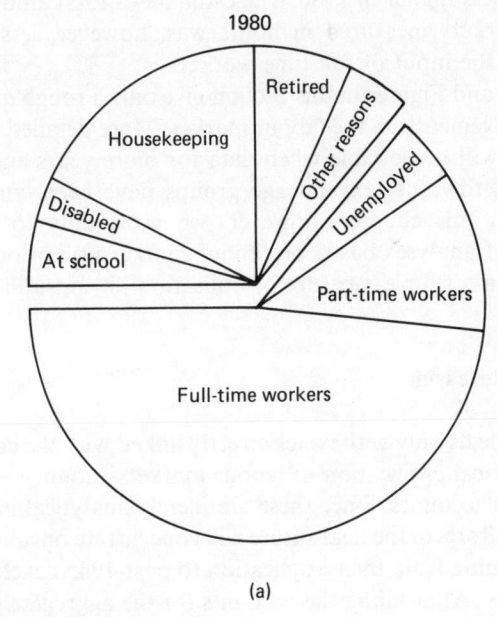

1960

1980

(a)

(a) Deployment of labour force time.

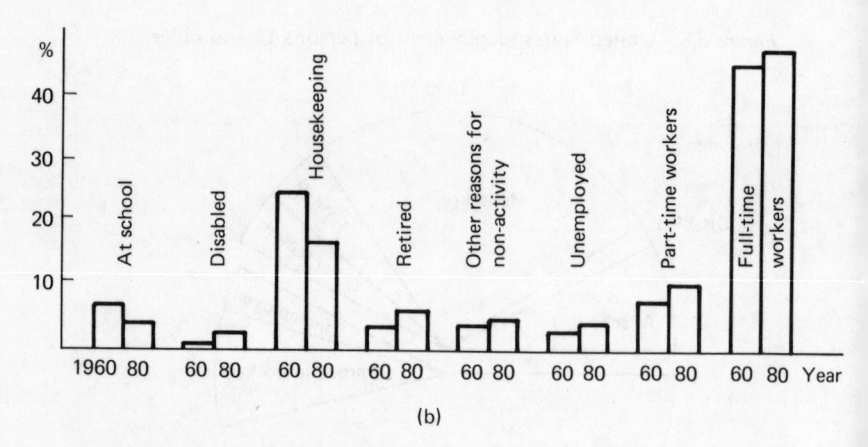

(b) Deployment of labour force time as percentage of total time available.

of total population aged 15 and over grew between 1960 and 1980. Particularly striking is the enormous decline of housekeeping as reason for non-activity and the growing importance of retirement and disablement. Part-time work was already important in 1960, but its percentage was nevertheless higher in 1980. The estimate of total labour input by part-time workers measured in hours was, however, less important compared to the input of full-time workers.

The Tables and Figures in this Section give only a rough indication of the actual movements on the labour market. More detailed description and analysis will be possible when data for more years and countries disaggregated towards sex and age groups have been compiled and computed. In this chapter, however, we want only to sketch the possibilities of analyses based on labour market utilisation accounts, rather than on a simple measure of utilisation or non-utilisation.

(e) **Further Research**

This chapter deals only with issues directly linked with the construction and the empirical application of labour market accounts – specifically the utilisation accounts. Since these are merely analytical instruments, our research efforts in the near future will concentrate on analysis of the insights stemming from their application to post-1945 developments in eight countries. After filling the accounts for the aggregate population and labour force and for several interesting disaggregations such as sex,

Figure 6.9 United States: deployment of labour force time (1960–80)

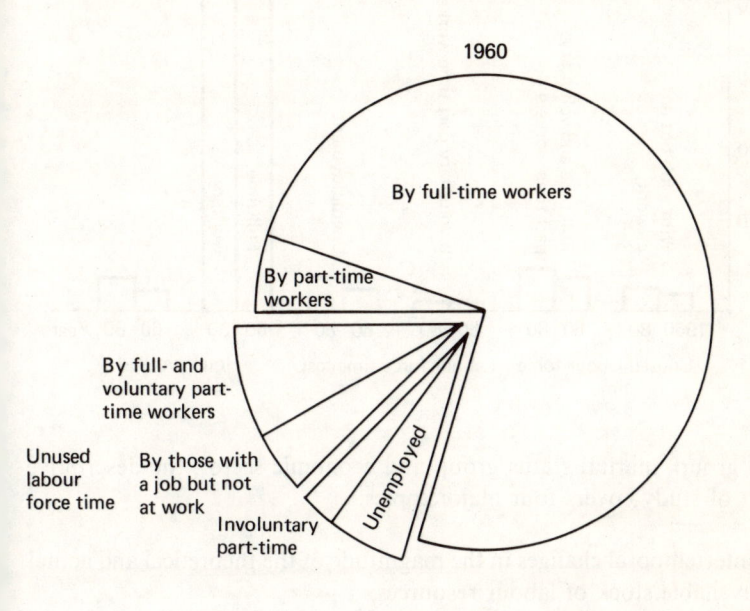

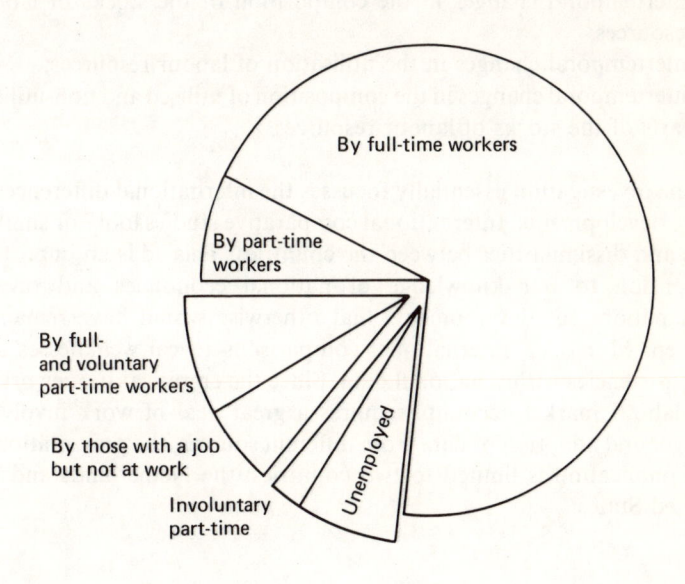

(a)

Figure 6.9(b)

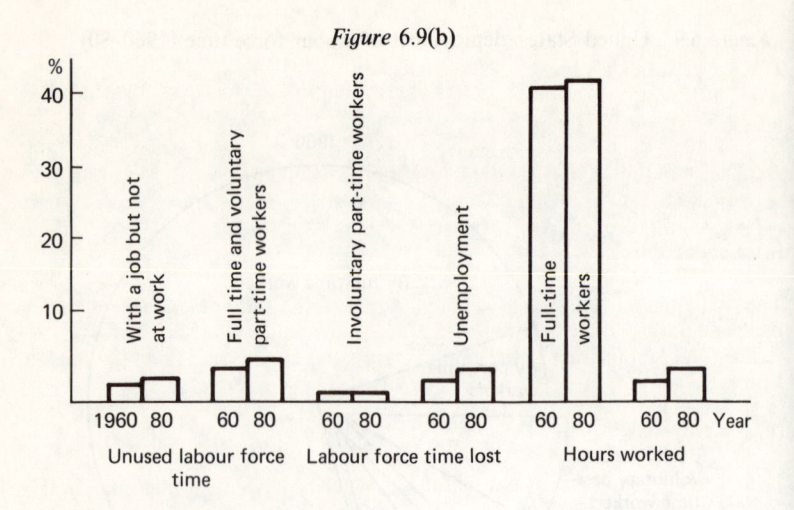

[Bar chart showing percentages for years 1960 and 80 across categories: "With a job but not at work", "Full time and voluntary part-time workers" (under Unused labour force time); "Involuntary part-time workers", "Unemployment" (under Labour force time lost); "Full-time workers", and a final pair (under Hours worked).]

age group, marital status group and economic sector, the descriptive part of study covers four major topics:

1. intertemporal changes in the magnitude of the theoretical and actual available stock of labour resources;
2. intertemporal changes in the composition of the stocks of labour resources;
3. intertemporal changes in the utilisation of labour resources;
4. intertemporal changes in the composition of utilised and non-utilised parts of the stocks of labour resources.

The investigation essentially focusses the international differences in these developments. International comparative studies look for similarities and dissimilarities between the countries. This adds an important dimension to our knowledge of national economies and reveals explanations for developments that otherwise would have remained hidden. Moreover, international comparisons reveal weaknesses and inconsistencies within national data. Since the empirical framework of the labour market accounts requires a great deal of work involving merger and adaption of data from different sources, the presentation in this publication is limited to two countries: the Netherlands and the United States.

Appendices

A 6.1 LABOUR FORCE, EMPLOYMENT AND UNEMPLOYMENT: THE ILO DEFINITIONS (Partial text)[28]

(a) Labour Force

The civilian labour force consists of all civilians who fulfil the requirements for inclusion among the employed or the unemployed, as defined below.

The total labour force is the sum of the civilian labour force and the Armed Forces.

(b) Employment

1. Persons in employment consist of all persons above a specified age in the following categories:

    (a) At work: persons who performed some work for pay or profit during a specified brief period, either one week or one day.
    (b) With a job but not at work: persons who, having already worked in their present job, were temporarily absent during the specified period because of illness or injury, industrial dispute, vacation or other leave of absence, absence without leave, or temporary disorganization of work due to such reasons as bad weather or mechanical breakdown.

2. Employers and workers on own account should be included among the employed and may be classified as 'at work' or 'not at work' on the same basis as other employed persons.
3. Unpaid family workers currently assisting in the operation of a business or farm are considered as employed if they worked for at least one-third of the normal working time during the specified period.

(c) Unemployment

1. Persons in unemployment consist of all persons above a specified age who, on the specified day or for a specified week, were in the following categories:

    (a) Workers available for employment whose contract or employment had been terminated or temporarily suspended and who were without a job and seeking work for pay or profit.
    (b) Persons who were available for work (except for minor illness) during the specified period and were seeking work for pay or profit, who were never previously employed or whose most recent status was other than that of employee (i.e., former employers, etc.), or who had been in retirement.
    (c) Persons without a job and currently available for work who had made arrangements to start a new job at a date subsequent to the specified period.
    (d) Persons on temporary or indefinite lay-off without pay.

A6.2 CALCULATION OF 'AGGREGATE HOURS LOST BY THE UNEMPLOYED' AND 'AGGREGATE HOURS LOST BY PERSONS ON PART-TIME FOR ECONOMIC REASONS' (Appendix to Table 6.3)

	Average weekly hours of voluntary part-time workers^a (1)	Number of unemployed looking for part-time work (× 1000) (2)	Hours lost by the unemployed looking for part-time work (column (1) × (column (2)) (3)	Number of unemployed looking for full-time work (× 1000) (4)	Aggregate hours lost by the unemployed (column (4) × 37.5) + column (3)) (5)	Persons on part-time for economic reasons (6)	Average weekly hours of persons on part-time for economic reasons (7)	Aggregate hours lost by persons on part-time for economic reasons (column (5) × 37.5 column (7)) (8)
1956	16.9					2248	21.3	36 418
57	17.0					2469	21.5	39 504
58	16.5					3280	22.0	50 840
59	16.3					2640	20.7	44 352
60						2860		
61						3142		
62						2661		
63		568		3305		2620		
64		596		3178		2455		
65		575		2791		2209		
66		560		2315		1894		
67	17.8	683	12 157	2293	98 145	2163	21.4	34 824

68	17.9	679	12 154	2138	92 329	1970	20.8	32 899
69	18.0	689	12 402	2142	92 727	2056	20.9	34 130
70	17.8	887	15 789	3201	135 826	2443	21.4	39 332
71	18.0	1044	18 792	3949	166 880	2675	21.1	43 870
72	18.2	1071	19 492	3769	160 830	2624	20.9	43 558
73	18.3	1013	18 538	3291	141 950	2519	21.0	41 564
74	18.3	1134	20 752	3941	168 540	2943	21.2	47 971
75	18.4	1393	25 631	6437	267 019	3748	21.4	60 343
76	18.4	1414	26 018	5874	246 293	3540	21.2	57 702
77	18.5	1423	26 326	5432	230 026	3530	22.3	53 656
78	18.6	1341	24 943	4706	201 418	3428	21.4	55 191
79	18.8	1325	24 910	4639	198 873	3478	21.5	55 648
80	18.8	1341	25 211	6108	254 261	4214	22.0	65 317
81	18.8	1449	27 241	6631	275 904	4658	21.7	73 596

[a]Voluntary part-time workers defined as persons who usually work part-time for other than economic reasons.
Sources: See Appendix A6.3.

A 6.3 SOURCES FOR TABLE 6.7

United States : *Current Population Reports* (various issues). Used are estimates of total population including armed forces overseas, Alaska, Hawaii and the District of Columbia; mid-year estimates of 15 year olds.

Japan : *Japan Statistical Yearbook* (post-war volumes). Estimates of 15 year olds as of 1 October.

France : *Annuaire Statistique de la France* (1950–81 issues). Estimates of 15 year olds as at 1 January.

Germany : *Statistiches Jahrbuch* (post-war volumes). Estimates of 14 year olds as at 31 December of the previous year. Until 1963, figures exclude (West) Berlin.

United Kingdom : *Statistical Abstracts* (1950–81). Mid-year estimates of those aged 15 years.

Sweden : *Statistical Abstract of Sweden* (1950–81) Estimates of 15 year olds as at either 31 December of previous year or 1 January.

Netherlands : *Maandstatistiek voor Bevolking en Gezondheid* (1953–82); *Bijzondere Statische Opgaven* (1950–2) 1009, 1013, 1015.
Estimates of 14 year olds as at 31 December of the previous year.

For the definition of working age the solutions of Moy and Sorrentino (1982, p. 5) are adopted. If 1 January or 31 December figures were available, the cohort on the verge of belonging to the working age group is selected: in the case of mid-year estimates the group which was about to enter this category. In the case of Japan, with a datum date at 1 October, the cohort which effectively had entered the working age group is chosen.

Columns (2), (4) 1963–79 : *Handbook of Labor Statistics* (1980), p. 19.

Columns (6) 1957–79: *Handbook of Labor Statistics* (1980), p. 56.

Columns (1), (2), (4), (5), (7) 1980–1 : *Employment and Earnings* (1959–82) (January issues); *Annual Report on the Labor Force* (1950–8 issues).

A 6.4 : BASIC SOURCE DATA FOR THE NETHERLANDS : LABOUR MARKET ACCOUNT

(a) Sources for Table 6.11 and Table A6.4 (in persons)

All figures are for 31 December, unless otherwise specified.
1. Sources: *Bevolking van Nederland 1830–1969*; *Statistical Yearbook for the Netherlands 1971, 1981*; *Maandstatistiek Bevolking en Volksgezondheid 1972*.
2. Row 1 minus row 3.
3. Sources: for 1960, Census 31 May 1960; for 1970, census at 28 February 1971; for 1972–80, Department of Justice.
4. See row 1.
5. Row 1 minus row 4.
6. See row 1.
7. Figures for 1970–80 provided by CBS. The figure for 1960 from 'Arbeidsvolume en geregistreerde arbeidsreserve 1950–1966' is for 31 May 1960, and is expressed in man years.
8. Row 6 minus row 7.
9. Row 5 minus row 6.
10. Row 5 minus row 15.
11. Figures at 1 December. Sources: *De Nederlandse jeugd en haar onderwijs; Statistiek van het wetenschappelijk onderwijs;* Moll, *Verborgen werkloosheid in Nederland*.

    In connection with the subscription boycott on the universities, there are no reliable numbers of students for the years 1972–3 and 1973–4. By means of interpolation the numbers of students in 1972–3 has been estimated be at 112 925 and in 1973–4 at 112 978 (excluding 'extraneï'). The figures for 1979 and 1980 have been reduced with 4000 part-time students but include 'extraneï' : All figures relate to full-time students.
12. Sources: Annual reports of the *Gemeenschappelijke Medische Dienst*.
13. Moll, *Verborgen werkloosheid in Nederland*.

    The figures consist of:

    1. Beneficiaries of the IW (Invaliditeitswet), the OW (Ongevallenwet, including persons 65 and older) and the IWI (Interimwet Invaliditeistsrentetrekkers). All abolished in 1966.
    2. Beneficiaries of a disability pension of the ABP (Government pension fund). From 1965 onwards
    3. Beneficiaries of a disability pension of the railway pension fund. From 1968 onwards.
    4. Beneficiaries of a disability pension of the unlitary pension fund. From 1968 onwrds.

    The figures on the disability pensions of the railway pension fund from 1976 and the government pension fund for 1980 are provided by the respective funds. The figure for the unlitary pension fund from 1976 onwards is held constant at the level of 1976.

Table A6.4 The Netherlands: labour market utilisation account in persons and in hours (1960)

		Persons × 1000	Theoretically available yearly labour stock in hours[a]	Yearly hours available[b]	Yearly hours worked[c]	Yearly hours lost[d]	Sums hours worked	Sums and saldi hours lost
1.	Total population	11556						
2.	domestic	11438						
3.	net migration	118						
4.	population < 15	3464						
5.	Total population > 15	8092	1861	1861			791	1070
6.	population > 64	1049	241				24	217
7.	population > 64 active	106			24			
8.	population > 64 pension + non-active	943				217		
9.	Total population 15 > 65	7043						
10.	non-active	3973						914
11.	at school	364				84		
12.	disabled (WAO)	—						
13.	disabled (other)	160				37		
14.	other reasons for non-activity	3449				793		
15.	labour force (active > 15)	4119			29		791	156
16.	military	124					29	
17.	civilian	3995						
18.	foreign	n.a.						
19.	national	n.a.						
20.	employed total	3946						
21.	actual at work total	3414					762	
22.	full-time	3220			461		760	
23.	employees	2121						
24.	self employed + family	1099			279			
25.	part-time	194					22	
26.	employees	121			13	15		23

27.	self employed + family	73	9	8	
28.	with a job not at work total	532			122
29.	public holidays	99		23	
30.	bad weather	21		5	
31.	paid leave	209		48	
32.	illness	201		46	
33.	industrial disputes	2		0	
34.	unemployed total	49		11	11

Notes:

[a] Product hours worked by full-time workers in base year and persons.
[b] Product hours worked by full-time workers in observation year and persons.
[c] Product hours worked by corresponding population category in observation year and persons.
[d] Product hours worked by full-time workers in observation year and persons.

14. Row 10 minus row 11 up to row 13.
15. Figures provided by the CBS and Maddison (1980).
16. Sources for 1960, census at 31 May 1960. For 1961–3 : Labour force statistics OECD (1958–9), reduced with those employed at the Ministry of Defence (*Statistical Yearbook for the Netherlands 1965–1966*). From 1964 onwards: Labour force statistics OECD (1968–79). The figure for 1980 is held constant at the level of 1979. All figures are in man years. The figures have been compared with ACDA figures in persons, sustaining the reliability of the former.
17. Row 15 minus row 16.
19. Number of valid labour permissions for foreign labourers, being employed in the Netherlands no longer than five years. Figures at 15 June. Source: *Sociale maandstatistiek* (1980).
20. Row 15 minus row 34.
21. Row 20 minus row 28.
22. Up to and including 27: Figures provided by the EIM (Nederlands Ekonomisch Instituut voor Midden- en Kleinbedrijf), adjusted for agriculture and government sector.
28. Sum of row 29 up to and including 33.
29. Up to and including 32: calculated from figures provided by the EIM in days and hours.
33. Industrial disputes in man days/260. Source: *Sociale Maandstatistiek* (1980).
34. Calculated from percentage given in Maddison (1982).

The figure for 1980 has been estimated at 6.7 per cent.

(b) Sources for Tables 6.12 and 6.13 and for Table A6.4 (hours)

Data calculated from Table 6.11 and Table A6.5 and estimates of hours worked and lost provided by the EIM, adjusted for inclusion of agriculture and fishery and the government sector.

A 6.5 BASIC SOURCES AND DATA FOR THE UNITED STATES: LABOUR MARKET ACCOUNT

(a) Table A 6.5

Sources: (a) *Persons*
Population estimates are derived from *Current Population Reports* 314 (1965).
Labour force figures are derived from *Employment* and *Earnings* (June 1962), and *Handbook of Labor* Statistics (1980).
The sub-categories of the non-active population and the unemployed are calculated with the use of the 1963 rates.

(b) *Hours*
Average hours found in *Employment and Earnings* (June 1962); part-time hours derived from estimates of non-agricultural hours of 1959 and 1961; to be found respectively in *Employment and Earnings* (May 1960 and January 1964).
All labour force figures refer to the population aged 14 and over.

(b) Table 6.14

Sources: Population estimates are derived from *Current Population Reports* 870 (1980); for the population older than 64 and younger than 16 years of age, the 1979 estimates are used. The labour force statistics are taken from *Employment and Earnings* (January 1981). Net migration (line 3) equals the 1979 figure from *Statistical Abstracts of the US* (1981).

(c) Table 6.15

Sources: Persons are the same as in Table 6.14. Average weekly hours are from *Employment and Earnings* (January 1981).

Notes to all Tables
(a) *Full-time workers* refer to workers on full-time schedules (e.g., they include the strictly full-time workers *and* the part-time workers, working part-time for other than economic reasons, usually working full-time). However, the theoretically available yearly labour stock, the yearly available hours and the yearly hours lost are based on the hours of those strictly working full-time (e.g., excluding any part-time worker).
(b) *Voluntary part-time* workers are taken to be those part-time workers working part-time for other than economic reasons, usually working part-time; *involuntary part-time* workers are those working part-time for economic reasons.
(c) *Military* are assumed to work the same hours as the strict full time workers.

Table A6.5 United States: labour market utilisation account in persons and in hours (1960)

		Persons ×1000	Theoretically available yearly labour[a] stock in hours	Yearly hours available[b]	Yearly hours worked[c]	Yearly hours lost[d]	Sums hours worked	Sums and saldi hours lost
1.	Total population	180 684						
2.	domestic	180 357						
3.	net migration	327						
4.	population < 14	53 349						
5.	Total population > 13	127 335	304.3	304.3			139.6	164.7
6.	population > 64	16 658						
7.	population > 64 active	3194						
8.	population > 64 non-active	13 464						
9.	non-active > 13 total	54 208						129.6
10.	Institutional	2057				4.9		
11.	at school	9334				22.4		
12.	housekeeping	32 647				78.0		
13.	disabled	1682				4.0		
14.	retired	5163				12.4		
15.	discouraged	560				1.3		
16.	other reasons for non-activity	2765				6.6		
17.	labour force	73 127						
18.	military	2154			6.0		6.0	
19.	civilian	70 613						
20.	employed total	66 682						18.0
21.	actual at work total	63 450			124.7	38	133.6	
22.	full-time	53 745			9.0	14.2		
23.	part-time	9705						
24.	voluntary	6845			5.9			
25.	involuntary	2860			3.1			
26.	with a job not at work total	3231						
27.	vacation	1576				3.8		7.7

208

28.		bad weather	168	0.4
29.		illness	942	2.2
30.		industrial disputes	40	0.1
31.		all other	505	1.2
32.		unemployed total	3931	9.4
33.	full time		3385	8.1
34.	part-time		546	1.3

Notes:

[a] Product hours worked by full-time workers in base year and persons.
[b] Product hours worked by full-time workers in observation year and persons.
[c] Product hours worked by corresponding population category in observation year and persons.
[d] Product hours worked by full-time workers in observation year and persons.

(d) Average *yearly hours* are calculated by multiplying weekly hours by 52.
(e) *Institutional population* is calculated as the difference between the estimates provided by the *Current Population Reports* and the total non-institutional population provided in the *Handbook of Labor Statistics*; this figure may, therefore, also reflect differences in definition. The 1980 figure is set to the 1979 figure.

A 6.6 ILO DEFINITION: 'ACTUAL HOURS WORKED PER PERSON EMPLOYED'

Actual hours of work are defined in the current international definitions (see a resolution of the Tenth International Conference of labour Statisticians convened in Geneva in October 1962) as follows:
Statistics of hours actually worked should include:

(a) Hours actually worked during normal periods of work.
(b) Time worked in addition to hours worked during normal periods of work, and generally paid at higher rates than normal rates (overtime).
(c) Time spent at the place of work on work such as the preparation of the workplace, repairs and maintenance, preparation and cleaning of tools, and the preparation of receipts, time sheets and reports.
(d) Time spent at the place of work waiting or standing-by for such reasons as lack of supply of work, breakdown of machinery, or accidents, or time spent at the place of work during which no work is done but for which payment is made under a guaranteed employment contract.
(e) Time corresponding to short rest periods at the workplace, including tea and coffee breaks.

Statistics of hours actually worked should exclude:

(a) Hours paid for but not worked, such as paid annual leave, paid public holidays, paid sick leave.
(b) Meal breaks.
(c) Time spent on travel from home to work and vice versa.

Source: ILO (1976).

Notes

1. See the discussion in the *Review of Economics and Statistics*, February 1950, pp. 49–79.
2. It is significant that the Thirteenth International Conference of Labour Statisticians, held at the ILO in Geneva (1982), devoted the major part of its agenda to a revision of the ILO recommendations on employment and unemployment, largely unaltered since 1954.
3. Maddison (1980) illustrates that in France, in the United Kingdom and especially in Germany, governments stimulate work-sharing in order to diminish the number of unemployed.
4. This also implies that the proportion of labour input by part-time workers is overstated in Tables 6.5 and 6.6 – see p. 000.
5. Antos, Mellow and Triplett (1979) review and criticise these investigations. This discussion of the decomposition of underlying effects relies on their article.
6. Easterlin (1982) develops an interesting theory on intergenerational income distribution, referring to this 'crowding out effect'.
7. Demographic groups may be substitutes. This renders adjustment as described in this paragraph even more difficult.
8. Bednarzik and Klein (1977) discuss long-term changes in the participation rate by sex, age group and marital status for the United States.
9. See Flaim (1979), Perry (1970), Wachter (1976) and Cain (1979).
10. Illustrated for Sweden by Sorrentino (1978).
11. This correction was also suggested earlier by Hitch (1951), Lebergott (1954) and Perry (1970).
12. See Gastwirth (1973), Mincer (1973), Shiskin (1976).
13. See p. 000 above.
14. See also Bancroft (1962).
15. The weighted unemployment rate in full-time equivalent units and the unemployment rate adjusted for discouragement in full-time equivalent units, parallel U-6 and U-7 as developed by Shiskin (1976).
16. See Gilroy (1975).
17. See weighted index of unemployment severity' (Gilroy, 1975, pp. 21–2).
18. Although an increase in the difference can be observed in recent years, this may be due to a relative increase in part-time unemployment for economic reasons.
19. Shiskin, 1976, p. 6.
20. Leon (1981), Steinberg (1976), Shiskin (1976).
21. See Leon (1981) and Steinberg (1976) for a more detailed discussion.
22. See the discussion in the *Review of Economics and Statistics*, February 1950, pp. 49–79.
23. An overview of recent political initiatives is given in Bruche and Casey (1982) and in Deroose, Vandeweghe and Vroman (1983). The Internationales Institut für Management und Verwaltung, Forschungseinheit Arbeitsmarktpolitik publishes quarterly the *Internationale Chronik zur Arbeitsmarktpolitik* (Berlin).
24. See OECD (1982) for a recent discussion of the work-sharing issue.
25. I am rather sceptical about the viability and the effectiveness of that measure (see de Neubourg, 1983).

26 Also in Switzerland efforts are made to construct labour market flow accounts (for Switzerland Mordasini, 1983). Recently Lindley started an investigation to construct labour market flow accounts for several EEC countries (Lindley, 1983). An ambitious research programme in this field is found in Stone (UN, 1975).
27. Interesting empirical contributions to the analysis of microeconomic labour market behaviour on the basis of flow data are made amongst others, by Tiokka, Scanlon and Holt (1977) for the United States and Denton, Feaver and Robb (1976) for Canada. Pioneering work has been done by Sonnet (1982) for Belgium: she estimates flows on the basis of stock data and projects future developments on the market.
28. ILO (1976), pp. 28–9.

References

AARTS, L., BRUINSMA, H. and DE JONG, P. L. (1982) *Arbeidscapaciteit van WAO-toetreders* (Zoetermeer: Sociale Verzekeringsraad).

ANTOS, J., MELLOW, W. and TRIPLETT, J. E. (1979) 'What is a Current Equivalent to Unemployment Rates of the Past?', *Monthly Labor Review* (March), pp. 36–46.

Annual Abstract of Statistics (London: CSO) (various issues).

Annual Report on the Labor Force (Washington, D.C.: Bureau of the Census) (1950–8 issues).

Annuaire Statistique de la France (Paris: INSEE) (1950–81 issues).

'Arbeidsvolume en geregistreerde arbeidsreserve 1950–1966' (Voorburg: CBS).

BANCROFT, G. (1950) 'The Census Bureau Estimates of Unemployment', *Review of Economics and Statistics* (February) pp.

——— (1962) 'Some Alternative Indexes of Employment and Unemployment', *Monthly Labor Review* (February) pp. 167–74.

BARRET, W. J. (1932) 'Extent and Methods of Spreading Work', *Monthly Labor Review* (September).

BAX, E. H. (1982) 'De stijging van de arbeidsongeschiktheid in de jaren zeventig: Beleid en analyse', *Mens en Maatschappij* (May), pp. 117–44.

BEDNARZIK, R. W. and KLEIN, D. P. (1974) 'Labour Force Trends: A Synthesis and Analysis', *Monthly Labor Review* 100 (10) (October) pp. 3–12.

BEST, F. (1981) *Work Sharing: Issues, Policy Options and Prospects* (The Upjohn Institute for Employment Research).

Bevolking van Nederland 1830–1969 (Voorburg: CBS).

Bijzondere Statische Opgaven (Voorburg, CBS) (1950–2 issues).

VAN DEN BOSCH, F. A. J. and PETERSEN, C. (1982) *An explanation of the growth of social security disability transfers* (Rotterdam: Institute for Economic Research), discussion paper, 8209 G/P.

BOWEN, W. G. and FINEGAN, T. A. (1969) *The Economics of Labor Force Participation* (Princeton: Princeton University Press).

BRUCHE, G. and CASEY, B. (1982) 'Arbeitsmarktpolitik unter Stagflationsbedingungen. Ein internationaler Ueberblick über die wichtigsten Massnahmen seit der Weltwirtschaftskrise 1974/75', *Mitteilungen aus der Arbeitsmarkt- und Berufsforschung* 3, pp. 232–50.

BUTLER, A. D. and DEMOPOULOS, G. O. (1972) 'Labor Force Behavior in a Full Employment Economy', *Industrial and Labor Relations Review* (April), pp. 375–88.

CAIN, G. G. (1979) 'The Unemployment Rate as an Economic Indicator', *Monthly Labor Review* (March), pp. 24–35.

CLARKSON, K. W. and MEINERS, R. E. (1977) *Inflated unemployment statistics: the effect of welfare work registration requirements* (Miami: University of Miami School of Law, Law and Economic Center) (March).

COHEN, M. S. (1969) 'The Direct Effects of Federal Manpower Programms in Reducing Unemployment', *Journal of Human Resources* (Fall) pp. 491–507.

Current Population Reports: Population Estimats (Washington, D.C.: Bureau of the Census) (various issues).

DENTON, F. T., FEAVER, Ch and ROBB, L. A. (1976) *La Dynamique à Court-Terme du Marché du Travail au Canada* (Ottawa: Conseil économique du Canada).

De Nederlandse jeugd en haar orderivijs (Voorburg: CBS).

DEROOSE, S., VANDEWEGHE, R. and VROMAN, C. (1983) *Internationale Vergelijking van Arbeidsmarktsituaties*, paper presented at Zestiende Vlaams Wetenschappelijk Economisch Congres (Ghent) (April), pp. 133–225.

DUNLOP, J. T. (1950) 'Estimates of Unemployment: some Unresolved Problems', *Review of Economics and Statistics* (February), pp. 77–9.

EASTERLIN, R. A., (1982) *Birth and Fortune: the Impact of Numbers on Personal Welfare* (New York: Basic Books).

Employment and Earnings (Washington, D.C.: Department of Labor, Bureau of Labor Statistics) (various issues).

FLAIM, P. O. (1979) 'The Effect of Demographic Changes on the Nation's Unemployment Rate', *Monthly Labour Review* (March), pp. 13–23.

FRIEDMAN, J. (1975) *Newsweek* 4 August, p. 63.

GASTWIRTH, J. L. (1973) 'Estimating the Number of "Hidden Unemployed"', *Monthly Labor Review* (March), pp. 17–26.

GILROY, C. L. (1975) 'Supplemental Measures of Labor Force Underutilization', *Monthly Labor Review* 98(5) (May), pp. 13–23.

GORDON, R. A. and GORDON, M. S. (eds) (1966) *'Prosperity and Unemployment'* (New York).

GRANIER, R. (1982) 'La Sous-Utilisation du Facteur Travail en France (1973–1980)', Université de Droit, d'Economie et des Sciences d'Aix-Marseille (June) (mimeo).

────── and MADDISON, A. (1982) *Politiques de l'Emploi et Emploi*, Tome I: Approche Empirique (Arx en Provence: Centre d'Analyse Economique).

GREEN, C. (1977) 'The Employment Ratio as an Indicator of Aggregate Demand Pressure', *Monthly Labor Review* (April), pp. 25–32.

Handbook of Labor Statistics (Washington, D.C.: Department of Labor, Bureau of Labor Statistics) (various issues).

HARRIS, D. (1976) 'Assessment of Unemployment in the EEC', in Worswick G. C. N. (ed.) *The Concept and Measurement of Involuntary Unemployment* (London: Allen & Unwin).
HARRIS, S. E. (1950) 'How much Unemployed?', *Review of Economics and Statistics* (February), pp. 49–79.
HEDGES, J. N. (1977) 'Absence from Work: Measuring the Hours Lost', *Monthly Labor Review* (October), pp. 16–23.
HILL, M. J. (1976) 'Can we Distinguish Voluntary from Involuntary Unemployment?', in Worswick, G. D. N. (ed.) *The Concept and Measurement of Involuntary Unemployment* (London: Allen & Unwin).
HITCH, T. (1951) 'Meaning and Measurement of "Full" or "Maximum" Employment', *Review of Economics and Statistics* (February), pp. 1–11.
HOLT, CH. C. (1980) 'Wages and Job Availability in Segmented Labour Markets', in Malinvaud, E. and Fitoussi, J. P. (eds) *Unemployment in Western Countries* (London:).
ILO (International Labour Office) (1976) *International Recommendations on Labour Statistics* (Geneva: ILO).
——— (1982) *Thirteenth International Conference of Labour Statisticians*, Report II (Geneva: ILO).
Japan Statistical Yearbook (Tokyo: various issues).
Japanese Yearbook of Labour Statistics (Tokyo: various issues).
JÜTTNER, D. J. (1972) 'Arbeitspotential, Arbeitsmarktreserven und Vollbeschäftigung', *Zeitschrift für die gesamte Staatswissenschaft* 128 (1) (April).
KAHN, R. (1976) 'Unemployment as seen by the Keynesians', in Worswick, G. D. N. (ed.) *The Concept and Measurement of Involuntary Unemployment* (London: Allen & Unwin).
KILLINGSWORTH, C. (1963) 'Unemployment and the Tax Cut', *Nation's Manpower Revolution* (Washington, D.C.: US Senate, Committee on Labor and Public Welfare, Employment and Manpower, 88th Congress, 1st session, part 5, October 28), pp. 1787–94.
KNOX, F. (1979) *Labour Supply in Economic Development: the Future of Large Market Economies to the Year 2000* (Westmead: Saxon House).
Labour Force Sample Surveys 1973–1975–1977 (Luxemburg: Eurostat, 1979, 1980, 1981 issues).
LEBERGOTT, S. (1954) 'Measuring Unemployment', *Review of Economics and Statistics* (November), pp. 290–400.
LEON, L. B. (1981) 'The Employment–Population Ratio: Its Value in Labor Force Analysis', *Monthly Labor Review* 104 (2) (February), pp. 36–45.
LEONTIEF, W. W. (1982) 'The Distribution of Work and Income', *Scientific American* (September), pp. 152–164.
LEVITAN, S. and TAGGART, R. (1973) 'Employment–Earning Inadequacy: a Measure of Welfare', *Monthly Labor Review* (October), pp. 19–27.
LINDLEY, R. M. (1983) *Population Accounting for Labour Market Analysis and Policy: a European Initiative*, paper presented at the Seminar: Arbeitsmarktstrukturen und -Prozesse: Beiträge zu Analyse und Politik (Basel) (March).
Maandstatistiek voor Bevolking en Volnsgezondheid (The Hague: Voorburg, CBS). (1953–82 issues).

MADDISON, A. (1980) 'Monitoring the Labour Market: A proposal for a Comprehensive Approach in Official Statistics', *Review of Income and Wealth* (June).

———— (1982) *Phases of Capitalist Development* (Oxford: Oxford University Press).

———— (1983) 'Comparative Analysis of the Productivity Situation in the Advanced Capitalist Countries', in Kendrick, J. W. (ed.), *International Comparisons of Productivity and Causes of the Slowdown* (Washington, D.C.: American Enterprise Institute (AEI)).

———— and GRANIER, R. 'Proportions pour l'Etablissement de Comptes du Marche du Travail', (Aix en Provence: Universite d'Aix-Marseille) (January) (mimeo).

MARIE, S. M. S. T. and BEDNARZIK, R. W. (1976) 'Employment and Unemployment during 1975', *Monthly Labor Review* (February), pp. 11–20.

MERTENS, D., KLAUDÜ, W. (eds) (1980) Probleme der Messung und Vorausschätzung des Erwerbspersonenpotentials, *Beiträge zur Arbeitsmarkt- und Berufsforschung* 44 (Nürnberg).

MINCER, J. (1973) 'Determining Who are the "Hidden Unemployed"', *Monthly Labor Review* (March), pp. 27–30.

MINCER, J. (1966) 'Labour–Force Participation and Unemployment. A Review of Recent Evidence', in Gordon, R. A. and Gordin, M. S. (eds), *Prosperity and Unemployment* (New York).

MOLL, R. P. (1907) *Verborgen werkloosheid in Nederland* (Rotterdam: Erasmus University).

MOORE, G. H. (1973) *How Full is Full Employment?* (Washington, D.C.: American Enterprise Institute for Public Policy Research).

MORDASINI, B. (1983) *Eine Bevölkerungs- und Arbeitskräftegesamtrechnung für die Schweiz*, paper presented at the Seminar: Arbeitsmarktstrukturen und -Prozesse: Beiträge zu Analyse und Politik (Basel) (March).

MOTHERAL, G. and SUMMERVILLE, R. (1978) *The impact of federal policies on labor force participation and unemployment*, paper presented at Meeting of the Southern Economic Association (November).

MOY, J. and SORRENTINO, C. (1982) 'Unemployment and Labour Force: Trends in Ten Industrial Nations: an Update', Monthly Labor Review (November), pp. 17–21.

DE NEUBOURG, C. (1983a) *Arbeidstijdverkorting: een Instrument, geen Oplossing*, paper presented at the Annual Meeting of the Studiekring Post-Keynesiaanse Economie (April).

———— (1983b) *Peregrinations in the land of Dreams, Needs and Data*, comment on R. Lindley's paper on the Seminar Arbeitsmarktstrukturen und -Prozesse: Beiträge zu Analyse und Politik (Basel) (March).

OECD (1982) *Labour Supply, Growth Constraints and Work Sharing* (Paris: OECD).

PERRY, G. L. (1970) 'Changing Labor Markets and Inflation', *Brookings Papers on Economic Activity*, pp. 411–448.

PHELPS, E. S. (ed.) (1970) *Microeconomic Foundations of Employment and Inflation Theory* (London: Macmillan).

REYHER, L. and BACH, H. U. (1980) 'Arbeitskräfte-Gesamtrechnung: bestände und Bewegungen am Arbeitsmarkt', *Mitteilungen aus der Arbeitsmarkt- und Berufsforschung* 4, pp. 498–513.

ROBINSON, J. (1937) *'Essays in the Theory of Employment'* (New York).

SHISKIN, J. (1976) 'Employment and Unemployment: the Doughnut or the Hole'?, *Monthly Labor Review* (February), pp. 3–10.

SIMLER, N. J. and TELLA, A. (1968) 'Labor Reserve and the Phillips Curve', *Review of Economics and Statistics* (February), pp. 32–49.

SMALL, S. S. (1972) 'Statistical Effect of Worktraining Programmes on the Unemployment Rate', *Monthly Labor Review* (September), pp. 7–13.

SMITH, R. (1973) 'Manpower Programms and Unemployment Statistics', *Monthly Labor Review* (April), pp. 63–5.

Sociale Maandstatistiek (1980) (The Hague: CBS) (December), p. 18.

SONNET, A. (1982) *La dynamique du Marché du Travail de 1970 à 2020 en Belgique* (Brussels: CRISP).

SORRENTINO, C. (1978) *International Comparisons of Unemployment* (Washington, D. C.: Department of Labor, Bureau of Labor Statistics).

Statistical Abstract of Sweden (1950–81) (Stockholm: Statistics Sweden, various issues).

Statistical Abstracts (1950–81) (London: CSO).

Statistical Abstracts of the US: 1981 (Washington, D.C.: US Bureau of the Census).

Statistical Yearbook for the Netherlands (1965–6, 1971, 1981) (Voorburg: CBS).

Statistiches Jahrbuch (Wiesbaden: Statistiches Bradesambt) (various issues).

Statistiek van het wetenschappelijk onderwijs (Voorburg: CBS)

STEINBERG, E. I. (1976) 'The Employment Ratio', *Survey of Current Business* (December), pp. 13–16, 50.

STRAND, K. and DERNBURG, T. (1964) 'Cyclical Variation in Civilian Labor Force Participation', *Review of Economics Statistics* (November), pp. 378–91.

TAYLOR, J. (1976) 'The Unemployment Gap in Britain's Production Sector, 1953–73', in Worswick, G. D. N. (ed.) *The Concept and Measurement of Involuntary Unemployment* (London: Allen & Unwin).

TELLA, A. (1964) 'The Relation of Labor Force to Employment', *Industrial and Labor Relations Review* 17 (April), pp. 454–69.

——— (1965) 'Labor Force Sensitivity to Employment by Age and Sex', *Industrial Relations* (February), pp. 65–83.

——— (1976) 'Analyzing Joblessness', *New York Times* (27 October).

TIOKKA, R., SCANLON, W. J. and HOLT, Ch. C. (1977) 'Extensions of a Structural Model of the Demographic Labor Market, in Ehrenberg, R. G. (ed.) *Research in Labor Economics* (Vol. 1) (Greenwich, Conn.), pp. 305–32.

UN (1975) *Towards a System of Social and Demographic Statistics*, Studies in Methods Series F 18 (New York: Statistical Office of the United Nations).

WACHTER, M. L. (1976) 'The Changing Cyclical Responsiveness of the Wage Inflation', *Brooking Papers of Economic Activity* 1, pp. 115–59.

WALDMAN, E., GROSSMAN, A. S., HAYGHE, H. and JOHNSON, B. L.

(1979) 'Working Mothers in the 1970s: a Look at the Statistics', *Monthly Labor Review* (October), pp. 39–49.

WORSWICK, G. D. N. (1976) *The Concept and Measurement of Involuntary Unemployment* (edited for the Royal Economic Society) (London: Allen & Unwin).

7 Full-capacity Employment, Unemployment and Labour Hoarding
Joan Muysken[1]

INTRODUCTION

In this chapter we integrate UV analysis – which determines unemployment due to market imperfections – and macroeconomic vintage analysis – which determines full-capacity employment. The resulting analysis enables us to distinguish between two types of structural unemployment: one type due to market imperfections, the other due to a shortage of capacity demand for labour. In Dutch discussions in the 1970s these two types were referred to respectively as 'qualitative' and 'quantitative' structural unemployment. Since the analysis enables us to distinguish between actual demand for labour and capacity demand, we can also observe labour hoarding. As a consequence, for a given supply of labour the under-utilisation of labour can be measured and decomposed into several components. These components are cyclical unemployment, quantitative and qualitative structural unemployment and labour hoarding.

The importance of distinguishing between these components lies in the differences between underlying causes and the implied consequences for economic policy.[2] However, it is hard to define a consistent framework in which the several components are analysed simultaneously. In this chapter, we propose such a framework.

The central element of our analysis is the employment function. This function implies a UV curve, which enables us to analyse unemployment due to imperfections on the labour market. The function can also be used to determine full-capacity employment from full-capacity demand for labour, which in its turn stems from a vintage model. As a consequence, we can also distinguish between cyclical unemployment and structural unemployment due to deficient capacity demand for labour. Finally, the distinction between actual demand for labour and capacity demand enables us to determine labour hoarding. This is elaborated in the next Section.

Next we apply our analysis to the Netherlands for the years 1967–81, by combining several empirical results in our framework. Since these results are taken from different empirical studies, our conclusions are of a tentative nature. Finally, we make some concluding remarks. However, before discussing the analytical framework, we elaborate on the decomposition of employment and on its underlying causes.

(a) A Decomposition of Unemployment with respect to its Causes

When analysing unemployment, the Central Planning Bureau distinguished in the mid-1970s between cyclical and structural unemployment. Cyclical unemployment results from under-utilisation or over-utilisation of productive capacity due to deficient (or too large an) effective demand (*MEV*, 1987, p. 58). The remaining unemployment is structural unemployment in a broad sense. Subtraction of seasonal and frictional unemployment yields structural unemployment in a narrow sense. In first instance, this type of unemployment is explained as a consequence of a deficient capacity demand for labour compared to labour supply (*MEV*, 1974, p. 58).

Later on, causes of a more qualitative nature also are recognised. Apart from seasonal and frictional unemployment, unemployment amongst disabled persons is introduced as a separate category. In the remaining structural unemployment in a narrow sense, a distinction is made between unemployment which results from qualitative discrepancies between supply of (and demand for) labour, and unemployment which results from deficient capacity demand for labour – i.e., qualitative and quantitative structural unemployment (*CEP*, 1975, p. 95). Quantitative structural unemployment results from scrapping of obsolete machinery. To the extent that the resulting fall in employment is not fully compensated by employment resulting from new investments, it can be explained by means of a vintage model. Qualitative structural unemployment has many different causes which are not further analysed.

The above decomposition of unemployment has been estimated by the Central Planning Bureau for the years 1970–6, the results are presented in Table 7.1. In 1976, the publication of such a decomposition was terminated without further explanation. In that decomposition cyclical unemployment is measured by correlating actual unemployment with a parabolic trend and a cyclical indicator (*MEV*, 1975, p. 85). The cyclical

Table 7.1 Decomposition of unemployment according to the Central Planning Bureau: the Netherlands (1970–6)

	1970 (1)	1971 (2)	1972 (3)	1973 (4)	1974 (5)	1975 (6)	1976 (7)
Cyclical unemployment	−25	−10	10	10	25–30	75–80	70
Disabled persons	15	15	15	15	15	15	15
Seasonal unemployment	13	13	13	13	13	13	13
Frictional unemployment	45	45	50	50	50	50	50
Structural unemployment in a narrow sense	5–10	5–10	25–30	30	35–40	55	90–95
Total	56	59	115	117	143	210	240

Source:
Columns (1)–(5): *Werkgelegenheidsnota* (1975), p. 19.
Columns (5)–(7): *MEV* (1976), p. 89.

indicator is the difference between actual production and full-capacity production, measured by peak-to-peak interpolation of production in manufacturing. Employment amongst disabled persons and seasonal unemployment are also influenced cyclically. For these components of structural unemployment in a broad sense, therefore cyclical neutral values are estimated (*CEP*, 1975, p. 96). By definition, frictional unemployment is very brief, a 'normal' search time of one or one and a half months is assumed (*CEP*, 1975, p. 97). Finally, the remaining unemployment is assumed to be structural unemployment in a narrow sense. No further distinction is made between quantitative and qualitative structural unemployment.

It is obvious that there is no theoretical framework in which the several components of unemployment are determined simultaneously. This holds in particular for the distinction between quantitative and qualitative structural unemployment; we present such a framework below.

THE NATURE OF UNEMPLOYMENT: AN ANALYTICAL FRAMEWORK

The centrepiece in our analytical framework is the employment function which is discussed below. The employment function implies a UV curve, which can be used to determine qualitative structural unemployment. This is explained first. The employment function is also used in the estimation of vintage models, which enables us to distinguish between employment, actual demand for labour and full-capacity demand for labour. As a consequence, cyclical unemployment and quantitative structural unemployment can be distinguished and labour hoarding can be determined. This is the subject of the next Section. The final Section summarises the analytical framework.

(a) The Employment Function

The employment function explains actual employment, E, as a result of the interaction between labour demand, N, and labour supply, $\bar{N}$. An obvious formulation results from the assumption that employment is determined by the minimum of supply and demand for labour – i.e., $E = \min(N, \bar{N})$. However, it is very possible that this minimum will not be reached due to imperfections on the labour market. For that reason, we prefer the more general specification of the employment function:

$$E = g(N, \bar{N}). \tag{7.1}$$

We assume that the function g has the following properties:

1. the function is homogeneous of the first degree in N and $\bar{N}$, hence:

$$g\left(\frac{N}{E}, \frac{\bar{N}}{E}\right) = 1 \tag{7.2a}$$

holds, or

$$\frac{E}{\bar{N}} = f\left(\frac{N}{\bar{N}}\right) = g\left(\frac{N}{\bar{N}}, 1\right) \tag{7.2b}$$

2. the function f in equation (7.2b) has the following properties:

$$f(0) = 0 \qquad 0 \leqslant f(x) \leqslant 1, \quad x > 0 \qquad \lim_{x \to \sim} f(x) = 1$$

$$0 \leqslant f'(0) \leqslant 1 \qquad 0 \leqslant f'(x) \leqslant 1, \quad x > 0 \qquad \lim_{x \to \sim} f'(x) = 0 \tag{7.3}$$

$$f''(x) \leqslant 0, \qquad x \geqslant 0$$

The general form of the employment function is depicted in Figures 7.1 and 7.2: The specification $E = \min(N, \bar{N})$, represented by the line ABC, obviously is a boundary case.

Figure 7.1 The employment function (equation (7.2a)) and the *UV* curve

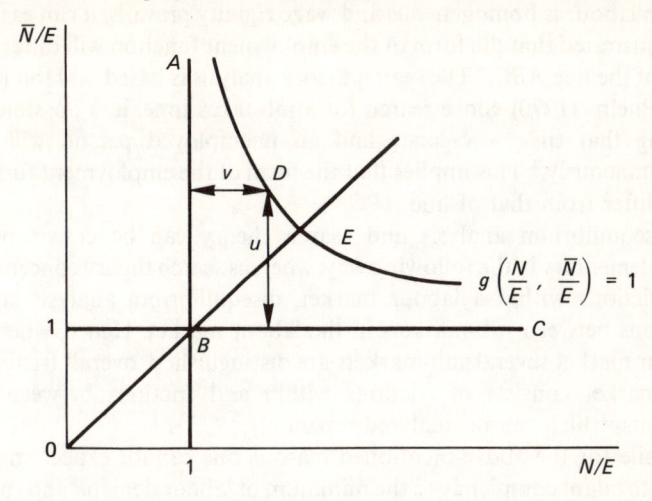

Figure 7.2 The employment function (equation (7.2))

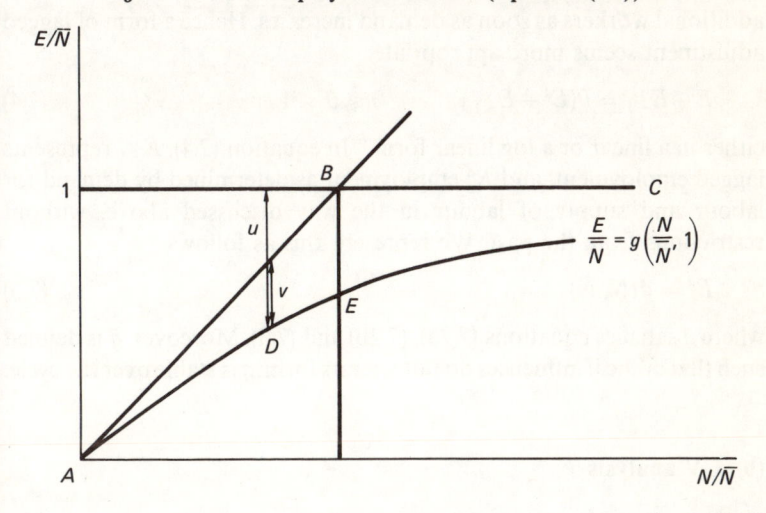

That the form of the employment function differs from that of the line *ABC* can be explained from two points of view, which do not exclude each other: disequilibrium analysis and search theory. The disequilibrium approach is presented in Hansen (1970), who distinguishes sub-markets in the labour market, with imperfect mobility between them. When labour is homogeneous and wage rigidity prevails, it can easily be demonstrated that the form of the employment function will differ from that of the line ABC.[3] The search theory analysis is based on Holt (1970) and Phelps (1970). Since search for a job takes time, it is possible that during that time a vacancy and an unemployed person will exist simultaneously.[4] This implies that the form of the employment function will differ from that of line ABC.

Disequilibrium analysis and search theory can be considered as complementary in the following way: whereas search theory concentrates on frictions within a labour market, disequilibrium analysis studies frictions between sub-markets in the labour market. Hence, when in a labour market several sub-markets are distinguished, overall friction on the market consists of frictions within and frictions between sub-markets, which can be analysed separately.[5]

While for the above-mentioned reasons one cannot expect employment to adapt completely to the minimum of labour demand and supply, one can also hardly expect employment to adapt instantaneously to changes in labour demand and supply: firms will not fire redundant workers immediately when demand falls, nor will they be able to hire additional workers as soon as demand increases. Hence a form of lagged adjustment seems more appropriate:

$$E - E_{-1} = \theta(E^d - E_{-1}) \qquad 0 \leqslant \theta \leqslant 1 \qquad (7.4)$$

either in a linear or a log linear form.[6] In equation (7.4), E_{-1} represents lagged employment, and E^d employment as determined by demand for labour and supply of labour in the way discussed above, without restrictions from the past. We represent this as follows:

$$E^d = \tilde{g}(N, \bar{N}) \qquad (7.5)$$

where $\tilde{g}$ satisfies equations (7.2a), (7.2b) and (7.3). Moreover, $\tilde{g}$ is defined such that cyclical influences do not alter its form: $\tilde{g}$ is stable over the cycle.

(b) UV analysis

As we discussed above, the employment function implies the simultaneous existence of vacancies and unemployment on the labour market. This can be elaborated by deriving from the employment function the UV curve – i.e., the relationship between unemployment and vacancies.

The UV curve can be derived by substituting in the employment function (7.2a) the definitions of unemployment, U, and vacancies, V:

$$U = \bar{N} - E \quad \text{and} \quad V = N - E \tag{7.6}$$

or as a percentage of employment:

$$u = \frac{U}{E} = \frac{\bar{N}}{E} - 1 \quad \text{and} \quad v = \frac{V}{E} = \frac{N}{E} - 1 \tag{7.7}$$

This yields the following UV curve:

$$g(1+v, 1+u) = 1 \tag{7.8}$$

The relation between the employment function (7.2a) and the UV curve (7.8) is presented in Figure 7.1. The function g in Figure 7.1 represents the UV curve using AB and BC as axes. Again the line ABC is a boundary case.

The UV curve often is used to measure imperfections on the labour market. These imperfections express themselves in the fact that unemployment and vacancies occur simultaneously on the labour market. If one for that reason should take the minimum of U and V as a measure of these imperfections, 'market imperfection is not a structural phenomenon ... [it] could be combated by an expenditure policy ... and the real cause of the relevant form of unemployment is not tackled' (Kuipers and Buddenberg, 1978, p. 395). The real cause of this kind of unemployment should be of a structural nature: one should concentrate on those imperfections which are part of the structure of the economy. This implies that 'the level of unemployment, existing when "true" unemployment, and vacancies are equal is uniquely qualified to serve as a measure of the imperfection of the labour market' (Brown, 1975, p. 140). This level can be found from, the UV curve by calculating the unemployment, U^*, for which holds $U = V$. The level of unemployment U^* often is used 'as a measure of structural disequilibrium in the labour market' (Hansen, 1970, p. 10). Even 'it has been maintained ... that the equality of unemployment and vacancies defines a zero cyclical unemployment level' (Hansen, 1970, p. 18).

However, when using the UV curve to measure imperfections on the labour market two problems arise. The first problems arises from the observation that around the UV curve 'cyclical swings (at a given structural situation) take place in a counterclockwise movement along a closed circuit' (Hansen, 1970, p. 7). As a consequence, the value of U^* measured in the upswing exceeds that measured in the downswing of the cycle. This is consistent with the dynamic specification of the employment function (7.4) (Hansen, 1970, equation (10)). The problem can be solved by allowing for cyclical influences when estimating the UV curve, and next deriving the long-run steady-state UV curve by eliminating these influences. Hence, the long-run employment function underlying equation (7.4) is $E = E^d$ – i.e., equation (7.5). As a consequence, the long-run UV curve is:

$$\tilde{g}(1+v, 1+u) = 1 \tag{7.9}$$

U^* can then be calculated from the long-run curve.

The second problem then is that even this long-run UV curve may shift: 'there may not exist a single-valued UV curve along which the labour market moves up and down though the cycle – even given the structural disequilibrium in the labour market' (Hansen, 1970, p. 20). As a consequence, even the employment function (7.5) may not be stable in the course of time.

For the moment, we shall ignore the second problem. We assume that the long-run UV curve (7.9) represents the 'given structural situation' well. Moreover, we denote by $\tilde{N}$ the structural labour supply, from which cyclical elements have eliminated. Finally, N^* represents the demand for labour at which structural imperfections on the labour market occur at the level U^*. That is, the demand for labour for which $U = V$ holds, and as a consequence:

$$N^* = \tilde{N}. \tag{7.10}$$

Substitution of equation (7.10) in the employment function (7.5) yields the employment, E^*, which is consistent with structural imperfections on the labour market of U^*. Hence:

$$E^* = \tilde{g}(1, 1) \cdot \tilde{N} = g(N^*, \tilde{N}) \tag{7.11}$$

holds, and U^* is given by:

$$U^* = \tilde{N} - E^* \tag{7.12}$$

or, as a percentage

$$u^* = \frac{1}{\tilde{g}(1, 1)} - 1. \tag{7.13}$$

When we read $\tilde{g}$ instead of g, this percentage is represented in Figure 7.2 by the line BE: at that line, unemployment equals vacancies.

(c) Vintage Models

As we indicated above, cyclical unemployment results from deviations in capacity utilisation from the level of full capacity due to changes in effective demand. Hence, in order to measure this type of unemployment is it relevant to know labour demand at full-capacity utilisation, N^c, and full-capacity output, X^c. An elegant way to determine X^c and N^c simultaneously is provided by vintage models. A clay-clay model was introduced and estimated for the Dutch economy by the Central Planning Bureau in the mid-1970s (den Hartog and Tjan, 1976). Since then, this model has been refined in many ways and putty-clay models have been estimated, too.[8]

The levels of aggregate output and demand for labour at full-capacity are an important characteristic of the 'given structural situation' of an economy. Hence, we can calculate from equation (7.5) the level of employment at full capacity, E^c:

$$E^c = \tilde{g}(N^c, \tilde{N}). \tag{7.14}$$

Effective demand can always be stimulated in such a way that employment E^c can be realised, given structural labour market imperfections. It then is clear that cyclical unemployment, U', is measured by the difference between actual unemployment, $\bar{N} - E$, and unemployment at full-capacity utilisation, $\tilde{N} - E^c$. Hence, cyclical unemployment is given by:

$$U' = (\bar{N} - \tilde{N}) + (E^c - E). \tag{7.15}$$

Now we can also measure unemployment, U^c, that results from a structural quantitative shortage of demand for labour. One might be inclined to identify this with unemployment at full-capacity utilisation, $\tilde{N} - E^c$. However, one then ignores unemployment as a result of imperfections on the labour market. For there exists structural quantitative shortage of demand for labour only when an increase in capacity demand for labour leads to a structural higher level of employment. And this is possible only when E^c lies below E^*. As a consequence unemployment due to a quantitative shortage of demand for labour is given by:

$$U^c = E^* - E^c. \tag{7.16}$$

When E^c exceeds E^* we have a structural excess demand for labour. It is then not possible to utilise productive capacity fully, due to the presence of market imperfections. Since there is a quantitative excess demand for labour, U^c is negative.

Finally, it should be noted that demand for labour can be derived from the vintage models by assuming that capacity demand for labour is utilised to the same rate as capacity output is. This gives the demand for labour which is necessary to produce current output, N^p. Denoting the utilisation rate by $q = X/X^c$, we have:

$$N^p = q \cdot N^c. \tag{7.17}$$

However, actual demand for labour will usually exceed N^p. Firms will hire more labour than is strictly necessary, in order to be able to deal with unexpected increases in demand. For that reason they will increase their demand by a fraction γ.[9] Moreover, actual demand for labour will also be influenced by past employment: It seems reasonable to assume that firms can only partly adjust actual demand to desired demand, $(1+\gamma)N^p$. Denoting the adjustment parameter by λ, this leads, for example, to the following specification of demand for labour:

$$N = \lambda(1+\gamma) \cdot N^p + (1-\lambda) \cdot E_{-1} \quad 0 < \lambda < 1, \quad \gamma > 0. \tag{7.18}$$

The phenomenon that firms will demand more labour than is strictly necessary for the production of current output is called 'labour hoarding'. Labour hoarding, L, is defined by

$$L = N - N^p \tag{7.19}$$

Substitution of equation (7.18) in (7.19) yields:

$$L = \lambda \cdot \gamma \cdot N^p + (1-\lambda) \cdot (E_{-1} - N^p). \tag{7.20}$$

This equation shows that the extent to which past employment exceeds strictly necessary current demand for labour has a positive influence on labour hoarding, as might be expected. This influence is the larger the slower the speed of adjustment – i.e., the lower λ is.

(d) The Sub-division of Unemployment

The UV analysis and vintage models discussed in the preceding sections provide an analytical framework for the sub-division of unemployment presented at the beginning of the chapter. However, we shall ignore seasonal unemployment and unemployment of disabled persons.[10]

The analytical framework can be discussed in the context of Figure 7.3. In Figures 7.3, g represents equation (7.4) in the downswing of the cycle,

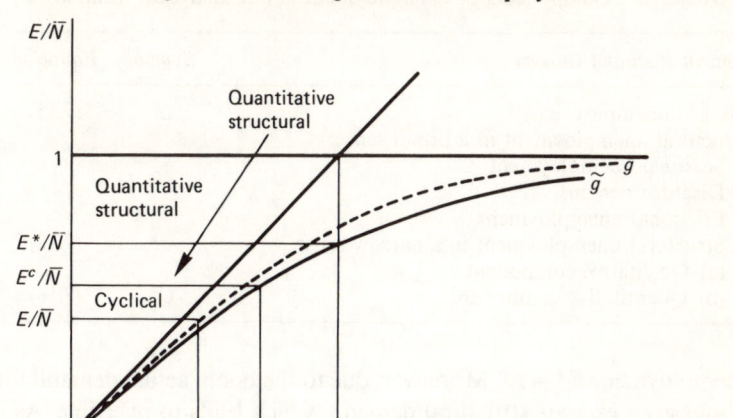

Figure 7.3 Decomposition of unemployment

assuming $\bar{N}$ and E_{-1} to be given. The function $\tilde{g}$ represents equation (7.5)–i.e., a cyclical neutral situation with labour supply at $\tilde{N}$.[11] In a vintage model, capacity demand for labour, N^c, and the utilisation rate, q, have been calculated. Actual demand for labour, N, then can be derived from equation (7.18), and the corresponding employment, E, from equation (7.4). The employment, E^c, corresponding to full-capacity operation is derived from equation (7.14). Finally, unemployment and vacancies are equal in a structural sense, at labour demand N^* and corresponding employment E^* (see equation (7.11)).

It is obvious that stimulation of effective demand increases E up to E^c. Accounting for a cyclical influence in labour supply, cyclical unemployment therefore is equal to $(E^c - E) - (\tilde{N} - \bar{N})$. To reduce unemployment any further, productive capacity has to be increased. When this capacity is increased such that demand for labour equals supply, employment increases from E^c to E^*. Hence structural unemployment due to deficient demand is $E^* - E^c$. The remaining structural unemployment, $\tilde{N} - E^*$, is due to market imperfections.

When Figure 7.3 would be drawn such that $E > E^c > E^*$, the subdivision would not change. Structural unemployment due to market imperfections still is $N - E^*$. However, demand for labour exceeds supply due to the high level of productive capacity, and these imperfections do not manifest themselves in unemployment. There is a structural excess demand for labour, resulting in a negative quantitative structural

Table 7.2 Components of unemployment in our analytical framework

Central Planning Bureau	Symbol	Equation
Cyclical unemployment	U'	(7.15)
Structural unemployment in a broad sense:		
1. Seasonal unemployment	–	–
2. Disabled persons	–	–
3. Frictional unemployment		
4. Structural unemployment in a narrow sense	U^*	(7.12)
(a) Qualitative component		
(b) Quantitative component	U^c	(7.16)

unemployment $E^* - E^c$. Moreover, due to the boom actual demand for labour even exceeds structural demand, which leads to overtime. As a consequence, cyclical unemployment, $(E^c - E) - (\tilde{N} - \bar{N})$, is negative too.

From the above one sees that total unemployment, U, can be subdivided into cyclical unemployment, U', quantitative structural unemployment, U^c, and unemployment due to market imperfections, U^*, such that:

$$U = U' + U^c + U^* \tag{7.21}$$

holds. The separate components of unemployment have been respectively defined in equations (7.15), (7.16) and (7.12). They have been defined independently, in an analytical consistent way. The sub-division of employment is summarised in Table 7.2.

THE NATURE OF UNEMPLOYMENT IN THE NETHERLANDS 1967–81

The analytical framework presented above essentially combines a vintage model, in which capacity demand and actual demand for labour are explained, with an employment function, in which employment is explained from demand and supply of labour. The employment function should have the properties described above (p. 222). However, although several vintage models and employment functions or UV curves have been estimated for the Netherlands, the combination of both can be found only in the most recent model of the Central Planning Bureau (CPB, 1983). Unfortunately, we are not yet able to include the results of this model in our analysis.[12]

As a consequence we have to combine the results of several vintage models which have been estimated for the Netherlands with those of several UV analyses, in order to get an indication of the sub-division of unemployment. The drawback of this procedure is that in the vintage models very crude unemployment functions have been used to obtain estimation results. Since these employment functions are not consistent with the more elaborate functions used in UV analysis, the empirical results cannot be fully consistent. However, we shall demonstrate below that the estimated values of E^c and E^* are quite robust with respect to the specification of the underlying vintage models and employment functions. This suggests that the inconsistency which stems from using separate results of vintage models and UV analysis is not too large a bias.

We now present the estimation results of the vintage models and those of the UV analyses. We combine these results in the final Section, where we estimate the several components of unemployment for the Netherlands.

(a) Capacity Demand for Labour

In discussing capacity demand for labour in the Netherlands, we use the estimation results of three recent models: Kuipers, Muysken and van Sinderen (1978)[13], den Hartog and Tjan (1980) and Kuipers and van Zon (1982). We will indicate these models below by *KMS*, *HT* and *KZ*, respectively. These models have been estimated from the same data, although for different periods. They all estimate (or predict): values of N^c for the period 1970–80.[14] These estimated values are presented in Figure 7.4, together with N and $\bar{N}$.[15]

From Figure 7.4 one sees that capacity demand for labour decreases from 1970 to 1976, first it declines slowly, later on quickly. From 1976 onwards capacity demand increases again. However, it remains below the level of 1970. The results of *KMS* and *KZ* are remarkably close to each other, except for the years 1973–4. *HT* shows a similar development in capacity demand for labour as *KMS* and *KZ* do, but the absolute level is estimated to be about 400 000 man years higher. Since this is not very plausible, as the authors admit themselves (*HT*, p. 182), we ignore this difference.

The three models differ in several respects. *KMS* and *HT* are clay-clay models, whereas *KZ* is a putty-clay model. The specification of *KZ* therefore differs strongly from that of *KMS* and *HT*. Moreover, *HT* differs from *KMS* because *HT* assumes a variable capital–output ratio

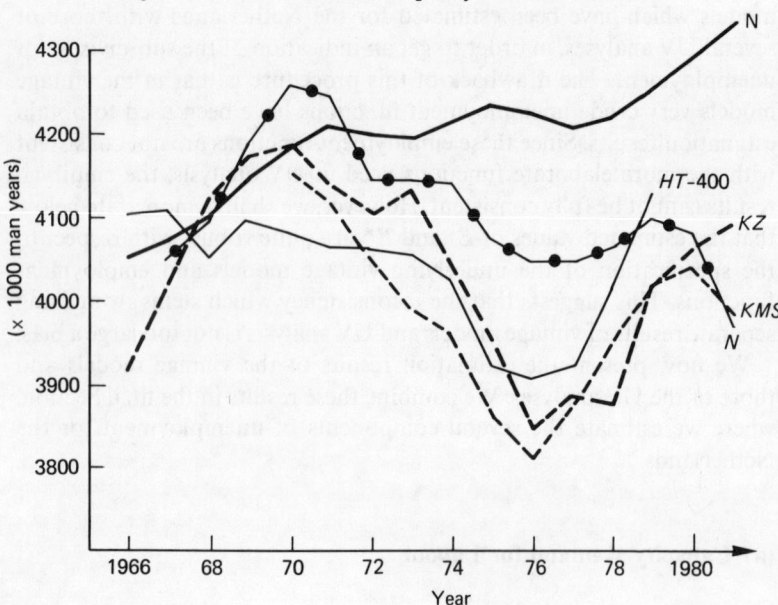

Figure 7.4 Estimations of capacity demand for labour

and *KMS* a constant one. Nonetheless the results with respect to N^c are remarkably similar. In each of the models an employment function is estimated in the form of equation (7.4)–*HT* use the log linear specification.[16] The models differ with respect to the specification of E^d.

$$KMS \ E^d = \beta . q . N^c + (1-\beta) . N^c \quad (7.22a)$$

$$HT \ \ln E^d = \beta \ln q . N^c + (1-\beta) \ln qN^c_{-1}, \quad \beta = 1/(1-\theta) \quad (7.22b)$$

$$KZ \ E^d = \beta . q . N^c. \quad (7.22c)$$

In spite of the differences in specification, the estimated value of θ hardly differs: 0.2 in the case of both *KMS* and *KZ*, and 0.25 in the case of *HT*. The estimated value of β is almost zero (0.045) in the case of *KMS* and almost unity (1.03) in the case of *KZ*. These parameter values are found by substituting equation (7.22) in equation (7.4), and estimating the resulting equation. For instance, in the case of *KZ*:

$$E = \theta . \beta . q . N^c + (1-\theta) . E_{-1} \quad (7.23)$$

is estimated, from which the values of θ and β can be identified.

In the vintage models no distinction is made between employment and demand for labour. Since labour hoarding as a result of past employment should appear somewhere, we are inclined to interpret equation (7.22) as a specification of desired demand for labour, $(1+\gamma).N^P$, in the case of KMS and KZ. Actual demand for labour then is found by substituting equation (7.22) in equation (7.18). This yields for KZ:

$$N = \lambda.\beta.q.N^c + (1-\lambda)E_{-1}. \tag{7.24}$$

Using this interpretation, equation (7.23) can be understood very well in terms of our previous analysis. We then have to assume that $E^d = N$ holds. $E^d = N$ is the specification of g in the form of $g(N, \bar{N}) = \min(N, \bar{N})$, as long as $N < \bar{N}$. Using this assumption, equation (7.24) can be substituted in equation (7.4) which gives:

$$E = \theta.\lambda.\beta.q.N^c + (1-\theta.\lambda).E_{-1}. \tag{7.25}$$

In this equation the same parameters are estimated as in equation (7.23). However, their interpretation differs: we find $\beta = 1.03$ – i.e., $\gamma = 0.03$ – and $\lambda.\theta = 0.2$. In order to identify the values of θ and λ separately, equation (7.24) should be estimated too.

In the period under study (1967–81), supply of labour exceeds demand except for three years, 1969–71. In those years, demand and supply hardly differ. This is consistent with the assumption $E^d = N = \min(N, \bar{N})$. We can therefore use equation (7.25) – at least as an approximation of the relevant employment function – to calculate E^c. The function g then is defined by a cyclical neutral equation (7.24) – i.e., at full-capacity level. And E^c can be calculated from:

$$E^c = \lambda.\beta.N^c + (1-\lambda).E^c_{-1}. \tag{7.26}$$

We do not know the value of λ. However, since employment has been decreasing from 1970 onwards we are inclined to interpret the decline of employment as a structural phenomenon in the 1970s. As a consequence, the estimation result of KZ of $\theta.\lambda = 0.2$, λ will lie close to 0.2. We use $\lambda = 0.2$ and $\beta = 1.03$.[17] It is obvious that the calculated value of E^c will hardly differ when we use the estimation results of KMS. For both models estimated $\lambda.\theta = 0.2$ and the estimated value of N^c lie close to each other. Moreover, β in equation (7.26) lies close to one. Hence, the values of E^c are quite robust with respect to the specification of the vintage model.

Finally, the results of KZ enable us to estimate labour hoarding in a straightforward way. Since q and N^c are estimated by KZ, N^P can be calculated according to equation (7.17). The difference between observed demand for labour and N^P then yields labour hoarding, by definition of equation (7.19). The calculated data on labour hoarding are presented in Table 7.3. As a percentage, of employment, labour hoarding decreases from 7.3 per cent in 1969 to 5 per cent in 1971, it further decreases to zero in 1974 and increases steadily afterwards to 8.1 per cent in 1980. As is not surprising, labour hoarding varies inversely with the utilisation rate. The sharp increase in labour hoarding in the late 1970s is obviously due to the decrease in employment. The tremendous increase in unemployment after 1980 can therefore be explained by a shakeout of redundant employees: while unemployment was at the very high level of 263 000 man years in 1980, labour hoarding was 236. Unemployment rose to about 400 000 man years in 1981, and over 800 000 man years in 1983.

(b) Labour Market Imperfections

As we explained above, the employment function can be used to analyse imperfections in the labour market. It is obvious that the employment function in the preceding Section is a crude one, assuming $E^d = N$.

We therefore turn to other studies in which more sophisticated employment functions are estimated. Kooiman and Kloek (1979), Kreijger (1981) and Heijke (1982) directly estimated employment functions for the Netherlands.[18] This function has been estimated indirectly, in the form of a UV curve, in Ministerie van Sociale Zaken (1978), Driehuis (1978), Kuipers and Buddenberg (1978), Muysken and de Neubourg (1981) and van den Berg (1982). In these studies, the following UV curve is estimated:

$$u = A.v. \tag{7.27}$$

Most studies include a trend in term in A, sometimes shift parameters are added too. In some studies the UV curve is estimated for absolute levels in U and V, in other U and V are related to the labour force.

All of the above-mentioned studies conclude that the UV curve or the employment function in the Netherlands shifted around 1967, indicating an increase in structural imperfections on the labour market. It is remarkable that in the same period a similar shift has been observed in Great Britain. The causes of that shift have been discussed extensively.[19] Gujariti (1972) stresses the influence of changes in the social security system, Taylor (1972) mentions labour hoarding as an important cause and both Forster (1973), and Bowers, Chesire and Webb (1970) draw attention to structural changes in demand for labour between regions

Figure 7.5 Estimations of unemployment due to labour market imperfections

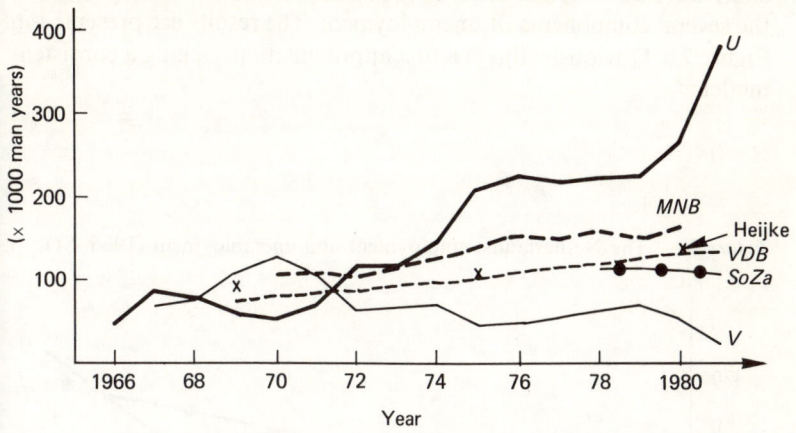

and occupational groups. The foundations of UV analysis also became a subject of this discussion: 'In no sense is the vacancy rate the determinant of the unemployment rate'.[20] However, as we discussed above, UV analysis can be explained very well, both in the context of search theory and in that of disequilibrium analysis.

In order to measure imperfections on the labour market, we will use van den Berg (1982). He used the same data as those which have been used in the estimation of the vintage models. Moreover, unemployment due to imperfections on the labour market estimated by van den Berg lies close to that found by Heijke (1982) and Muysken and de Neubourg (1981).[21] The various estimates of U^* for the Netherlands, 1970–81, are presented in Figure 7.5.[22] From Figure 7.5, one sees that from 1975 onwards unemployment due to market imperfections is about half of total unemployment, and it increases steadily in the course of time. According to the Ministerie of Social Zaken (1982) U^* decreased since 1979. However, this is a result of a cyclical downswing. Van den Berg (1982) explicitly eliminated cyclical influences, which is consistent with equation (7.13). Hence we will use his results.

(c) Components of Unemployment in the Netherlands

We demonstrated above that the estimated values of E^c and E^* are quite robust with respect to the underlying vintage models and employment functions. In our view, this justifies the use of these estimates in our analytical framework in order to get an impression of the magnitude of the several components of unemployment. The results are presented in Figure 7.6. Obviously, this is a first approximation, lacking a consistent model.[23]

Figure 7.6 The Netherlands: employment and unemployment (1966–81)

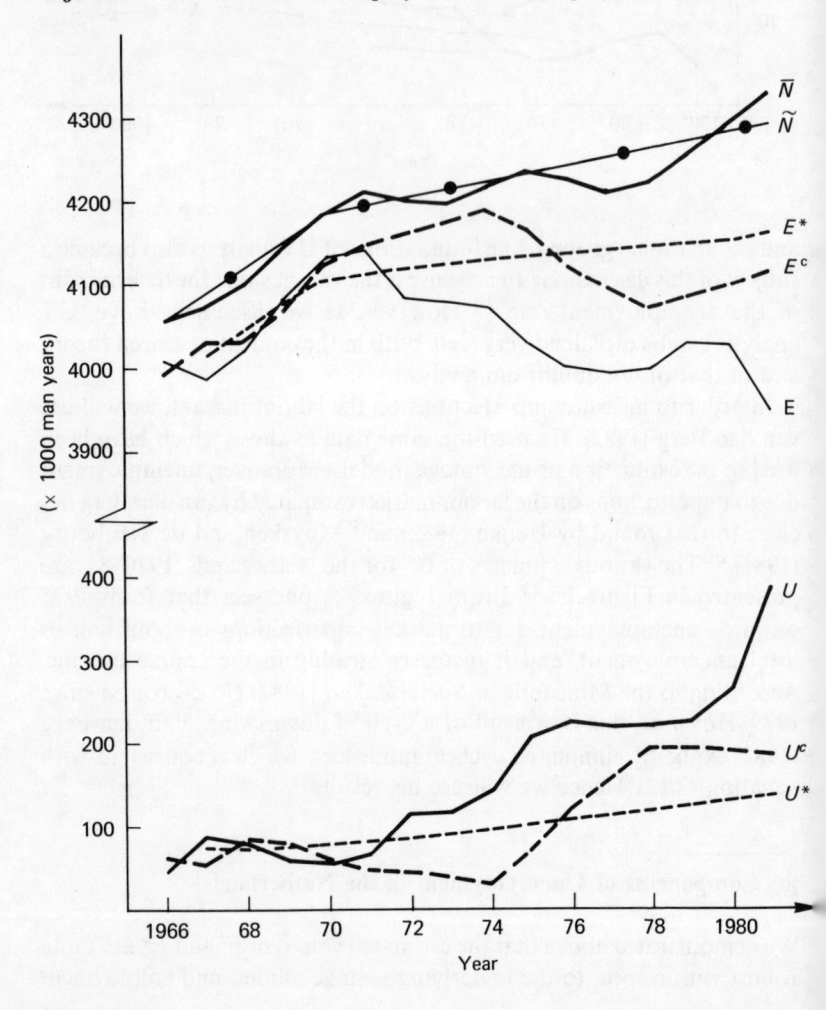

From Figure 7.6 one sees that employment at full-capacity utilisation increases steadily in the period 1966–74. Actual employment, however, declines from 1971 onwards. A similar development occurs in employment at full-capacity utilisation after 1974. The subsequent fall in both in E and in E^c coincides with a sharp decline in capacity demand for labour. Next to cyclical influences, structural influences therefore also play an important role in the period 1971–8. The recovery of capacity demand for labour in the period 1976–81 first induces stabilisation and even some recovery in employment. However, employment falls again in the years 1980–1. This is due to under-utilisation of productive capacity, since employment at full-capacity continues to increase.

The development of cyclical unemployment is related to the development described above, and to that of supply of labour. On the average, labour supply increased at 0.24 per cent per year over the period 1970–80. However, in 1978 the growth in labour supply accelerated: from that year, the average growth rate was 1 per cent. This increase in growth rate cannot be ascribed to cyclical influences, whereas the fall in labour supply behind its trend in the years 1976–9 probably is of a cyclical nature. For that reason, the level of cyclical unemployment is low in the period 1976–9. It increases in 1980 and 1981, partly as a result of decreased utilisation of productive capacity. Under-utilisation of productive capacity – although to a lesser extent – also explains cyclical unemployment in the period 1971–5. Finally, the years 1966–70 are characterised by a small level of negative cyclical unemployment, mainly due to a cyclical fall in labour supply.[24]

Unemployment due to market imperfections increases steadily from 75 000 man years in 1967 to 133 000 in 1981. As a consequence of the decrease in employment at full-capacity utilisation in the mid-1970s, which did not recover sufficiently in the late 1970s, structural unemployment is not only due to market imperfections: since 1976 it is complemented by quantitative structural unemployment. As a consequence structural unemployment increases from 60 000 man years in 1974 to 200 000 in 1978, and stabilises itself at that level till 1981.

Finally, in order to get a complete picture of under-utilisation of labour, data on unemployment should be complemented with data on labour hoarding. As we discussed above (p. 234), labour hoarding is high in the periods 1967–71 and 1979–80, which are characterised by a low rate of capacity utilisation. The high levels of labour hoarding in the late 1970s are also caused by the decline in employment.

The several components of unemployment are summarised in Table 7.3, together with data on labour hoarding. We stress again the

Table 7.3 Components of unemployment and labour hoarding: the Netherlands (1967–81)

| | | | Unemployment | | |
| | | | | Structural | Labour |
Year	Total	Cyclical	Quantitative	Imperfections	hoarding
1967	87	33	−21	75	292
68	80	−5	11	74	236
69	62	−18	5	75	230
70	55	−5	−20	80	189
71	69	22	−35	82	209
72	115	71	−41	85	133
73	117	78	−52	91	42
74	143	109	−62	96	−5
75	206	136	−31	101	182
76	224	102	14	108	102
77	218	61	44	113	142
78	221	30	72	119	208
79	225	33	68	124	266
80	263	77	54	132	326
81	380	203	44	133	

tentative nature of this sub-division of unemployment, since the results of different empirical studies have been combined.

CONCLUDING REMARKS

We developed a consistent analytical framework to analyse underutilisation of labour, given labour supply. Labour hoarding and unemployment are analysed simultaneously, together with the decomposition of unemployment in several components. These components are summarised in Table 7.2, where we distinguish between cyclical and structural unemployment – either caused by labour market imperfections or by deficient capacity demand for labour. The centrepiece of our analysis is the employment function. This function enables us to estimate unemployment due to imperfections on the labour market by equating U and V. Moreover, this function enables us to derive employment at full-capacity operation from capacity demand for labour, which is derived using a vintage model. As a consequence, cyclical unemployment and unemployment due to deficient capacity demand for labour can be distinguished. Moreover, labour hoarding can be measured. Hence the combination of a vintage model and an employment function provides a fruitful analytical framework.

Several vintage models have been estimated for the Netherlands. However, the employment functions used in these models have always been rather crude, for computational reasons. Since the estimation of a vintage model together with an elaborate employment function falls outside the scope of the present analysis – it is a matter for further research – we combined the results of different empirical studies in our framework in order to get an impression of the under-utilisation of labour. The result is presented in Table 7.3.

Although our analytical framework provides a better decomposition of unemployment than that of the Central Planning Bureau in the mid-1970s, an important lacuna remains: the explanation of supply of labour. Whereas demand for labour is explained from vintage analysis and the interaction of demand and supply from the employment function, supply of labour should be explained in a similar way. The integration of such an explanation in our analytical framework would make the analysis of under-utilisation of labour complete.

Appendix

The data used in this chapter are presented in Table A7.1

$\tilde{N}$ Structural labour supply. 1965–9 yearly growth of 0.79 per cent from $\tilde{N}_{1965}$; 1970–81 yearly growth of 0.23 per cent from $\tilde{N}_{1970}$.

$\bar{N}$ Labour supply in manufacturing (*CEP*, 1981, Annex C1).

N Demand for labour in manufacturing ($E+V$).

E Employment in manufacturing (*CEP*, 1981, Annex C1).

E^c Capacity demand for labour calculated according to $E^c = 0.199\,N^c + 0.806\,E_{-1}$ for the period 1966–70 and $E^c = 0.199\,N^c + 0.806\,E^c_{-1}$ for the period 1971–81.

E^* Employment consistent with structural imperfections on the labour market ($\tilde{N} - U^*$).

q^* Rate of capacity utilisation (Kuipers and van Zon, 1982).

N_{kz} Capacity demand for labour (Kuipers and van Zon, 1982).

N_{kms} Capacity demand for labour (Kuipers, Muysken and van Sinderen, 1978). From 1977, corrected on the difference $E_{cep} - E_{kms}$.

N_{ht} Capacity demand for labour (den Hartog and Tjan, 1980, Appendix 9.14 – and for N^c/N after 1973 Table 8.3 and Figure 8.1). From these data we subtracted 350.

U Unemployment ($N-E$).

U^* Due to imperfections on the labour market. Data on U^*/U from van den Berg, 1982, Table 5.

U^c Due to a shortage of capacity demand for labour ($N - E^c$).

U' Cyclical unemployment ($N - E - N + E^c$).

U^*_{mnb} U^*/U from van den Burg *et al.*, 1982; Table 3. U^*/U, both excluding disabled persons.

U^c_{cpb} U^c from *CPB* (1983), see also Table 7.1, p. 221 above.

V Vacancies (van den Berg, 1982).

Table A7.1 Data for Chapter 7

	$\tilde{\tilde{N}}$	$\tilde{N}$	N	E	E^c	E^*	q^*	N^c_{kz}	N^c_{kms}	N^c_{ht}	U	U^*	U^c	U'	U^*_{mnb}	U^c_{cpb}	V
1966	4054	4055	4009	4009	3992	0	0	3916	0	4154	46	0	62	−16	0	0	0
67	4086	4073	4054	3986	4032	4011	0.935	4023	0	4159	87	75	54	33	0	0	68
68	4118	4101	4098	4021	4033	4044	0.937	4122	0	4103	80	74	85	−5	0	0	77
69	4151	4145	4189	4083	4071	4076	0.949	4172	0	4142	62	75	80	−18	0	0	106
70	4184	4184	4256	4129	4124	4104	0.972	4184	4151	4123	55	80	60	−5	106	81	127
71	4194	4209	4247	4140	4147	4112	0.976	4137	4118	4111	69	82	47	22	110	79	107
72	4203	4197	4145	4082	4159	4118	0.978	4102	4046	4111	115	85	44	71	102	105	63
73	4213	4195	4145	4078	4174	4122	0.993	4132	3988	4102	117	91	39	78	118	107	67
?4	4222	4213	4139	4070	4188	4126	1.001	4140	3953	4074	143	96	34	109	125	118	69
75	4232	4232	4073	4026	4162	4131	0.985	3950	3863	3970	206	101	70	136	139	132	47
76	4242	4223	4046	3999	4120	4134	1.026	3844	3808	3955	224	108	122	102	151	160	47
77	4251	4209	4046	3991	4094	4138	1.004	3885	3874	3979	218	113	157	61	147	0	55
78	4261	4220	4062	3999	4070	4142	0.995	3873	3947	4069	221	119	191	30	158	0	63
79	4271	4254	4097	4029	4079	4147	0.955	4011	4017	4177	225	124	192	33	149	0	68
80	4281	4208	4078	4025	4095	4149	0.925	4056	4038	0	263	132	186	77	166	0	53
81	4291	4328	3969	3948	4114	4158	0	4090	3980	0	380	133	177	203	228	0	21

Notes

1. This chapter is a revised version of 'Structurele en conjuncturele werkloosheid' which appeared in *Maandschrift Economie* (1984), pp. 193–217.
2. See, for instance, *Ministerie van Sociale Zaken* (1975), p. 16 and *MEV* (1974) p. 58.
3. This is elaborated in Kooiman and Kloek (1979), who use the 'aggregation by integration' method of Muellbauer (1978). They assume that the distribution on sub-markets on the labour market is log normal in demand on and supply of labour. Aggregation then yields the following employment function:

$$E = \phi \cdot \bar{N} + (1-\phi)N - \delta \cdot \tfrac{1}{2}(\bar{N}+N) \quad 0 < \phi < 1$$

here δ is a friction parameter. The values of ϕ and δ depend on $\ln N/\bar{N}$ and on δ_f, the variance of the distribution.
4. This is elaborated in Kreijger (1981), who postulates that the period of being employed is exponential distributed with mean λ, and search time is exponential distributed with mean μ. λ is assumed to vary positive with $N/\bar{N}$ and μ negative. Assuming steady growth, Kreijger then derives the following employment function:

$$\ln\left(\frac{N}{\bar{E}} - 1\right) = \alpha + \beta \ln \frac{N}{\bar{N}} + \gamma \cdot t$$

5. In Muysken and de Neubourg (1981) and van den Burg *et al.* (1982) we measure frictions on the Dutch labour market for the period 1955–79. We distinguish between sub-markets with respect to both occupational groups and regions and measured frictions between and within these sub-markets. Our conclusion was that frictions are concentrated for the largest part within sub-markets (see also van den Burg *et al* (1982)).
6. See the vintage models discussed on p. 231, see also Hansen (1970) and Sneesens (1983).
7. The analysis can also be presented when U and V are related to labour force, but our choice seems more appropriate, since we see no reason why V should be related to $\bar{N}$.
8. See the models discussed on p. 234.
9. One might assume that γ varies in a negative way with q. For instance, when desired demand is $\theta \cdot qN^c + (1-\theta) \cdot N^c$, then:

$$\gamma = \theta + (1-\theta)/q.$$

This equation is used in Kuipers, Muysken and van Sinderen (1979) and in *CPB* (1983).
10. Both have a cyclical component (which will be measured under cyclical unemployment), and a structural component (which probably will be measured under unemployment due to market imperfections).
11. In Figure 7.3 we do not distinguish between N and $\bar{N}$.
12. The data used in the estimation of the model were not published at the time of writing this article. In Muysken and Meijers (1986), the analysis is performed using the data and results of the FREIA model.

13. A similar model has been published in Kuipers, Muysken and van Sinderen (1979).
14. *KMS* has been estimated for the period 1959–76 and predicts the period 1977–81, *HT* has been estimated for the period 1959–73 and predicts the period 1977–81, and *KZ* has been estimated for the period 1950–77 and predicts the period 1978–80.
15. The data are presented in the Appendix.
16. In these vintage models employment functions are used for estimation purposes. For a given set of parameters of the model the vintage models generate data on X^c and N^c, whereas data are available on X and E. That set of parameters is chosen which minimises some relationship between X and X^c on the one hand, mostly $\Sigma_t(q_t - 1)^2$, and between N^c and E on the other. In the latter case, an employment function is assumed of which the residuals – corresponding to least squares estimation using generated data on N^c – are to be minimised.
17. Unfortunately we were not able to find satisfactory results, when estimating equation (7.23) for the data of *KZ*.
18. Heijke (1982, pp. 232–6) uses the following employment function:

$$E = (N^{-\lambda} + N^{-\lambda})^{-1/\lambda}$$

19. For a summary, see Bewley (1979).
20. Holden and Peel (1975, p. 251). Warren (1977), Parikh (1977) and Bewley (1979) commented on this.
21. Muysken and De Neubourg (1981) find consistently a higher value of U^*. This is due to the use of different data – excluding, for instance, unemployment of disabled persons.
22. The data are presented in the Appendix. One should realise that the registration of vacancies – and that of unemployment, too – is far from perfect (Muysken and de Neubourg, 1981, pp. 3–4). For that reason the data on U^* should be interpreted with care.
23. The construction and estimation of such a model has a high priority in our research.
24. These estimations of cyclical unemployment exceed those of the Central Planning Bureau, presented in Table 7.1. The reason is that the Central Planning Bureau estimates cyclical unemployment by fitting a trend to actual unemployment – allowing for some influence of the utilisation rate, whereas *KZ* estimate capacity demand for labour and the corresponding employment.

References

AZARIDES, C. (1975) 'Implicit contracts and underemployment equilibria', *Journal of Political Economy* 83.
BAILEY, M. N. (1976) Contract theory and the moderation of inflation by recession and by controls', *Brookings Papers on Economic Activity*.

VAN DEN BERG, D. J. (1982) 'The specification and the estimation of the unemployment vacancy curve, in the period 1956–1979', *De Economist* 130, pp. 397–420.

BEWLEY, R. A. (1979) 'The dynamic behaviour of unemployment and unfilled vacancies in Great Britain: 1958–1971', *Applied Economics* 11, pp. 303–8.

BOWERS, J. K., CHESIRE, P. C. and WEBB, A. E. (1970) 'The change in the relationship between unemployment and earnings increases: a review of some possible explanations', *National Institute Economic Review* pp. 44–63.

BROWN, A. J. (1975) 'UV analysis', in Worswick, G. D. N. (ed.), *The Concept and Measurement on Involuntary Unemployment* (London: Allen & Unwin) pp. 134–45.

VAN DER BURG, H., KUIPERS, S. K., MUYSKEN, J. and DE NEUBOURG, C. (1982) *The Volume and Composition of Structural Employment in the Netherlands, 1950–1980* (The Hague, NPAO).

CPB (Centraal Planbureau) FREIA (1983) (The Hague).

CEP Centraal economisch plan (The Hague: Centraal Planbureau).

DRIEHUIS, W. (1978) 'Labour market imbalances and structural unemployment', *Kyklos* 31 (4), pp. 638–61.

FORSTER, J. I. (1973) 'The behaviour of unemployment and unfilled vacancies: Great Britain 1958–1971, A Comment', *Economic Journal* 83.

GUJARITI, D. (1972) 'The behaviour of unemployment and unfilled vacancies: Great Britain: 1958–1971', *Economic Journal* 82, pp. 195–204.

HANSEN, B. (1970) 'Excess demand, unemployment, vacancies and wages', *Quarterly Journal of Economics* 84, pp. 1–23.

HARPER, I. R. (1980) 'The relationship between unemployment and unfilled vacancies in Australia, 1952–1978', *Economic Record* 56, pp. 231–43.

HARTOG, J. (1980) *Tussen vraag en aanbod* (Leiden: Stenfert Kroese).

DEN HARTOG, H. and TJAN, H. S. (1976) 'Investment, wages, prices and demand for labour', *De Economist* 124, pp. 32–55.

────── (1980) 'A clay-clay vintage model approach for sectors of industry in the Netherlands', *De Economist* 128, pp. 129–88.

HEIJKE, J. A. M. (1982) 'Arbeidsallocatie en loonstructuur', in: WRR *De wisselwerking tussen schaarsteverhoudingen en beloningsstructuur* (The Hague) pp. 207–308.

HOLDEN, K. and PEEL, D. A. (1975) 'The determinants of unemployment and the UV relationship', *Applied Economics* 7.

HOLT, C. C. (1970) 'Job search, Phillips' wage relation and union influence: theory and evidence', in Phelps, E. S. *et al. Micro Foundations of Employment and Inflation* (London: Macmillan) pp. 53–124.

KOOIMAN, P. and KLOEK, T. (1979) 'Aggregation of micro markets in disequilibrium', paper presented at ESEM 1979 (Rotterdam: ESEM).

KREIJGER, R. J. (1981) *UV analysis, labour demand and supply: an integrated approach*; Report AE 5 (Amsterdam: Faculty of actuarial science and econometrics).

KUIPERS, S. K. and BUDDENBERG, F. H. (1978) 'Unemployment on account of market imperfections in the Netherlands since the second wrld war', *De Economist* 126(3), pp. 380–412.

────── MUYSKEN, J. and VAN SINDEREN, J. (1978) 'De werkgelegenheidsontwikkeling in Nederland sinds 1970: een nadere analyse', *ESB* pp. 648–510

——— MUYSKEN, J. and VAN SINDEREN, J. (1979) 'The Vintage Approach to Output and Employment Growth in the Netherlands, 1921–1976', *Weltwirtschaftliches Archiv* 115(3), pp. 485–507.
——— and VAN ZON, A. H. (1982) 'Output and employment growth in the Netherlands in the postwar period: a putty-clay approach', *De Economist* 130(1), pp. 38–70.
LENDERINK, R. S. and SIEBRAND, J. C. (1976) *A disequilibrium analysis of the labour market* (Rotterdam: University Press).
MEV Macro Ekonomische Verkenning (The Hague: Centraal Planbureau).
Ministerie van Sociale Zaken (1975) Nota inzake de werkgelegenheid (The Hague).
——— (1978) Rapportage arbeidsmarkt (The Hague).
——— (1982) Rapportage arbeidsmarkt (The Hague).
MUELLBAUER, J. (1978) 'Macrotheory *vs.* macroeconomics: the treatment of "disequilibri'm" in macro models', paper presented at ESEM (Geneva: ESEM).
MUYSKEN, J. and DE NEUBOURG, C. R. J. (1981) 'Qualitative structural unemployment in the Netherlands, 1955–1979', Memorandum from the Institute of Economic Research 75 (Groningen).
———DE NEUBOURG, C. R. J. and VAN DER BURG, H. (1982) Regional and occupational labourmarket imperfections, the Netherlands 1955–1980, Memorandum from the Institute of Economic Research 105 (Groningen).
——— and MEIJERS, H. (1986) 'Conjunctuur en structuur werkloosheid in Nederland 1970–1985', working paper no. 86005 (Maastricht: University of Limburg).
PARIKH, A. (1977) The relation between unemployment and vacancies: a comment, *Applied Economics*, 9, pp. 77–90.
PHELPS, E. S. (1970) 'Money wage dynamics and labour market equilibrium', in Phelps, E. S. et al. *Micro Foundations of Employment and Inflation* (London: Macmillan).
SNEESENS, H. T. (1983) 'A macroeconomic rationing model of the Belgian economy, *European Economic Review* 20, pp. 193–215.
TAYLOR, J. (1982) The behaviour of unemployment and unfilled vacancies: Great Britain, 1958–71: an alternative view', *Economic Journal* 92, pp. 1352–65.
WARREN, R. S. (1977) 'The behaviour of unemployment and unfilled vacancies in Great Britain, a search-turnover view', *Applied Economics* 9, pp. 237–42.

8 Aggregate Unemployment and Labour Slack as Indices of Labour Utilisation

Chris de Neubourg[1]

Although in previous studies I preferred the use of multiple indicators to analyse the situation in the labour market and a thorough study of 'the dough, the doughnut and the hole' (de Neubourg, 1983, 1985), it makes sense to investigate whether the actual statistical apparatus allows the construction of a single indicator of the degree of non-utilisation of labour resources, that (partly) avoids the shortcomings of the traditional unemployment rate. This chapter defines a method to measure 'aggregate labour slack' on the basis of detailed labour market accounts and applies it to the post-1973 data for five countries. The estimates take into account the non-utilised labour capacity due to unemployment, due to changes of the number of hours actually worked and due to changes in registered labour force participation. This exercise does not imply that the application of other indicators – including the traditional ones – is not useful. It should rather be seen as the recognition that a single indicator is sometimes needed in econometric modelling, forecasting and policy evaluation; moreover the aestheticism of summary statistics is appealing.

The first section summarises the shortcomings of the traditionally used unemployment estimates and uses this information to formulate the prerequisites for the labour slack definition. Definitions previously met in the literature are discussed in the second Section, while the third Section explains the proposed labour slack measure and its components. Its empirical application based on the labour market accounts for five countries – Canada, Germany, the Netherlands, Sweden and the United States – is the content of Section four. A concluding Section is finally added.

SHORTCOMINGS OF THE UNEMPLOYMENT RATE AS GUIDELINES FOR THE DEFINITION OF AGGREGATE LABOUR SLACK

A critical appraisal of the traditional concepts – labour force, employment and unemployment – reveals that four major shortcomings are relevant in this context (see de Neubourg, 1983, 1985):

1. The net effect of the discouraged worker effect, the additional worker effect and related registration effects, affects the size of the registered labour force; consequently cyclical movements in the unemployment rate (with a cyclically varying 'labour force' in the denominator) are no longer the sole product of variations in the share of unemployed in the labour force; this diminishes the reliability of the unemployment rate as a cyclical indicator.
2. Labour hoarding and dishoarding are not reflected in the unemployment rate since the latter is expressed in persons: a cyclical bias of the unemployment rate results.
3. Differences in the impact of legislation and government policy upon the labour force and the number of unemployed introduce problems of intertemporal and international comparability.
4. Significant changes in the real number of hours worked and in the share of part-time workers are masked when labour force and (un-)employment are measured in persons, and therefore the unemployment rate underestimates real labour slack.

A ratio – which permits consistent comparison of the degree of nonutilisation of labour resources over time – requires an adequate measurement of the population at working age which offers labour services to the economy. Two reasons can be given why the difference between the registered labour force and the sum of the individuals supplying labour is too much influenced by economic changes – such as cyclical fluctuations or economic growth – to use the measured labour force as a reliable estimate of the 'labour market relevant population'. The first reason is especially relevant for short-term fluctuations; the second for the evaluation of long-term changes. First, the cyclical 'enter and quit' behaviour of the population at working age – reflected by the discouraged worker effect and the additional worker effect – results in the exclusion from the registered labour force of a notable part of the population that offers (sometimes) labour services to the economy.

Second, persistent and significant changes in labour force participation rates occur, induced by long-term economic and social changes. New entrants (or re-entrants) become thus increasingly important and enlarge the gap between the real and the registered labour force (Sorrentino, 1978). Both observations lead to the conclusion that the 'labour market relevant population' (= the number of people that, under certain conditions, supply labour) is significantly higher than the registered labour force. The measurement of labour force attachment by some kind of active behaviour (working or looking for a job) seems to be a very poor demarcation criterion. Empirical research in the United States shows, for example, that a sixth of the persons *not* in the labour force during the last quarter of 1975 worked for some time during the preceding 12 months; over the same period nearly 10 per cent of the population not counted as belonging to the labour force reported that they wanted jobs but did not look for them for a variety of reasons (including discouragement over job prospects – Shiskin, 1976). The results of a (United States) 'Work Experience Report' indicate a growing attachment to the labour force by many so-called secondary workers (Gastwirth, 1973). Mincer (1973) reports that by far the larger part of new job holders (entrants and re-entrants) comes from outside the official labour reserve, and that the available labour reserve is, therefore, much larger than the official estimate.

The same conclusions can be drawn from similar data for the other countries. In Germany, for example, employment diminished by 1.7 million during the recession of 1974–7, while unemployment rose 'only' by 900 000; after corrections are made for net emigration and changes in the age structure of the population at working age, more than half a million of persons dropped out of the registered labour force during that period. Quite the reverse could be observed during the relatively prosperous years 1978 and 1979 – employment increased by half a million while registered unemployment declined by 150 000 persons; after corrections for demographical changes are made, 60 000 individuals, who did not belong to the registered labour force, are said to re-enter employment (Autorengemeinschaft, 1979; Klauder, 1982).

These theoretical and empirical observations lead to the first requirement to be met by a new labour slack estimate: the *span of the definition* should stretch beyond the traditional labour force count, and should take the *entire labour market relevant population* into account. In previous studies it is extensively argued that estimates of the volume of the effects described above are unreliable – those based on surveys as well as those based on econometric modelling (de Neubourg, 1983, 1985; Mincer, 1973; Gastwirth, 1973).

The only way to deal with this part of the apparent labour capacity is by not excluding it *a priori* from the analysis, and to start with a demographic concept of labour supply rather than with a defective behavioural definition of who 'belongs' to the labour force. There exists an additional reason why a demographic concept of labour supply is to be preferred above the traditional labour force definition. Many governments – faced with mass unemployment in the late 1970s and the early 1980s, adopted policies to stimulate people to withdraw from the registered labour force by stimulating emigration, by promoting early retirement, by prolonging the stay of young people in education and training, or by restricting the registration of older unemployed workers. In some countries, people are discouraged to enter the workforce by raising income taxes for some groups of workers. One of these policy measures (or a combination of them) are applied in Belgium, France, Germany, the Netherlands and Sweden. It is clear that these policies by no means improve the utilisation of labour resources, although the traditional (and official) unemployment rate suggests they do. A labour slack estimate based on a demographic definition avoids this kind of statistical delusion.

The second major requirement to be fulfilled by a new labour slack estimate relates to the *units of measurement*. The unemployment rate is expressed in persons, and is therefore unable to account for major shifts in the *average actual hours worked per person per year*. From empirical investigations, it is known that the yearly hours actually worked per person declined drastically in the post-1945 period. Moreover, time actually spent on the job decreased more rapidly during the 1970s and the early 1980s, since many governments used work-sharing by means of longer holidays, shorter work weeks and more part-time employment to divert labour slack into channels other than overt unemployment (Maddison, 1980; de Neubourg, 1984; de Neubourg and Kok, 1984). Since work-sharing cannot be seen as an amelioration of the aggregate utilisation of labour capacity, but should rather be interpreted (at best) as a redistribution of the non-utilisation, a reliable labour slack estimate should account for these changes. This can be done only if the labour slack estimate is expressed in hours. After a brief review of labour slack estimates found in the literature, these two major requirements will be translated into an operational definition.

LABOUR SLACK ESTIMATES IN THE LITERATURE

Earlier work on alternative definitions of the degree of non-utilisation of labour resources discusses mainly adjustments to the traditional concepts.[2] Either the suggested adjustments try to account for changes in the yearly hours worked, or they try to extend their range of observation beyond the registered labour force. The time weighted unemployment rate (Hitch, 1951; Lebergott, 1954; Perry, 1970), the full-time equivalent unemployment rate (Bancroft, 1962) and the labour force time lost (Bancroft, 1962; Gilroy, 1975) belong to the first category; the unemployment rate adjusted for discouragement (Gastwirth, 1973; Mincer, 1973) and the employment population ratio (Moore, 1973) form the second.

Earlier efforts to use broader measures of labour slack on lines similar to the approach developed by Maddison (1980) and Granier and Maddison (1982) are found in Gordon (1970), Taylor (1974) and Lal (1977). The discussion in this Section, however, is confined to the important contributions of various authors of the German 'Institut für Arbeitsmarkt- und Berufsforschung' and to the other labour slack definitions that meet the two requirements, set in the previous section, simultaneously.

The 'Institut für Arbeitsmarkt- und Berufsforschung' (IAB) has paid attention very early to the definition and measurement of the potential labour force, the potential labour resources and the degree of utilisation of both ('Auslastung des potentiellen Arbeitsvolumens') (see, for example, Autorengemeinschaft Institut für Arbeitsmarkt- und Berufsforschung). It developed labour market accounts to provide the basic data for its estimates (see, for example, Autorengemeinschaft Institut für Arbeitsmarkt- und Berufsforschung; Reyher and Bach, 1980). In this context, however, its contributions to the definition and measurement of the concept 'potential labour resources' are highly relevant. The potential labour force is defined as the sum of the employed, the unemployed (together the registered labour force) and what is called the 'Stille Reserve' ('hidden reserve'); the definition and the estimate of the latter concept is especially interesting when labour slack estimates are studied. The 'Stille Reserve' is said to estimate that part of the population that does not belong to the registered labour force, but that would supply labour to the economy when no constraints were met. The concept is assumed to take the net effect of the discouraged worker effect and the additional worker effect and other types of hidden unemployment into account.

Operationally the potential labour force is measured by a trend extrapolation of the aggregate labour force during the prosperous years 1961–5 and 1970, corrected for changes in the sex–age structure of the population, for changes in sex and age specific participation rates and for 'special influences' ('Sondereinflüsse' – for details see Klauder and Kühlewind, 1980). The 'Stille Reserve' is then defined as the difference between the calculated potential labour force and the registered labour force. Transformation of the data calculated with persons as units of measurement into potential labour resources measured in hours is done by multiplying the count in persons by the 'average potential yearly working time per worker'.

Once the average *actual* yearly working time per person is known, the degree of utilisation – and, complementarily – the degree of non-utilisation of the potential labour capacity – hence labour slack – can easily be calculated.

Table 8.1 compares the degree of utilisation measured in persons and in hours (columns 1 and 2) and the degree of non-utilisation in persons and in hours (columns 3 and 4) with the official unemployment rate (1970–83). From Table 8.1 it can be seen that the estimate of the labour slack given in the column is systematically higher than the official unemployment rate; this effect can be attributed to the effect of the fact that the 'Stille Reserve' is taken into account (column 3), and to the gap between the number of hours potentially available and those actually worked.

Table 8.1   Germany: utilisation of labour capacity (1970–81) (definitions IAB)

	Utilisation in persons	Utilisation in hours	Non-utilisation in persons	Non-Utilisation in hours	Unemployment rate
1970	99.4	98.3	0.6	1.7	0.7
71	99.0	97.5	1.0	2.5	0.8
72	98.6	96.8	1.4	3.2	1.1
73	98.4	96.0	1.6	4.0	1.2
74	97.1	94.1	2.9	5.9	2.6
75	94.2	90.8	5.8	9.2	4.7
76	93.9	90.8	6.1	9.2	4.6
77	93.8	90.5	6.2	9.5	4.5
78	94.1	90.5	5.9	9.5	4.3
79	94.6	91.1	5.4	8.9	3.8
80	94.4	90.7	5.6	9.3	3.8
81	91.8	87.2	8.2	12.8	5.5

Source: Autorengemeinschaft (1981).

Although the method developed by the IAB meets the basic requirements formulated in the previous section, its application may be criticised on four points.

In the first place the peak-to-peak extrapolation used to estimate the 'Stille Reserve' raises some difficulties when long-lasting recessions are met. More specifically, no peak can be seen after the last 'Hochkonjunkturjahr' (1970). Consequently, the estimate of the volume of the 'Stille Reserve' relies entirely on the trend extrapolation of the curves between the peak of 1965 and 1970. As the distance between the year of the last peak and the observation year grows, the estimate of the 'Stille Reserve' risks becoming more unreliable, a problem increased by social and economic changes induced by the recession itself and affecting the age and sex specific participation rates structurally.[3] A second problem with the labour slack estimate of the IAB relates to long-term changes in the participation rates of quantitatively important subgroups of the population. Since the definition of the 'Stille Reserve' takes the labour force participation rate in the prosperous years as the standard, it is implicitly assumed that the participation rate reaches its maximum in those years.

Given the fact that both the aggregate participation rate and the participation rates for various sub-groups of the population change significantly in the longer term (see de Neubourg, 1983), this implicit assumption may be violated and may render the estimate of the 'Stille Reserve' unreliable. Dominant trends in the participation rates of married woman and older male workers in recent decades are especially relevant in this context (though these trends are less outspoken in Germany than in other countries – de Neubourg, 1983). The more important these trends are, the more they affect the reliability of the estimates.

The labour slack definition of the IAB cannot account for changes in the government policy (of the type discussed in the previous section), that affect the aggregate labour market participation. Changes in pension plans, in the age or retirement and in the school-leaving age are important in this respect. These changes have proved to be important in recent years.

The calculation of the impact of the discrepancy between the IAB estimates of the number of hours potentially available and the number of hours actually worked, finally, may be criticised on theoretical grounds (although both basic quantities are estimated very carefully – see Reyher et al., 1983 for details). The difference between the two estimates can be attributed to various factors that diminish the number of hours actually worked (including absence from the job, holidays and changes in the number of part-time workers). However, it is theoretically not defensible to regard every decrease of the number of hours actually worked as an economically significant non-utilisation of labour capacity. If this were the case, the utilisation of labour resources would nowadays be half of what it had been about a century ago. Nevertheless, few authors would agree that the utilisation labour capacity during the 1960s was dramatically worse than it was a hundred years ago. This means implicitly that the degree of (non-)utilisation of labour cannot be judged from the gap between the number of hours total available labour resources potentially could have worked and the number of hours actually worked only, since a part of that discrepancy may be due to changes (actually an increase) in labour productivity. Strictly speaking, a decrease in the number of hours actually worked, that is, compensated for by an offsetting increase in labour productivity, should not be regarded as a significant loss of productive capacity. The calculations of the IAB do not take this effect into account, and therefore become troublesome when the period of observation is extended.

Maddison (1980) adopts an approach similar to that of the IAB in order to avoid the under-estimate of unemployment by official figures and to correct them for other dimensions of labour slack. He distinguishes two separate accounts: the monitoring account and the use of potential account. The former estimates the number of hours actually worked in the economy.

The 'use of potential account' builds up an estimate of the total labour slack in an economy by calculating a hypothetical total hours potentially workable and subtracting from it the total hours worked. The total hours potentially workable, in turn, are computed by multiplying the activity rate, the employment ratio and the average number of hours worked per year per employee in 'a normal past year of high economic activity' (Maddison, 1980) with the potential population of working age (which equals an estimate of population of working age in absence of migration restrictions).

By means of the monitoring account and the use of potential account, Maddison estimates the labour slack in France, Germany and the United Kingdom for the period of 1973–8. In 1978, the overall labour slack was about 4 per cent in the United Kingdom, 8.6 per cent in Germany and 7.3 per cent in France. Unemployment in 1978 was 6.1 percent in the United Kingdom, 3.8 per cent in Germany and 5.2 per cent in France.

Granier and Maddison (1982) and Granier (1984) basically use the same approach to calculate a 'ratio of under-utilisation of the 'normal' labour input' ('taux de sous-utilisation de l' input 'normal' de travail'), applying the formula:

$$1-(L_0/L_0') \simeq 1-(E/E')+1-(J/J')+1-(h/h')$$

where:

L_0 = labour input effectively used
E = employment
J = number of days worked per year per employed
h = number of hours worked per day per employed
L_0', E', J' and h' = their non-primed equivalent in a 'normal'
(= high economic activity) year

with E/E', J/J' and $h/h' \geqslant 1$.

The results of Granier and Maddison are similar to those of Maddison (1980): the ratio of under-utilisation of labour input equals 7.3 per cent in 1978 and 8.82 per cent in 1980, indicating that the unemployment rate accounts for respectively 70.15 per cent and 71.09 per cent of total labour slack and sustaining the argument that the unemployment count significantly underestimates the real under-utilisation of labour.

Although the basic ideas of Maddison can be regarded as an important contribution to the development of a labour slack estimate, some reservations have to be made. Generally, the remarks made concerning the IAB estimates apply also to the work of Maddison and Granier. The estimate of labour slack relies heavily on two crucial assumptions: one concerning the effect of the absence of migration restrictions (necessary to calculate the potential population of working age), and the second regarding the arbitrary definition of 'a normal year of high economic activity' (needed to estimate potential labour input). The volume of the estimated labour slack is dependent on the choice of the 'standard year': this is illustrated by the fact that there is no labour slack except unemployment in 1973 by definition because 1973 was chosen as the 'normal' year. Maddison, in fact agrees that his calculations have to be seen as illustrations rather than as models; he invites other researchers to apply more sophistication, more detail and different judgements about what constitutes 'full employment'. The integration of his proposal into a wider system of sociodemographic monitoring would allow more sophistication in calculating the 'standard available labour resources'. This standard is crucial in the estimate of which part of the resources are left unused. Moreover, more specific insight should be sought in order to determine where and how exactly this part is lost.

THE DEFINITION OF LABOUR SLACK

In order to fulfil the two requirements specified in the first Section, the definition of a labour slack estimate should take the fact that the labour market relevant population is significant larger than the registered labour force into account. On the other hand it should be defined in hours as units of measurement. The solutions to the first requirement chosen by the IAB and by Maddison and Granier are not really satisfactorily, because the definitions of the total labour resources depend in both cases on the definition of 'full employment years' ('Hochkonjunkturjahre'). The resulting labour slack estimate therefore risks becoming based partly on arbitrary judgement; moreover, it cannot account for long-term changes in the labour force participation rates.

The second requirement is not a problem by itself, but the interpretation of the discrepancy between the amount of hours that potentially could have been worked in a certain year and to the amount of hours that actually has been worked, introduces some problems related to the fact that the non-utilisation of hours directly compensated for by a rise in labour productivity should not be interpreted as an economically relevant form of labour slack. The definition proposed in this chapter solves these matters in a specific way.

The first element to be defined can be described as the 'actually available labour resources' (abridged further as AALT, where T stands for 'time' to indicate that the units of measurement are hours). In order to avoid the arbitrariness of the solutions chosen by the IAB and Maddison, a demographic definition of the available labour resources (LR) is preferred. This implies that all persons over a certain age (16 years) are supposed to form the labour resources potentially available for the economy, except those following full-time education, those who are disabled and those who are staying in institutions for mental or penal reasons. Since in most European countries people aged 65 and over are supposed to retire entirely (and in practice do retire), this category of persons is also deducted from the total labour resources.

LR (labour resources – in persons) is thus defined as the population aged 16 years and over minus the full-time students, the disabled, the institutional population and the retired persons aged 65 and over.[4] LR is the equivalent of the registered labour force, defined traditionally as the sum of employed and unemployed workers and indicated in this context as RLR which stands for 'registered labour resources'. The multiplication of LR with the 'average annual contractual working time per full-time worker ($FAACWT$) defines the volume of 'actually available labour resources' – AALT.

The non-utilised labour resources (or the absolute volume of labour slack expressed in number of hours) is the next element to be defined. Consistent with what has been argued previously, the labour slack in hours (LST) is composed of three major parts: the non-utilised labour resources due to unemployment ($NULT^u$), the non-utilised labour resources due to non-participation ($NULT^p$) and the non-utilised labour resources due to changes in the average annual actual working time per worker ($NULT^h$) ($AAAWT$).

$NULT^u$ can easily be defined as the multiplication of the number of unemployed by the average annual contractual working time per full-time worker ($FAACWT$). Since the calculation of the labour slack estimate is based on the detailed labour market accounts developed in previous research (de Neubourg, 1983), and since these accounts are also calculated in hours, the amount of $NULT^u$ – can be derived directly from these accounts: this applies to most of the definitions discussed in this Section (see also Appendix A8.1). The non-utilised labour resources due to non-participation ($NULT^p$) is defined as the labour resources (in hours) left unused by the non-active members of the labour resources (LR); this implies the labour resources left unused for other reasons than full-time education, disablement, retirement over the age of 65 and institutional exclusion from active life.

The definition of the non-utilised labour resources due to changes in the average annual working time per worker is somewhat more complicated ($NULT^h$ and $AAAWT$). The latter component ($AAAWT$) measures the average annual time of all workers actually spend at their jobs. This means that the theoretical yearly working time is corrected for free Saturdays and Sundays, holidays and vacations, time lost due to other reasons for absence from the job (bad weather, illness, industrial disputes, personal and other reasons) and the number of part-time workers and their average annual theoretical working time. This implies that the sum of the non-utilised labour resources due to changes in the $AAAWT$ (= $NULT^h$) consists of three components: the non-utilised labour resources (in hours) due to absence from work ($NULT^a$), the non-utilised labour resources due to part-time work ($NULT^{pt}$) and the non-utilised labour resources due to changes in the $FAACWT$ ($NULT^s$). The latter, in turn, is defined as the difference between the total number of hours contractually supplied by all full-time workers and the total number of hours that full-time workers would have supplied contractually if $FAACWT$ in year $t = FAACWT$ in year $t-1$.

As has been argued previously, not every decline in the total number of hours actually worked can be regarded as an economic loss of productive labour capacity (if this line, nevertheless, were defended, it would be logical to define the total available labour resources as the number of people available for work multiplied by 24 hours a day). A good deal of the decline in the total number of hours worked can be attributed to a significant increase in labour productivity. In order to avoid an overestimation of the labour resources time lost due to shorter working hours, $NULT^h$ should be corrected for changes in productivity. In the definition of labour slack presented here, this is done by subtracting the annual percentage change in labour productivity from the annual percentage change in $NULT^h$. Labour productivity is defined as GDP/ULT, where ULT stands for utilised labour resources (in hours) – measured, in turn, by the product of the employed persons and $AAAWT$.

Labour slack time can now be defined by means of the components described above as:

$$LST = NULT^u + NULT^p + (NULT^h_{t-1} + (NULT^h_t - NULT^h_{t-1})$$
$$\left[\frac{\left(\frac{NULT^h_t - NULT^h_{t-1}}{NULT^h_{t-1}} \cdot 100\right) - \left(\frac{GDP_t/ULT_t - GDP_{t-1}/ULT_{t-1}}{GDP_{t-1}/ULT_{t-1}} \cdot 100\right)}{\left(\frac{NULT^h_t - NULTH^h_{t-1}}{NULT^h_{t-1}} \cdot 100\right)} \right]$$

To express the total volume of labour slack as a percentage of the actually available labour resources, LST should be divided by $AALT$ to become a labour slack estimate that can be interpreted similarly to the unemployment rate: $LST/AALT$.

Labour slack time can also be expressed either in 'full-time equivalents' or in persons. To obtain to former ratio LST is divided by $FAACWT$; the latter is obtained by dividing LST by $AAWT$ (which in turn stands for the average annual working time per person).
Thus:

$$LSE = LST/FAACWT$$

$$LSP = LST/AAWT.$$

For the sake of completeness, five more useful key volumes that can be defined on the basis of the labour market accounts – in persons and in hours – are given. The employed labour resources (ELR) logically consist of the sum of all employed persons, while the non-employed labour resources ($NELR$) are defined as $LR - ELR$. The non-employed labour resources due to unemployment ($NELR^u$) equals aggregate registered unemployment. The non-utilised labour resources time ($NULT$) is defined as the difference between $AALT$ and ULT. The registered available labour resources time ($RALT$), finally, forms the product of RLR and $FAACWT$.

EMPIRICAL APPLICATION OF THE LABOUR SLACK ESTIMATE: SOME PRELIMINARY RESULTS

The empirical application of the definitions discussed in the previous section yields a number of summary figures and ratios for every single country, as illustrated in Appendix A 8.2. The Appendix gives the figures for the Netherlands 1973–82. It is clear that the very extent of the data does not allow an easy interpretation. The discussion in this chapter is therefore confined to the main topics: (i) can the labour slack estimate, as developed in the previous section, be regarded as a valuable indicator of the cyclical situation; (ii) is the labour slack estimate a valuable instrument to study international differences in the (non-)utilisation of labour capacity? The first issue will be discussed referring to the data for the Netherlands. Figures for five countries are used to illuminate the second topic. An initial warning should be made: the empirical part of this research is still in progress, and since some of the calculations are based on preliminary estimates for certain data in the labour market accounts, the absolute figures should be interpreted with caution.

Taking a glance at the Figures 8.1a and 8.1b and comparing the plots of LST and the aggregate unemployment ($NELR^u$) for the Netherlands, it can be seen that LST shows more fluctuations and increases earlier, though both have the same overall trend. Figure 8.2 – where the effect of differences in the scaling is eliminated by dividing LST and $NELR^u$ by their standard deviations – reveals the same results. This confirms our expectations: an increase in the non-utilisation of labour resources does not necessarily take the form of overt unemployment.

Early in the downswing of the cycle, employers tend to cushion fluctuations in the production by diminishing the number of hours worked (especially by reducing overtime). When the recession shows persistence, governments will try to convert overt unemployment into other types of labour slack – more specifically by reducing the average number hours worked per worker (by means of work-sharing, part-time work, etc.) and by reducing labour market participation (by means of earlier retirement, fiscal discouragement, etc.). The cyclical sensitivity of

Figure 8.1 The Netherlands: aggregate unemployment and plots of *LST*

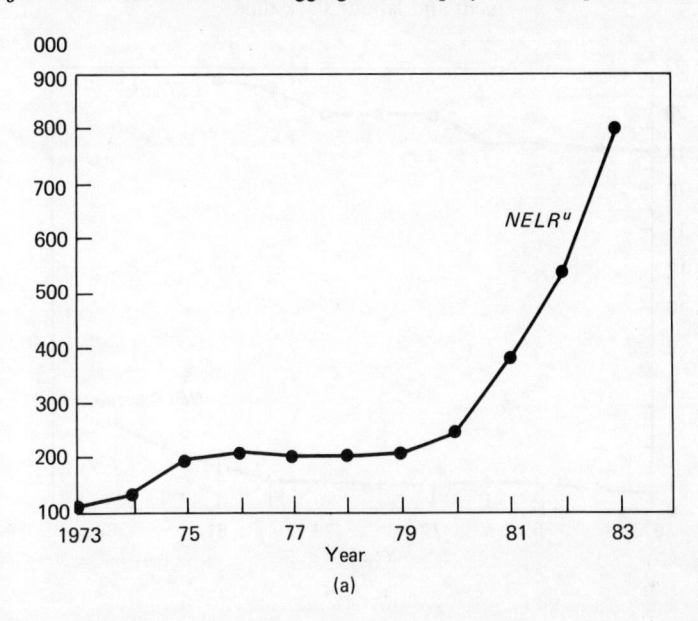

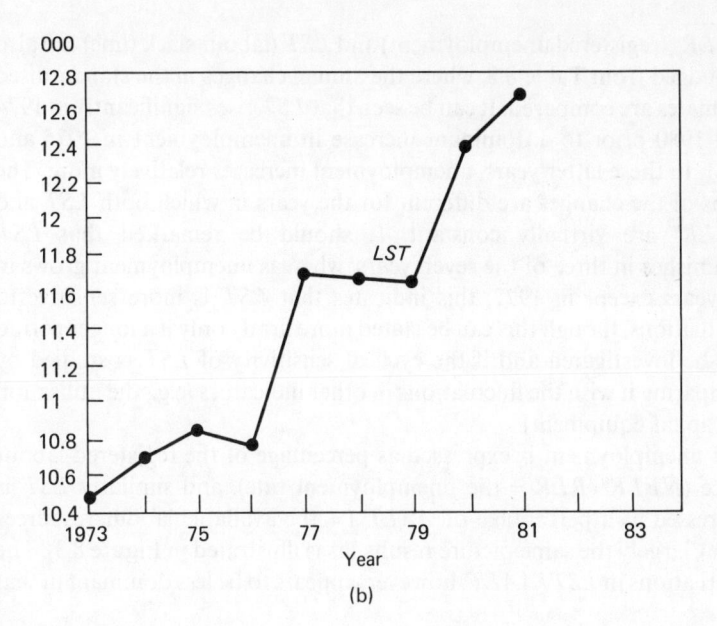

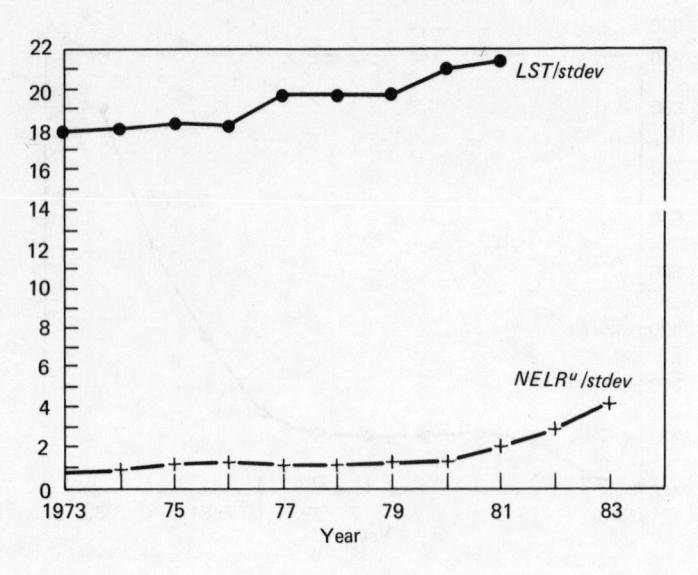

Figure 8.2 The Netherlands: standardised estimates of registered unemployment and labour slack time

$NELR^u$ (registered unemployment) and LST (labour slack time) can also be judged from Table 8.2, where the annual changes in the standardised estimates are compared. It can be seen that LST rises significantly in 1974 and 1980 prior to a dominant increase in unemployment in 1975 and 1981. In these latter years, unemployment increases relatively more. The signs of the changes are different for the years in which both LST and $NELR^u$ are virtually constant. It should be remarked that LST diminishes in three of the seven years, whereas unemployment grows in all years except in 1977; this indicates that LST is more sensitive to fluctuations, though this can be stated more firmly only if a longer period can be investigated and if the cyclical sensitivity of LST is studied by comparing it with the fluctuations in other indicators (e.g., the utilisation of capital equipment).

If unemployment is expressed as percentage of the registered labour force ($NELR^u/RLR$ = the unemployment rate), and similarly LST is expressed as a percentage of $AALT$ (= the available labour resources time), largely the same picture results (as is illustrated in Figure 8.3). The fluctuations in $LST/AALT$, however, appears to be less dominant in that

Table 8.2 Annual changes in standardised LST (labour slack time) and $NELR^u$ (unemployment: the Netherlands (1974–81)

	1974	75	76	77	78	79	80	81
$NELR^u$	0.14	0.33	0.09	−0.04	0.01	0.01	0.21	0.74
LST	0.35	0.26	−0.07	1.56	−0.03	−0.04	1.16	0.47

Figure 8.3 The Netherlands: unemployment rate and percentage labour slack

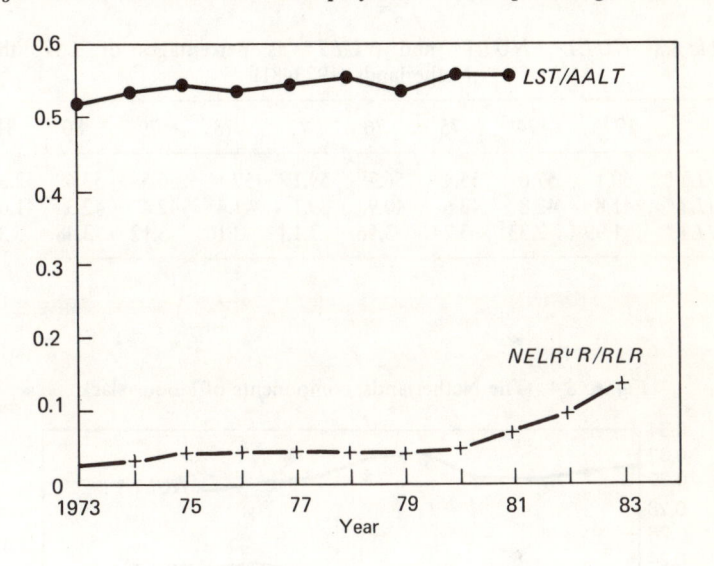

case; this has to be explained by the fact that *AALT* is defined as the product of *LR* and *FAACWT*. To the extent that the average number of hours worked by full-time workers is influenced by the cyclical situation (which might be the case if governments reduce the number of hours worked weekly for all workers or if 'overtime' is a popular instrument to react upon short-time fluctuations in production), the ratio *LST/AALT* has to be less sensitive for cyclical changes, since their effects appear also in the denominator. Therefore *LST/AALT* cannot be regarded as an ideal cyclical indicator.

It is interesting to study changes in the components of *LST*. This is done in Table 8.3 and in Figure 8.4. In Table 8.3 $NULT^p$ (non-utilised labour resources time due to non-participation), $NULT^h$ ($NULT$ due to changes in the hours actually worked) and $NULT^u$ ($NULT$ due to unemployment) are expressed as percentages of the aggregate labour slack estimate. $NULT^p$ and $NULT^h$ form the larger components of LST, though the share of $NULT^u$ increases between 1973 and 1975 and between 1980 and 1981. The share of $NULT^p$ diminishes significantly between 1973 and 1981, while both $NULT^p$ and $NULT^h$ as percentages of LST show significant year-to-year changes. Figure 8.4 gives some more details, including the changes in the major components of $NULT^h$,

Table 8.3 $NULT^p$, $NULT^h$ and $NULT^u$ as percentages of LST: the Netherlands (1973–81)

	1973	74	75	76	77	78	79	80	81
$NULT^p$	60.1	57.6	55.4	56.7	59.1	57.1	56.5	53.4	52.3
$NULT^h$	41.8	42.8	42.6	40.9	39.1	41.4	42.4	42.3	41.6
$NULT^u$	1.99	2.33	3.24	3.56	3.13	3.10	3.12	3.48	5.32

Figure 8.4 The Netherlands: components of labour slack

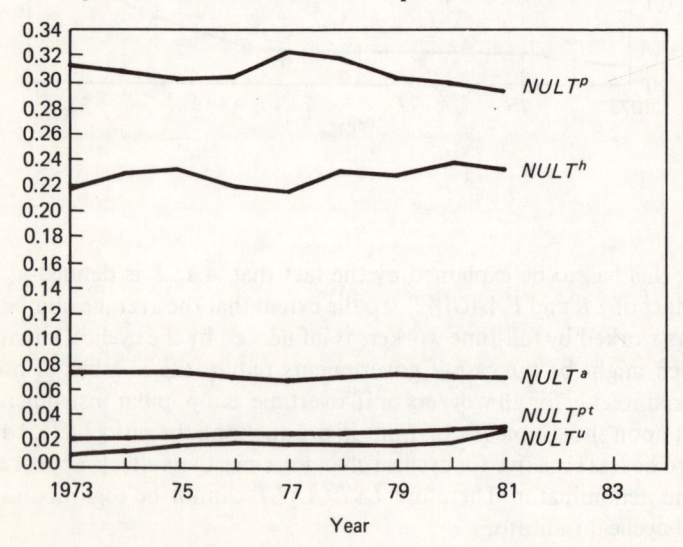

namely $NULT^{pt}$ and $NULT^a$ (respectively $NULT$ due to part-time work and $NULT$ due to absence from the job). The data are now expressed as a percentage of $AALT$, the actual available labour resources time. The graphs conform the results of Table 8.3. Additionally, it can be seen that the impact of part-time work increases, but not very fast (from other data we know that huge increases can be observed after 1981.

An additional question should be raised related to the cyclical sensitivity of LST. As demonstrated in the previous section, $NULT^h$ is corrected for yearly productivity changes to estimate LST. The contribution of $NULT^h$ in LST is therefore increased (or diminished) according to whether productivity increased (or decreased) in the observation year (as can be seen by comparing the ratios 20 and 20b in Appendix A8.2). This might introduce a problem when productivity changes very rapidly (though in none of the calculations made for the five countries does this appear to be the case). An alternative correction for productivity changes should, therefore, be contemplated. Introducing annual changes in a smoothed productivity time series might offer a viable alternative, though other ratios should also be experimented with.

Finally, the use of LST and $LST/AALT$ in internationally comparative studies should be discussed. It is clear that their relevance is influenced by the difference in government policies. As the latter have an important impact upon the extent to which overt unemployment is mitigated in other types of labour slack, the traditional unemployment rates may be a misleading indicator to compare the non-utilisation of labour resources internationally. This is illustrated in the bottom lines of Table 8.4, comparing $LST/AALT$ and the unemployment rate ($NELR^u/RLR$) for five countries in 1981. It can be seen that the same level of unemployment rates of Canada, the Netherlands and the United States are paralleled by largely differing $LST/AALT$ estimates, indicating that, for example, in the Netherlands overt unemployment is more cushioned by the policy measures mentioned previously. Similar $LST/AALT$ estimates, as those for Germany and the Netherlands are also combined with highly different unemployment rates, indicating that different instruments are used in the two countries. To explain the background of these differences, a detailed study of the underlying components should be made. For completeness sake, Table 8.4 lists some important ratios in this respect. A detailed discussion of the 47 summary figures and ratios and their changes between 1973 and 1983 for five countries, however, goes far beyond the scope of this chapter.[5] It is, nevertheless, possible to conclude that the labour slack estimates

Table 8.4 Summary figures and ratios (1981)

	Canada	Germany	Netherlands	Sweden	United States
6. $AAWT$	2115	2290	2036	1924	1824
7. $FAACWT$	2129	2154	2319	2695	2024
8. $AAAWT$	n.a.	2090	1562	1565	1621
23. RLR/LR	0.71	0.79	0.59	0.78	0.73
25. $NELR/LR$	0.34	0.24	0.45	0.24	0.32
26. $NELR^u/LR$	0.05	0.03	0.04	0.02	0.05
29. $RALT/AALT$	0.71	0.73	0.59	0.78	0.75
31. $NULT/AALT$	0.37	0.50	0.45	0.35	0.51
33. $NULT^p/AALT$	0.27	0.39	0.31	0.17	0.30
34. $NULT^{pt}/AALT$	0.05	0.02	0.04	0.06	0.06
35. $NULT^a/AALT$	0.05	0.07	0.07	0.10	0.07
36. $NULT^u/AALT$	0.05	0.03	0.03	0.02	0.13
42. $NULT^h/AALT$	0.10	0.09	0.25	0.17	0.13
38. $LST/AALT$	0.42	0.50	0.59	0.36	0.49
41. $NELR^u/RLR$	0.08	0.04	0.07	0.02	0.07

Note: n.a. = Not available.

produced in this chapter yield a more trustworthy basis for international comparative labour market research.

CONCLUSIONS

Since a single labour market indicator is sometimes useful and necessary, and since the traditional unemployment rate is criticised in this context, it makes sense to develop an alternative labour slack estimate. The definitions found in the literature contain elements of arbitrary choice related to the question of what should be regarded as a cyclical neutral level of activity. The labour slack estimate developed in this chapter tries to avoid this arbitrariness by adopting a demographically based definition.

$LST/AALT$ (labour slack time as a proportion of total actual available labour resources time) can be seen to be useful in international comparative studies. It is, however, not more than it is intended to be: a summary figure; this means that a discussion of the underlying developments is useful, if not necessary. *LST* appears to be a sensitive cyclical indicator, when applied to a single country; $LST/AALT$, however, is unsuitable as a cyclical indicator since $AALT$ is not defined to be cyclically independent. Moreover, the correction for productivity changes, incorporated into the definition of LST, may cause interpretation problems when the yearly changes in productivity are large or volatile. Solutions to these problems may be found by introducing smoothed yearly changes in productivity rather than crude changes, and by defining $AALT$ as cyclically neutral by means of peak-to-peak intrapolations. These solutions, however, introduce again the problems of arbitrary choice. Further research should enlighten the empirical usefulness of ameliorated labour slack estimates.

Appendices

A8.1 DEFINITIONS OF THE SUMMARY FIGURES AND RATIOS IN TERMS OF THE LABOUR MARKET ACCOUNTS FOR THE UNITED STATES

The numbers in the definitions refer to the corresponding numbers of the lines of the labour market accounts for the United States, reprinted on the following pages, where (p) stands for the account in persons and (h) stands for the account in hours.

Summary figures in 1000 persons

1. $LR = 7(p) - [10(p) + 11(p) + 12 > 65(p)]$ — Labour resources
2. $RLR = 14(p)$ — Registered labour resources
3. $ELR = 15(p) + 17(p)$ — Employed labour resources
4. $NELR = LR - ELR$ — Non-employed labour resources
5. $NELR^u = 42(p)$ — Non-employed labour resources due to unemployment

Summary figures in hours

6. $AAWT = \dfrac{[14(h) + 19(h)]}{[15(p) + 17(p)]}$ — Average annual working time per worker

7. $FAACWT = \dfrac{[15(h) + 19(h)]}{[15(p) + 18(p)]}$ — Average annual contractual working time per full-time worker

8. $AAAWT = \dfrac{14(h)}{[15(p) + 17(p)]}$ — Average annual actual working time per worker

9. $Retro = [15_t(p) + 18_t(p)] * FAACWT_{t-1}$ — Number of hours that full-time workers would have worked in year t if $FAACTW_t = FAACTW_{t-1}$

Summary figures in million hours

10. $AALT = 2(h) - [3(h) + 7(h) + 8(h) + 9(h) > 65]$
    $\cong LR * FAACWT$ — Actually available labour resources time

11. $RALT = 11(h)$ — Registered available labour resources time

12. $ULT = 14(h)$ — Utilised labour resources time

13. $NULT = 19(h) + 6(h) + 10(h)$
    $+ 40(h) + 39(h)$
    $+ [9(h) - 9(h) > 65]$ — Non-utilised labour resources time

14. $NULT^s = [15(h) - 19(h)] - \text{Retro}$ — $NULT$ due to diminishing of the average yearly contractual hours worked by full-time workers

15. $NULT^p = 6(h) + 10(h)$
    $+ [9(h) - 9(h) > 65]$ — $NULT$ due to non-participation

16. $NULT^{pt} = 16(h)$ — $NULT$ due to part-time work

17. $NULT^a = 19(h)$ — $NULT$ due to absence from job

18. $NULT^h = NULT^s + NULT^{pt} + NULT^a$

19. $NULT^u = 40(h)$ — $NULT$ due to unemployment

Persons

1. *Total population*
2. Domestic population
3. Net migration
4. Population < 16
5. Population > 16
6. Institutional
7. Non-institutional
8. Non-active population
9. Keeping house
10. Going to school
11. Unable to work
12. Retired
13. Other reasons
14. Active population
15. Military labour force
16. Civilian labour force
17. Employed
18. Full-time
19. Part-time
20. Voluntary part-time
21. Involuntary part-time
22. Wage and Salary workers
23. Self-employed
24. Unpaid family workers
25. Actual at work
26. Voluntary part-time
27. Part-time for economic reasons
28. Full-time
29. On full-time schedules, working part-time
30. Vacation
31. Illness
32. Bad weather
33. Industrial disputes
34. Legal or religious holiday
35. Other reasons
36. With a job, not at work
37. Vacation
38. Illness
39. Bad weather
40. Industrial disputes
41. Other reasons
42. Unemployed
43. Looking for full-time work
44. Looking for part-time work
45. 15 weeks and longer

Hours

USA, hours
1. Theoretically available[a]
2. Available
3. Lost by institutional
4. Lost by non-institutional
5. Lost by non-active
6. Lost by keeping house
7. Lost by going to school
8. Lost by unable to work
9. Lost by retired
9a. Lost by retired 65+
10. Lost by other reasons
11. Available by the active population
12. Available by the military labour force
13. Available by the civilian labour force
14. Worked by the employed (excluding with a job not at work)
15. Worked by persons on full-time schedules
16. Worked by persons on part-time schedules
17. Worked by persons on voluntary part-time
18. Worked by person on part-time for economic reasons
19. Lost by the employed
20. Lost by vacation
21. Lost by illness
22. Lost by bad weather
23. Lost by industrial disputes
24. Lost by legal or religious holiday
25. Lost by other reasons
26. Lost by persons with a job, not at work
27. Vacation
28. Illness
29. Bad weather
30. Industrial disputes
31. Other reasons
32. Lost by persons on full-time

Persons

46. 14 weeks and shorter
47. job losers and leavers
48. new (re)entrants
49. household heads
50. no household heads

Hours

schedules working part-time
33. Lost by vacation
34. Lost by illness
35. Lost by bad weather
36. Lost by industrial disputes
37. Lost by legal or religious holiday
38. Lost by other reasons
39. Lost by persons on part-time schedules
40. Lost by the unemployed

[a] Base year 1968.

A8.2 SUMMARY FIGURES AND RATIOS FOR THE NETHERLANDS 1973–81

	1973	74	75	76	77	78	79	80	81
Summary figures in 1000 persons									
1. LR	8229	8276	8330	8399	8934	8953	9033	9156	9250
2. RLR	4905	4944	4991	5038	5089	5153	5234	5348	5464
3. ELR	4682	4699	4687	4721	4784	4844	4919	5035	5055
4. $NELR$	3547	3577	3643	3678	4150	4109	4114	4121	4195
5. $NELRu$	110	135	195	211	204	206	210	248	385
5a. $NELRu/stdev$	0.60	0.73	1.06	1.14	1.11	1.12	1.14	1.34	2.09
5b. $K5a(t)-K5a(t-1)$	0.01	0.14	0.33	0.09	−0.04	0.01	0.02	0.21	0.74
5c. $K5b(t)/K5a(t-1)$	0.02	0.23	0.44	0.08	−0.03	0.01	0.02	0.18	0.55
Summary figures in hours									
6. $AAWT$	1876	1828	1779	1793	1771	1731	1703	1706	1716
index 1973 = 100	100	97	95	96	94	92	91	91	92
7. $FAACWT$	2459	2424	2396	2391	2400	2355	2408	2419	2452
index 1973 = 100	100	99	97	97	98	96	98	98	100
8. $AAAWT$	1468	1420	1365	1389	1356	1319	1261	1264	1267
index 1973 = 100	100	97	93	95	92	90	86	86	86
9. Retro (+1000)	10368	10314	10058	9902	9922	10152	9908	10280	10243

Summary figures in million hours

10. *AALT*	20 232	20 058	19 956	20 085	21 442	21 080	21 753	22 151	22 683
index 1973 = 100	100	99	99	99	106	104	108	109	112
11. *RALT*	12 060	11 982	11 957	12 048	12 214	12 133	12 604	12 938	13 399
index 1973 = 100	100	99	99	100	101	101	105	107	111
12. *ULT*	6875	6671	6398	6559	6488	6391	6205	6365	6403
index 1973 = 100	100	97	93	95	94	93	90	93	93
13. *NULT*	8631	8525	8415	8522	9443	9181	9357	9494	9613
index 1973 = 100	100	99	98	99	109	106	108	110	111
14. NULT^s	2469	2655	2686	2506	2591	2847	2766	3021	3004
15. *NULT^p*	6300	6161	6016	6103	6907	6670	6585	6619	6628
index 1973 = 100	100	98	95	97	110	106	105	105	105
16. *NULT^{pt}*	424	443	458	515	553	519	602	649	711
index 1973 = 100	100	105	108	122	131	123	142	153	168
17. *NULT^q*	1484	1477	1483	1389	1430	1472	1567	1577	1563
index 1973 = 100	100	100	100	94	96	99	106	106	105
18. *NULT^h*	4377	4576	4627	4410	4574	4839	4935	5247	5278
index 1973 = 100	100	105	106	101	105	111	113	120	121
19. *NULT^u*	208	250	351	383	366	362	364	431	674
index 1973 = 100	100	120	169	184	176	173	175	207	323

Labour slack

20	LST (1000)	10479	10693	10850	10769	11693	11676	11652	12394	12674
20a.	$LST/stdev$	17.75	18.11	18.37	18.24	19.80	19.77	19.73	20.99	21.46
20b.	$LST(K15+K18+K19)$	10885	10987	10995	10896	11847	11870	11885	12297	12580
20c.	$K20(t)-K20(t-1)$	54	102	8	−99	951	23	15	412	283
20d.	$K20c(t)/K20(t-1)$	0.00	0.01	0.00	−0.01	0.09	0.00	0.00	0.03	0.02
21.	LSE	4262	4412	4529	4503	4872	4959	4839	5123	5168
22.	LSP	5586	5849	6098	6007	6603	6747	6844	7264	7384
22a.	$LSP/stdev$	7.94	8.32	8.67	8.54	9.39	9.59	9.73	10.33	10.50

Ratios

23.	RLR/LR	0.60	0.60	0.60	0.60	0.57	0.58	0.58	0.58	0.59
24.	ELR/LR	0.57	0.57	0.56	0.56	0.54	0.54	0.55	0.55	0.55
25.	$NELR/LR$	0.43	0.43	0.44	0.44	0.46	0.46	0.46	0.45	0.45
26.	$NELR^u/LR$	0.01	0.02	0.02	0.03	0.02	0.02	0.02	0.03	0.04
27.	ELR/RLR	0.95	0.95	0.94	0.94	0.94	0.94	0.94	0.94	0.93
28.	$NELR/ELR$	0.76	0.76	0.78	0.78	0.87	0.85	0.84	0.82	0.83
29.	$RALT/AALT$	0.60	0.60	0.60	0.60	0.57	0.58	0.58	0.58	0.59
30.	$ULT/AALT$	0.34	0.33	0.32	0.33	0.30	0.30	0.29	0.29	0.28
31.	$NULT/AALT$	0.43	0.43	0.42	0.42	0.44	0.44	0.43	0.43	0.42
32.	$ULT/NULT$	0.80	0.78	0.76	0.77	0.69	0.70	0.66	0.67	0.67
33.	$NULT^p/AALT$	0.31	0.31	0.30	0.30	0.32	0.32	0.30	0.30	0.29
34.	$NULT^{pi}/AALT$	0.02	0.02	0.02	0.03	0.03	0.02	0.03	0.03	0.03
35.	$NULT^q/AALT$	0.07	0.07	0.07	0.07	0.07	0.07	0.07	0.07	0.07
36.	$NULT^u/AALT$	0.01	0.01	0.02	0.02	0.02	0.02	0.02	0.02	0.03
37.	$ULT/RALT$	0.57	0.56	0.54	0.54	0.53	0.53	0.49	0.49	0.48
38.	$LST/AALT$	0.52	0.53	0.54	0.54	0.55	0.55	0.54	0.56	0.56
38a.	$LST'/AALT$	0.54	0.55	0.55	0.54	0.55	0.56	0.55	0.56	0.55

39.	LSP/LR	0.21	0.22	0.23	0.22	0.24	0.22	0.23
40.	LSE/LR	0.28	0.29	0.31	0.30	0.32	0.31	0.33
41.	$NELR^u/RLR$	0.02	0.03	0.04	0.04	0.04	0.04	0.07
42.	$NULT^hAALT$	0.22	0.23	0.23	0.22	0.23	0.23	0.23
43.	$LST/AALT$ (%)	−0.52	2.93	1.98	−1.38	1.56	−3.29	4.45
44.	LSP/LR (%)	−0.50	4.42	3.17	−1.20	3.53	−5.44	3.98
45.	LSE/LR (%)	1.69	5.61	4.80	−2.12	3.93	−1.70	4.23
46.	$NELR^u/RLR$ (%)	1.44	21.76	43.08	7.20	−0.27	0.36	15.58
47.	19 as % 20	1.99	2.33	3.24	3.56	3.10	3.12	3.48

GDP (index)	714.2	739.5	731.8	770.8	789.1	810.3	824.6	829.3	819.3
							GDP index	4396	
							POP (1000)	14030	
GDP	53418522	55310833	54734912	57651914	59020660	61675880	6E+07	620274166	1279466

Notes

1. For statistical assistance I am indebted to Harry van Oostroom.
2. See de Neubourg (1983, 1985) and Shiskin (1975) for a detailed review.
3. Further research by means of detailed surveys and econometric estimates, revealed that the latter effect is very small for the period 1970–80 – see Brinkman (1980); Gross et al. (1980); Blazejczak (1980); and Görzig and Klauder (1982).
4. Appendix A8.1 defines the components of the labour slack estimates in terms of the labour market accounts for the United States (as developed in de Neubourg, 1983).
5. This discussion should also be complemented with a discussion of the basic labour market account data, since some policy effects are by definition removed from the *LST* estimates. This is, for example, the case with the effects of social security policy related to disablement. As I argued elsewhere (de Neubourg 1983, 1985) huge international differences may result.

References

Autorengemeinschaft (1979) Der Arbeidsmarkt in der Bundesrepublik Deutschland im Jahre 1979, 1980, 1981, *Mitteillungen aus der Arbeitsmarkt- und Berufsforschung* (January issues 1979, 1980, 1981).

BANCROFT, G. (1962) 'Some Alternative Indexes of Employment and Unemployment', *Monthly Labor Review* (February), pp. 167–74.

BLAZEJCZAK, J. and GÖRZIG, B. (1980) Bestimmungsgründe für das Erwerbsverhalten der verheirateten Frauen, in Mertens, D. and Klauder, W. (eds) *Probleme der Messung und Vorausschätzung des Erwerbspersonenpotentials*, Beiträge zur Arbeitsmarkt- und Berufsforschung 44 (Nürnberg: IAB).

BRINKMANN, Ch. (1980) Erwerbsbeteiligung und Arbeitsmarktverhältnisse: Neue empirische Ergebnisse zur 'Entmutigung' und zusätzlichen 'Erwerbspersonen', in Mertens, D. and Klauder, W. (eds) *Probleme der Messung und Vorausschätzung des Erwerbspersonenpotentials*, Beiträge zur Arbeitsmarkt- und Berufsforschung 44 (Nürnberg: IAB).

EGLE, F. (1980) Modellrechnungen zur Erklärung und Projektion des Erwerbspotentials, in Mertens, D. and Klauder, W. (eds) *Probleme der Messung und Vorausschätzung des Erwerbspersonenpotentials*, Beiträge zur Arbeitsmarkt- und Berufsforschung 44 (Nürnberg: IAB).

GASTWIRTH, J. L. (1973) 'Estimating the Number of "Hidden Unemployed"', *Monthly Labor Review* (March), pp. 17–26.

GILROY, C. L. (1975) 'Supplemental Measures of Labor Force Underutilization', *Monthly Labor Review* (May), pp. 13–23.

GORDON, R. J. (1970) The recent Acceleration of Inflation and Its lessons for the Future, *Brookings Papers on Economic Activity* (1), p. 21.

GRANIER, R. and MADDISON A. (1982) *Politiques de l'Emploi*, Tome I: Approche Empirique (Aix en Provence: Centre d'Analyse Economique).

GROSS, J., ROSENBERG, P. and SARRAZIN, T. (1980) Zum Problem der Schätzung des Erwerbspersonenpotentials und der 'Stillen Reserve', in Mertens, D. and Klauder, W. (eds) *Probleme der Messung und Vorausschätzung des Erwerbspersonenpotentials*. Beiträge zur Arbeitsmarkt- und Berufsforschung 44 (Nürnberg: IAB).

HITCH, T. (1981). 'Meaning and Measurement of "Full" or "Maximum" Employment', *Review of Economics and Statistics*. (February), pp. 1–11.

KLAUDER, W. (1982) Arbeitskräfte- Potentialrechnung, in Mertens, D. (ed.), *Konzepte der Arbeitsmarkt- und Berufsforschung*, Beiträge zur Arbeitsmarkt- und Berufsforschung (Nürnberg: IAB). pp. 99–119.

———— and KÜHLEWIND, G. (1980) Ueberblick über das Erwerbspersonenpotentialkonzept des I.A.B., in Mertens, D. and Klauder, W. (eds) *Probleme der Messung und Vorausschätzung des Erwerbspersonenpotentials*, Beiträge zur Arbeitsmarkt- und Berufsforschung 44 (Nürnberg: IAB).

LAL, D. (1977) *Unemployment and Wage Inflation in Industrial Economies* (Paris: OECD).

LEBERGOTT, S. (1954) 'Measuring Unemployment', *Review of Economics and Statistics* (November), pp. 290–400.

MADDISON, A. (1980) 'Monitoring the Labour Market: A proposal for a Comprehensive Approach in Official Statistics', *Reivew of Income and Wealth* (June).

MINCER, J. (1973) 'Determining Who are the "Hidden Unemployed"', *Monthly Labor Review* (March), pp. 27–30.

MOORE, G. H. (1973) *How Full is Full Employment?* (Washington, D.C.: American Enterprise Institute for Public Policy Research).

de NEUBOURG, C. (1983) *Peregrinations in the land of Dreams, Needs and Data*, comment on R. Lindley's paper on the Seminar Arbeitsmarktstrukturen und Prozesse: Beiträge zu Analyse und Politik (Basel, March).

———— (1984) *What a Difference a Day Makes: Figures and Estimates on Work-time Reduction*, Memorandum from The Institute of Economic Research 141 (University of Groningen, Faculty of Economics).

———— (1987) see chapter 6 above.

———— and KOK, L. (1984) *Arbeidstijdverkorting* (Utrecht: Aula, Het Spectrum).

PERRY, G. L. (1970) 'Changing Labor Markets and Inflation', *Brookings Papers on Economic Activity* 0, pp. 411–48.

REYHER, L. and BACH, H. U. (1980) 'Arbeitskräfte-Gesamtrechnung: bestände und Bewegungen am Arbeitsmarkt', *Mitteilungen aus der Arbeitsmarkt- und Berufsforschung* (4), pp. 498–513.

SHISKIN, J. (1976) 'Employment and Unemployment: the Doughnut or the Hole?', *Monthly Labor Review* (February), pp. 3–10.

SORRENTINO, C. (1979) *International Comparisons of Unemployment* (Washington, D.C.: Department of Labor, Bureau of Labor Statistics).

TAYLOR, J. (1974) *Unemployment and Wage Inflation* (London: Longman).

9 Average Weekly Hours of Work in the United Kingdom 1948–80: A Disaggregated Analysis

A. J. Neale and R. A. Wilson

INTRODUCTION

In Bosworth and Westaway (1986) a number of hypotheses were outlined to explain the determination of average weekly hours, concentrating on the aggregate manufacturing sector. In this chapter, the analysis is at a much more disaggregated level, distinguishing many different industries and categories of worker in the labour market.

One of the key questions addressed is the impact on hours worked of a cut in the length of the normal working week. As noted in Bosworth and Westaway, one would expect that normal hours (that is, hours paid for at a basic rate of pay) would be at least in part determined by economic forces both from the supply and from the demand side. Nevertheless, the position adopted here is that normal hours, in the long run, are exogenously determined as a result of a complex bargaining procedure between employers and employees. In the longer term the influence of technological factors which determine the underlying necessities of the production process in various industries is undoubtedly of crucial importance in determining the pattern of hours worked. On the supply side, the pressure to take at least part of the fruits of economic growth in the form of lower hours has lead to downward pressure on negotiated hours.

Pressure on the level of normal hours from the supply side has been discussed in Wilson (1982). Leslie (1978) attempts to introduce the supply side into a model of hours by assuming that firms are faced by a constraint to maintain a certain minimum level of utility for their workforce. The employee welfare function is taken to include hours of leisure and income as arguments. The firm is assumed to minimise its costs subject to this and the conventional production function constraint. The level of hours that will minimise costs is thereby given to the firm by the wage structure it faces (in terms of straight time hourly wages, overtime premia, fringe benefits, bonous payments, shift premia, etc.) which in turn reflect the employee utility function. In this model optimal hours may depart from *normal* hours, in either direction, depending on workers tastes for income and leisure. If, at the normal working week, they prefer income to leisure then this could explain the 'permanent' overtime working phenomenon discussed by commentators.

Many other reasons have been identified why the length of the actual working week differs from the normal working week in the aggregate. At the simplest level, average hours are connected to normal hours by the identity

$$AH = NH + OH*POT - SH*PST \qquad (9.1)$$

where :

AH = average hours worked per person per week
NH = normal hours per person per week
OH = overtime hours worked per person per week
SH = short time hours lost per person per week
POT = the proportion of persons working overtime
PST = the proportion of persons on short time.

Inspection of the data reveals that for most of the post-war period the positive effect of overtime working has far outweighed the negative impact of hours lost through short-time working (see Wilson, 1982). One of the most interesting aspects of the development of hours worked since the war is the reason for the apparently permanent level of overtime worked.

As noted in Bosworth and Westaway (1986) the many explanations for this phenomena may be divided into two main schools of thought which Leslie and Wise (1980) characterise as the 'institutionalists' and the 'economists'. Proponents of the first school of thought include Ullman (1968), Whybrew (1968) and Clegg (1962). Whybrew, for example, concludes that overtime patterns in Britain can best be explained in ways that have little or nothing to do with production demands. There is much more evidence that overtime growth is influenced by relative pay factors, so that it is highest in industries and groups that have low average hourly earnings. Far from making possible essential additional output, much of British overtime now seems to arise out of a desire to waste time at work in order to obtain a living wage (Whybrew, 1968, p. 2). However, as is pointed out in Bosworth and Westaway (1986), such conclusions are not reached on the basis of an empirically testable model of hours of work and the evidence is usually little more than suggestive. The institutionalists have not attempted to build an integrated framework to show how such factors come to dominate. The onus of proof falls on the economic models whose failure is claimed as support for the institutional school. To the extent that this is an economic argument, it is a purely supply-side one.

Proponents of the economic school hold, to a greater or lesser extent, that overtime working is a rational response of a firm attempting to minimise costs (or maximise profits) subject to a production function constraint and a wage structure which reflects the costs of persuading the workforce to work long or unsocial hours. As such, this literature is largely demand-side orientated although attention is paid to supply factors. The early work in this field by Feldstein (1967) and Craine (1973) adopted a production function approach and was mainly concerned with the importance of treating employment and hours separately. Their results suggested that the returns to hours at the margin significantly exceeded the marginal returns to employment. This was attributed, first, to the fact that increasing hours are positively correlated with an increase in capital utilisation (not offset by increased capital costs); and second, to the existence of 'setting-up' time. Given the assumption that returns to hours and employment are different in the production function it is easy to demonstrate that a cost-minimising firm faced with a quadratic cost function relating wages to the level of average hours worked will have optimal (cost-minimising) hours different from normal hours. This reflects the fact that it is not optimal to minimise the hourly wage rate when hours are more productive than persons. The optimising condition is that costs of working an additional hour relative to employing one more person should equal the ratio of their marginal productivities, (although, as Leslie and Wise (1980) note, hours are not a factor of production, per se, but a conversion factor changing the arguments of the production function from stocks to flows).

Leslie and Wise (1980) present regression results which suggest that once differences in inter-industry efficiency are allowed for the high returns to hours compared to employment disappears and that in fact the returns to the stock and flow variables for labour services are virtually identical. Their introduction of industry shift dummies may be picking up various kinds of cross-sectional differences between industries. Because of technological differences one would expect differences in the optimal level of hours in different industries in the long-run (see the discussion below for details). This probably explains the 'success' of the industry dummies introduced by Leslie and Wise. Clearly while some of these industry-specific 'efficiency effects' are not related to optimal hours certain other ones are, because for technological reasons it will be efficient for some firms to work relatively long hours. By allowing for such effects Leslie and Wise are able to concentrate on the response of output to a change in hours worked. However, they constrain this elasticity of output with respect to hours to be the same across all industries. It is questionable whether this is valid in a model based on a pooled time series–cross section data set. It is unclear whether they have tested this restriction or not, but it is possible that such effects are being spuriously picked up by the industry specific time trend dummies present in their specification. Furthermore, a second implicit restriction in their model is that persons and hours are hoarded at equal rates, which would affect the estimates of the respective returns to these inputs. As Knight and Wilson (1974) have suggested, hoarding can take a variety of forms and it is not clear that the assumption made by Hughes and Leslie (1975) is the appropriate one. This is particularly important in view of Leslie and Wise's argument that previous authors (especially Feldstein and Craine) have obtained high estimates of the return to hours by ignoring labour hoarding. However, although Leslie and Wise find returns to hours and persons are (approximately) equal, when they introduce various dummy variables and an unemployment proxy to control for hoarding, they find that the hoarding variable has no effect on the estimated hours coefficient (Leslie and Wise, p. 81). This, in itself, is a rather disturbing result and probably arises because any such effect has been swamped by the dummies. In any case while it is clear that the efficiency effects can explain the high returns to hours in a cross-sectional data set it is not possible to explain the results obtained by Craine who used time series data to test a similar hypothesis.

Other recent studies including those by Hughes and Leslie (1975), Hart and Sharot (1978) and Bosworth and Wesaway (1986) have moved away from the production function approach and estimated hours functions directly. In doing so they tend to place a great deal more stress on the use of hours as a means of adjusting the input of labour services in the short-term. These authors have developed various additional hypotheses to explain the observed divergence between actual and normal hours. For Hughes and Leslie the reason is the existence of fixed costs of employment. These relate only to the level of employment and include, for example, national insurance contributions. They are distinct from costs associated with the adjustment of employment levels such as training, hiring and firing costs which are discussed below. Given the assumption of fixed costs of employment even where returns to hours and persons are equal, the presence of such costs drives a wedge between the ratios of marginal costs and marginal returns to the stock, employment, and the flow, utilisation. As a result, working at a level of utilisation consistent with normal hours is sub-optimal and optimal hours exceed normal hours.

For Bosworth and Westaway the rationale for continuous overtime working lies more in the capital savings that can be made by utilising capital more intensively. Their chapter casts some light on this issue in its discussion of shiftworking. In Bosworth and Dawkins (1982) it is argued that the number of shifts and their duration will depend not only on the relative costs of different work patterns but also on the technical nature of the production activity in that particular sector. The important factor which they identify is the level of capital savings to be made by running plant more intensively than that consistent with working normal hours. In continuous process industries such as chemicals and iron and steel, and those industries with continuous production lines such as motor vehicles, there are high opportunity costs attached to stopping production on one day and starting it up again the next. In some cases continuous shiftworking may therefore be a technical necessity. Furthermore the length of each shift may be dictated by the production technology in use.

Since Leslie (1978) starts from the assumption of a Cobb–Douglas production function the expression he obtained for optimal hours is independent of the level of output. This result is common to other work in this area, notably that of Nadiri and Rosen (1969), who derive a theoretical model in which desired hours are independent of output levels (although their empirical model reinstates it as an independent variable). Intuitively it seems plausible that all long-run scale phenomena should be embodied in stock demand functions (e.g., employment) rather than their service flows per unit of stock (e.g., hours per person). Thus if output doubles one might expect employment and capital to double (given constant returns to scale) while hours and capital utilisation remain constant. In the short run, however, there are equally obvious reasons for expecting firms to use hours as a means of adjustment to unexpected fluctuations in output. Some kind of output or activity level variable would seem to be necessary to represent such effects although, as discussed below, it should take a rather different form from the type of variable included in the stock demand function.

Even in the long run there may be reasons for expecting scale effects on hours worked. Leslie (1978) notes, for example, that size of plant may exert an indirect influence if this affects the utility of workers and hence their preferred level of hours. Shorey (1978), amongst others, has presented evidence of such disutility in relationship to larger plants. Scale effects can be justified in the hours equation even more simply by revoking the assumption of a Cobb–Douglas production technology, (see, for example, the model derived by Hart and Sharot, 1978). It is easy to demonstrate that the exclusion of an output term is dependent on the assumption of the form which the production technology takes. A production technology which is less restrictive than the Cobb–Douglas form would allow for the possibility of an output term to be included.

The remainder of this chapter is structured as follows. In the next section a theoretical model of the demand for hours of work is developed, drawing on the ideas outlined above. In the following section the theoretical model suggested is developed into a form suitable for estimation, and also in this section we discuss our data. In most previous studies of hours of work attention has focused on the hours of manual workers. We estimate models, for each of forty different industries, and various categories of worker. First there is a disaggregate analysis concentrating upon manual males, and full-time manual females. This is followed by an aggregate analysis covering all workers. The results are discussed in the concluding section.

A MODEL OF THE DEMAND FOR HOURS

The theoretical model developed in this section draws from a number of the ideas outlined above. The model is implicitly a recursive one in which a firm firstly makes a decision regarding its desired factor input levels in a cost-minimising way given their desired production function and the perceived product demand. The cost-minimising problem is:

$$\min_{v} w'.v \quad s.t \quad f(v) = q \tag{9.2}$$

where:

q = output

$f(v)$ = a production function defined over a vector of v inputs where $f(\cdot)$ is assumed to possess continuous first and second order derivatives with a negative definite Hessian.

The vector w defines the input prices. The first order conditions yield factor demands as functions of input prices and output. Typically, depending on the precise assumptions made about the form of $f(\cdot)$, the hours/utilisation solution is derived solely as a function of factor prices, w (e.g., Leslie, 1978, see also the discussion in the previous section). Under certain very restrictive assumptions desired hours can be derived as a constant equal to normal hours (e.g., Ball and St Cyr, 1966). However, relaxation of some of Ball and St Cyr's more restrictive assumptions (such as the very specific form of the wage function) can allow for the possibility of optimal hours (H^*) being different from normal hours (HN).

As discussed in Bosworth and Westaway (1984) 'capital savings' can be made by working at levels of utilisation (of labour and capital) in excess of that commensurate with normal hours, thereby reducing the amount of capital stock required to produce a given amount of output. This result arises naturally out of the minimisation problem (9.2) and emphasises the importance of differences in the returns to the various factor inputs in the production function. If the returns to capital are relatively low compared to those for persons and hours, then using large amounts of capital in the production process is a relatively inefficient way of producing output and it is optimal to work with a small capital stock but to use it relatively intensively to reap the gains from the relatively high returns to hours.

Clearly the whole issue hinges on what 'normal' hours are considered to be. 'Optimal' hours are obviously the overall cost-minimising level of utilisation but normal hours are almost invariably taken as the level of utilisation which minimises the hourly wage rate. These will only be equal under restrictive assumptions. (See, for example, the model of Ball and St Cyr, 1966, where there are no fixed employment costs and returns to factors of production are equal in the production function.) Without these assumptions there is nothing 'normal' about 'normal hours' as usually defined in the literature. Since the industries in the United Kingdom vary widely in terms of the returns to factors of production and fixed costs of employment and capital which they face, it is interesting to note not only the wide existence of apparently permanent overtime, but also importantly, the relatively small variation in the level of normal hours across industries as negotiated between employers, employees and trade unions.

The complex bargaining procedure by which these groups arrive at an agreed normal working day/week (usually) is, however, clearly related to optimal hours through technical (and hence cost) considerations. This is evidenced by the role of shiftworking in continuous process industries, the long hours worked by those in high capital cost ventures which have prohibitive shiftworking costs such as the extraction of North Sea oil and the role of part-time (especially female) labour, in service sectors which have peak-level periods.

The concept of optimal hours may also be extended to incorporate effects from the supply side. As noted in the introduction, Leslie (1978) has suggested that firms may face an additional constraint imposed by the need to maintain a contented workforce. This may involve working a certain minimum level of overtime on a semi-permanent basis. For example, employers may view continuous overtime working as a cost-minimising strategy in that it may minimise proneness to strikes. There is some evidence to suggest that overtime is greatest in industries and sectors where the basic rate of pay is lowest (Whybrew, 1968). Employers may trade off the costs of raising basic wage rates against the costs of overtime working in order to keep their workforce satisfied and to prevent them striking for higher pay. Such a strategy keeps the workforce satisfied by giving it some flexibility in selecting how long it wishes to work and may also be seen as a means of raising workers incomes in the presence of incomes policies. Under such an interpretation the existence of such overtime may not be as economically irrational as Whybrew (1968) implies. It is not that overtime working is an institutional feature, rather that the level of normal hours are.

The level of optimal hours will clearly be dependent upon the numbers of factors including various price terms reflecting overtime premia, shift premia, etc. Owing to the paucity of data on the relevent prices we cannot make a direct estimate of H^*, as discussed above and below. Furthermore, we also recognise that hours of work may not be instantaneously adjustable and so the following section also discusses the modelling of short-run adjustment of actual hours towards the desired level. In the empirical analysis which follows we take H^* as datum. We need to consider ways of proxying this variable. Leslie (1978) has suggested several possible measures.

$$H^* = a.NH^b \tag{9.3}$$

$$H^* = a + b.NH \tag{9.4}$$

and

$$H^* = a + b.TIME \tag{9.5}$$

Furthermore, Hazeldine (1978) has suggested that H^* can be measured by interpolating the values of actual hours between peaks in the output per person/hour series. However, in view of the steplike nature of the normal hours (NH) time series it is unlikely that either of Leslie's procedures (9.3) or (9.4) would be very useful. On the other hand, equation (9.5) implies that optimal hours bears no relation to normal hours at all, which seems unnecessarily wasteful of useful information since one would clearly expect H^* to be related to negotiated basic hours in the long run. Moreover, the interpolative procedure suggested by Hazledine suffers from all of the usual problems associated with this technique such as unequal strengths of peaks in the time series, assumptions of linear (or log linear) interpolation, etc.

The procedure we adopt here is rather more general than any of those suggested above, namely,

$$H^* = H^*(HN, TREND, CONSTANT) \tag{9.6}$$

so that optimal hours may exhibit constant and trend divergences from normal hours within the log linear specification we adopt for $H^*(\cdot)$. Our measure of normal hours is also converted into a five-year moving average in order to remove the steplike elements in the time series of normal hours which is unlikely to reflect more continuous movements over time of optimal hours. Equation (9.6) and the problems associated with it are discussed further in the next section on data and estimation.

A number of reasons can be identified why the length of the actual working day or week may differ from the optimal length. The main issues to be considered here are the accuracy with which employers forecast their product demands (when carrying out the minimisation problem (9.2)), the labour services required to produce them and the degree and speed with which these can be adjusted. In part this is a technological issue, for if new workers are required, their training and learning of the job will depend upon the production technology in use. Clearly the slower the process of introducing new workers into the workforce the greater the need for working high average hours if product demands are to be met. In an upturn of economic activity, the greater are the fixed costs of adjusting employment, the more actual hours will exceed optimal hours. This aspect of the problem has been emphasised by Hart and Sharot (1978) who develop a model in which hours depend on the lagged adjustment of employment towards its desired level. The work of Nadiri and Rosen (1969) was important in emphasising that hours of work provide a rapid means of adjusting factor inputs to meet an output target. We envisage a similar role for hours here in meeting short-run fluctuations that arise in the face of a fixed capital stock. We assume that any deviation in output from its forecast level, in the first instance, is met largely through an adjustment to hours of work (ignoring variations in intensity of work effort). Actual employment levels may not instantaneously adjust to the desired levels, and so any shortfall here is made up through hours of work. Therefore, as we demonstrate in the next section, the level of desired hours will also depend on current and lagged values of employment. Hence equation (9.7) gives desired actual hours as a function of optimal hours, employment and output forecast errors,

$$H^d = H^d(E(q)/q, H^*, E) \tag{9.7}$$

DATA AND ESTIMATION

The model of the preceding section is now developed into a form suitable for estimation. The model is estimated on various sets of annual data on hours worked that run from 1948–80 for forty industries. The categories of the labour force considered include full-time manual males, full-time manual females, and all workers. This is the same data set as used in Wilson (1982). A complete description of the sources and methods used can be found there. A brief summary of this and the other data series used is as follows.

E = Total employment by industry, mid-year estimates based on the Department of Employment's Census of Employment and continuous series. Estimates prior to 1959 were based on the national insurance card count adjusted to form a continuous series with Census of Employment based series.

Q = Gross output by industry, based on estimates from the Cambridge Growth Project model (MDM3), updated using information from the CSO commodity accounts.

H = Average weekly hours per employee, by industry and by seven categories of worker. The series for manual workers are based primarily on the Department of Employment's Earnings and Hours survey, weighting together the April and October estimates. After 1968 this is supplemented by information from the New Earnings Survey (NES). The series for part-time manual women is truncated and only runs from 1959 onwards. Analysis of this category is therefore restricted to the shorter period 1959–80. The series for non-manual workers are much more limited because of lack of data. Empirical analysis is therefore restricted to very simple models (e.g., fitting of time trends). Their main importance is in providing the means to construct a comprehensive measure of hours worked for all workers. This is based on the series for the seven individual categories (full-time manual men and women, full-time non-manual men and women, part-time men and part-time manual and non-manual women). They are combined together using employment weights which are also used in empirical analysis (see below).

NH = Average weekly normal hours for which a basic rate of pay was received. This series comes from the same source as actual hours and is available for manual workers only. However, it is regarded as a good proxy measure for negotiated basic hours of all workers.

PM = The proportion of manual workers, by industry. For earlier years Census of Population data was interpolated and for more recent years information is taken from the NES.

PT = The proportion of part time workers, obtained from the Censuses of Population, the Department of Employment's Earnings and Hours survey and the Census of Employment.

PF = The proportion of female workers, by industry, based on the Department of Employment Census of Employment and continuous employment series.

The previous section suggested a model of the form given in equation (9.7) so that actual hours deviate from their optimal value due to errors in output forecast and employment adjustments. In our empirical work H^* is proxied by a variable based on normal hours, a constant and a time trend as described in equation (9.6). Together these terms are intended to represent the effect of institutional and supply side pressures on the length of the normal working week as well as any economic cost terms behaving in a trend-like fashion, which have encouraged long-term changes in work patterns towards a greater use of overtime and different shift systems. For this purpose NH is formed as a five-year moving average of the normal hours series (centred on the third observation). On the other hand, the level of optimal hours for non-manual and part-time workers may be less than that for manual workers. This, together with the trends in changing composition of the workforce make the expected signs on both constant and trend ambiguous and dependent on the relative strengths of these factors. *A priori* a positive coefficient is expected on the NH variable, but given the tendency towards growth of overtime work it is likely to be less than unity.

The output errors variable is proxied by the term QD. This attempts in a very simple way to measure output forecast errors. It is constructed as Qt/Q where Qt are the fitted values of regressing the natural log of output against a constant and a time trend. Clearly trend output may not be a rational forecast of expected output, certainly in the short-term but it seems more reasonable in the annual model we are considering here. Although this specification is not very sophisticated its advantage lies in its simplicity of construction and interpretation, and ease of use in a forecasting mode. Moreover in view of the general distributed lag structure which we adopt, our method of measurement of forecast errors is not unduly restrictive. This is because the expected level of output does not fully adjust straight away if the distributed lag structure on QD is considered to be the ratio of two polynomial lag structures on Qt and Q. Given the way in which the variable is constructed we would *a priori* expect a negative coefficient because as output rises above trend average hours would tend to increase.

Following Hart and Sharot (1978), in spirit, if not in detail, the recursive nature of the adjustment of hours and employment is recognised by the inclusion of an employment term. Hart and Sharot argue that any excess or shortfall in employment *vis-à-vis* its desired level cannot be met immediately through employment adjustments. The difference must be made up through utilisation or average hours worked. In their model the current difference between desired and actual employment is incorporated in the hours equation. In order to measure this difference an estimate of desired employment is first derived from an employment function. It is, however, easy to demonstrate that taking the simple partial adjustment mechanism assumed by Hart and Sharot (assuming the variables are all in logs),

$$E_t - E_{t-1} = (E_t^d - E_{t-1}).\lambda \tag{9.8}$$

then $E_t^d - E_{t-1}$ is given by the expression

$$E_t^d = \left(\frac{1-\lambda}{\lambda}\right)(E_t - E_{t-1}) \tag{9.9}$$

The adjustment process can therefore be represented by including the term $E_t - E_{t-1}$ in the hours equation.

The general form of our model is therefore as follows:

$$H = H(NH, QD, E, C, T) \tag{9.10}$$

where the expected derivatives are, $H_{HN} > 0$, H_{QD}, $H_E < 0$

Finally, in the equations which we estimate for the all workers category we clearly have to take into account some of the important changes in the structure of employment, within each industry, which have taken place over our estimation period; in particular, the declining proportion of manual males (who tend to work the longest hours), and the increasing shares of female and part-time employment (both of these categories tend to work lower than average hours). Three variables are included to measure these compositional effects. The proportion of manual males (PM) is, in general, expected to have a positive coefficient, although there may be certain exceptions in industries where they work lower than average hours. Subject to similar caveats, we would expect the proportion of females (PF) and the proportion of part-timers (PT) to have negative coefficients. The final estimating equation contains first order lags on all of the economic variables to capture features of less than instantaneous adjustment. Initially at least the coefficients on E_t and E_{t-1} are not restricted to be the same. In the case of the expectations error variable we have already discussed some of our motivations for introducing a lag structure in the previous section. More generally, a lag on QD is expected to reflect the continuing importance of past errors in affecting current decisions. A lagged dependent variable appears to reflect the costs of adjusting the level of hours while optimal hours may adjust slowly due to costs associated with changing work patterns. Hart and Sharot argue that hours may be adjusted almost instantaneously and exclude lag terms in hours. We prefer to regard this as an empirical question and include such terms in our initial estimating equation. Our unrestricted model, estimated by OLS is as follows (note that in the case of 'all workers' the specification also includes terms in PM, PF and PT. A log linear specification was adopted throughout).

$$H_t = C + a.NH_t + b.QD_t + d.E_t + e.H_{t-1} + f.NH_{t-1} \\ + g.QD_{t-1} + h_{t-1} + j.T + e_t \qquad (9.11)$$

where e_t is a white noise error.

Simplifying the equation as far as legitimately possible and adopting the attitude that intertemporal issues would be better represented by equation dynamics rather than error dynamics. This was done as the spirit of the model is more consistent with gradual adjustment using likelihood ratio tests and Chow stability tests with attention given to the economic interpretation of the model. The model was estimated over the period 1948–77, retaining three observations on which to test parameter constancy. The results are discussed in the following section.

RESULTS

The model was estimated for each of forty industries and for three main categories of workers. The results for manual males, the group upon whom previous research has concentrated and where the data is at its most reliable are discussed first. We then consider the results of applying the model to full-time manual females and all workers.

(a) Results for Manual Males

For manual males the final equations selected are generally very successful over a range of criteria. As Table 9.1 shows, the multiple correlation coefficients (R^2) exceeds 95 per cent in eleven cases, is between 90–95 per cent in fourteen cases and is less than 90 per cent in fourteen industries. The autocorrelation properties of the estimated equations, measured by the *D.W.* or '*h*' statistics are generally quite satisfactory. The tests of structural stability over the 'forecast' period 1978–80 are reasonable in most cases. However, there are clearly some industries for whom the hypothesis of no structural change at conventional significance levels is rejected, such as agriculture, tobacco and iron and steel. However, these tend to be cases where the data for these years is particularly uncertain and likely to be subject to revision. Furthermore they also tend to occur where the properties are otherwise satisfactory.

In terms of the structure of the preferred equations, the most common form selected involves terms in normal hours and the first-difference of the output errors variable. Terms in employment, and the time trend are rarely important. This type of specification supports our hypothesis that it is not the level of output but the deviation from trend which plays a role in determining average hours. Furthermore since, in most instances, a first difference form of the output error variable has been accepted and the lagged dependent variable has a coefficient less than unity the equations possess steady state solutions in which average hours are a function of optimal hours only. Thus average hours of manual males are generally determined by a stable error correction mechanism (*ECM*) structure. The variable *QD* can be given a further interpretation. Namely, that it is not so much instances of output forecast errors $QD \neq 1$ that affect the level of average hours of manual males, but the relative growth of trend compared to actual output. This suggests that firms'

Table 9.1 Results for manual males

	Constant	NH	QD	E	H1[d]	NH1[d]	QD1[d]	E1[d]
Agriculture	−1.586[a]	1.423[a]	0.166[b]				−0.226[a]	
Coal mining	0.602	2.206			0.694[a]	−2.053		
Oil & natural gas	−0.202	−1.182			0.830[a]	1.420		
Mining n.e.s.	0.195	−1.164			0.817[a]	1.307		
Cereal processing	2.205[a]	0.440[b]	−0.090[b]					
Food processing n.e.s.	0.689	0.219			0.781[a]	−0.175		
Drink	1.021[b]	−0.383				1.124[a]		
Tobacco manufacture	4.151[a]	−2.429[b]		−0.344[b]	0.181	2.505		
Coke ovens	1.317[c]	3.276[a]			0.528[b]	−2.827[b]		
Mineral oil refining	−1.348[c]	0.941[a]			0.432			
Chemicals	0.182	0.286[a]			0.674[a]			
Iron & steel	4.012[a]	0.406[b]	−0.257[a]	−0.267[a]				
Non-ferrous metals	−1.118[c]	1.314[a]	−0.184[a]					
Mechanical engineering	0.157	0.361[a]			0.607[a]			
Instrument engineering	0.428[c]	0.364[b]			0.529[a]			
Electrical engineering	−0.085	0.256[a]			0.772[a]			
Shipbuilding	0.013	0.362[a]			0.634[b]			
Motor vehicles	1.003[a]	0.533[a]			0.210			
Aerospace equipment	−0.461[c]	−0.554			0.629[a]	1.054[c]		
Vehicles n.e.s.	−0.433	1.023[b]	0.016	−0.123[b]	0.287		−0.104	
Metal goods	0.062				0.675[a]	0.315[a]		
Textile fibres	0.979[a]	1.325[b]			0.467[a]	−1.048[c]		
Textiles n.e.s.	−0.166	−0.018			0.688[a]			
Leather, clothing etc.	0.450[b]	0.307[a]			0.575[a]			
Bricks	0.284	0.704[c]			0.759[a]	−0.531		
Timber & furniture	−0.025				1.006[a]			
Paper & board	−0.049	0.065[c]			0.949[a]			
Printing & publishing	0.007	0.120[b]			0.723[a]			
Rubber	0.197				0.659[a]	0.398[a]		
Manufactures n.e.s.	0.282	0.207[a]			0.725[a]			
Construction	0.246		−0.127[a]		0.600[a]	0.346[a]		
Gas	2.031[a]		−0.004		0.281	0.198[b]		
Electricity	−0.154	0.363	−0.132	−0.151	0.735[a]			
Water	1.395[a]		−0.050		0.262	0.384[a]	−0.023	
Transport	0.617	0.098			0.750[a]			
Communications	1.794[a]	2.583[a]			0.331[b]	−2.370[a]		
Distribution	0.567[b]				0.625[a]	0.233[a]		
Insurance	0.981[a]	0.246[a]			0.503[a]			
Professional services	2.415[a]				0.390[a]	0.334[b]		−0.242[a]
Miscellaneous services	0.630[b]	0.208[b]			0.627[a]			

output will, in the very short term (i.e. one period), be supply constrained when $QD < 1$ so that additional hours are needed on a sufficient scale to meet output demands when there are shortages of factor stocks (capital and labour). However, by the following period sufficient flexibility has been achieved. When output demand is relatively low $QD > 1$ overtime working may not be reduced immediately and there is some hang-over effect whereby high levels of overtime working persists until the following period. 'Institutionalists' may take some support from this evidence of a hangover effect. However, as the presence of a

Trend	DQD[d]	DNH[d]	DE[d]	Corrected R^2	D.W.	F-test	n	e
0.004[a]				0.978	1.92	(3,24) 7.75	1.4230	−0.0600
	−0.240[a]			0.936	−0.50	(3,24) 0.87	0.5000	0
	−0.007			0.863	0.07	(3,24) 1.38	1.4000	0
	−0.086[b]			0.886	0.03	(3,24) 1.94	0.7814	0
0.002[b]				0.673	1.39	(3,25) 3.86	0.4400	−0.0900
−0.001	0.037			0.953	−0.33	(3,23) 2.17	0.2009	0
0.002[a]	−0.134			0.835	1.80	(3,24) 5.74	0.7410	0
−0.003[c]	−0.226[c]		AR1	0.816	0.38	(3,22) 11.14	0.0928	0
	−0.014		0.668[b]	0.950	—	(3,21) 0.32	0.9513	0
	−0.005			0.946	−1.61	(3,25) 1.49	1.6567	0
	−0.168			0.953	0.52	(3,25) 1.10	0.8773	0
−0.006[a]				0.947	1.98	(3,24) 9.34	0.4060	0.2570
0.002[b]				0.939	2.04	(3,25) 2.67	1.3140	−0.1840
	−0.149[b]			0.922	0.73	(3,25) 1.57	0.9186	0
	−0.053			0.911	−0.80	(3,25) 2.17	0.7728	0
	−0.158[a]			0.973	0.02	(3,25) 1.58	1.1228	0
	−0.165[a]	−0.115		0.932	−0.18	(3,24) 2.89	0.9891	0
	−0.103[a]			0.814	0.26	(3,25) 3.17	0.6747	0
	−0.042[c]			0.960	−0.63	(3,24) 0.74	1.3477	0
−0.006				0.907		(3,22) 1.08	1.4348	−0.1234
	−0.145[a]			0.932	−1.31	(3,25) 0.71	0.9692	0
	−0.091[a]			0.866	0.20	(3,24) 2.04	0.5197	0
0.001	−0.208			0.966	0.56	(3,23) 3.09	−0.0577	0
	−0.148			0.954	1.01	(3,25) 0.54	0.7224	0
	−0.158[a]			0.956	−0.48	(3,25) 4.64	0.7178	0
	−0.088[a]			0.933	−1.28	(3,26) 1.60	0.0000	0
	−0.226[a]	−0.165[a]		0.974	−0.04	(3,24) 1.45	1.2745	0
	−0.149[a]	−0.150[c]		0.823	0.92	(3,24) 3.69	0.4332	0
	−0.166[a]			0.962	−0.09	(3,25) 1.78	1.1672	0
	−0.151[a]			0.950	0.80	(3,25) 2.59	0.7527	0
			AR1	0.925	0.45	(3,25) 0.55	0.8650	0.3175
			0.278[a]	0.582	—	(3,24) 3.25	0.2750	−0.0040
				0.939	0.89	(3,23) 2.06	1.3698	−0.4981
			−0.022	0.793	1.38	(3,23) 1.75	0.5203	−0.0990
	−0.264[c]			0.750	0.77	(3,24) 0.88	0.3920	0
	−0.825[a]			0.615	−0.58	(3,24) 2.50	0.3184	0
	−0.102[c]			0.940	0.02	(3,25) 0.43	0.6213	0
	−0.064			0.829	−0.47	(3,25) 0.07	0.4950	0
0.007[a]				0.835	0.96	(3,24) 2.71	0.5475	0
	−0.061			0.953	0.60	(3,25) 3.42	0.5576	0

Notes:
[a] Significant at the 10% level.
[b] Significant at the 5% level.
[c] Significant at the 1% level.
[d] A 'D' prefix indicates a first difference and a '1' suffix a one-period lag. AR1 indicates autoregressive estimation of order one.
[e] Long-run elasticity of average hours with respect to output deviations.
[n] Long-run elasticity of average hours with respect to normal hours.

lagged dependent variable in many of the specifications indicates, the costs of adjusting average hours may well be the cause of this. Such costs might include uncertainties attached to future expectations of product demand as well as affects arising from a relative loss of productivity of the type cited by Feldstein (1967) and Craine (1973).

Table 9.2 Full-time manual females

	Constant	NH	QD	E	H1^d	NH1^d	QD1^d	E1^d
Agriculture	0.206	0.594^a			0.353^c			
Coal mining	1.578	0.605^c	−0.234^a					
Oil & natural gas	1.322	0.330			0.328^c			
Mining n.e.s.	0.169	0.228			0.730^a			
Cereal processing	0.332^b	0.902^b	−0.054^c					
Food processing n.e.s.	0.797^b	0.779^a						
Drink	0.892^a	0.750^a						
Tobacco manufacture	1.282^c	0.662^a						
Coke ovens	0.802^c	2.169^a				−1.325^b	−0.121	−0.083^c
Mineral oil refining	1.045^c	0.723^a	−0.017^c					
Chemicals	0.274	1.016^a		−0.061^b				
Iron & steel	0.011	1.087^a		−0.066^b				
Non-ferrous metals	0.354^c	0.888^a						
Mechanical engineering	−0.413^a	0.605^a			0.500^b			
Insurance engineering	−0.468^a	1.113^a	−0.038^b					
Electrical engineering	−0.606^a	0.916^a			0.236^c			
Shipbuilding	−0.224	1.049^a						
Motor vehicles	0.449	0.806^a						
Aerospace equipment	−0.505^a	0.679^a			0.451^a			
Vehicles n.e.s.	0.778^c	0.779^a						
Metal goods	−0.110	1.012^a						
Textile fibres	−0.096	1.106^a	−0.109^a	−0.098^a			0.024^c	
Textiles n.e.s.	−0.307^b	0.737^a	0.203^a		0.331^a		0.129^a	
Leather, clothing etc.	0.042	0.383^a			0.596^a			
Bricks	1.493^a	0.731^a		−0.092^a				
Timber & furniture	−0.003	0.982^a	−0.074^b					
Paper & board	0.027	0.373^a			0.618^a			
Printing & publishing	0.110^c	0.529^a			0.438^b			
Rubber	0.476^b	0.861^a						
Manufactures n.e.s.	1.434^a	0.686^a		−0.061^b				
Construction	3.702^a							
Gas	4.698^a			−0.195				
Electricity	1.271^a	0.494^a		−0.098^b	0.290^c		−0.063	
Water	2.418^a	0.327^b						
Transport	0.975^a				0.747^a			
Communications	−2.700^a	1.691^a	−0.640^b				0.343^c	
Distribution	0.938^c	0.062			0.688^a			
Insurance	−0.233^c	0.276^b			0.784^a			
Professional services	1.881^a	0.135^c			0.511^a			−0.096^b
Miscellaneous services	1.081^a	1.630^a			0.336^c	−1.265^a		

Trend	DQD^d	DNH^d	DE^d	Corrected R^2	D.W.	F-test	n	e
				0.93	1.89	(3,20) 1.11	0.918	0
-0.0008^a				0.97	1.25	(3,25) 0.63	0.605	-0.234
-0.0003^b	-0.009			0.94	0.88	(3,24) 2.58	0.490	0
				0.85	-1.26	(3,26)14.63	0.843	0
				0.98	1.61	(3,26) 0.62	0.902	-0.057
-0.0013^b				0.98	1.54	(3,26) 2.02	0.779	0
				0.81	2.56	(3,27) 1.78	0.750	0
-0.003^c				0.90	1.59	(3,26) 5.21	0.662	0
-0.002^a				0.96	2.11	(3,23) 4.94	0.844	-0.121
-0.003^b				0.91	1.64	(3,25) 2.34	0.723	-0.017
	-0.055^b			0.98	1.41	(3,25) 3.31	1.016	0
	-0.064^a			0.96	1.96	(3,25) 1.47	1.087	0
	-0.063			0.92	1.64	(3,26) 1.51	0.888	0
		-0.159^a		0.98	-1.09	(3,25) 1.49	1.210	0
				0.97	1.70	(3,26) 6.09	1.113	-0.038
	-0.088^b			0.97	1.01	(3,25) 0.22	1.199	0
				0.87	1.76	(3,27) 5.55	1.049	0
	-0.068^a			0.93	1.95	(3,26) 0.17	0.866	0
				0.97	0.66	(3,26) 0.23	1.237	0
-0.001^c	-0.033^c			0.93	1.56	(3,25) 7.56	0.779	0
	-0.053^b			0.97	1.86	(3,26) 0.02	1.012	0
				0.96	1.52	(3,24)10.45	1.106	-0.085
				0.99	-0.53	(3,24)26.60	1.102	0.496
	-0.112^a			0.97	1.20	(3,25) 3.63	0.948	0
-0.002^a	-0.059^b			0.99	1.82	(3,24) 6.72	0.731	0
				0.96	2.23	(3,26) 0.77	0.982	-0.74
	-0.079^a			0.97	0.64	(3,25) 2.50	0.976	0
	-0.069^a			0.98	1.00	(3,25) 1.35	0.941	0
	-0.061^a			0.97	1.98	(3,26) 1.83	0.861	0
	-0.072^a			0.99	1.51	(3,25) 0.88	0.680	0
-0.0029^a				0.68	1.31	(3,27) 3.36	0	0
-0.008^a				0.68	1.84	(3,26) 3.52	0	0
				0.92	0.38	(3,24) 4.47	0.696	-0.089
		-0.111		0.23	1.39	(3,26) 0.22	0.327	0
-0.0012^a	-0.1196			0.91	-0.99	(3,25)10.03	0	0
0.005^a		-0.360^c		0.88	2.30	(3,23) 2.03	1.691	-0.297
-0.001	-0.119^c			0.96	0.98	(3,24) 1.10	0.199	0
	-0.016			0.97	-1.08	(3,25) 0.25	1.277	0
				0.98	-1.17	(3,25) 0.58	0.276	0
	-0.057			0.97	0.26	(3,24) 0.16	0.550	0

Notes: [a]Significant at the 10% level. [b]Significant at the 5% level. [c]Significant at the 1% level. [d]A 'D' prefix indicates a first difference and a '1' suffix a one-period lag. AR1 indicates autoregressive estimation of order one. [e]Long-run elasticity of average hours with respect to output deviations. [n]Long-run elasticity of average hours with respect to normal hours.

By comparison with the role played by output in our model, the employment terms are generally insignificant. There seems to be little independent role for the adjustment of hours to discrepancies between desired and actual employment over and above the role of the output forecast error terms. However, in those industries in which they do appear (eight cases in all) they are always of the correct sign and usually significant at the conventional 95 per cent confidence level. One of the features of the coefficients on $NH_{t-i}(i = 0, 1)$ which is of interest is the long-run elasticity of this variable with respect to average hours. This elasticity is the product of the elasticity of hours with respect to optimal hours and the elasticity of optimal hours with respect to the normal hours variable. *A priori* one might expect that the first elasticity should be close to unity while the long-run behaviour of normal and actual hours suggests the latter may be less than unity. In practice since optimal hours as such are not observed we cannot measure these separate elasticities but only the compound one.

The estimated long-run values of these elasticities are tabulated in the column headed '*n*' for each industry. They generally appear quite reasonable, giving support to our specifications. The weighted average elasticity across all industries is 0.67 (at the mean). This suggests that in the long-run reductions in normal hours have resulted in a reduction in average hours of about two thirds the size (in percentage terms). This reflects the tendency for the proportion of overtime working to increase as negotiated hours have fallen. Across manufacturing industries the average elasticity is slightly higher at 0.73 and in services it is rather lower at 0.52 although in both instances this does disguise some rather differing estimates for individual industries.

The sectors with lowest response elasticities appear to be the food industries, textiles and transport and communications. The greatest response is found in agriculture, chemicals, engineering and construction. However, the calculated elasticities are typically all less than unity. These results imply that the potential scope for raising employment by reducing normal hours will be limited because of the tendency for overtime to rise. This issue is discussed in more detail in Whitley and Wilson (1986).

(b) Results for Full-time Manual Females

Many of the comments made above regarding the structure of the preferred equations for manual males carry over to manual female category. However the difference of the output error variable is less prevalent in the case of manual females as reported in Table 9.2. The current value (Q^t/Q) alone is found more frequently. Generally speaking, the output effects, whether in their unrestricted or first-difference form, possess coefficients which are roughly half the size (in modulus) of those for manual males. This suggests from the employers point of view, that the hours of manual females are not a primary source of labour utilisation adjustment when output deviates from its trend level. Compared to the results for manual males though, there is evidence of a more important role for the adjustment of manual female hours in response to general labour shortages (as represented by the employment terms). The role of the lagged dependent variable is somewhat more limited than for manual males, suggesting, as we might expect, that the costs of adjusting the hours of female manual labour are less important for the employer than are those for manual males.

By far the most overwhelming determinant level of average hours of manual females is the level of NH_t, the main component of 'optimal' hours. The average elasticity of average hours with respect to this variable across all industries is 0.86 compared to 0.67 for manual males.

Across manufacturing industries the estimated elasticity for manual females is 1.03 and in the service sector it is 0.63 compared to 0.73 and 0.52 respectively, for manual males. Thus the pattern is the same for manual females in that the greatest response is found in manufacturing. The most responsive sectors are found to be metal goods, engineering, textiles and transport and communication. In the case of engineering this finding is commensurate with that for manual males whilst in the case of textiles and transport and communication the conclusions on responses are reversed.

As we mentioned earlier, the response to the output-error variable is more limited in the short run for manual females than it is for males. However, the preferred equations for manual females do contain a number of cases in which some long-run effect is present. The size of the long-run elasticities however, are negligible, reiterating that the role of such a term is primarily a short-run one, whichever category of worker we are considering.

(c) Results for All Workers

Structurally, the preferred results for the all workers category, contained in Table 9.3, are again very similar to those for manual males and females with the first difference specification of the output-errors term being prevalent. Hence the similar comments apply here as were made for

Table 9.3 Results for all workers

	Constant	PM	PF	PT	NH	QD	E	$H1^d$	$NH1^d$	$QD1^d$
Agriculture	1.058^a		-0.291		-0.381				0.729^c	-0.193^b
Coal mining	0.514				1.698			0.242^b	-1.583	
Oil and natural gas	-2.308^b							0.753^b		-0.008
Mining n.e.s.	3.214^a	3.101^a		0.047^b	1.673^a	-0.003^a	-0.030^a	0.002	-0.620^b	
Cereal processing	2.243^a				0.204		-0.075	0.594^a	-0.325^c	-0.029
Food processing n.e.s.	1.001^b	0.347^b	-0.058	-0.138^c	0.517^a	-0.177^a		0.331^c		-0.072^a
Drink	-0.350	-0.202	0.133	-0.532^a	0.113	-0.126	0.254^a	0.566^a		0.207^b
Tobacco manufacture	2.175^a				0.631		-0.213^a	0.011^b		
Coke ovens	1.371				0.628^a	-0.007		0.706^a	-6.557^a	
Mineral oil refining	-2.082^b	-1.978			3.616^a			0.350^b		
Chemicals	-0.015	1.001^a		-0.078	1.197^a	-0.067^b		0.797^a	-0.794^a	0.113^a
Iron and Steel	4.617^b	3.860^b	0.026	-0.195^b	0.164	-0.233^a	-0.269^a			
Non-ferrous metals	-0.572^b			0.084^c	1.192^a			-0.113^a		
Mechanical engineering	-0.223	0.494^a			0.441^a			0.621^a		
Instrument engineering	0.710				0.461^a			0.354^a		
Electrical engineering	0.700	0.557^a		-0.044	0.803^a			0.564^a	-0.559^a	
Shipbuilding	0.014				1.009^a	-0.065		0.742^a	-0.749^a	0.150^a
Motor vehicles	0.099		0.118^a	0.149^b	1.046^b	-0.001				-0.056^b
Aerospace equipment	1.422^a	2.005	0.006	-0.270^a	0.610^a	-0.064^a				
Vehicles n.e.s.	2.655	-3.458		0.039	1.711^a		0.012			

Table 9.3 (Contd.)

	$E1^d$	Trend	DQD^d	DNH^a	DE^d	Corrected R^2	D.W.	F-test	n	e
Agriculture						0.9950	1.213	18.28	0.459	−0.255
Coal mining		0.000^b	-0.216^a			0.9482	−0.3153	1.00	0.466	0
Oil and natural gas			-0.073^b			0.7705	−0.4617	1.09	1.676	−0.006
Mining n.e.s.						0.9292	−0.994	2.22	−1.025	0
Cereal processing		-0.003^c				0.9891	6.5763	1.76	0.287	−0.221
Food processing n.e.s.						0.9964	1.198	5.16	0.260	−0.166
Drink		0.003				0.9642	−0.650	3.66	0.638	0.082
Tobacco manufacture		-0.004^a	−0.112			0.9671	1.884	7.04	0.628	0
Coke ovens	2.829^b					0.9553	1.557	4.77	−0.381	−0.024
Mineral oil refining			−0.016			0.9756	−0.830	2.03	1.842	0
Chemicals		−0.001				0.9861	0.042	1.12	−3.911	0.227
Iron & Steel						0.9833	2.531	12.64	0.164	−0.233
Non-ferrous metals						0.9676	1.978	1.03	1.071	0
Mechanical engineering			-0.103^b			0.9686	0.574	0.93	1.164	0
Instrument engineering			0.021			0.9867	−0.116	0.12	0.714	0
Electrical engineering			-0.057^b			0.9886	−0.843	0.46	0.560	0
Shipbuilding						0.9613	−0.988	5.37	1.008	0.329
Motor vehicles						0.8898	2.154	3.29	1.046	−0.057
Aerospace equipment		0.003				0.9871	2.304	0.74	0.610	−0.064
Vehicles n.e.s.			−0.003			0.9493	2.196	0.61	1.711	0

Table 9.3 (Contd.)

	Constant	PM	PF	PT	NH	QD	E	H1^a	NH1^a	QD1^a
Metal goods	3.497^a	1.847^a	0.273^a	0.159^b	0.258^b					
Textile fibres	−0.398	−1.944^b	−0.079^b		1.058^a			0.247	−0.250	
Textiles n.e.s.	0.754^b	0.328^b			0.250^a			0.450^a		
Leather, clothing etc.	1.497^a	0.342^a	0.209	−0.140^b	0.525^a					
Bricks	0.720^c	0.398^c			0.817^a			0.569^a	−0.568^a	
Timber and furniture	1.386^a	0.811^a			0.639^a			0.613^a	−0.609^a	
Paper and board	2.135^a	0.852^b		−0.216^a	0.363^a	−0.122^a				0.016
Printing and publishing	0.433	1.539^a	0.070		2.186^a			0.150	−1.416^a	
Rubber	1.322^a	0.589	0.069		0.682^a	−0.105^a				
Manufactures n.e.s.	1.641^a	0.571^a		0.166^b	1.131^a			0.304^b	−0.800^c	
Construction	−0.216	5.646^a	−0.137		1.054^a			0.335^a	−0.462	
Gas	3.323^a	3.375^a	0.066^c		−0.038		0.056		0.150	
Electricity	1.851	7.616^a	0.232^c	0.228^a	0.747^b	−0.042		0.513^a	−0.517^a	
Water	3.227^a	4.907^a	0.107^b	−0.367^b	0.094	−0.047				
Transport	−1.183		0.053	−0.811^a	0.490^a			0.559^a		
Communications	0.660^a				0.817^a	−0.113^a		0.015^a		0.435^a
Distribution	−0.431		−0.092^c		1.073^a	−0.013		0.611^a	−0.599^a	
Insurance	0.832^b	0.452^a			0.757^a			0.371^b	−0.359^b	
Professional services	1.979^b	0.889^a		0.736^a	0.522			0.488^a	−0.505	
Miscellaneous services	−1.600^a		−0.124^b	0.091^a	1.123^a			0.275^b		

Table 9.3 (Contd.)

	$E1^d$	Trend	DQD^d	DNH^d	DE^d	Corrected R^2	D.W.	F-test	n	e
Metal goods			-0.063^a			0.9789	2.111	0.83	0.253	0
Textiles fibres			-0.069^a			0.9362	-0.950	2.97	1.073	0
Textiles n.e.s.			-0.150^a			0.9874	0.662	9.47	0.636	0
Leather, clothing etc.						0.9846	1.698	0.11	0.525	0
Bricks			-0.109^a			0.9841	-0.081	2.90	0.578	0
Timber and furniture			-0.053^a			0.9791	-0.354	2.35	0.078	0
Paper and board						0.9866	1.856	0.68	0.363	-0.106
Printing and publishing		0.004^a	-0.077^a			0.9893	-0.156	8.96	0.906	0
Rubber			-0.082^a			0.9770	1.648	0.41	0.682	-0.105
Manufactures n.e.s.		0.015^a				0.9903	0.735	1.21	0.476	0
Construction						0.9847	1.012	25.02	0.890	0
Gas			-0.006			0.9613	1.522	2.29	0.112	0
Electricity		0.005^c				0.9798	0.116	1.85	0.472	-0.086
Water		0.010^b	-0.179^c			0.9522	2.103	2.87	0.094	-0.047
Transport						0.9583	0.857	8.02	1.111	0
Communications						0.9278	0.489	1.90	0.829	0.327
Distribution						0.9956	0.109	0.10	0.219	-0.033
Insurance			-0.007			0.9922	0.073	0.23	0.633	0
Professional services			-0.248			0.9802	0.104	1.14	0.033	0
Miscellaneous services						0.9970	0.957	1.44	1.549	1.549

Notes:
[a] Significant at the 10% level.
[b] Significant at the 5% level.
[c] Significant at the 1% level.
[d] A 'D' prefix indicates a first difference and a '1' suffix a one period lag.

manual males; namely that there exists a stable long run solution and that the adjustment properties are similar. Compared to the manual male and female coefficients, those for all workers have a very similar long-run response (i.e. little or no effect). In the short run the all workers output coefficients are generally in line with those of manual females and therefore smaller than manual males.

The long-run values of the estimated elasticities of normal hours with respect to average hours are tabulated in the column headed 'n' and they generally appear quite reasonable. The average elasticity across all industries is 0.63 suggesting a limited correspondence between cuts in the normal working week and the average working week, and reflecting the tendency for overtime working to increase as negotiated hours have fallen. Across manufacturing industries the average elasticity is rather lower at 0.35 and in services it is rather higher at 0.79, although in both instances this does disguise some rather differing estimates for individual industries. However, it does show that average hours in the service sector are more responsive to cuts in the normal working week than in manufacturing (a feature not found for the individual manual male or female estimates discussed above, suggesting the importance of compositional effects such as the role of non-manual workers). The lowest estimates are found in the (nationalised) public utilities, gas, electricity and water (and also in transport). In several industries these elasticities are rather implausible. In coke ovens considerable difficulty was experienced in finding a satisfactory specification and in this case a second order lag had to be added to the unrestricted model to make the equation plausible.

Compared to the manual male and female groups, therefore, the response elasticities for the all workers category is rather different. In particular, manufacturing is less responsive than services. This is almost certainly due to the other, non-manual and part-time components of the all workers category.

Turning now to some of the other variables; the employment and trend terms are generally not very important and in most cases are excluded from the preferred specifications. In the case of the employment variables there seems to be little independent role for the adjustment of hours to discrepancies between desired and actual employment over and above the role of the output forecast error terms in leading to adjustments to actual hours. Furthermore, in the few industries in which employment terms do appear they are often poorly determined and have the wrong sign. Similarly, the time trend coefficient is rarely significant and even when it is contained in the preferred equation it is usually very small.

The compositional variables, which are designed to take account of the changing structure of industrial employment, are most significant for the changing proportion of manual workers. These terms are highly significant in many industries and, with several exceptions, have the expected positive sign. They are particularly significant in the non-service sectors of the economy where manual workers formed a large proportion of the workforce for much of our estimation period.

The effects of the proportion of part-time workers and of female workers are not very important. In view of the significant changes in the proportion of part-time female workers who on average work just under half the average level of hours this result is somewhat surprising. These variables, when included, frequently have positive coefficients where we would, *a priori*, expect a negative effect, in view of the tendency for these groups to work less than average hours. However, these trends are relatively recent phenomena (since the middle of the 1960s) and consequently in our estimation period (1948–77) they may not weigh so heavily. The Census of Population information reported in Table 8 of Wilson (1982) illustrates this point. It shows that it is only at some point after 1961 that the proportions of females and part-time workers begin to show any significant changes, whereas the changes in the manual share of employment is a much longer-term phenomenon. Nevertheless, the positive coefficients are somewhat disturbing and must be regarded as a criticism of the model in this case. In part the unsatisfactory nature of the coefficients for the proportion of females and part-timers may arise because of measurement error in the dependent variable, since data on the categories other than full-time manual workers are relatively weak.

For the all workers category, average hours are least responsive to changes in normal hours in the public utilities sector, agriculture and coal mining, followed by the manufacturing sector, and highest in the service sector. This reverses the conclusions reached for manual males for whom manufacturing was found to be more responsive than services.

CONCLUSIONS

This chapter has sought to examine some of the main economic determinants of average weekly hours for various categories of worker in the labour market. We have argued that there are various reasons why employers might find it profitable to work its labour force at a rate of utilisation exceeding normal hours in the long-term. For the main groups, where the data is at its most reliable, the empirical models which have been estimated have shown a remarkable degree of consistency in their findings and specifications. The main findings indicate the importance of overtime working as an adjustment factor, made mainly through manual males, to unanticipated changes in output. The results indicate that although in the long-run hours worked are independent of output this is an important factor in the short term.

References

BALL, R. J. and St CYR, E. B. A. (1966) 'Short Term Employment Functions in British Manufacturing Industry', *Review of Economic Studies* (July), pp. 179–207.

BOSWORTH, D. L. and DAWKINS, P. J. (1982) *Optimal Capital Utilisation in British Manufacturing Industry*, report to the Leverhulme Trust.

────── and Westaway, A. J. (1986) Hours of work and employment in UK manufacturing industry: an empirical analysis, Chapter 2 in Wilson (1986) pp. 32–61.

CLEGG, H. (1962) 'Implications of the Shorter Working Week for Management', *British Institute for Management*, occasional paper 8.

CRAINE, R. (1973). 'On the Service Flow from Labour', *Review of Economic Studies* (January) pp. 39–46.

FELDSTEIN, M. S. (1967) 'Specification of the Labor Input in the Aggregate Production Function, *Review of Economic Studies* 34 (October), pp. 375–386.

HART, R. A. and SHAROT, T. (1978) 'The Short-run Demand for Workers and Hours: A Recursive Model', *Review of Economic Studies* 45. pp. 299–309.

HAZLEDINE, T. (1978) 'New Specifications for Employment and Hours Functions' *Economica* 45, pp. 179–193.

HUGHES, B. and LESLIE, D. (1975) 'Hours of Work in British Manufacturing Industries', *Scottish Journal of Political Economy*, XXII 3, pp. 293–304.

KNIGHT, K. G. and WILSON, R. A. (1974) 'Labour Hoarding, Employment and Unemployment in British Manufacturing Industry', *Applied Economics* 6 (December). pp. 303–10.

LESLIE, D. (1978) A supply and demand analysis of the structure of hours of work for UK production industries (University of Manchester: Discussion Paper 5).

────── and WISE, J. (1980) 'The Productivity of Hours in UK Manufacturing and Production Industries', *Economic Journal* 90 (1), pp. 74–84.

NADIRI, M. I. and ROSEN, S. (1969) 'Interrelated Factor Demand Functions', *American Economic Review* 59 (September), pp. 457–71.

SHOREY, J. (1978) 'Time series analysis of strike frequency', *British Journal of Industrial Relations* xv (1), pp. 63–75.

ULLMAN, L. (1968) Collective bargaining and industrial efficiency, in Caves, R. E. (ed.) *Britain's Economic Prospects* (London: George Allen & Unwin), pp. 324–80.

WHITLEY, J. D. and WILSON, R. A. (1984) 'The impact on employment of a reduction in the length of the working week: results of simulations using a macroeconomic model of the UK economy', *Cambridge Journal of Economics*, 10 (1), pp. 43–60.

WHYBREW, E. G. (1968) Overtime working in Britain, Royal Commission on Trade Unions and Employee Associations, Research Paper 9 (London: HMSO).

WILSON, R. A. (1982) 'Average weekly hours 1948–81: changes in the pattern of hours worked', paper presented at a conference on 'Hours of Work and Employment', University of Warwick (16–17 September). Chapter 1 in Wilson (1986), pp. 6–31.

——— (ed.) (1986) *Hours of Work* (University of Warwick: Institute for Employment Research).

10 Estimating the Relationship Between Output and Hours Worked in United Kingdom Manufacturing and Production Industries

Richard T. Baillie and Mick Silver[1]

INTRODUCTION

The concern of this chapter is with the estimation of the marginal productivity of hours worked for British manufacturing industries. Such estimates are of particular interest when considering the policy option of reducing average hours worked to increase employment (i.e., the number of employees). The approach taken is separately to specify the numbers of employees and hours worked in a production function.

Overtime work is generally paid at a higher rate than normal hours. This recognises the advantages of increasing the utilisation of existing capital and not having to incur the costs of hiring and training new employees and the fixed element in the wage bill. However, there are *a priori* grounds for believing the marginal productivity of overtime hours is different from that of normal hours. Less employees may work overtime than normal time and (depending on whether an optimal capital to labour ratio was in force in normal hours) this may lead to differences in the productivity of overtime hours compared with normal hours. Worker fatigue may also impose (and lead to) diminishing returns. Denison, in his United States growth accounting studies, used a guesstimate that a small change in average hours worked for full-time, non-farm wage and salary workers led to 30 per cent offset in output per man hour (Denison, 1974, p. 39). Leslie and Wise (1980) cite the TUC's judgement of the elasticity of output with respect to hours worked as 0.6. This figure was used as part of the TUC's case for a shorter working week.

This chapter is concerned with the econometric evidence and questions certain aspects of existing studies for United Kingdom manufacturing industries, and provides new estimates. Particular attention will be directed to inter-industry variation in the marginal productivity of hours worked, thus arguing for caution in the use of 'blanket policies' on changes in the length of the working week.

SOME EVIDENCE FROM ECONOMETRIC STUDIES

Craine (1973) used United States time series data for total manufacturing to separately specify hours worked and number of employees in a Cobb–Douglas production function, of the form:

$$Q = A H^\alpha L^\beta K^\gamma e^{\phi t} \tag{10.1}$$

where:
- Q = net output
- A = a constant
- H = hours worked
- L = number of employees
- K = capital stock.

The last term is an attempt to replicate the effects of technical progress over a time trend, t.

The resulting value of α was 2.02. However, as Hazledine (1981) noted, the estimated model suffered from autocorrelation and the output index used for most of the sample period was constructed largely from man hour interpolations – see also Sims (1974) p. 707.

Feldstein (1967) estimated a Cobb–Douglas production function with hours and employees separately specified using cross-section (two-digit SIC industrial level) data for the United Kingdom. This assumed the production function to be the same for all industries, and consequently ignored possible inter-industry variation if α. Feldstein's results for α, whilst mostly insignificant, were on average 2.13. Explanations for their higher values may lie with losses in output in normal time due to the waste involved in setting up the production process, which does not appear in overtime work (assuming setting-up time to be greater than closing-down time). Another explanation may lie with specification or estimation problems in the models used, and already mentioned in the above reference to Craine's (1973) study. Leslie and Laing (1978) have argued that α may be tracking a labour-hoarding phenomenon with industries working high overtime rates hoarding less labour. Leslie and Wise (1980) put forward a further explanation, arguing that industries working with high overtime rates are more efficient than other industries. The hours worked variable would thus also track variation in efficiency between industries. In their model the value of A in equation (10.1) above was allowed to vary between industries and was identified as not being constant. With the effects of the variable efficiency parameter included in the model, α was found, as will be seen, to settle down to a value less than unity.

Leslie and Wise (1980) provide the most sophisticated estimates of α. They utilised net output, employment, hours worked and capital stock for 28 United Kingdom production industries over the period 1948–68 as given by Stone (1974). Their estimated model is given by:

$$\ln Q_{it} = a_1 + \sum_{j=2}^{28} a_j d_j + \alpha \ln H_{it} + \beta \ln L_{it} + \gamma \ln K_{it}$$
$$+ b_1 t + \sum_{j=2}^{28} b_j d_j t + \delta UN_t + u_t \qquad (10.2)$$

where Q_{it} is net output of the ith industry in year t and $a_j d_j$ is the efficiency parameter of the jth industry relative to the first industry a_1 ($d_j = 1$ for the jth industry, zero otherwise). H_{it}, L_{it} and K_{it} refer to hours, labour and capital respectively. The next two terms capture the effect that there are separate rates of technical progress in each of the industries; b_j represents technical progress in the jth industry relative to technical progress in the first industry b_1, ($d_j = 1$ for the jth industry, zero otherwise). The last variable (UN) is an adjusted unemployment series intended to measure excess demand over time and thus capture cyclical effects. The study by Leslie and Wise (1980) represents a distinct advance on previous work by:

1. including a proxy to replicate the effects of labour hoarding which the variable 'hours worked' might otherwise spuriously track in time series work;
2. including separate industry specific 'efficiency' terms which might otherwise be picked up by the 'hours worked' variable in previous cross-sectional (industry) studies;
3. including separate rates of technical change for each industry.

The value of α was estimated to be 0.64 and was identical to the estimate of β. When the equation was estimated without separate industry effects for efficiency and technical progress, α was found to be 1.16; thus supporting the concern that Feldstein's high value for α arose because it tracked inter-industry efficiency variations, which were in turn correlated with hours worked.

INTER-INDUSTRY VARIATION IN THE MARGINAL PRODUCTIVITY OF HOURS WORKED

As noted at the start of this chapter, our interest primarily lies with inter-industry variation in the marginal productivity of hours worked – a topic comparatively neglected by previous studies. Leslie and Wise (1980) actually assume in their model (equation (10.2) above) that the coefficients for hours, employees and capital *are constant across industries*. They compared the pooled or restricted model with the unrestricted model of separate equations. This yielded an F statistic of 2.93, which was significant at the 1 per cent level. Whilst the test rejects their assumption of $\alpha_i = \alpha$, $\beta_i = \beta$, $\gamma_i = \gamma$ for $i = 1, \ldots g$ industries, they note:

> We do in fact consider that variation among these parameters does exist, but it is not so great as to cast doubt on the usefulness of pooling. The calculated value of F is not particularly large viewed in this light and [our model] can be defended as a reasonable description of the data set. The pooled estimates are comparatively precise in terms of their estimated standard errors, incomparably more so than the separately estimated parameters, and agree with other types of information such as that available from distributive shares data. Whilst a full analysis of covariance might provide additional detail, we doubt that such an analysis would alter the central substantive economic conclusions reached above, namely that there are separate industry effects which when excluded cause a large, upward bias on the hours coefficient, and that allowance for these effects in estimation leads to a well-behaved production function in good agreement with the evidence from institutional sources and industrial relations experts (Leslie and Wise, 1980, pp. 82–3).

However, Leslie and Wise were able to provide an explanation of the high value of α obtained in previous studies, and gave an improved estimate in their study. Yet, the rejection of the pooled model is worrying and adds further reason for the search for the inter-industry variation in the model.

In this study, we replicated Leslie and Wise's data set, and considered fifteen manufacturing industries, which accounted for 94.9 per cent of manufacturing net output (average of 1948 and 1968).[2] A number of further developments in estimating production functions (unrelated to the hours worked element), are candidates for further investigation. Namely:

1. The use of the dual cost function as opposed to the production function (Fuss and McFadden, 1978).
2. The use of gross output as opposed to net output as the dependent variable, the latter implying material and energy are weakly separable (Bruno, 1978; Diewert, 1978).
3. Relaxing the restrictions that α, β and γ are constant across industries.
4. Acknowledge that disturbance term of the production function for each industry is likely to be contemporaneously correlated, thus requiring Zellner's (1962) (SURE) estimator.
5. The use of flexible functional forms as opposed to the restrictive Cobb–Douglas form (Berndt, 1981; Berndt and Khaled, 1979).
6. The estimated function (by *OLS*) may suffer from bias because of the endogeneity of employment and hours worked. There is some evidence in Muellbauer (1984) that such bias is small.

Data constraints precluded an examination of 1 and 2. It was considered of interest to relax the constancy assumptions (3) with the use of SURE (4) to help provide better estimates of the separate equations.

The results of the OLS estimates for each industry are given in Table 10.1. Table 10.2 presents the results of estimation of the fifteen industries by the SURE estimator. The main differences between the results in Table 10.1 and 10.2 concern the estimated standard errors of parameter estimates. In general more of the SURE estimates are significant, although a number carry the wrong sign. The hypothesis of equal elasticities of hours worked is given by:

H_0: $\alpha_i = \alpha$ $i = 1, \ldots g$

v.

H_1: $\alpha_i \neq \alpha$

This was formally tested by the statistic

$$F = \frac{\hat{\beta}'R'[R(X'\hat{\Omega}_1^{-1}X)^{-1}R']^{-1}R\hat{\beta}/(g-1)}{(Y-X\hat{\beta})'\Omega_1(Y-X\hat{\beta})/(Tg-K)}$$

Table 10.1 Estimation of industry level production functions by OLS

Industry	Constant	Hours Worked	Numbers Employed	Capital Stock	Unemployment	Time	$\hat{\sigma}^2$
Food processing	40.18 (0.84)	−5.27 (0.72)	0.39 (0.32)	−0.72 (0.11)	0.11 (0.54)	0.06 (0.21)	0.387 $(10)^{-1}$
Drink and tobacco	17.90 (1.49)	−2.25 (1.50)	1.14 (2.93)	−0.82 (1.50)	0.05 (1.32)	0.09 (4.99)	0.107 $(10)^{-2}$
Chemical	41.63 (6.20)	4.01 (6.95)	0.65 (2.17)	2.64 (3.06)	−0.11 (3.21)	−0.06 (1.34)	0.819 $(10)^{-3}$
Iron and steel	−11.27 (1.72)	2.22 (2.02)	1.67 (3.11)	−1.08 (2.35)	0.21 (2.93)	0.11 (5.43)	0.289 $(10)^{-2}$
Non-ferrous metals	−6.61 (1.13)	2.09 (1.81)	0.91 (1.70)	−1.08 (1.03)	0.14 (1.67)	0.11 (2.13)	0.606 $(10)^{-2}$
Engineering	−15.44 (2.30)	2.05 (5.04)	0.68 (2.41)	0.60 (0.55)	−0.04 (1.25)	0.04 (0.72)	0.755 $(10)^{-3}$
Shipbuilding	2.89 (0.52)	1.87 (3.27)	0.46 (3.56)	−2.00 (2.46)	0.04 (0.66)	0.08 (4.60)	0.247 $(10)^{-2}$
Motor Vehicles	−7.10 (3.00)	1.29 (4.39)	1.39 (7.85)	−0.16 (1.80)	0.06 (1.48)	0.08 (4.99)	0.858 $(10)^{-3}$
Aircraft	−7.16 (1.44)	0.91 (0.92)	0.98 (3.96)	0.20 (0.45)	0.08 (1.60)	0.05 (2.15)	0.144 $(10)^{-2}$
Metals n.e.s	−14.82 (1.40)	1.39 (2.53)	0.94 (3.43)	0.98 (0.69)	−0.13 (3.99)	0.02 (0.49)	0.877 $(10)^{-3}$
Textiles	−1.45 (0.14)	−0.67 (0.49)	0.82 (2.29)	0.80 (0.95)	−0.06 (0.81)	0.03 (4.65)	0.266 $(10)^{-2}$
Leather, etc.	14.04 (2.73)	−0.20 (0.39)	0.05 (0.26)	−1.17 (2.62)	−0.14 (4.08)	0.05 (14.76)	0.494 $(10)^{-3}$
Building Materials	−2.51 (0.31)	0.00 (0.00)	1.82 (6.42)	−0.44 (1.05)	−0.02 (0.36)	0.07 (3.34)	0.102 $(10)^{-2}$
Timber	2.39 (0.73)	−0.33 (0.87)	0.61 (1.93)	0.19 (0.59)	−0.05 (1.50)	0.04 (4.39)	0.527 $(10)^{-3}$
Paper, printing	−23.88 (9.69)	2.43 (1.98)	1.17 (3.04)	1.11 (1.18)	−0.12 (2.71)	0.16 (0.51)	0.151 $(10)^{-2}$

Notes: t-statistics are presented in parenthesis beside parameter estimates.

Table 10.2 Estimation of industry level production functions by SURE

Industry	Constant	Hours Worked	Numbers Employed	Capital Stock	Unemployment	Time
Food processing	57.80 (2.54)	−5.37 (1.50)	0.57 (1.24)	−3.42 (1.10)	0.12 (0.65)	0.17 (1.26)
Drink and tobacco	17.88 (2.53)	−2.07 (2.33)	1.01 (4.06)	−0.89 (2.73)	−0.05 (1.68)	0.09 (8.64)
Chemical	−40.97 (11.69)	3.93 (11.00)	0.86 (5.62)	2.44 (5.80)	−0.11 (4.08)	−0.05 (2.36)
Iron and steel	−9.46 (2.63)	1.81 (3.14)	1.79 (8.16)	−1.07 (5.61)	0.20 (3.94)	0.10 (12.49)
Non-ferrous metals	−8.24 (2.48)	2.19 (3.57)	1.04 (4.14)	−1.01 (2.65)	−0.14 (2.02)	0.10 (5.20)
Engineering	−13.14 (3.75)	1.64 (6.59)	0.81 (5.06)	0.50 (0.91)	−0.04 (1.52)	0.04 (1.44)
Shipbuilding	−1.10 (0.32)	1.97 (6.13)	0.35 (5.80)	−1.33 (2.85)	0.02 (0.50)	0.06 (6.62)
Motor Vehicles	−7.76 (9.02)	1.37 (12.21)	1.39 (27.34)	−0.59 (−5.82)	0.06 (2.08)	0.08 (14.53)
Aircraft	−7.82 (4.26)	1.08 (3.00)	1.00 (10.82)	0.10 (0.64)	−0.07 (1.91)	0.05 (6.52)
Metals n.e.s.	−14.54 (4.29)	1.38 (4.73)	1.15 (10.33)	0.75 (1.69)	−0.13 (4.70)	0.03 (1.96)
Textiles	−7.16 (1.26)	−0.51 (0.77)	0.81 (4.94)	1.42 (3.04)	−0.04 (0.72)	0.03 (7.30)
Leather, etc.	14.30 (5.99)	−0.41 (1.49)	0.13 (1.75)	−1.11 (5.83)	−0.13 (5.98)	0.05 (26.76)
Building Materials	−1.42 (0.30)	−0.10 (0.18)	1.84 (11.02)	−0.54 (2.07)	−0.02 (0.64)	0.07 (5.67)
Timber	0.33 (0.19)	−0.18 (0.72)	0.90 (6.98)	0.08 (0.52)	−0.04 (−1.56)	0.05 (9.80)
Paper, printing	−23.09 (8.10)	2.12 (6.68)	1.29 (11.07)	1.16 (6.01)	−0.13 (3.64)	0.01 (1.83)

Notes:
t-statistics are presented in parenthesis beside parameter estimates.

where:

$$R = \begin{bmatrix} 1 & -1 & & & & \\ & 1 & -1 & & 0 & \\ & & \cdot & \cdot & & \\ & & & \cdot & \cdot & \\ & & & & \cdot & \cdot \\ & 0 & & & 1 & -1 \end{bmatrix}$$

which is of dimension $(g-1) \times gk$, k is the number of exogenous variables in each equation and $\hat{\beta}$, is the usual Zellner SURE estimator applied to the stacked regression model, so that:

$$Y = X\beta + u \qquad E(uu') = \Omega_1.$$

Under the null hypothesis the test statistic, F, will have an $F_{g-1, g(Tk)}$ distribution. In our case $k = 6$, $g = 15$ and T (the sample size) is 21.

Exactly analogous procedures can be used to test the hypotheses of equal inter-industry elasticities of numbers employed and capital stock. The computed F statistics of equal α, β and γ were 18.41, 30.25 and 16.63 respectively. Since $F_{14, 225}$ (0.01) = 2.17 it is clear that all these tests imply clear rejections of the constant elasticities hypotheses. Inter-industry variation thus appears considerable.

A test of the use of SURE against OLS is provided by the maximum likelihood test statistic, given by:

$$\lambda = T(\ln|\Omega_0| - \ln|\Omega_1|)$$

where Ω_1 is the unrestricted SURE error covariance matrix and Ω_0 is the corresponding OLS error covariance matrix. Under the null hypothesis that OLS is adequate, Ω_0 is restricted to being a diagonal matrix and λ has an asymptotic chi-squared distribution with $g(g-1)/2$ degrees of freedom. For our study $g = 15$ and $\lambda = 252.21$ being significant at a 0.1 per cent level, thus justifying the use of the SURE estimator.

The results in Table 10.2 (compared with Table 10.1) clearly represent better estimates in that many more of the coefficients are significant. However, the estimated equations for each industry are not always satisfactory in that many coefficients possess the wrong sign. The estimates for the chemicals, engineering, aircraft, and paper and printing industries appear to be quite reasonable (though for the chemical industry the experimental time trend is negative, obviously capturing factors other than technical progress). In all of these five industries the hours worked as elasticities are significant (at the 1 per cent level), positive and greater than unity with a quite high variability between these industries. The iron and steel, non-ferrous metals, shipbuilding and motor vehicles industries again all have significant (at the 1 per cent level), positive elasticities of hours worked greater than unity. However, in these cases the capital stock elasticities all have the wrong sign whilst significant. In addition, the signs are wrong and the coefficients significant for the unemployment series in the iron and steel and motor vehicles industry. For the remaining six industries the elasticities of hours worked were negative – though in only one case (drink and tobacco) significant.

The Cobb–Douglas model is a particularly restrictive functional form, and there is much to be gained from using flexible functional forms. In particular the transcendental logarithmic (translog) form includes the Cobb–Douglas form as a special case – see Christensen, Jorgensen and Lau (1973). A disadvantage of flexible functional forms is the substantial increase in the number of parameters to be estimated and hence the corresponding reduction in the degrees of freedom. This study focusses on the hours worked variable only, and allows its specifications to be more flexible in the sense of including its square and a single cross-product with labour. However, this did little to benefit the final model, and the results are not repeated here, although they are available from the authors on request.

What is apparent from the above is that the elasticities of hours worked does vary between industries, and there is a body of evidence to suggest that it may well be greater than unity for many industries. However, these high elasticities may in turn be derived from a misspecification error. There has recently emerged a body of work on this point which will now be discussed.

EXPANDING THE MODEL

Muellbauer (1984) (though see also Mendis and Muellbauer, 1984) has argued that the considerable reduction in normal hours in the 1950s and early 1960s would bias the results if not included in the model. Also the hours worked variable is based on an average of only two periods in each year and a more annually representative series would improve the results (though such data is not available to test this.) Leslie (1984) has warned of the danger of the average hours series also reflecting changes in the composition of the workforce. The growth in part-time working and full-time female employment are two important secular changes referred to.

Table 10.3 Results for textiles and paper, printing, etc. industry

	Constant	Number of employees	Capital stock	Adjusted unemployment	Time trend	Normal hours	Hours worked	Proportion female	Adjusted hours worked	Quality adjusted hours	$\bar{R}^2$	DW
Textiles	−5.37 (−0.69)	0.52 (3.24)	0.02 (0.03)	−0.002 (−1.40)	0.02 (2.60)	−0.002 (−0.24)	1.41 (1.72)	—	—	—	99.8	1.52
Paper, printing, etc.	35.26 (−3.19)	1.35 (3.96)	1.37 (1.75)	−0.003 (−2.02)	−0.02 (−0.97)	−0.01 (−1.00)	4.05 (3.87)	—	—	—	99.2	1.61
Textiles	−4.51 (−0.55)	0.53 (3.21)	−0.04 (−0.05)	−0.002 (−1.38)	0.02 (2.49)	−0.001 (−0.07)	1.30 (1.51)	−0.12 (−0.52)	—	—	99.8	1.48
Paper, Printing, etc.	−26.59 (−2.35)	−1.64 (−0.54)	0.70 (0.81)	−0.004 (−2.52)	−0.02 (−0.66)	−0.01 (−0.54)	2.86 (2.13)	−1.16 (−0.99)	—	—	99.0	1.67
Textiles	22.86 (2.45)	−0.21 (−0.54)	−1.87 (−1.99)	−0.006 (−2.91)	0.03 (3.33)	−0.02 (−2.65)	—	−0.20 (−0.68)	0.01 (2.36)	—	97.0	1.89
Paper, printing, etc.	0.33 (0.04)	0.69 (0.50)	−0.24 (−0.32)	−0.006 (−3.68)	−0.001 (−0.54)	−0.003 (−0.02)	—	−2.13 (−1.85)	0.014 (1.32)	—	98.7	1.89
Textiles	7.27 (0.95)	0.35 (0.83)	−0.52 (−0.56)	−0.004 (−1.91)	0.02 (2.02)	−0.01 (−1.17)	—	−0.15 (−0.47)	—	0.46 (0.75)	99.2	1.78
Paper, Printing, etc.	−7.73 (−1.16)	3.14 (2.55)	−1.03 (−1.17)	−0.007 (−4.91)	0.02 (0.70)	0.01 (1.23)	—	−3.45 (−3.02)	—	−0.61 (−0.58)	99.7	2.21

Notes:
t-statistics are presented in parenthesis beneath parameter estimates.

Finally, Heathfield (see Chapter 13) has argued in this context for the inclusion of a variable on the utilisation of capital and that electricity based measures (see Heathfield, 1972) might be usefully employed for this purpose. Unfortunately, the unavailability of such data at an industry level for the period in question precluded the empirical examination of this point.

Our concern lies now with the effect of including variables on normal hours and the composition of the workforce into the model. Comparable data was readily available for only two industries – textile and paper, printing and publishing. Normal hours excludes overtime and refers to those quoted in national agreements or laid down by the wage boards and councils (Department of Employment, 1971). Data are not available for the period in question on the proportion of females in employment. However, the proportion of females in the labour force (employed and registered unemployed) is known at an industry level and can be used as a proxy. An alternative approach is to utilise estimates by Buxton (1972). These first, (albeit crudely) adjust indices of hours worked (which were based only on manual workers) to take account of non-manual workers. A second series is provided which weights changes in the hours worked by each category of employee (male manual, female manual and all non-manual) according to their relative labour remuneration.

The results are given in Table 10.3. The method of estimation was *OLS*, though in a number of cases the models suffered from autocorrelation and a maximum likelihood iterative technique (Beach and MacKinnon, 1978) was employed. The inclusion of hours worked, whilst improving the estimates given in Table 10.1, increased the coefficient of hours worked, as suggested by Muellbauer (1984). Including the proportion of females in the labour force, though not significant in itself, leads to a fall in the hours worked elasticity. The adjusted hours worked series provides a very small figure, though it is significant only for the textile industry. The quality-adjusted hours worked series was not significant for either of the two industries, though the equating of relative remuneration with marginal rates of transformation must be considered dubious. In general, there appears to be good theoretical reasons for expanding the model to improve the estimates, though this very limited experiment was unable to provide substantial empirical evidence.

CONCLUSION

This chapter has been concerned with the estimation of the marginal productivity of hours worked for United Kingdom manufacturing and production industries. In particular, our interest lay with deriving separate estimates for individual industries. We showed that assumptions of constant elasticities for hours worked across industries (and for that matter, capital stock and number of employees) were invalid. Such assumptions were invoked by Leslie and Wise (1980) in their important study of this area. One of the reasons for their use of this assumption was the difficulty in obtaining satisfactory estimates of the production functions (with hours worked) for individual industries. We utilised the more efficient SURE estimation system (given *a priori* grounds to expect the residuals for each industry to be contemporaneously correlated – since all industries experience the effects of macro social and economic changes). The use of SURE substantially improved the efficiency of the estimates, and showed values of the marginal productivities of hours worked to vary, and to be greater than unity. This is in contrast with the overall results for manufacturing industries by Leslie and Wise (1980). Improvement to the specification of the equations by making the functional form more flexible had little impact on the results – the restrictive Cobb–Douglas form not (in this case) being so restrictive after all. However, for many industries the estimates remained poor with many variables possessing the wrong sign. We improved the specification of the model for two industries, though this did not lead to any considerable improvements in the model.

Notes

1. Derek Leslie kindly provided some of the data utilised in this study, and some helpful references.
2. These comprised food processing (MLH, Standard Industrial Classification 1958 (211–3, 214–8, 219, 229); drink and tobacco (231, 239–40); chemicals (263, 271–7); iron and steel (311–3); non-ferrous metals (321–2); engineering (331–9, 341–2, 249, 351–2, 361–5); shipbuilding (370); motor vehicles (381); aircraft (383); metals n.e.s. (391–6, 399); textiles (001 part), 411–9, 421–3, 429); leather, etc. (431–3, 441–6, 449, 450); building materials (461, 464, 469); timber, etc. (471–5, 479); paper, printing, etc. (481–6, 489).

References

BEACH, C. M. and MacKINNON, J. G. (1978) 'A Maximum Likelihood Procedure for Regression with Autocorrelated Errors', *Econometrica* 46, 51–8.

BERNDT, E. R. (1981) 'Modelling the simultaneous demand for factors of production', in Hornstein, Z., Grice, J. and Webb, A., (eds) *The Economics of the Labour Market* (London: HMSO), pp. 127–42.

────── and KHALED, M. S. (1979) 'Parametric productivity measurement and choice among flexible functional forms', *Journal of Political Economy* 87 (6), pp. 1220–65.

BRUNO, M. (1978) 'Duality, Intermediate inputs and value-added', in Fuss, M. and McFadden, D. *Production Economics: A Dual Approach to Theory and Application* 2 (Amsterdam: North-Holland).

BUXTON, A. J. (1972) 'Calculation of labour service in UK manufacturing', *Working Paper* 18 *Centre of Industrial Economic and Business Research* (University of Warwick: (July)).

CRAINE, R. (1973) 'On the service flow from labour', *Review of Economic Studies* (January) pp. 39–45.

CHRISTENSEN, L. R., JORGENSEN, D. W. and LAU, L. J. (1973) 'Transcendental logarithmic production frontiers', *Review of Economics and Statistics* LV (February) pp. 28–45.

DENISON, E. F. (1974) *Accounting for United States Economic Growth 1929–1969* (Washington, D.C.: The Brookings Institution).

Department of Employment (1971) *British Labour Statistics, Historical Abstract* (London: HMSO).

DIEWERT, W. E. (1978) 'Hicks' aggregation theorem and the existence of a real value-added function', in Fuss, M. and McFadden, D. *Production Economics: A Dual Approach to Theory and Application* 2 (Amsterdam: North-Holland).

FELDSTEIN, M. S. (1967) 'Specification of labour input into the aggregate production function', *Review of Economic Studies* (October) pp. 275–386.

FUSS, M. and McFADDEN, D. (1978) *Production Economics: A Dual Approach to Theory and Application* 2 (Amsterdam: North-Holland).

HAZLEDINE, T. (1981) ' "Employment function" and the demand for labour in the short run', in Hornstein, Z., Grice, J., and Webb, A. (eds) *The Economics of the Labour Market* (London: HMSO) pp. 149–81.

HEATHFIELD, D. F. (1972) 'The measurement of capital utilisation using electricity consumption data', *Journal of the Royal Statistical Society* (Series A) 35, pp. 208–20.

LESLIE, D. G. (1984) 'The productivity of hours in US manufacturing industry', *Review of Economics and Statistics* LXVI (August) pp. 486–90.

—— and LAING, C. (1978) 'The theory and measurement of labour hoarding', *Scottish Journal of Political Economy* (February) pp. 41–56.

—— and WISE, J. (1980) 'The productivity of hours in UK manufacturing and production industries', *Economic Journal* 90 (357) pp. 74–83.

MENDIS, L. and MUELLBAUER, J. (1984) 'British manufacturing productivity 1955–1983: Measurement problems, oil shocks and Thatcher effects', *Centre for Economic Policy Research* 32.

MUELLBAUER, J. (1984) 'Aggregate production functions and productivity measurement: A new look', *Centre for Economic Policy Research* 34.

SIMS, C. A. (1974) 'Output and labour input in manufacturing', *Brookings Papers on Economic Activity* (3).

STONE, R. (1974) 'Structural changes in the British economy 1948–1968', in *A Programme for Growth* (vol. 12) (Cambridge: Cambridge University Press).

ZELLNER, A. (1962) 'An efficient method of estimating seemingly unrelated regressions and tests for aggregation bias', *Journal of the American Statistical Association* (June) 348–68.

11 Industrial Capacity and Employment Promotion in Developing Countries: Some Conclusions

N. Phan-Thuy[1]

In the development process of the Third World there are no doubt few facts which are more paradoxical than the gross and durable under-utilisation of scarce capital resources coexistent with dramatic under-utilisation of labour. It is hardly acceptable that, while fixed industrial capital remains largely unused, further investment increases the capital stock whereas unemployment and poverty grow worse every day.

It was not until the early 1970s that the question of excess capacity in developing countries began to receive wider attention. A number of concrete studies on Third World countries (mainly by the World Bank, the Centre for Latin American Development Studies of Boston University and the ILO) have contributed to a better understanding of this complex problem, and the object of the following statement is to present some conclusions drawn from the research carried out by the ILO[2] in some selected developing countries.

It scarcely needs to be said that, in the context of the new international economic order (NIEO), an even more determined effort has to be made to find ways of ensuring full utilisation of industrial capacity in the developing countries. However, there are on the one hand conceptual difficulties in defining and measuring capacity under-utilisation, and on the other specific features in the economic structure and the fabric of society of each country which, in practice, make the problem extremely complex.

CONCEPTS OF UNDER-UTILISATION OF INDUSTRIAL CAPACITY AND MEASUREMENT PROBLEMS IN DEVELOPING COUNTRIES

While it is generally recognised that there is under-utilisation of industrial capacity – in the sense of under-utilisation of installed

Table 11.1 Capital utilisation rates

	Direct measure (hr)	Indirect measure (quantity)
Maximum level Socially optimal level (Socio-economic target)	$T = 8760$ hr	
INTENDED (EX ANTE) CAPITAL UNDER-UTILISATION $= f$ (ECONOMIC POLICIES) Financially optimal level (Private target at the time of investment)	a^*: desired no. of hr of plant operation	Q^*: capacity output $\longleftrightarrow$?
UNINTENDED (EX POST) CAPITAL UNDER-UTILISATION $= f$ (SUPPLY + DEMAND BOTTLENECKS) Actual level	a: actual time of operation a^1: a adjusted for sectional variations in intensity of operation	Q: level of output actually produced
Zero level		

$U_1 = \dfrac{a}{T}$ = Actual time utilisation of K

$1 - U_1$ = Actual idleness of plant

$U_2 = \dfrac{a'}{T}$ = Actual time intensity/utilisation of K

$1 - U_2$ = Actual idleness of plant adjusted for sectional variation of intensity of operation

$U_5 = \dfrac{a^*}{T}$ = Desired time Utilisation of K

$1 - U_5$ = Intended plant idleness

$U_6 = \dfrac{a}{a^*}$ = $\dfrac{\text{Actual time}}{\text{Desired time}}$

$1 - U_6$ = Unintended plant idleness

$U_3 = \dfrac{Q}{Q^*}$ = Actual capacity utilisation

$1 - U_3$ = Excess capacity

$1 - U_3$ = Unintended plant idleness

$U_4 = \dfrac{U_1}{U_3} \equiv \dfrac{a/T}{Q/Q^*}$

$U_4 = \dfrac{\text{Actual time}}{\text{Actual capacity}} \dfrac{U}{U}$

$1 - U_4$ = Desired plant idleness

capital – in developing countries, it is not always easy to estimate its extent. The approach adopted by the ILO is a microeconomic one in the sense that reference is made to 'micro-capacity' – which is to say capacity at the level of the firm – and especially to 'effective' capacity – an economic concept which involves the notion of optimal utilisation of resources.

Effective capacity corresponds to the output achieved at the lowest average cost, and therefore takes into account the prices of the various production inputs. In developing countries, where the market prices of the production inputs are sometimes distorted as a result of government policies or economic imbalances, financial effective capacity (or commercial capacity) – which is determined by the entrepreneur according to financial and technical criteria – has to be distinguished from socioeconomic effective capacity (or social capacity), the calculation of which will have to take into account the distortions in the prices of the production inputs.

As shown by Table 11.1, two types of under-utilisation of capital can be distinguished: *unintended* capital under-utilisation (which results in excess commercial capacity) and *intended* or structural capital under-utilisation (which results in excess social capacity). The first case arises when there are unforeseen bottlenecks on the demand side, on the supply side or on both, which prevent a factory from producing at the level which the entrepreneur considers to be optimal. The second arises when the market prices of the various production inputs differ significantly from their real costs and the entrepreneur fixes his full capacity target according to his production costs estimated at market prices – i.e., lower than it would be if there were no price distortion. We consider the under-utilisations of industrial capacity in developing countries as the sum of these two types.

Sample surveys were conducted in the manufacturing sector of Morocco, Nigeria and Sri Lanka to measure these two types of capital under-utilisation and to identify the factors responsible. The unintended capital under-utilisation is measured in terms of time and intensity of operation of machinery, while the intended capital under-utilisation is measured in terms of number of shifts.

At present, it is recognised that there are still some deficiencies in the measurement of capital under-utilisation. First, the questionnaire set up is sometime ambiguous so that the survey replies are often subject to the respondent's subjective guesses. Second, the country studies undertaken, are based upon sample surveys and, to obtain aggregate data for the whole manufacturing sector, simple summations of data obtained at plant level are carried out which do not take into account the interdependence of various industries, nor output and employment displacement effects within an industry. Third, while it was attempted to estimate social capacity through optimum shift coefficients, there still exists some arbitrariness in its measurement.

Therefore, even though it is more important to aim at determining the causes of excess capacity and the steps to be taken to increase utilisation than at estimating precisely the actual level of utilisation, it is nevertheless useful to pursue further research to improve the collection and analysis of data.

POLICY GUIDELINES FOR PROMOTING EMPLOYMENT THROUGH FULLER UTILISATION OF INDUSTRIAL CAPACITY

The country studies undertaken, recognise that capital under-utilisation seems to be common to semi-industrialised developing countries, and that there is no single necessary cause of capital under-utilisation; several causes share simultaneously in the causation of particular cases of under-utilisation.

No single measure could therefore solve the problem of under-utilisation; rather a combination of economic, fiscal, legal and social measures could act simultaneously on the various simultaneous causes. The measures must aim at reducing both unintended and intended under-utilisation of capital.

The measures aiming at reducing the unintended under-utilisation of capital should help firms to reach their own targets (commercial full capacity targets) by removing bottlenecks. These bottlenecks can come either from the demand side (such as lack of foreign and local demand) or from the supply side (such as shortage of imported and local raw materials, spare parts, electricity and machine breakdowns, lack of working capital, scarcity of technical, managerial and supervisory staff), or from both. They can be external as well as internal to the firms. Because of this multi-dimensional nature, policy measures should also be multi-dimensional, ranging from general to selective in order to cope with the problem.

For instance, to boost the foreign demand for products manufactured in firms with excess capacity, it is suggested that there is a need to revise the export regulations which end up favouring the large capital-intensive firms using imported materials and to have an effective policy of international marketing to improve the quality of products, the sales and after-sales service in small industrialising countries. Apart from these government measures of a general nature, consideration should be given to the scope for sub-contracting, at both national and international levels.

The supply or production bottlenecks are countless and vary from one industry to another, and from one firm to another. They vary with the activity, the organisation, the size and the nature of the firm. So no general macroeconomic policies can remove them. The policy measures must be selective and aim at each individual bottleneck affecting a particular firm. They require close co-operation with firm's managers who should check periodically the productive capacity of different departments and production lines of their enterprise and detect the possible production bottlenecks.

The results of the country studies also suggest that firms seem to set up targets lower than they should be socially because they compute their optimal level of production on the basis of market prices of inputs – mainly capital and labour. These market prices in developing countries diverge from their real prices: unwarranted penalty costs for operating at specific times of the day or week or year, general wage levels that are (economically speaking) too high, and capital prices that are too low to reflect the scarcity of resources in semi-industrialised economies where labour is abundant and capital scarce.

These price distortions result from some present social and industrial policies which are designed to accelerate industrialisation without paying enough attention to the misallocation of resources. So, by reorienting or modifying their industrial investment incentive policies (such as industrial investment codes, export promotion policies, credit policies, exchange rate systems, etc.) and by including the objective of fuller utilisation of existing productive capacity in their economic planning, governments would be able to redress these distortions and to induce firms to increase their capacity utilisation targets by using more fully their installed equipment with more shifts worked.

Furthermore, the concept of a double-day shift system should be introduced and promoted either through the 'big push' strategy or through the 'selective push' strategy. The big push strategy consists of stimulating the demand for factories' products through export promotion and moving the whole industrial sector to a double-shift basis to satisfy the increase in demand. However, it seems to be quite ambitious as a quick solution to the problem, and can also have a high probability of failure with the ongoing world recession.

The 'selective push' strategy consists of a package of measures aiming at promoting the double-shift system by making it more profitable to firms, and also more acceptable to workers. These measures can be fiscal incentives – such as tax rebates proportional to employment of casual workers or of workers hired from a government sponsored pool of shift workers; depreciation allowances calculated according to the number of shifts, direct subsidy or tax credit for each worker employed on a second shift; labour legislation reforms – such as a flexible hire and fire policy, minima for wage premiums, lesser number of working hours for the second shift, a productivity based incentive bonus after 6 or 7 p.m., a rotating change of workers on each shift, etc.; social measures – such as improving public transportation for those people working early and late hours, subsidies for meals and housing for shift workers.

CONCLUSION: SUGGESTIONS FOR A PROGRAMME OF ACTION

We have seen through a selected number of country studies how the promotion of employment through the fuller utilisation of installed industrial capacity can be facilitated by a wide variety of measures, none of which should be overlooked if the desired goal is to be achieved. What each country should do, in fact, is to adopt a programme of action based on practical research; for this purpose, it might be desirable to set up within the planning ministries a small unit responsible for increasing capacity utilisation.

The first task would be to collect systematically, keep up to date and analyse data on capital under-utilisation and on the extent of shift work, and at the same time to conduct surveys investigating workers' attitudes to this form of work organisation. It would then be possible to establish for each branch of industry the optimal shift work pattern and to fix goals for increasing the shift coefficient (1.3, 1.5, etc.) for the duration of the development plan, together with the output targets.

Second, the 'discriminatory' aspects of existing economic and social policies should be identified and corrective measures proposed. This would involve, for example, determining the measures to be taken as regards short-term credits to facilitate the financing of working capital, while at the same time eliminating or reducing subsidies on fixed capital. Consideration should also be given to the effect of laws relating to night work, overtime pay and differentials for work performed outside normal hours. What is needed, in fact, is a regular re-evaluation of industrial promotion policies, taking into account existing excess capacity and the price distortions of labour and capital.

Third, specific measures to increase capacity utilisation should be formulated within the framework of overall economic planning. Generally speaking, this will involve analysing and stimulating both local and foreign demand, while at the same time encouraging firms to increase the number of shifts rather than the acquisition of new machines.

Fourth, the adoption and implementation of all these measures will require legislative and administrative action. The tax and labour laws, the regulations governing short-term credit, the training of the necessary administrative staff, technicians and skilled workers for additional shifts, all demand a series of sustained efforts in the institutional field. Such efforts are amply justified by the importance of the problem of industrial capacity under-utilisation and the gravity of unemployment and under-employment in developing countries, the industrial sectors of which are already substantial.

Finally, the success of a policy programme for a fuller utilisation of industrial capacity depends first on the consciousness of governments, employers and workers about the importance of increased capital utilisation for national economic development; second, on the close co-operation between governments, employers' and workers' organisations to work out an appropriate policy package; and third, on the popularity and acceptance of a double day shift system by employers and workers as 'normal' if the demand and supply conditions are favourable to the introduction of a second shift to increase capital utilisation.

An effective way to do it is through 'exhortation'. This would consist of an intensive campaign explaining and publicising the possibilities of additional profits and the importance of increased capital utilisation in developing countries for national economic development. This campaign must be based on concrete and in-depth studies carried out in as many developing countries as possible to convince governments, employers and workers of the importance of increased capital utilisation.

Notes

1. Economist, Emergency Employment Schemes Branch, Employment and Development Department, International Labour Office, Geneva, Switzerland. Opinions expressed in this paper are those of the author, and do not necessarily represent the views of the International Labour Organisation.
2. N. Phan-Thuy et al. (1981).

Reference

PHAN-THUY, N., BETANCOURT, R. R., WINSTON, G. C. and KABAJ, M. (1981) *Industrial Capacity and Employment Promotion: case studies of Sri Lanka, Nigeria, Morocco and overall Survey of other developing countries* (London: Gower).

12 The Percentage Utilisation of Labour Index (PUL)
A. Bennett and S. Smith-Gavine[1]

INTRODUCTION

The Index of PUL (= Percentage Utilisation of Labour)[2] uses a statistically representative Panel of 171 factories and 131,500 operatives at full. It thus refers to the manufacturing industry of Great Britain. It shows the fluctuating intensity of specifically and narrowly human effort per worked hour.[3] This entity is typically the basis of all factory planning and hour by hour control.[4] It is briefly explained in the third paragraph below and at length throughout the fourth section of the chapter.

The PUL phenomenon is not confined in its importance to the administration of factories: it is, in fact, a powerful and sensitive macroeconomic parameter. A glance at Figure 12.1 shows the huge swings of the PUL sub-indices for particular branches of industry[5] which (prior to the monetarist experiment) chase each other round in a manner reminiscent of the accelerator principle well known to first-year students of economics.[6] Again, a look at Figure 12.2 shows the important influences of the main PUL Index – which is a weighted average of these sub-indices – upon output. It is seen there how, in spite of slight timelags, the tiny fluctuations of PUL about its succession of trendings explain many of the similar tiny fluctuations in output.[7] It is also seen how the succession of PUL trendings themselves take the dominant share, alongside employment[8] and average weekly hours worked per operative and (unshown) technological productivity growth, in explaining output's changing course through the chart.

It is clear that an index of the PUL phenomenon can have three main uses to the macroeconomist. *First*, if successive proportionate changes in it are subtracted from the corresponding proportionate changes in an index of output per operative hour (based on official data,[9] there must emerge an index of underlying 'technological'[10] productivity as seen in

Figure 12.1 PUL sub-indices of consumer, intermediate and capital goods

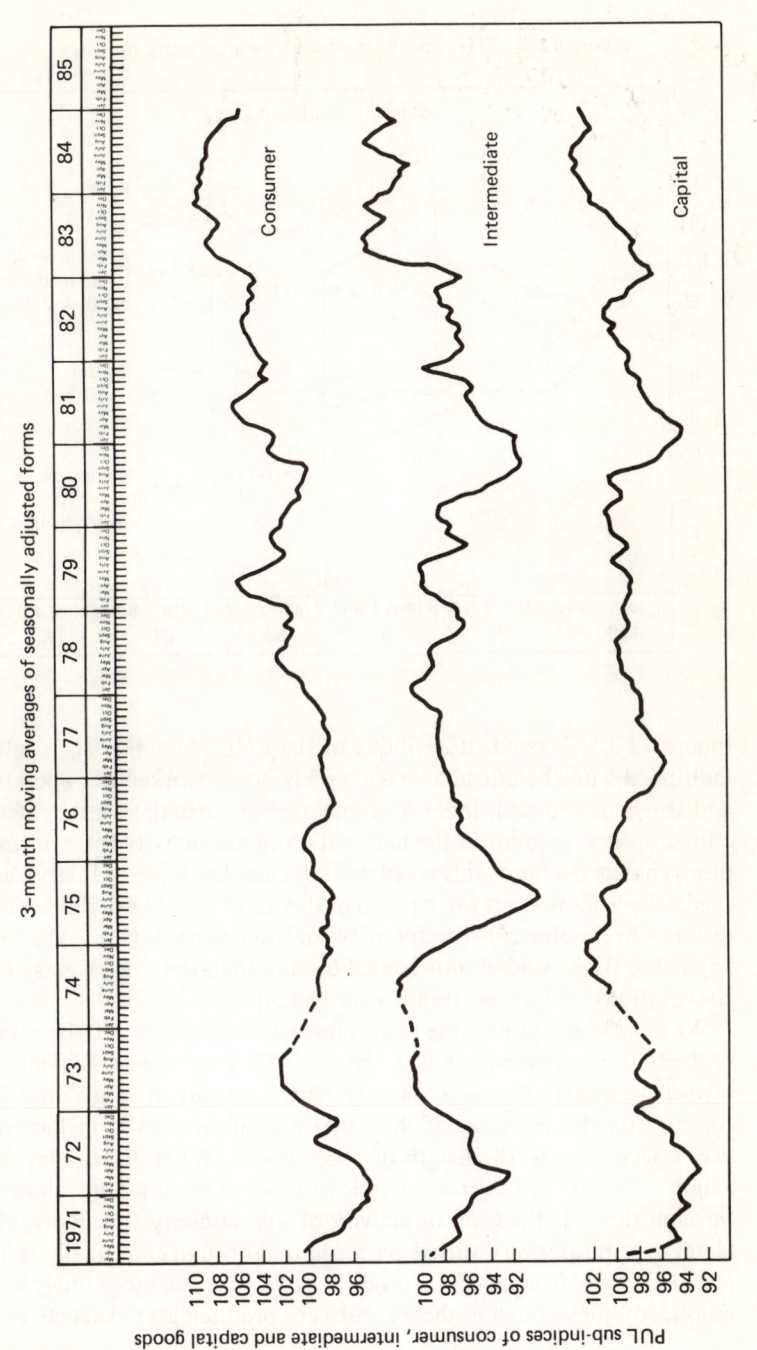

3-month moving averages of seasonally adjusted forms

PUL sub-indices of consumer, intermediate and capital goods

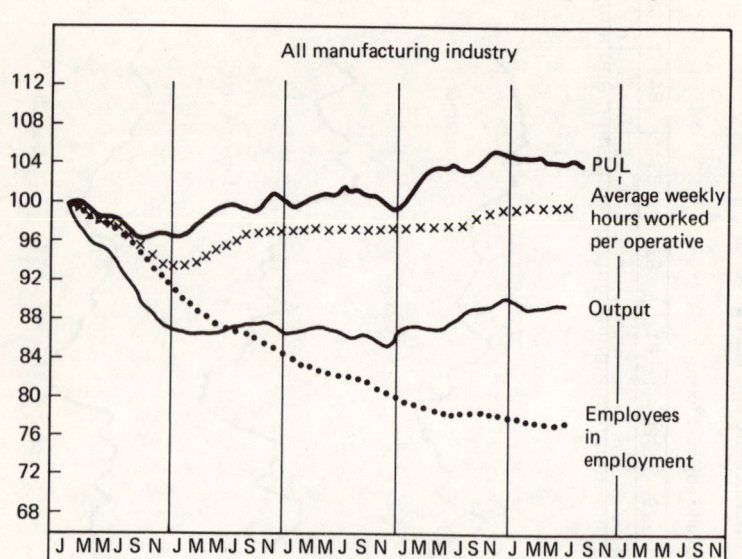

Figure 12.2 PUL and output: all manufacturing industry

Figure 12.3.[11] Second, if an index of the PUL phenomenon is intermultiplied with the offical average weekly hours worked per operative and also with a suitable index of employment,[12] then there must emerge a final or 'net' account of the national economic activity (or 'temperature') change (so far as this is reflected in manufacturing industry); and this entity is termed net work put in in Figure 12.5.[13] Third, if these two results – 'technological' productivity and net work put in – are then applied to the nowadays much cited total output, the true origins of its convolutions and longer trends may be laid bare.

We must keep our promise to explain in a single paragraph the nature of the PUL phenomenon in factories (pp. 353–8 below gives the full and proper account). Technical factory terms are put in single inverted commas on the occasion of their first appearance. PUL in factories varies according to the length of order books. What determines that length is, in part, the microeconomic fortunes of the firm; but, showing through these, is the level of activity of the economy. The work of a factory – typically very varied yet repeating through continually resurrected 'batches' of a particular product – consists of an exceedingly large number of 'jobs'. Each of these consists of producing an exact effect by

Figure 12.3 Output per operative hour; PUL and 'technological' productivity; gross fixed investment in plant and machinery

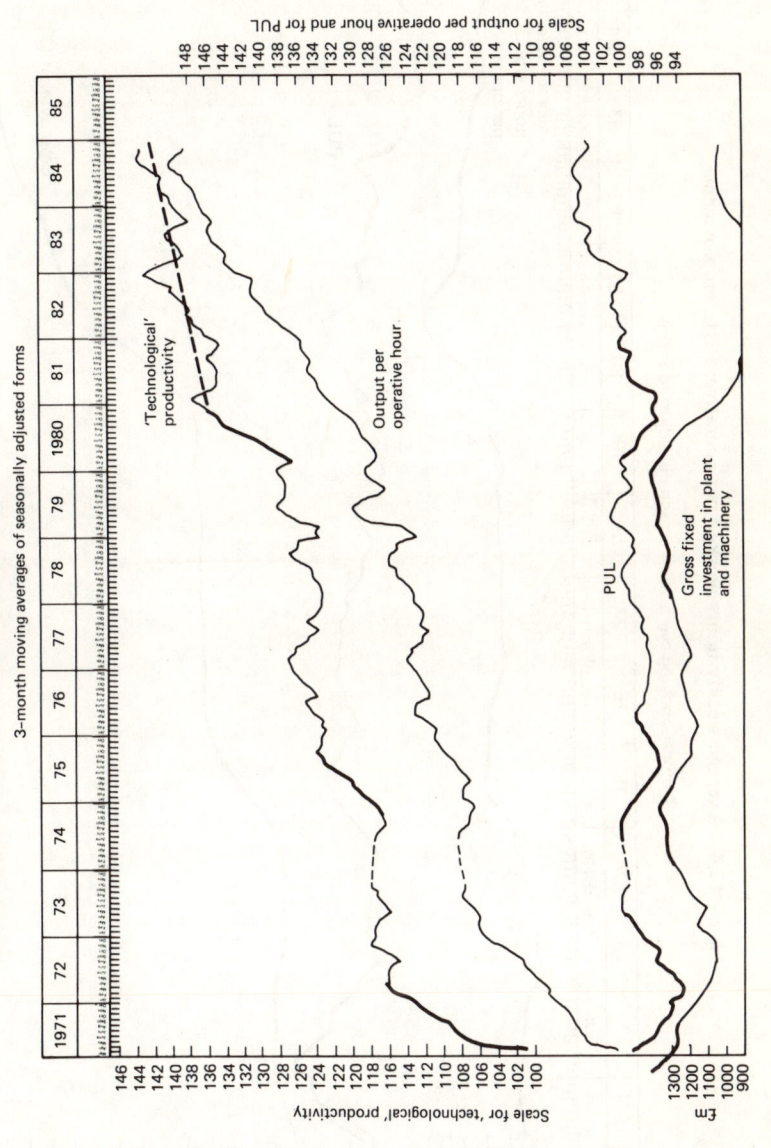

3-month moving averages of seasonally adjusted forms

Figure 12.4 Average weekly hours worked per operative; PUL; employment

3-month moving averages of seasonally adjusted forms

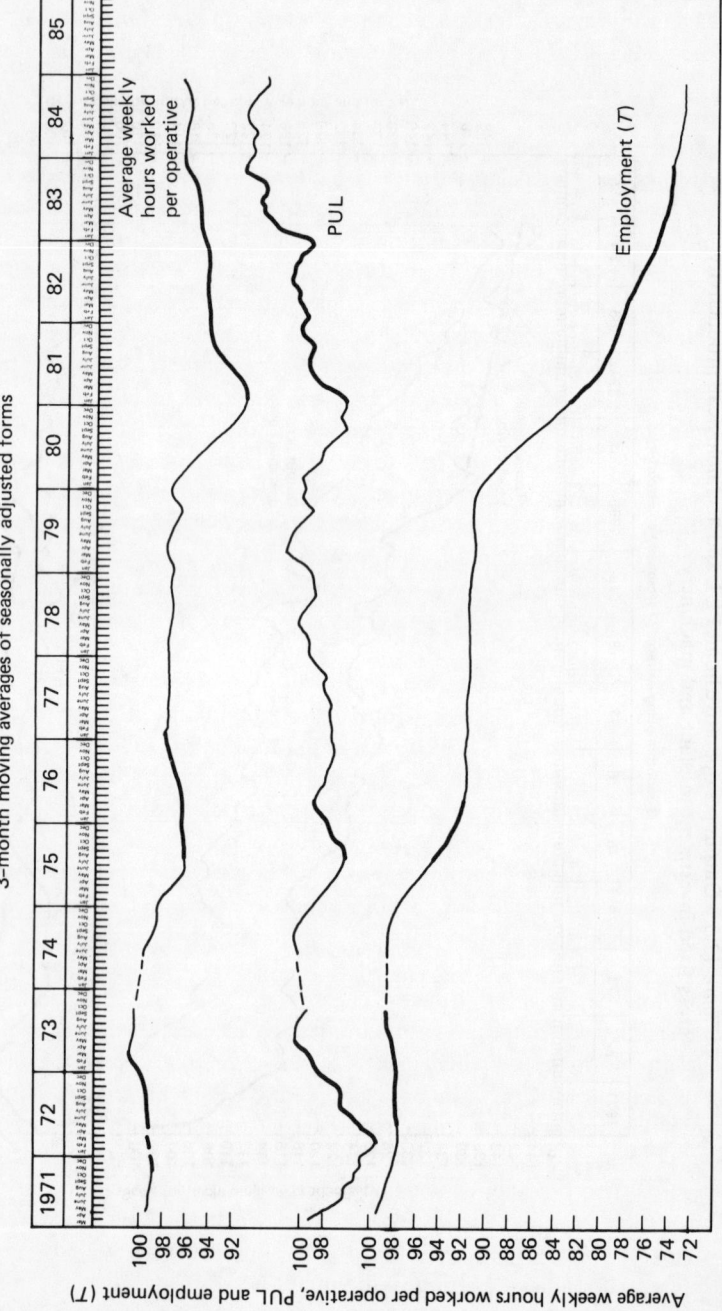

exact equipment. (If either is changed, a new job is declared.) It will have been assessed for its 'standard minute' content by work measurement personnel sometime in the past. Now a standard minute is *not* a period of time; and it is *not*, of course, a unit of real output irrespective of the power of the equipment with which it is produced. It is, in fact, a psychophysiological quantum – the amount of effort a standard operative would expend in a minute. Incentive payments are for standard minutes, so that operatives do want to 'achieve' as many per 'minute of time' as reasonably possible. But, as order books shorten, they will not be able to and the ratio will fall. Typically, an operative will enter 'time started' and 'time finished' on cards as he does each job at his 'workpost'. When, at the end of the week, such data is aggregated in various directions, it not only enables operatives to be paid the right amounts but is also the backbone of factory administration in every respect (see pp. 356–9). The key statistic of 'standard hours achieved per hour of time' will bind together the complex data of some 'factory summary sheet' at the end of each week. And it is a copy of this which is forwarded by the Panel to the Index of PUL monthly.

Those who wish only a brief impression of the results of the PUL Index could turn without further ado to p. 336 below. But others, wishing the deeper foundations necessary to appreciate detail, may care to finish this present Section.

The actual PUL phenomenon must obtain in all sectors of economic life. Nevertheless, it is largely only in manufacturing industry that work is sufficiently definable for its varying intensity to be recorded. Indeed, it is only amongst operatives there that it is usually so recorded.[14] Accordingly, those used to taking output per person hour (*vide* the official category all employees) as a starting point of various analyses may realise that, although PUL change amongst staff (the remaining relevant official category) may be approximately inferred in the short run, yet the impossibility of an actual PUL Index in their case means that the doubtlessly varying rate of rise of their underlying 'technological' productivity (computerisation of office processes and the like) can hardly be traced through time.

Attempts have always been made since 1945 to separate out, by indirect mathematical inference, the PUL and underlying 'technological' productivity elements in some such series as output per operative hour. When it comes to wide comparisons with other countries which may sport no direct measure of the PUL phenomenon (or with earlier times at home when a measure was similarly not available), such inferential studies remain paramount. It is believed, however, that the direct empirical approach of the Index of PUL will also be welcomed.

One particular study in which the reader will have an interest parallel with his study of the Figures in this chapter is that recently undertaken by Lionel Mendis and John Muellbauer. Although it runs back some 16 years prior to the commencement of the Index of PUL in 1971 and, for the moment, ends in 1983, yet there are 12 years in common between the two studies. As those authors point out, the agreement between the courses appointed by them for both the PUL and underlying 'technological' productivity phenomena and those found in the Figures in this chapter are striking. An early account of the Mendis and Muellbauer research is: 'Has There Been A British Productivity Breakthrough? Evidence From An Aggregate Production Function For Manufacturing' (discussion paper 170, Centre for Labour Economics, London School of Economics). Another one is: 'British Manufacturing Productivity 1955–83: Measurement Problems, Oil Shocks And Thatcher Effects' (discussion paper 31, Centre for Economic Policy Research. (Here comparison is made, not only with the Index of PUL but also with the Confederation of British Industry capacity utilisation data). And a further account is a forthcoming article in the *Economic Journal* for which the reader should certainly be watching out.

The Index of PUL was started during the Heath administration of 1970–4 and was intended to add to the statistical series on which a still largely accepted 'fine tuning' of the economy was based. The authors have been surprised and intrigued by the fact that it is under the monetarist experiment – an event which, perhaps, could not have been foreseen – that it has achieved a role as passive monitor rather than contributory guide.

The role of the Index of PUL is to supply additional raw data to fellow economists and analysts of all kinds. It is purely factual and quite unassociated with any school of economic thought; and commentary is intended only to link the results into the wider economic controversies of the day, and not to attempt to strike net conclusions.

It has only been within the last few years that the authors have contacted fellow economists. The reason for the delay was that, although they began by intending simply to ascertain the facts of each passing moment, certain patterns in regard to both underlying technological productivity growth and also the changing level of economic activity began to emerge. It therefore seemed important that time should be allowed to elapse to see whether or not their existence was confirmed – which, indeed, it has very strikingly been. Such patterns are not merely of scientific interest: they are of great practical significance because – amidst the otherwise very differently behaving phenomena under the monetarist experiment – they show a certain important persistence. The practical and pragmatic, it seems, cannot be separated from the scientific and underlying.

A few words must now be said about the processing of the PUL data received from a Panel factory; about the interpretation of the detail of the charts; and about the stratification of the Panel.

To begin, then, with the processing of the material received. This is typically in the form of the number of standard hours achieved per hour of time (see again p. 331 and pp. 353–8) during the month. This, however, is actually taken by us as a percentage of an estimated absolute maximum thereof (assessed at the initial interview). Now such an absolute maximum is not likely to be achieved in most cases and certainly not in the whole Panel; and so, relating PUL magnitude on that basis to employment and average hours magnitudes upon it where such a thing is (or is nearer to being) achievable is very arguably inappropriate. Accordingly, PUL magnitude in the Sub-panels (and hence in the Panel) is multiplied by a factor of 5/4 to relate it to the more practical maximum which was early found to be about 80 per cent of the hypothetical absolute maximum;[15] and this practical maximum has always been shown as 100 in the charts. (To make the matter more complicated still, the rise in PUL during the monetarist experiment has meant that this so-judged practical maximum has actually been exceeded by a small amount!).

The absolute PULs of a factory are not used for the Index. If that were done, there would be the danger (in all but the largest sample) that a factory quitting the Panel might, for some reason specific to its exact manufacturing processes, have had habitual PUL levels slightly (say) less than most; that the replacing recruit might have one higher than most; and that the Index would therefore go up invalidly. Accordingly, what are used for the Index are the changes in each factory's PUL from one month to the next.

Let us now turn to make the key points about the interpretation of the charts. First, it will be realised that series such as PUL itself, employment and average weekly hours worked per operative, etc., are (either in known fact or simply in principle) subject to a 100 per cent ceiling level. However, for comparability between series, the percentage figure in March 1981 is set at 100 (see below). Second, all graphs are of seasonally adjusted figures. In the case of government series, the adjustments are the official ones. In the case of PUL, they are nowadays the same for each Sub-index and hence also for the main Index.

Third, all graphs are of three-month moving average figures. However, there was a good deal of movement on in PUL between March and April 1971 and, in order to give the reader some representation of this fact, it is the score for the individual month of March which has been set at the 100 level and the three-month moving average figure for April (even though it contains that March score) is shown in contrast to it – by a dotted line. We hope the reader will endorse this deviation from logic made in an exceptional case in the interest of some representation of additional factual material. For comparability, the same has been done with series other than PUL.

Fourth, in all graphs the period September 1973–March 1974 is covered by a dotted straight line. This was a period which included major strikes so that the detail of various graphs within it would be misleading. Fifth, the meaning of the graph heading, Employment (T) was explained above.[16] Sixth, the relationship between the two net work put in graphs in Figure 12.5 was also explained above.[17]

Seventh, a point of logic concerning the method of representing output per operative hour and 'technological' productivity must be explained. Phenomena like these rise forever. Now suppose one such – say, 'technological' productivity – has recently arrived at 150. It now goes up by 3 to 153. One is tempted to call this – and graph it as – a 3.0 per cent rise. But really, of course, it is 3.0 per cent only in terms of the graph's – and the economy's – starting level long, long ago. The fair and relevant level to measure the rise against is the 'advantageous' height of 150 from which it started. And this gives a rise of only 2.0 per cent. This, in fact, is how the chart represents the matter; and so a glance along it will give a valid impression of when 'technological' productivity was doing comparatively well or badly. (The disadvantage of this representational device is more abstract: the distance between the little divisions on the chart, and the numerical values of those distances, do not mean the same absolute things – though, over a few years, the inconsistency is negligible).

Finally, a quick word about the stratification of the Panel of factories underlying the Index. This is by region, factory size and product. In fact, early research showed the first two factors – although still catered for as closely as possible when replacing defections from the Panel for one reason or another – seem to carry so small importance as to be statistically undetectable. By constrast – and as the reader will see from Figure 12.1 –, the third factor is of overwhelming importance. Accordingly, the movements of the Sub-indices for Consumer, Intermediate and Capital Goods respectively are weighted into the main

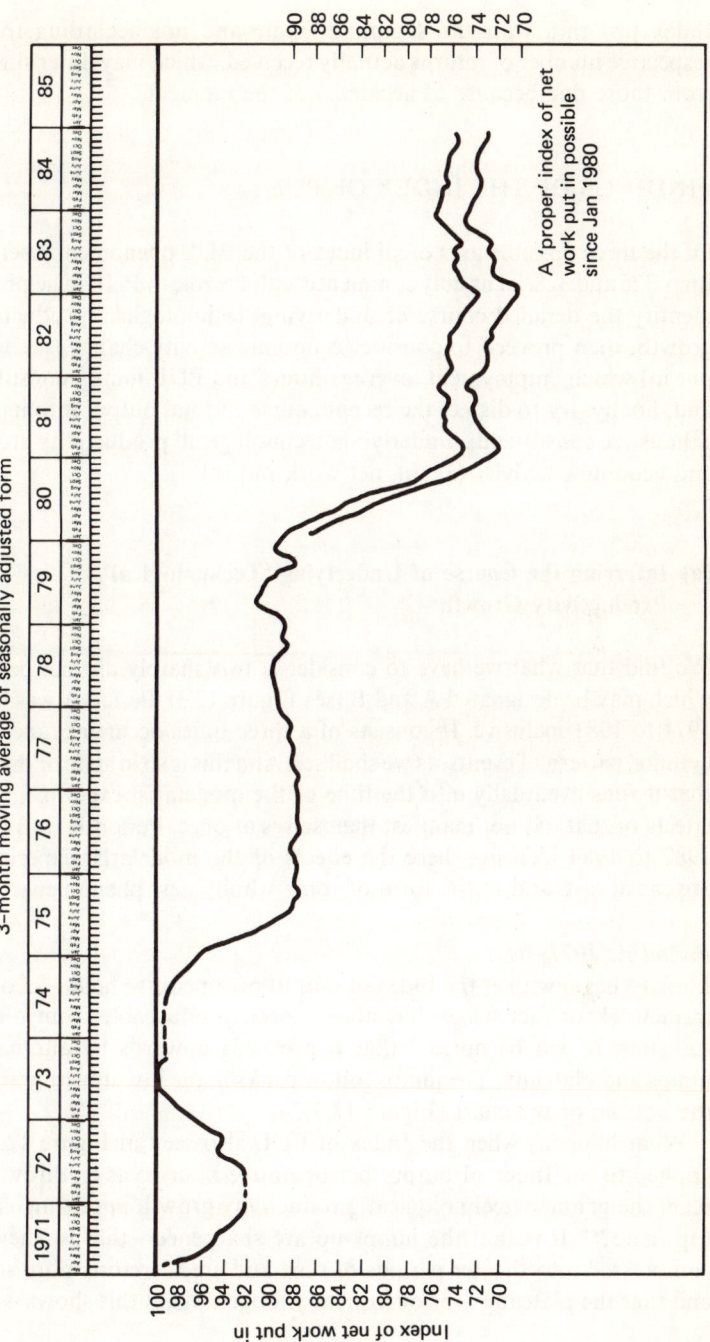

Figure 12.5 Index of net work put in

3-month moving average of seasonally adjusted form

A 'proper' index of net work put in possible since Jan 1980

Index of net work put in

Index pro rata with the sampling frame and not according to the respective number of returns actually received, which may differ slightly from those due because of accidents of the moment.

FINDINGS OF THE INDEX OF PUL

Of the three possible uses of an index of the PUL phenomenon set out on p. 326 and 328, let us duly commence with the role of PUL in helping to identify the detailed course of underlying 'technological' productivity growth; then proceed to consider economic activity change (net work put in) which employment, average hours and PUL jointly constitute; and, finally, try to dissect the recent course of total output into its two exhaustive constituents, underlying 'technological' productivity growth and economic activity (again, net work put in).

(a) Inferring the Course of Underlying 'Technological' Productivity Growth

We find that what we have to consider is two sharply distinct periods which may be designated A and B (see Figure 12.3). Period A was from 1971 to 1981 inclusive. It consists of a three times occurring, and very definite, pattern of events, as we shall see. And this is so in spite of the fact that it runs eventually into the time of the monetarist experiment: the effects of that did not manifest themselves at once. Period B runs from 1982 to 1984 inclusive: here the effects of the monetarist experiment appear at last, and in the form of some wholly new phenomena.

Period A: 1971–81
Look to begin with at the Index of output per operative hour – an outer framework of fact which has always been produceable from official statistics. It will be noticed that it proceeds upwards by alternating jumps and plateaux. The jumps follow peaks in the investment graph at the bottom of the chart (Figure 12.3).

What happens when the Index of PUL also seen in Figure 12.3, is applied to the Index of output per operative hour so as to throw into relief the genuine 'technological' productivity growth appearing at the top there?[16] It is that the jumps up are sharpened – that is, they are compressed into shorter periods of time and are therefore more acute; and that the plateaux are consequently longer. What this shows is that 'technological' productivity is even more closely associated with investment than might have been inferred from the course of output per operative hour. (The phrase 'associated with', rather than 'caused by', is used since some may feel that the constant relationship is explicable in terms of some more indirect causative route.) It is interesting to see how the rhythm extends by some 18 months even into the period of the monetarist experiment.

The way in which the alternation of steep jumps and gently upward-sloping plateaux comes about is readily seen from blacked-in segments on the graphs. Soon after the burst of investment, output per operative hour rises; but PUL *falls*. This means that the rise in underlying 'technological' productivity is early and acute. There is then no further such acute rise by 'technological' productivity; but output per operative hour continues to rise because PUL recovers and so unloads 'technological' productivity which it has been holding as a potential, on to it.

Period B: 1982–4

In this period we see a powerful and steadfast climb by output per operative hour and, in a moment, we shall see that this is primarily due to the novel feature of a PUL rising far beyond its previous ceiling level – a phenomenon, it may be assumed, which is due in one way or another to the arrival of the monetarist experiment. But we must note here a 'psychological' point. It is that this climb by output per operative hour gains in impressiveness from the fact that it is smoothly continuous with one occupying 1980 and 1981. Yet this was only the latest case of the three times occurring pattern of Period A just mentioned, and so probably nothing much to do with the monetarist experiment itself.

Putting that 'psychological' point aside and coming to the actual years 1982 and 1984 inclusive, we will examine first the ceiling-breaking climb in PUL which was primarily responsible for the imposing rise in output per operative hour during those years; and we will turn only later to the degree of underlying 'technological' productivity growth which – following after the meteoric jump up in 1980 – also contributed (but in a smaller way).

What, then, can be said concerning the ceiling-breaking rise in the PUL phenomenon? That phenomenon is unlike 'technological' productivity growth, in that it cannot rise forever. Accordingly, in so far as a climb in output per operative hour is found to be due to it, there is immediately some regret: the beginnings of an accelerated long-term growth are not present after all. In addition to this there is the consideration that it is arguably the natural economic function of PUL to take the impact of 'temperature' change in particular branches of industry (see Figure 12.1) and in industry as a whole (see Figure 12.4); and that it is therefore hardly to be wished for to have PUL rammed permanently up to some ceiling level and to leave average hours and – more importantly – employment to do the short-term fluctuating.

However, it could be argued that a PUL rise of some 4 per cent above its previous ceiling level is still a 'productivity' growth gain within the wide sense of the word; that it had been high time that it was achieved: and that the new ceiling ought – in spite of the remark at the end of the last paragraph – to be permanently maintained. How far can this approach be substantiated? It has earlier been noted how, prior to the monetarist experiment, there was a tendency for the Sub-indices for Consumer, Intermediate and Capital Goods respectively to chase one another round in a manner reminiscent of the well-known accelerator principle (see again Figure 12.1). During that experiment, however, there seems to have been a tendency to synchronised behaviour. Part, therefore, of the 4.0 per cent or so surpassing of its previous ceiling by the main Index is due to the mere fact that Intermediate and Capital Goods, although not individually exceeding their previous highs, have come up level with those at the same time as each other (and hence may both go down together as they did in 1980). Although this result of the monetarist experiment is technically intriguing, it does not amount to an increase in that rather special sort of 'productivity' that would have consisted in several PULs being individually higher through time.

It is, however, the case that one of the Sub-indices – Consumer Goods – not only peaked in the same general period as its companion Sub-indices: it also did exceed its previous high. This last fact, then, is an increase in this Sub-panel's inherent PUL. Could it, in any possible way, represent an increase in underlying 'technological' productivity of a sort which should properly go into the graph of that name?

The reader will be very clear in mind about the following *general* principle: A PUL rise is an increase in human effort per hour within an exact given context of physical equipment and all the methods pertaining to it; and therefore it does not include the fruits of an improved work context itself.

There is, however, a *special* sort of change in the work context whose fruits will, after all, get themselves entered into PUL change. It is to do with 'waiting-time' as the factory term is (approximately 10 per cent) – that is, the (say) decreasing proportion of their time that operatives spend waiting for work to arrive at their workpoint. Such falling proportion does go into factory records as an element within a rise in the

PUL phenomenon and accordingly – and by request of the Index – is submitted as such.

There is, in fact, practical logic in this. The usual and natural reason for waiting time decreasing (and hence for greater intensity of human work per day, if not actually per any one hour) has been a rehabilitation of the activity of the factory for (apart from its own microeconomic fortunes) economic 'temperature' reasons.

What, however, we are confronted with in the case of the Consumer Goods Sub-index is a rise in PUL which breaks its previous ceiling. It may, therefore, be that, as the result of the abrasive influence of a much deeper and longer depression than formally, there has been an enhanced resolve by management to reduce any part of waiting time which had resulted simply from weak organisation and administration – a resolve, that is to say, greater than the one always present under competitive market forces.

Now, if such improved organisation (and day-to-day administration of it) has come about, then the ceiling-breaking rise in PUL in Consumer Goods – or some judged portion of it – would logically belong to 'technological' productivity growth. In that case, when we look along Figure 12.3 and survey the 4.0 per cent or so ceiling breaking rise in the main PUL Index there, we could recall that, whilst a good deal of it is due merely to the nowadays synchronised behaviour of the three Sub-indices, yet there is a ceiling-breaking rise in Consumer Goods which may – or in some part may – be due to 'technological' productivity. We are, however, here getting down actually to 'boxes within boxes within boxes', and we may feel that this hardly supports a view that the ceiling-breaking rise in the main PUL Index is really a vast and heartening increase in 'technological' productivity in disguise.

Let us, then, turn away from the small element of 'technological' productivity which may have leaked, in this scientifically annoying way, into the Index of PUL. Let us look instead at the graph of that name (still Figure 12.3) where the phenomenon may be properly found.

When we look at that graph covering out Period B – 1982 to 1984 inclusive – we see certain very angular small fluctuations. This is clearly a case for trying to draw a trend line through them; and, as a help, we may as well include in our view the year 1981 at whose beginning the earlier sharp jump in 'technological' productivity gives way to the gently upward trending, if angularly fluctuating, plateau.

The elimination of small, angular fluctuations by drawing a trend line would, indeed, seem reasonable. It is, of course, just conceivable that 'technological' productivity may actually fall. Devastation of industrial equipment by war is a far-fetched fulfilment of the logical point. There may also be those who, looking at the prolonged low level of investment since early 1981, may argue that 'technological' productivity is ready to fall slightly now: they may argue, that is to say, that investment now contains no 'net' on balance – the actual improvements at one point being outweighed by deteriorations elsewhere. But what – surely? – is certain is that it cannot go bouncing up and down every six months or so in the manner of the angular little oscillations in the graph since early 1981.

Now that jagged course is generated by the application of a markedly varying PUL graph to a rather smoothly behaving output per operative hour. Should we, then, say 'smooth is probable', and that the PUL graph, though true in its ceiling breaking upward trend, contains spurious fluctuations? It would seem not. In the first place, the PUL phenomenon is just the thing that does fluctuate (down as well as up) short-term in factories: it is a shock absorber (see pp. 353–8).

In the second place, the period from September 1982 to April 1983 may be taken as a clinching example of how – although official statistics underlying the Index of output per operative hour provide a firm long-term framework without which no private research could hope to succeed – the Index of PUL with its homogeneous data (again see p. 353–8) and monthly reports from factories, can highlight very short-term developments. We see how a valley in PUL between these dates, because it is not accompanied by a quite sufficient hiatus in the climb of output per operative hour,[17] generates the disfiguring gable in the 'technological' productivity graph. Yet the valley in PUL is well evidenced: from Figure 12.1 we see that ones occurred at about that time in all the Sub-indices for the three branches of industry shown; and, in fact, each of these is internally well evidenced also.

Altogether, therefore, the jagged oscillations in the 'technological' productivity graph should not be taken as representative of the real situation which must certainly be smoother. Accordingly, the dash-dash trend line shown – which, amongst other things, passes through points in late 1982 and early 1983 lower than the offending gable – may be entertained as a suitably smooth course.[18]

Having drawn our reasoned smooth dash-dash graph line, what can we now say about 'technological' productivity growth in our Period B (1982 to 1984 inclusive)? We noted earlier that, in our Period A (1971 to 1981 inclusive), there was a clear pattern of behaviour and that this included an alternation by 'technological' productivity of spectacular jumps and only very gently upward sloping plateaux. It is obvious to the eye that the gently rising plateau from 1982 to 1984 inclusive does not compare with any of the blacked-in jumps up that have occurred. So how does it compare with previous plateaux? It is, in fact, a rise of about 1.5 per cent a year; and this compares with one of possibly 1.0 per cent a year over the plateau of mid-1975 to 1979 inclusive; and one of conceivably 0.4 per cent a year over the plateau of 1972 inclusive to mid-1974.

There is, then, in our Period B (1982 to 1984 inclusive), a slightly higher rate of 'technological' productivity growth than during previous plateaux. One possible reason that many may spot is that, though the preceding peak in investment was no higher than the earlier ones, it certainly lasted longer: hence the usual jump up in 'technological' productivity may have left effects still to be manifested. If this view be taken, then the very low investment since early 1981 would suggest that 'technological' productivity growth is about to peter out – and, some might hazard, even fall slightly.

There are, however, some four possible reasons for the slightly higher rate of underlying 'technological' productivity growth during the 1982 to 1984 inclusive plateau which do not have to do with the height or duration of the preceding peak in investment.

First, as is frequently argued, there has been the high bankruptcy rate amongst firms, and (since these may contain an above average proportion of low productivity ones) the level of those remaining may be raised.

Second, it is possible that investment, though much lower in volume, has been more apt in an important regard. This is that there has been a move by many firms towards concentration upon a limited number of products (and of sizes and models of each) so that high productivity special purpose equipment (see p. 357) has been replacing low productivity general purpose at a higher rate than through longer years. The adventurous marketing policy required for this is, perhaps, not to be particularly expected in a period of exceptional recession: but it is conceivable.

Third, it is possible that, even apart from the point just made, investment undertaken has been more carefully selected.

Fourth, it is often argued that there have been improvements which do not involve physical equipment. And it could be here argued that, if these have typically been instituted evenly over all departments in a factory, then they would not show up as an increased PUL in subsequent departments (less waiting time there) and so the confinement of the ceiling-breaking rise in PUL in one Sub-index only mentioned above would be no criticism of the hypothesis. Such a view, then, could possibly be upheld. Yet those not too familiar with the factory world may care to reflect that, just because higher management in Britain may have been less dynamic in aggregate in instituting major new investment than in many other countries, it does not necessarily mean that middle management – charged with the task of using the investment in front of them – brave competitive pressures in a particular case to the extent of having these resources in administrative disarray.

Suppose, however, that each and all of these four possibilities are admitted as real. We must still not lose sight of the fact that all they are being called upon to explain is say an additional mere 0.5 per cent a year – that is, the difference between the 1.5 per cent obtaining during the plateau from 1982 to 1984 inclusive and the 1.0 per cent during the one from mid-1975 to 1979 inclusive. The trivial addition of 0.5 per cent to 1.0 per cent, then, has to be compared with the dominating blacked-in jumps up seen at times along the chart and adding respectively about 15.0 per cent, 7.0 per cent and 11.0 per cent a year to any presumed basic 1.0 per cent.

(b) Changes in the Level of Economic Activity

Let us now pass on to the different subject of the 'temperature' or 'level of activity' of the economy (so far as this obtains in manufacturing industry and is registered in terms of operatives there). This is clearly a matter, in part, of employment as a percentage of those available for work.[19] It is also a matter, in part, of the average weekly hours worked by such operatives as are employed taken as a percentage of a hypothesised maximum. (Such employment and such average hours together, of course, give total hours worked as a percentage of a maximum.) Finally, the level of economic activity is a matter, in part, of the intensity of work throughout the total hours worked – per any one hour, that is to say: and this is the PUL phenomenon. When these three embodiments of economic 'temperature' change are compounded together (by inter-multiplication of the several indices) they yield the entity (correspondingly of a percentage type) which has been termed net work put in.

Look at the net work put in graph in Figure 12.5.[20] Beginning with modern times, it will be seen how there was a cliff face fall in 1980 and how from 1981 to 1984 inclusive there was a stubbornly horizontal trend with just very small fluctuations about it.

Now turn to Figure 12.4 where the three constituents of net work put in – employment, average weekly hours worked per operative, and PUL of course – are shown separately. It will be seen that use is made of blacked and unblacked segments – the purpose, however, being unrelated to that in Figure 12.3 examined earlier.

During 1980 – the year of the cliff face drop in net work put in in Figure 12.5 –, all three graphs in Figure 12.4 are falling. The cliff face drop is, in fact, the sum of these falls:[21] there is no question, that is to say, of a fall (or rise) being a matter of transfer of existing 'coldness' in the economic temperature from one graph to another. And this pure circumstance is indicated by the segments concerned being *un*blacked.

Now come to the years 1981 to 1983 inclusive. Here the graphs are blacked-in to show that this is a period of exchanges of 'coldness' between them. The fall in employment – still continuing – is now merely due to the fact that average hours and PUL are unloading their shares of the earlier arrived 'coldness' (mentioned in the above paragraph) on to it. There is, then, no fall in the overall economic 'temperature' as is seen from the horizontalness of the trend of the Index of net work put in during these three years.[22]

Surveying the combined period of 1980 and of 1981 to 1983 inclusive, we now see the danger of reckoning the course of economic activity by the single parameter of employment. If we had done that, we should have been impressed by the fact that the fall was at first sharp and then progressively decelerated; and, with a kind of scientific instinct, we might have concluded that it – supposedly embodying the whole of economic 'temperature' change – was destined to come up again by a mirror image of the course by which it had gone down. But, when we see the true course of economic activity change as shown by net work put in in Figure 12.5, the impression is more discouraging – a sudden drop followed by a horizontal trend setting hard with the continuing passage of time and with only trivial and hapless fluctuations around it.

Again surveying the combined period of 1980 and of 1981 to 1983 inclusive, we find a further point of importance. It is that this is the third case of a three times occurring pattern. This pattern consists, of course, of all three parameters – average hours, PUL and employment – first falling together in response to a wave of 'coldness' striking the whole system; and of the first two later tending to pass their shares of it across to employment so that it may need to continue its fall. But this pattern – though dominating and obvious for all to see – is surrounded by features differing from time to time and even sports some variation within itself. Take the occurrence of the pattern between mid-1974 and (say) late 1976: here we see employment levelling off after the usual continuation of the fall within the pattern, whereas in the recent occurrence of the pattern (1980 to 1983 inclusive) it starts a further fall – unblacked to indicate additional 'coldness' now entering the system.[23] Take also the occurrence of the pattern from 1971 included to mid-1973: when average hours and PUL recover, though employment fulfils the 'spirit' of the pattern by recovering less, it does nevertheless not do the usual outright fall. But, of course, that partly deviant behaviour was because the authorities were actually beginning a reflation which might ultimately have taken all 'coldness' right out of the system.

Clearly, the awareness of any such self-willing pattern is likely to be of use to policymaking in one way or another. For example, if PUL and average hours recover after a fall, it may not be right to say: 'Ah, these are leading the way up: employment must surely follow shortly'. That was true only in the earliest of the three occurrences of the pattern and when actual reflation was being undertaken by the authorities. It is more likely to be right to say: PUL and average hours are going up and, as figures show, employment is going down. This unloading process may leave employment lower for a long time to come. In fact, since the position is only 'temperature neutral', there may even be a further wave of 'coldness' on its way into the system'. These thoughts, then, are the ones more likely to be justified by the second and third occurrences of the pattern.

(c) The Dissection of Recent Total Output Changes into 'Technological' Productivity Growth and Fluctuations in Economic Activity

A frequently quoted statistic these days is 'total output' (typically of manufacturing industry). As a matter of fact, this can be a somewhat confusing concept. Total output is an amalgam of two quite different things. On the one hand, there is the increasing 'fruitfulness' of a given operative hour worked with a given PUL – that is, the underlying 'technological' productivity seen in Figure 12.3. On the other, there is the fluctuating *number* of operative hours intermultiplied with fluctuating PUL out of a maximum possible of all that – that is net work put in, shown in Figure 12.5.

Incongruous amalgam as total output might seem, there are, however, two possible reasons for its popularity. The first is as follows. Prior to a direct measurement of the PUL phenomenon such as the present Index aims to provide, the 'technological' productivity element in the always available output per operative hour could not be pinpointed to stand in its own right; and similarly the PUL element could not be singled out to be combined with employment and with average hours to show the level of economic activity. The only clue to either of them lay in surveying total output, and assessing respective contributions.

The second possible reason for the popularity of the concept of total output may flow from an at least popular 'monetarist' stance that 'all good things go together'. Thus, it seems to be argued, the sight of a rising underlying 'technological' productivity is likely to encourage other businessmen to keep in the race by investing more themselves; and all such investment will also raise the level of economic activity. And, in return, the rising level of economic activity itself will encourage investment which will further raise underlying 'technological' productivity.[25]

But whatever the causes of the popularity of the total output statistic – and it is, of course, an outermost empirical fact from which we must all begin –, there is little doubt that dissection into its 'technological' productivity and its economic activity (net work put in) elements is desirable.

How, then, is the behaviour of total output accounted for in recent time? In Figure 12.6a – the relation with Figure 12.6b will be explained in a moment – look first at the year 1980. It contains a fall of about 15.0 per cent. Net work put in is seen to fall approximately by a gigantic 22.0 per cent. But 'technological' productivity did its meteoric jump up remembered from Figure 12.3 and (p. 337) (a) above but here shown as about 7.0 per cent because of the exact months chosen. Hence, the 15.0 per cent fall in total output.

Once the bottom was reached at the end of 1980, output began on a low-lying course. The small detail of that course is open to reasoned argument, as we shall see in a moment. But the basic principle might be said to be thus: 'A slow upward trend in "technological" productivity is played upon by a gently oscillating net work put in. When net work goes down, it offsets (or more than offsets) the effect of the current instalment of "technological" productivity growth upon output. When it goes up again it lets out this potential it has acquired and does so on top of the then current instalment of "technological" productivity growth so that output rises quite well'. And the consequent warning might be added: 'One should not be too pessimistic when falls in output occur. Equally, one should not seize upon the subsequent larger rise as a sort of joint take-off into growth by "technological" productivity and the level of economic activity: "technological" productivity is climbing only slowly

Figure 12.6 Behaviour of total output

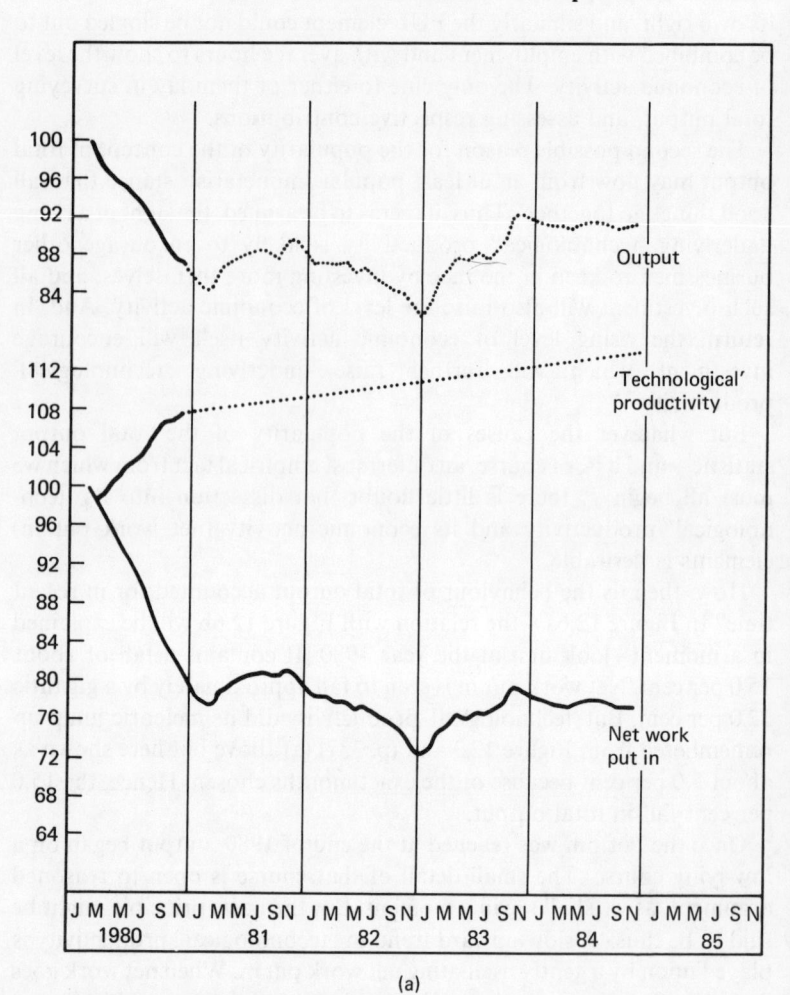

(a)

and the level of economic activity is oscillating trivially'.

Although we have shown the raw data in Figure 12.6b, the construct in Figure 12.6a may both illustrate that principle better and also strike the reader as a possibly useful one. We came to a conclusion above[26] that the official statistics underlying the graph of output per operative hour, with their vast samples and in spite of the inherent difficulties of some of the incoming data, were 'good at' the long term; and that the Index of

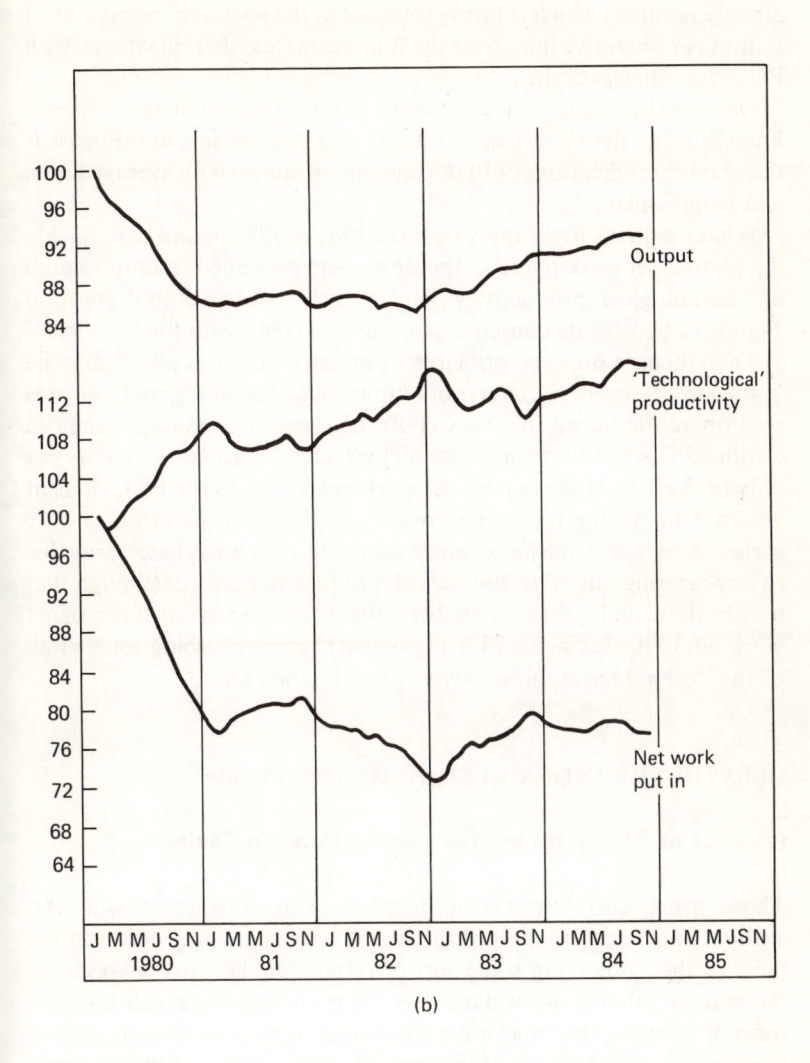

[Figure 12.6(b): Graph showing Output, 'Technological' productivity, and Net work put in from 1980 to 1985]

PUL, with its homogeneous data of standard hours per hour of time (see pp. 328 and 321 above and pp. 353–8 below) reported for the exactly relevant time period, was 'good at' the very short term. In the construct of Figure 12.6a we try to exploit these respective strengths.

On the one hand, we use the dotted part of the 'technological' productivity graph (reproduced from Figure 12.3 with which we are already familiar) which is firmly founded in the *long-term* behaviour of output per operative hour over the four years (together, of course, with PUL over that period).

On the other hand, we use net work put in which can here contribute knowledge of the *short-term* positions of a year or so's duration: it is based on the indications of PUL (together of course with average hours and employment).

What we do is simply apply over the 1981 to 1984 period that quickly fluctuating net work put in to the slow – and presumed smooth – climb of 'technological' productivity. And we arrive at the output graph in Figure 12.6a with its consequential upward trend with fluctuations.

This, then, is how the principle in inverted commas above may be argued to determine the course of output. But, even in Figure 12.6b, it is seen operating (albeit in a very confused form). For example, the rise during 1983 is not due to any take-off by 'technological' productivity but only to the fluctuations up by net work put in and to the PUL element within it unloading the 'technological' productivity growth of a little earlier. And, again, the flattening of output in 1984 is not necessarily due to any petering out of 'technological' productivity growth (though that may be the actual case) but possibly rather to the fluctuation down of net work put in (including its PUL ingredient) again absorbing some or all of the 'technological' productivity growth going on.

USES OF THE INDEX RESULT TO THE FIRM[27]

(a) Uses of PUL Data in Management Decision Taking

Those firms, currently 171 in number, who collaborate with the authors in the construction of the Index, understandably do so on the basis of their obtaining some sort of return for the work involved in the regular submission of data. For many the pay-back will take the form of knowing that they are contributing to the flow of information concerning the behaviour of the manufacturing sector of the economy and that improved knowledge must help rather than hinder the effectiveness of policymaking and implementation.

In most cases, however, collaborating firms could, and often do, obtain a return of a more direct kind. The data that inform a general readership of decisiontakers, analysts and commentators can, in the first place, extend the understanding by management of the economic environment of their own company; in the second place, the information might be used as an element in the assessment of comparative performance; and in the third place, the relationships between the PUL Index and their own individual labour utilisation experience, taken together with the movement of other indicators reproduced in the Bulletin, might be found to serve a predictive purpose.

These uses will be examined individually.

(b) Improved Knowledge of the Economic Environment

Managers with significant decisiontaking involvement should be able to add to their existing general knowledge of their economic environment by referring to the level and trend of PUL in its main graph form and as disaggregated in the Sub-panels for Consumer, Intermediate and Capital Goods and also the Sub-sub-panels for Current and Durable Consumer Goods provided in the Bulletins.

A high and sustained level of PUL may be taken as an additional indicator of what might be called a favourable economic temperature and particularly of a degree of 'full employment' of those hours that are actually being worked. Other configurations of PUL would, of course, be differently and appropriately interpreted.

Another aspect of the overall economic environment would be illuminated by the contribution of the labour utilisation factor to productivity growth. Conditions in which PUL was a major determinant of such growth might be interpreted as being characterised by deficient or inappropriate investment or organisational change.

(c) Assessment of Comparative Performance

By calculating its own PUL values – typically standard hours produced as a proportion of direct attended hours – a firm may compare the periodic changes in intensity of labour utilisation. By and large, a firm may expect to correspond individually to the sample figures shown in either the all industry graphs or in those that relate to disaggregations by major market segment.

Should there be significant deviations from trend then a manager might be expected to initiate some investigation, as he might also do if there were significant variations in the contribution of PUL to overall productivity in his firm as compared with industry at large.

With the revealed possibility of PUL not only experiencing cyclical movements (note 1971–81), but shifts in the level of activity (1982–3), it is clear that changes in circumstances susceptible to managerial influence are very likely to affect PUL and, in turn, overall productivity, and – presumably – other corporate performance indicators, such as profitability.

(d) PUL as an Instrument of Prediction

As has been explained, movements in PUL may have a predictive implication. For example, an upward movement in PUL may be predictive of an increase in hours worked – probably through an increase in overtime – and ultimately of an increase in employment. PUL is the most immediately sensitive of the possible reactions of employment, in its fullest sense, to changes in activity.

Similarly, a downward movment in PUL may be predictive of a reduction in hours worked, and then of a reduction in employment. PUL is therefore a leading indicator of economic recovery or recession, and such knowledge must, of course, improve the economic environmental understanding referred to under (a) above (p. 348).

An examination of the relationship between movements of PUL in the sector Sub-panels suggests, for example, that behaviour in the Intermediate Goods sector may serve as something of a leading indicator for PUL movements elsewhere. Firms identifying themselves as being of an intermediate type might, then, at least investigate this relationship in their own case.

In addition to these general effects, a firm might possibly develop predictive relationships of a more particular sort. For example, a movement in PUL among some identifiable group of firms might have to be associated in a regular way with some movement in the PUL (or at least in the business activity) of an individual firm.

As an illustration of a particular predictive purpose that might be served by PUL the case may be taken of a firm whose product is used by other firms at some relatively late stage in their production process. A rise in the PUL of the sub-sector appropriate to the latter might signal an eventual increase in their demand for the products of the first-mentioned business. Such evidence might well be built in to that firm's forward planning process. It is not suggested that such particular, and short-run, intertemporal relationships would be identifiable for any significant proportion of firms, but it would seem to be worthwhile for collaborating firms and other corporate readers to pay close enough attention to their own PUL and that of relevant subsectors of industry, so that any relationship of this kind may be identified and made use of.

In most cases, firms will probably obtain more information from general rather than particular predictive characteristics of the PUL Index – that is, those movements of PUL which may be suggestive of increases or decreases in hours worked and employment.

(e) Understanding of Factors Determining the PUL Behaviour of Individual Firms

Firms may extend their use of the PUL principle to identifying and investigating the sources of deviations of their own experience from the general PUL trend, and in doing so establish a basis for their own performance improvement. Of course, the outcome of such analysis would not only be of interest to the firm individually, or even to firms in general, but to all those interested in factors ultimately determining corporate performance – and, in turn, that of the industrial economy of the United Kingdom.

Movements in PUL essentially indicate variations in work intensity – all other things remaining unchanged. It might be expected that in any individual plant there will be some maximum level that such work intensity might attain – and in consequence in any grouping of plants, or sub-section of manufacturing industry, there will be some corresponding maximum.

Actual PUL might be expected to vary with reference to the relationship of employed labour and the demand for output, demonstrating greater or lesser fluctuations according to the expectations and practices existing at any particular time. With expectations of a generally high and steady demand for output – and, by derivation, for labour – PUL might be expected to fluctuate considerably, as short-run deviations from expected levels are coped with by reducing effort input, rather than the 'extensive' factors of hours and numbers employed. On the other hand, with less 'optimistic' expectations, it will be likely that PUL will follow a less variable trace, as adjustments to demand conditions are made by changes in hours and numbers.

Whilst at any one time (or during any single identifiable period – which may extend over several years) PUL in the individual plant, or in some group (which may be as large as all manufacturing industry), might be regarded as having a maximum level, yet there is every reason to believe that that level itself might change. Evidence from the sample of firms upon which the index is based suggests that such a change occurred in 1982–3, when the trend of PUL appeared to shift from one level to another. Such a change is independent of any technological (including major organisational) factors that would cause any revaluation of standards, but may be illustrative of a change in practices and attitudes within the existing framework of production.

Such a movement – which in 1982–3 was of an upward kind – is presumably reflective of changes in attitudes of both management and employees, and suggests a change in perception of the business environment.

Firms that have experienced such an upward movement from one 'plateau' of PUL trend to another might wish to consider what have been the causal factors in their case, and whether those factors are controllable. In other words, can the new and higher level of labour utilisation be purposely maintained – or is it some chance reaction to passing circumstances?

Those operations that have not experienced such a movement might find it worthwhile to investigate the possible reasons (as, of course, might those firms whose experience has significantly improved on the increment demonstrated by either the main Index or its appropriate subsection).

A seemingly fruitful field for further research is indicated by these movements of PUL. It is, of course, unlikely that there is unlimited (or even very significant) scope for further productivity improvements to arise entirely from the intensity element of employment, but the maintenance – and possible slight improvement – of present levels of PUL is clearly of great importance for the performance of the economy.

An understanding of the factors promoting shifts in PUL 'base' and a development of capabilities to control these factors, therefore appears to be essential for firms that are to maintain their competitiveness and hence to survive in the current economic environment.

Random indications are that the observable upward shift of PUL in 1983 was due to the manifestation of managerial determination and to the willingness of labour to improve its co-operation with management, particularly in the direction of much improved flexibility; and to actual increases in work effort associated both with routine production and with ancillary activities such as maintenance and materials handling cannot be ignored.

Much interest must centre on the extent to which such developments are permanent in nature: all the factors concerned are – unlike the elements of productivity arising from technological change – readily reversible in effect. Management's will to improve productivity may not be sustainable over time, and employee attitudes to co-operation may undergo change – and are clearly vulnerable to external environmental pressures. Furthermore, the pure 'increased effort' factor, inspired largely by fear of job loss, may wear off with any real, apparent or expected improvements in economic circumstances.

Such, then, are the uses of the PUL Index results to firms, as distinct from the general macroeconomic reading public. Further research into structural, organisational and behavioural factors is envisaged and it is hoped that both firms and also students of management may realise the benefit that should arise from such closer investigation of relationships.

FOUNDATION OF THE INDEX DATA IN FACTORY PROCEDURES

The PUL phenomenon may be defined as 'the fluctuating intensity of human exertion per hour by factory operatives as working specifically mandated equipment; as doing so according to stipulated methods and with only the needed and advised movements; and as working under carefully noted general circumstances'. Two things will at once be realised by the economist about this factory concept and the practice well-nigh universally mounted upon it.[28] First, the phenomenon is measureable in terms of the psychophysiological quanta (degrees of Marshallian disutility, indeed) per minute and under no circumstances whatever in terms of units of real output irrespective of the framework of equipment, of methods and of actual bodily movements currently involved in their production. Second, the operative may slavishly vary his intensity of exertion per hour[29] within this rigid and delicately specified framework obtaining for the time being, but no resourceful suggestion by him for an improved framework will be included in the reckoning of that exertion itself and of the incentive money payment due to him for it.[30]

There is, then, a logical and practical distinction between, on the one hand, the number of psychophysiological quanta per hour fluctuating between a maximum and minimum;[31] and, on the other, the slow (but non-reversing) improvement in the factory's framework within which that fluctuation takes place – improvement, that is to say, in underlying 'technological' productivity which makes a given psychophysiological quantum ever more fruitful in terms of the units of real output it gives rise to. This distinction has always been entertained in logic, and meticulously observed in practice,[32] in the various specialist industrial professions (such as cost and management accounting, process planning, production planning and control and work measurement). Similarly, the use of psychophysiological quanta has, as we shall see, been part of the basis of overall business decisions – the determination of quantities and prices (or, as the case may be, the submitting of tenders), the recruitment of additional labour and the amount and technical nature of new investment.

Although in what follows we shall use terms reminiscent of engineering industries (e.g., 'component', 'sub-component', etc.) for the sake of graphic exposition, yet the system of administration through psychophysiological quanta (called standard minutes as already mentioned, and as will soon be explained in detail) is in use in most industries using most materials – metal, wood, natural fibre material, glass, leather, clay, plastics, etc. The effects wrought by dipping, smoothing, painting, polishing, typing, etc. are just as much 'sub-components' requiring a 'job' (containing so many standard minutes) as are those wrought by shaping, drilling or joining in the case of metallic substances.

Let us now attempt nine points by way of description and analysis which may provide the user of the PUL. Index results with a sense of how factories are administered and hence how such an Index virtually creates itself from the statistics normally kept there.

1. The factory administrative term for a psychophysiological quantum is, as mentioned earlier, a standard minute (or second or hour). This is the amount of human effort that would be expended in a 'minute of time' (another term) by an operative of 'standard' disposition, motivated to a 'standard' extent by an incentive payment system and working on a task with which he had a 'standard' familiarity. (The reader may think of a light year in astronomy which is the distance that light would travel in a year if it behaved in a reasonable or 'standard' manner!) An operative, therefore, is recorded (see below) – possibly every half hour or so – as having 'achieved' (or 'generated') so many standard minutes per minute of time.

2. It would not be possible to administer a factory in terms of units of real output because it makes a large number of different products so that 'units' would be of different sizes; because one 'component' common to several products is not the same sized 'sub-unit' as another common to another several; and because even a genuine unit

(say, a 'component' common to several products and of constant nature through time) will be a smaller matter in terms of cost and time for more rather than for less powerful equipment which may, however, still operate side by side. Accordingly, homogeneous, atom-like psychophysiological quanta (standard minutes) are needed for building up into work of indefinitely varying sizes and kinds.

3. It is a little exceptional if a factory manufactures just one product, or a large number with no 'components' in common. Most produce quite a large number with one 'component' common to some, another to another, and so on in quite a complicated pattern. Such a 'component' may be exactly identical from one product to the next. But, even when it is not quite so, it will go through the same succession of 'shops' or 'production departments' (machining, assembling, etc.) and the same sub-specialist 'workpoints' within each. Now the exact tiny item of work done at an exact workpoint – that is to say, by exact and constant equipment and exactly specified methods and advised movements – on an exact 'sub-component' is, as we have mentioned earlier, termed a job. (If any of these features are minutely altered, a new job obtains.) In 'batch' production – the most frequent sort – it will be discontinued and taken up again and again through time.

4. The layman should, then, picture the work of a factory as tiny streams ('sub-components') running together to form rivers ('components') each of which runs in turn to help form not one but a number of large estuaries – an overall pattern, then, somewhere between unitary and infinitely varied. Within this pattern, it is only very small jobs of a minute or two's duration – whether fashioning some tiny sub-component or else making one of a succession of accurately specified contributions to the major process of joining large components finally together – that are assessed for their standard minute (psychophysiological quanta) contents. It is not, that is to say, work so protracted and complex as to be unvisualisable in terms of its human effort content that is so assessed. The reverse side of the coin must, of course, be that the number of assessments made is quite enormous; and the function of work measurement is, in fact, the key and indefatigably detailed preliminary to the production work of a factory ever taking place at all. But it must be remembered that jobs, once assessed, will occur again and again as batches of various products are periodically repeated so that what must be assessed in any current period is only a small part of the huge number of assessments being used at that moment.

5. A set of multi-coloured cards with carbons between will typically accompany work as it moves along from one workpoint to the next and gradually takes shape, and they will accumulate standard hour data. The following four objectives will be served by this:

   (a) As a batch (again see below) of a particular product takes its turn to go along the line of workpoints, the standard hours per hour of time taken can be compared with the 'standard' number. (This time the word 'standard' belongs to the discipline of cost and management accounting rather than work measurement.)

   (b) The standard minutes per minute of time achieved by each given operative happening to do a 'job' upon a given batch of a given product can be added at the end of the week to those he has achieved on batches of other products to determine his total pay.

   (c) Scheduling of work in the ideal sequence through workpoints – that is, with regard to customer urgency or to loads generated at subsequent workpoints – require a knowledge of the standard hour content of every job.

   (d) The total factory standard hours achieved per hour of time in the week will be calculated either from adding up operatives or jobs – and entered on some factory weekly summary sheet. The ratio will then be used to see, for example, whether more overtime must be prepared for, or even whether the recruitment of more labour may be required.

   A single statistic entered by an operative on his set of cards will, then, yield these and other control data. (It is, of course, the factory weekly summary sheet, or the like, of which copies are sent into the Index of PUL monthly)

6. Beyond the current objectives just mentioned under 5(a)–(d) standard minute and hour data is also required for basic planning:

   (a) Before any two prospective products can be compared in respect of their labour costs, the cheapest technical way in this regard of manufacturing every tiny sub-component in each must be carefully estimated in terms of standard seconds and minutes.

   (b) When that has been done, the respective labour costs in terms of standard hours for the two products will be noted: and when all other costs and marketing considerations have been taken into account the decision which to adopt may be taken.

   (c) Two alternative types of equipment and technical method may serve to contribute to a number of products. Which one has the lower labour cost in terms of standard minutes over all such products will be important in determining which type of investment is undertaken.

(d) Suppose it is intended to thin out the number of product lines or models or sizes of each and to aim 'aggressively' for the large market shares which would greatly increase the number of units, and lower the unit cost and price, of each. 'Special purpose' could then replace the more adaptable 'general purpose' equipment. (This is the oldest story in industrial history. But, if further growth in volume warranted it, successive jobs could be combined and intervention by the human hand eliminated and this might be termed 'automation'—partly a new story. But the difference between old and new stories is one of degree.) The calculation of whether such an adventurous step would be likely to succeed would depend on ascertaining the standard hours involved in the use of the proposed new investment.

7. The number of standard minutes per minute of time operatives will 'achieve' will differ according to:

(a) Abiding personal temperaments.
(b) Current moods.
(c) Practical snags at a previous workpoint (e.g., machine breakdowns).
(d) The microeconomic fortunes of the firm. (But hardly of the industry: the impact of so slow and major a change would be taken by the discharge of labour.)
(e) Fluctuations in the activity of the whole macroeconomy (so far as this reflects itself into the manufacturing sector, of course).

The degrees of fluctuation of the whole factory standard hours per hour of time due to the last factor may not be greater than those of all the others put together. But, throughout the Panel on which the Index of PUL is based, it is naturally thrown into relief as the others cancel one another out.

8. As noted above, the assessments of standard seconds (addable to standard minutes) of human effort in jobs are done by work measurement personnel. These have a basic theoretical training and long prior experience under a senior officer; and they are backed by tabulations for many typical tiny human movements. Also, they may take averages of tried and trusted operatives and on a large number of different occasions. There are, then, a number of mutually complementary methods so that the 'truth' may be tightly closed in upon.

Differences between two officers range at maximum only up to 10 per cent; and that extreme may obtain on only a very few of the very large numbers of different jobs done by an operative in a week or going to make a product or the whole output of the factory. Moreover, the assessments will have been made at different times in the past.

9. Pay bargaining (at factory and national level) is about money per standard-hour. It is not, of course, about standard hours per hour of time. Accordingly, the work of a work measurement officer is professional and technical and he tends not to be under diplomatic pressure from management or operatives.

With this brief description in mind concerning how a factory is naturally run, the reader may well appreciate how the Index of PUL does not break new ground. It merely highlights data which is already the backbone of factory administration for the use of the macroeconomist in his distinct but related concerns. The Panel underlying the Index of PUL is merely 'the national factory' – or, at least, a statistical proxy for it.

Notes

1. The possibility of an index of the PUL phenomenon in industry was first suggested by Sydney A. N. Smith-Gavine when he was on the staff of the Department of Political Economy of the University of Aberdeen (having been for a period in industry during his earlier career). Thanks are still due in long retrospect for conditions which made his preliminary work on the project possible. He removed to Leicester Polytechnic in order to be centrally placed for contact with industry. Sincerest thanks are due to the institution for a type of post uniquely favourable to the conduct of the research and for costly secretarial, computing and other services; and also to colleagues in respect of an inevitably heavier lecturing load from time to time.

   Smith-Gavine was joined at the outset by Alan J. Bennett of the University of Aston Management Centre who, in a long interim period in his academic career, had been general manager of an aluminium castings undertaking and who still kept in touch with industry through several part-time directorships. Sincere appreciation is expressed to the Centre for assistance with travelling expenses entailed in the research, for a period of sabbatical leave and for encouragement generally.

   Mrs Monica Cadwell became the research assistant at the Leicester end of the Index at an early date. It is no exaggeration to say that, without her minutely accurate labours, mathematical clarity of mind and resilience in the frequent times of peak loading, this intensely empirical research project could not have survived through long years until exciting patterns of economic behaviour were slowly unearthed and now continuously monitored. She is *de facto* a third partner in the research.

An inital grant for a feasibility study from the Economic and Social Research Council is recalled with gratitude from the time when the Index was about to be started.

The Esmée Fairbairn Charitable Trust, who have provided continuous funds from an early date, have recently again extended these further in time. The nature of an Index is that it should be absolutely unbroken and comparable through the years. It is, therefore, the unfailing character of the generosity of the Esmée Fairbairn trust which makes this additional source of prime economic data possible.

Finally, the sincerest appreciation is due to the Panel of factories who have supplied, month in and month out, the statistics – routine in factories but novel and tell-tale in the world of macroeconomists and the authorities – of which the Index quite simply consists.

Several times a year – determined by statistical considerations – Bulletins To Co-operating Firms of about 35 pages each are produced. These are intended also for general readership in the political, academic, civil service and journalistic, etc. spheres. No charge is made, and the authors would be delighted to hear from anyone who would like to be put on the mailing list. The address of Leicester Polytechnic is The Newarkes, Leicester LEI 9BH (telephone 0533-858643); and of the University of Aston Management Centre, Nelson Building, Gosta Green, Birmingham B4 7ET (telephone 021-359-3611).

The Index of PUL is not associated with any school of political or economic thought.

2. Although this name for the phonemenon was selected for the Index, factories use a number of terms of which this is just one.
3. Using the official statisticians' terms, out of 'all employees' the category concerned is not of course, 'staff': the work of these is usually too heterogeneous and 'abstract' to be the subject of the prior work measurement which is the basis of recording fluctuating intensity (see below – particularly pp. 353–8). The nearest official category concerned is 'operatives'. But, to be duly precise, it is really direct operatives (a factory and cost accountancy concept which the official statisticians do not sport). These are such operatives (the majority) as operate the machines to make the factory's products. Indirect operatives maintain the machines and run general production services: their work is not so usually subjected to work measurement (though where it is in the Panel the data is included).
4. Except in some factories in the process industries. Here the pace of 'work' may be determined by, for example, the laws of chemical nature so that it would be without point to offer incentive pay (which is one reason for work measurement – again see later) to human beings who are but 'midwives' to the process. (The layman to the factory world might be surprised, however, to see how frequently some incentive element of pay is 'wangled' in even here. Operatives like the feeling that there is at least something they may be able to do to increase their week's earnings; and managements are glad of anything which may make operatives look sharp in a general way and,

perhaps, hustle work between one process and the next.) In this type of factory – largely confined to the Intermediate Goods Sub-panel of the PUL Index (see note 5 below) – the per hour phenomenon of PUL, which is still an economic entity, must be detected by special methods. These are, however, clearly successful since the PUL graphs for these factories behave no differently from the ones for 'orthodox' factories maintained by the researchers.

5. The term 'Intermediate Goods' needs a word of explanation. They consist of: (i) goods which, although not consumed, or not immediately consumed, are closely linked to consumer goods industries (for example, chocolate boxes sold to confectionary firms for use or for stock); and (ii) goods which, whilst used solely in production, are nothing like so long lasting as capital goods (for example, oils, abrasives, etc.). (It was discovered in a very early stage of running the Index that the three branches of industry entertained had clearly specific PUL behaviours.)

6. To combine (for each Sub-panel) PUL, employment and average hours to arrive at a net work put in (see below) for it would be very interesting since the accelerator principle might be expected to be manifested more clearly in terms of that entity. There are, however, some difficulties in allocating employment and average hours to the branches of industry used in the PUL Index and this ancillary research has not yet been undertaken.

7. There have been certain revisions in official data since the chart was prepared.

8. The employment graph has a slightly different coverage, and is prepared on different principles (see note 24) from, the Employment (T) graph (see note 12) in Figure 12.4.

9. The official statisticians now produce an actual output per operative hour, but the one used from an early date in the PUL Bulletins To Co-operative Firms, although having a very slightly different coverage, is being maintained for the sake of consistency. The official statisticians have, however, always endorsed the logic with which their data is used.

10. The word 'technological' is always placed in its inverted commas to indicate that what is included is not only increases in productivity due to improved equipment (together with the changes in method which obviously accompany that), but also those rarer ones which are due to improved methods with the same equipment.

11. Ideally, the application of PUL to any Index of output per operative hour should purge out fluctuations from the latter and leave as an Index of 'technological' productivity a succession of smooth trends either up, horizontal, or (just conceivably) down. Whilst, that is to say, it is just possible that 'technological' productivity could trend down slightly for a time – for example, during a period of investment so low as not quite to cover replacement of equipment – it is incredible that it should bounce up and down in an angular fashion every six months or so. The graph of 'technological' productivity inferred in Figure 12.3 does, however, contain that defect. Wherein lies the explanation of such deviation from the ideal? The Index of PUL itself, whilst the underlying Panel can never equal the powerful ones available to the official statisticians, does have the advantage that the data is homogeneous (see pp. 353–8) and pertains to an exact time period stated. The official data of output and operative hours worked *per*

contra has the advantage of large samples, but many small snags operate against perfect accuracy in the short term. In general, it is possible to take the view that official data – without which the Index of PUL and its indications could simply not be achieved at all – is 'good at' the long term, whereas the Index of PUL is similarly 'good at' detecting at least the timing of little short-term jobs up and down.

12. This suitable measure is seen as Employment (T) in Figure 12.4. The 'T' stands for 'temperature'. That is to say, the graph's movements abstract from that exodus from manufacturing industry which is merely across to other sectors of the economy (and vice-versa); and also from that element of exodus into retirement (and from that element in the number of starters) which is due to various changes, present and past, affecting the size of the total working population.

13. In Figure 12.5 there is one edition of net work put in running the whole course and a 'proper' one running from 1981 only. The explanation of the matter has to do with the employment ingredient in that series. It will be remembered from note   , that the employment series logically required is Employment (T) – that is, one which abstracts from movements merely across to (or, for that matter, back from) employment in other sectors of the economy. Since official statistics do not show the proportion of operatives – the category of employee, of course, required – leaving manufacturing industry who are genuinely going down into unemployment, it was necessary until the beginning of 1980 to rely on 'all employees' concerning whom that proportion can at least be indirectly inferred. However, from 1980 onwards (until, at any rate, the middle of 1983), the exodus of 'all employees' was almost entirely downwards into unemployment. Hence, it could be concluded that that of specific operatives was so also. And hence the available official statistics of operatives' exodus could be used at last. It is these, then, which are the employment ingredient – proper for the first time – in the short-running net work put in. The reader will realise that the proportion of operatives leaving manufacturing who go down into unemployment cannot be expected to be the same as that in the case of staff – and hence of all employees – and he will therefore appreciate the concern with the point of principle. Equally, however, he may be relieved to notice that the 'proper' edition of net work put in differs from the long-running one by amounts which may not be of too great practical concern.

14. Strictly, direct operatives (see note 3 above).

15. Simply as an arithmetical process, the procedure described would, of course, be pointlessly circular. However, there are reasons for it of a practical nature. For example, at the interview respondents' assessments of a practical maximum are sometimes later seen to have been under-estimates whereas those of an absolute maximum may be safer. Again, in the type of factory described in note 4 above where pace is machine-orientated, an absolute maximum is a simple engineering fact and is often achieved, whereas the historical detail needed to find a sort of 'maximum long-term practical average' might not be readily available.

16. It will be recalled from note 11 that the ideally expected purging out of small fluctuations is often not achieved.

17. It is satisfying, however, how in the graph in Figure 12.2, there is a required

drop of at least some magnitude at about this period.
18. Of course, its linear character may not be correct. A changing trend, provided it was devoid of short-term fluctuations, could be hypothesised by those with views on economic influences at work.
19. The exactly relevant concept is Employment (T) in Figure 12.4 and this was explained in note 12.
20. See note 13.
21. More strictly speaking, the result of the intermultiplication of the three indices.
22. In this period of blacked-in stretches in Figure 12.4 for the year 1981, 1982 and 1983, Employment (T) – to take that as the example – enjoys this blacking-in to indicate that the mere transfer of 'coldness' between graphs mentioned above is the end-to-end circumstance. When, however, net work put in (Figure 12.5) was doing one of its little fluctuations down around its horizontal trend, Employment (T) should, very strictly speaking, be unblacked, to indicate that its fall was the result of new 'coldness' entering the economy for just that moment and compared just with net work put in's immediately preceding little hillock. But, if that were done, it would underestimate the end-to-end transfer. (The subtle logical point for any reader interested is that average hours and/or PUL, because they are trending upwards, will shortly afterwards have to rise by a larger amount than they fell to make net work put in fluctuate down; and part of this rise will be shown as a blacked-in transfer to the then segment of Employment (T) but part also as a return upward fluctuation in net work put in. Accordingly, that latter part may be regarded as validating the notion of 'mere transfer' to Employment (T) retrospectively.)
23. As explained earlier, unblacked segments during an occurrence of the pattern (with a mild degree of exception in the case of the first) indicate falls due to new 'coldness' entering the system; and, conversely, unblacked ones indicate transfers of a recently arrived 'coldness' between the graphs. It is not known yet whether the 1984 segments are really the ending of the third occurrence of the pattern or (say) the beginning – straight after the ending of the previous one, this time – of a fourth. If the former is the case – it (that is to say, average hours and PUL), is really still trending upwards in spite of momentary dips – then Employment (T) is basically continuing merely to receive transfers; and so those segments should be blacked after all. (There is no doubt that 'coldness' is entering the system during the very short period concerned – even though the downward oscillation by net work put in in Figure 12.5 does not take it below a previous one about its long horizontal trend. It is the converse case of the seeming paradox discussed in note 22 above that a trend movement and the sum of short-term movement therein make contradictory demands upon the blacking/unblacking device.) If, however, 1984 is the beginning of a fourth occurrence of the pattern, then the segments should be unblacked (with no seeming paradoxes this time).
24. As readers will recall, the employment content (genuine operatives, not all employees, of course, since January 1980) of net work put in Figure 12.5 is duly corrected for movements across into other sectors and also for changes in the size of the national working population. In Figures 12.6a and 12.6b, however, we are concerned with output which is total willy nilly; and hence

the edition of net work put in used duly restores those 'impurities' to the employment element within it.

25. Such a view is, of course in sharp distinction to the indications of the Keynesian formulae which relatively layman readers may recall from student days. These would indicate that, out of the increased real income caused by 'technological' productivity growth, the absolute amount – and probably even the proportion – saved from income would be greater. The level of income and economic activity would, therefore, actually have to *fall* – fall, that is to say, to the level at which savings had become small enough by this new route (and so in spite of the fruits of the higher 'technological' productivity) to be fully lapped up by the limited amount of investment being done.

26. See note 11.

27. After the rather close reasoning in some of the foregoing the reader may welcome the opportunity to relax just a little with this Section by Alan Bennett. It does not look at the Index so much from the point of view of those averages, aggregates and net sums which pertain to the analysis and control of the macroeconomy and the measurement of its success. It regards it rather from the standpoint of the individual business manager and his concern with relationships which may obtain in one case yet not in another. The Section is based on contact with executives in the Panel of factories more extensive than is involved in their recruitment and submissions to the Index. It should, therefore, be of interest to the academic student of management and of applied microeconomics, from any of whom the author would be delighted to hear.

28. But see note 4.

29. As will be seen shortly, according to personal mood but, more importantly, for operatives as a whole according to the amount of work available as the result of the microeconomic fortunes of the firm, and showing through these as they cancel out over all manufacturing industry as a whole the level of activity of the macroeconomy.

30. If he does make such suggestions, he will doubtless be quickly promoted to foreman and higher still in due course and enjoy the appropriate salaries. Again, if he is one of a committee of operatives who make such suggestions, he will doubtless get a merit award along with the rest. But, once a work framework is established, he will be paid for working within it and solely according to the varying number of psychophysiological quanta (identified to jobs by work measurement personnel) which he may 'achieve' from time to time.

31. On p. 326 there is mention of the huge degrees of swing in particular branches of industry. But those in an individual factory can be greater still.

32. Actually, since the last quarter of the 19th century when the techniques of more systematic work measurement, pioneered by Taylor and Gilbreth in the United States, spread gradually across the industrialised world.

Part III
Capital

13 Capital Utilisation, Capacity and Scrapping

David F. Heathfield

INTRODUCTION

This chapter considers three related issues. First an attempt is made to counter recent claims that capital utilisation should be omitted from estimates of production functions and productivity.

Second, a distinction is drawn between idle capital and scrapped capital: the latter determines capacity rather than productivity, and is to all intents and purposes immeasurable.

Third, and finally, it is argued that capital utilisation measures which are based on electricity consumption have much to recommend them and, with some 'weak' assumptions, can be made to measure capital services independent of errors in the measurement of capital stock.

THE NEED TO MEASURE CAPITAL UTILISATION

1. The arguments which will be countered in this Section seem to fall into two classes. The first is that capital stock is an ever-present productive asset and its productivity, or 'efficient use', should properly include 'better' utilisation. Thus if two firms (A and B) have the same capital stock and firm A uses its capital for twice as long as firm B, then the productivity of capital in firm A is deemed to be higher than that of firm B. To correct for utilisation, it is argued, will therefore detract from proper productivity differences.

   This seems to be the argument advanced for example by Kendrick (1973) which is quoted by Gollop and Jorgenson in Kendrick and Vaccara (1980):

   > In contrast to the human population the entire living population of capital goods is available for productive use at all times, and involves a per annum cost, regardless of degree of use. The purpose of capital assets is for use in production of current output and

income. The degree of capital utilization reflects the degree of efficiency of enterprises and the social economy generally. Hence in converting capital stocks into inputs we do not adjust capital for changes in rates of capacity utilization and thus these are reflected in changes in the productivity ratios.

The idea that 'the degree of capital utilization reflects the degree of efficiency of enterprises and the social economy generally' requires the rather strange abstraction of economic considerations from 'efficiency' measures. There is much theory and empirical evidence to show that the optimal level of capital utilisation is not 100 per cent but depends upon the technical characteristics of production *and* the rhythm of input prices over a day or over a week or over a year. (See for example, Winston and McCoy, 1974; Marris, 1964; Hamlin and Heathfield, 1983; Bettancourt and Clague, 1981; Bosworth and Dawkins, 1981).

The idea that capital is more efficiently used when its usage exceeds 'optimal' involves either a contradiction or a somewhat unusual and possibly misleading use of the words 'efficient' and 'optimal'. (This optimal usage is based on *ex ante* planning, with competitive markets, and hence is neither output-constrained nor Chamberlinian nor due to 'clay' capital.)

It seems wise, then, to distinguish between 'utilisation' and 'efficiency'. Indeed 'utilisation' may be more useful as an explanation of variations in 'efficiency'.

2. The second class of argument denying the usefulness of including capital utilisation in production functions seems to be based on the idea that if the utilisation of one input is included (typically that of labour) then this will serve for all inputs. To include capital utilisation as well as labour hours is thus to 'double count': capital utilisation is therefore redundant. This is the argument advanced by Denison (1974) and is also quoted in Gollop and Jorgenson:

> In the short run, the intensity of capital utilization fluctuates with variations in the pressure of demand, but in this respect capital input is not different from land input or labour input. The hours that capital is used may also change in the longer run but such changes, if they occur, are merely manifestations of changes in other output determinants that are separately measured so need not be given separate consideration.

In order to counter this argument it is necessary to specify a production function. By way of illustration we will look at three popular forms: a fixed coefficient function, a Cobb–Douglas function, and a CES function.

(a) The Fixed Coefficient Function

By 'fixed coefficient' is meant that a particular *stock* of capital (K_s) requires a particular *stock* of labour – or fixed crew size (L_s), and produces a fixed *flow* of output. (q units per shift).[1]
Thus:
$$Ls = \rho \times K_s \quad \text{and} \quad q = \gamma \times K_s$$
where:
 ρ = fixed crew/machine ratio
 γ = fixed output/machine ratio.

If we had data on crew size, capital stock and output per shift then their coefficients could be measured without reference to utilisation rates. However, the data available are typically the quantity produced over a number of shifts (Q) and the total number of workers employed on all shifts (L). Furthermore the length of the shift and the working of part shifts means that the usual measure of labour input is simply the number of worker hours per quarter.

$\therefore$ we have $Q = n.q$

and $L = nL_s$

where n is the number of shifts worked per quarter and L_s the shift size (i.e., crew size).

Now the fixed coefficients are defined in terms of L_s, K_s and q not in terms of Q, L and K.

$$\therefore \quad \gamma = \frac{q_s}{K_s} = \frac{Q}{nK_s}$$

and
$$\rho = \frac{L_s}{K_s} = \frac{L}{nK_s}.$$

In order to obtain estimates of the coefficients (γ and ρ) from data on Q, L and K_s, it is thus necessary to know how many hours (shifts) the capital is being used for – i.e., (nK_s). If n is not included then ρ and γ may take any value.

This is the exact opposite of Denison's argument, in that it is the inclusion (unavoidably) of labour utilisation which necessitates rather than obviates the need for a capital utilisation measure.

(b) Cobb–Douglas Function

The point becomes clearer if we consider the instantaneous flow Cobb–Douglas (C–D) function:

$$q = A_t L_s^\alpha K_s^\beta.$$

Once again, data are available only on Q and L, and cannot be disaggregated into q and n and L_s and n.

Thus:

$$\frac{Q}{n} = A_t \left(\frac{L}{n}\right)^\alpha K_s^\beta$$

$$Q = A_t n^{1-\alpha} L^\alpha K_s^\beta.$$

It is therefore necessary to include some measure of utilisation (n) into the estimation of the C–D function if labour hours and quarterly output data are used.

Note that if the C–D function has constant returns to scale, then:

$$Q = A_t L^\alpha K^\beta$$

where $K = nK_s$ – (i.e., capital utilisation (n) × capital stock = capital services.

(c) CES Function

It is also clear from the CES function that some measure of utilisation is necessary. Thus, for example:

$$q^{-\theta/m} = \gamma^{-\theta}\delta K_s^{-\theta} + \gamma^{-\theta}(1-\delta)L_s^{-\theta}$$

or

$$Q^{-\theta/m} = n^{\theta(1-1/m)}[\gamma^{-\theta}\delta(nK_s)^{-\theta} + \gamma^{-\theta}(1-\delta)(nL_s)^{-\theta}]$$

$$Q^{-\theta/m} = n^{\theta(1-1/m)}[\gamma^{-\theta}\delta K^{-\theta} + \gamma^{-\theta}(1-\delta)L^{-\theta}]$$

where:
K = capital *services* – i.e., $K_s \times n$.

Notice again that when the function has constant returns to scale ($m = 1$), we have:

$$Q^{-\theta} = \gamma^{-\theta}[\delta K^{-\theta} + (1-\delta)L^{-\theta}].$$

In all these cases, then, it is necessary to include a measure of capital utilisation *because* the data on output and on labour services cannot be disaggregated into that of each shift and the number of shifts. There is no systematic relationship between the flow of one variable and the stock of another.

If, indeed, the true relationship for the C–D function (say) is:

$$Q = A_t n^{1-\alpha} L^\alpha K^\beta$$

and it is estimated as:

$$Q = A_t L^\alpha K_s^\beta.$$

Then the omitted term will be $n^{1-\alpha}$, which will cause A_t to be misestimated and will induce a trend in it if n is not constant over time.

One final point may be made in this section of the chapter. Some investigations (e.g., Feldstein, 1967, but see Muellbauer, 1984) have entered labour hours and labour stock separately into the production function. Thus:

$$Q = A_t L_u^\alpha L_s^{\alpha_1} K_s^\beta.$$

The difference between coefficients α and α_1 were interpreted as indicating that an additional hour (L_u) would be more productive than an additional man (L_s). This is clearly mistaken.

First the partial derivative, w.r.t. L_u implies that L_s and K_s are fixed. This can mean only that the existing machines are worked for another hour. There seems no reason why the output in that additional hour should be any different from that of all other hours. Whatever that derivative might be, it is clearly not the marginal product of another hour's labour with labour stock and capital *services* fixed.

Second, the partial derivative w.r.t. L_s implies that L_u and K_s are fixed which could mean *either* that the same stock of machines is used more intensively, for a fixed period *or* that the same stock of machines is operated for slightly longer – i.e., the additional workers come on after the normal work force have finished (or some combination of the two). Thus unless the estimates are corrected for utilisation changes it is not possible to know whether the marginal productivities are due to the substitution of L_s for K_s in the correctly specified production function, or whether it is the result of working the same factor ratio for another hour.

The same point may be made in regard to returns to scale. Returns to scale occur through the increase in both L_s and K_s, not through the increase in L and K. Given the underlying instantaneous flow production function:

$$q = A_t L_s^\alpha K_s^\beta$$

then returns to scale are $\alpha + \beta$, and if L_s is simply replaced by L and K_s by K, then

$$Q = A_t L^\alpha K^\beta$$

which implies that simply doubling the number of shifts would cause output to

1. more than double if $\alpha + \beta > 1$
2. less than double if $\alpha + \beta < 1$
3. exactly double if $\alpha + \beta = 1$.

This is a rather strange assumption, since it is difficult to see why the process should become more or less productive simply because it is operated for two shifts rather than one.

It thus becomes necessary to distinguish between expansion in output due to an increase in utilisation and an increase due to larger scale. As is clear from above, this implies that the utilisation term should be used twice. Once to correct capital stock for utilisation ($K_s \to K$) and once to capture the returns to scale effects ($n^{1-\alpha-\beta}$). If there are constant returns to scale, increasing the number of machines and crews is thus exactly equivalent to increasing the number of shifts for existing machines and crews and $n^{1-\alpha-\beta}$ is 1.

When there are increasing returns to scale and L and K increase, the implied increase in output has to be moderated by the extent that the increase in L and K came about via utilisation rather than scale.

Similarly for decreasing returns to scale.

(d) Summary

The arguments in this Section are aimed at countering the view that capital utilisation is best omitted from production functions and productivity indexes. Its inclusion is necessary because the data on output and on man hours input cannot be rendered suitable for estimating the instantaneous flow production function, and because productivity measures should make allowance for variations in the optimal utilisation rate of capital rather than regard any deviation from maximum as an inefficiency.

SCRAPPING AND CAPACITY

The estimates of capital stock most frequently used in production function and productivity analysis are based on the perpetual inventory method (or a stochastic version of it) in which investments over the past D years are summed to yield current capital stock. (D is the estimated average life of the piece of capital.)

It is not entirely clear what is meant here by 'life'. It may be that the piece of capital will actually fall apart after D years (i.e., the 'one-hoss-shay' assumption), or it may be that the changing economic climate will render it 'uneconomic' after D years, irrespective of its physical existence as an operational machine.

In either case, the fixed life assumption is somewhat questionable. Physical deterioration can be postponed indefinitely with suitable repairs and maintenance and the obsolescence due to changing economic climate depends on just how swiftly and in what ways the economic climate does change.

This latter point has been made particularly important by the oil price shocks which represented a change of climate sufficient to distort any fixed economic life assumption. This gives rise to the argument that our estimates of capital stock are over-estimates, since they fail to take account of the 'losses' due to the severe price shocks. For example, part of the 'slowdown' may be due to the sudden loss of some capital assets, rather than to falling productivity of existing capital.

The important distinction to be drawn here seems to be that between *scrapped* capital and *idle* capital. If some capital is rendered uneconomic by recent price changes, it may well be switched of and left idle, but it is still available for duty if necessary. If, on the other hand, some capital is worn out and melted down, then it is no longer available, whatever the future climate may turn out to be.

'Scrapping' seems to imply an irreversible shutting down of capital – a permanent reduction in the economic ability to produce – i.e., a change in capacity. 'Obsolescence', on the other hand, merely implies a reversible shutting down of capital. Should the right economic climate come about again, then the capital is there ready for use – i.e., it is a change in idleness, not in capacity.

If there are indeed a number of vintages lying idle then the oil price shock may have caused as many previously idle machines to be switched on as it caused active machines to be switched off. The question therefore is one of optimal idleness, and not of scrapping or capacity.

Two final observations may be made here. First, if indeed the price shock caused a change in optimal utilisation of capital then some measure of it is necessary in the production function. To include a utilisation variable will remove the need to subtract the wholly idle capital from the capital *stock* input measure. It will also remove the need to try to estimate the capacity of the sector concerned. This bears on the second point: any attempt to measure all existing capital assets must end in failure. There are windmills which could still be operated if necessary. There are steam engines in York Museum and in private hands which could clearly be recruited to productive effort should the need arise. If 'capacity' is to be defined to cover all possible economic climates it must thus include *all* existing capital assets since they could clearly come into their own again under some configuration of demand and input prices. Estimating 'absolute' capacity in this way is as difficult as it is pointless. Pointless because there seems to be little point in estimating absolute capacity: it plays no part in the estimation of production functions and – we have argued – should play no part in the estimation of productivity and/or efficiency. The fact that we keep our old steam engines in idleness shouldn't be taken to mean that we are using our capital less efficiently than those who 'scrap' their old equipment. On the other hand, if capacity is to be confined to those processes which could become profitable under some 'reasonable' regime of demand and input prices then we are left with the question of what is 'reasonable'? There is unlikely to be any degree of agreement on what constitutes capacity output.

The CBI survey of capacity seems to fall into this second category – i.e., that of 'reasonable regimes'. By asking how much more could be produced without changing current prices (both for output and for input) the CBI is limiting the 'reasonable' range of climates to one – the current climate. The question therefore seeks to elicit how much capital is lying idle which could earn positive quasi-rents with existing prices. This is very similar to the Keynesian notion of involuntary idleness of labour – i.e., how much capital is seeking work at the going prices and is unable to find it?

The existence of involuntary unemployed capital seems to suggest price rigidity, but in any event it is clear that the particular measure of utilisation may change simply because the prices change rather than through any change in the number of machines actually in operation or the number of machines lying idle. For example, an idle machine is part of capacity when prices are such that it can earn a quasi rent but is not part of capacity if prices are such that it earns negative quasi rent. The CBI capacity measures are therefore open to several interpretations.

In this section it is argued that measuring capital utilisation – i.e., 'capital in use' is a rather more relevant and achievable aim than measuring 'capacity' and deviations from it. The idea of capacity is not well defined and would, in any of its guises, appear to be of little significance in the estimation of production functions or of measuring factor productivity.

The distinction between 'utilisation' and 'capacity' is paralleled by the distinction between 'idleness' and 'scrapping'. 'Scrapping' implies irreversible idleness and there seems to be little or no data available on 'irreversibility'. Even quite old capital (windmills, for example) could be regarded as part of capacity.

CAPITAL UTILISATION MEASURES

The measure of capital utilisation suggested here is that due to Foss (1963) and once favoured by Jorgenson and Griliches (1967) and derived for the United Kingdom by Heathfield (1972). The measure relies on the fact that most capital is now operated by electricity and that those units of capital which are driven by electricity have a specified 'rated wattage'. The rated wattage of a piece of capital is the maximum power which can be continuously extracted from it. If the capital were run continuously at maximum power it would thus consume 8.760 × rated wattage KW hours per year. By comparing this figure with the actual consumption, it should be possible to measure the utilisation rate of the capital.

In order for this to work, it is necessary that the electricity-consuming capital bears a constant ratio to non-electricity-consuming capital. Furthermore, to order to obtain some estimate of installed wattage it is necessary to assume something about the quantity of net investment (which is known for every year) and the installed rated wattage (which is not known for most years). Heathfield obtained two point estimates of installed wattage and calculated the incremental capital-installed wattage ratio (ICWR). By assuming a constant ICWR it is possible to interpolate and extrapolate those two point estimates of installed wattage to all years for which we have investment or capital stock data.

Whatever the shortcomings of this method may be, it does have a number of advantages over others. First, electricity cannot easily be stored. The input is timed to coincide with use. There can be no 'hoarding' as is the case with labour-based measures, sales-based methods or material input measures. Second, electricity is perfectly homogeneous and measurable in physical units – it therefore presents none of the usual problems of quality change or aggregation.

This method of measuring capital utilisation purports to yield an estimate of the absolute level of capital utilisation. For the United Kingdom engineering industry, for example, the level of utilisation is about 12.0 per cent. This is considerably lower than the utilisation rate reported, for example, by the CBI, thus reinforcing the earlier point that the CBI survey serves as an indication of involuntary idle capital rather than all idle capital.

The estimates also show considerable variation over time, which suggests that capital stock alone is not a good measure of capital services.

One criticism of this method is that the oil price shocks would cause:

1. A missestimate of existing capital stock and hence a missestimate of the installed wattage.
2. A switch to less energy-intensive methods of production, thereby disturbing the assumed constant ICWR.

Little can be done about 2. except to gather some new data on installed wattage by survey methods. Even so, it could be argued that as far as electric motors are concerned there is very little scope for substitution. Space and process heating may lend themselves to solid fuels and gas substitution, but fortunately these uses of electricity constitute – and for a long time have constituted – only a very small proportion of total electricity consumption (see Heathfield, 1972).

As for the criticism that the missestimation of capital stock will lead to a secondary missestimation of utilisation, it turns out that the errors are of offsetting rather than reinforcing.

Consider the method described above, we have:

$$W_t = W_0 + IWKR(K_{st} - K_{s0})$$

where:

W_t = installed wattage at time t
W_0 = installed wattage at time 0

$IWKR$ = incremented wattage–capital ratio
K_{st} = capital stock at time t
K_{s0} = capital stock at time 0.

From this, we get:
$$K_{ut} = \frac{E_t}{W_t \times T}$$
where:
K_{ut} = capital utilisation
E_t = electricity consumption over period T
W_t = installed wattage at time t
I = number of hours in period T.

Hence capital services:
$$K_{ut}K_{st} = \frac{E_t K_{st}}{W_t + T}$$
or
$$K_{ut}K_{st} = \frac{E_t K_{st}}{W_0 + IWKR K_{st} - IWKR K_{s0}}.$$

Now if the incremented wattage–capital ratio is quite close to the average wattage–capital ratio, we have:
$$K_{ut}K_{st} = \frac{E_t}{A.W.KR}$$
(since $W_0 = AWKR.K_{s0}$)

Electricity consumption alone thus provides a good measure of capital services independently of any measure of capital stock. This result, of course, depends on the acceptability of the assumptions, but does suggest that attempts at measuring capital utilisation may moderate some of the difficulties which spring from the hypothesised missestimation of stock due to price shocks.

It has been shown above that, provided there are constant returns to scale, a measure of capital services ($K_{ut} \times K_{st}$) is sufficient to estimate production functions. However, it is also clear that for non-constant returns a measure of utilisation is necessary. The solution offered in this section is thus 100 per cent satisfactory only for the CRTS case. The inclusion of a capital utilisation measure will of course be less successful in picking up the returns to scale effects if that utilisation measure is inaccurate. Nevertheless, its inclusion may be preferable to omitting it altogether.

SUMMARY AND CONCLUSION

In this chapter we have tried to show that some measure of capital utilisation is necessary if data on instantaneous output and crew size are not available. That although the electricity-based method suffers some shortcomings, it has a number of advantages over alternatives. The particular criticism that price shocks have destroyed the usefulness of capital stock estimates – and hence our utilisation estimates – are countered in two ways. First it is important to distinguish between 'scrapping' and 'idleness'. The former is relevant only to some rather esoteric measure of capacity. The latter is relevant to (and will be reflected in) our measures of capital utilisation. Any such price shock thus reinforces the arguments in favour of including utilisation rates. Indeed, as far as capital service measures ($K_u \times K_s$) are concerned, it can be shown that under some assumptions, our measure is independent of errors in capital stock figures.

For some applications (CRTS) a capital services variable is sufficient but, should a separate utilisation measure be necessary, it is argued that the electricity-based measure, though imperfect, is better than nothing.

Note

1. By 'shift' is meant the work time of a particular crew of workers.

References

BETANCOURT, R. R. and CLAGUE, C. K. (1981) *Capital Utilisation* (Cambridge: Cambridge University Press).
BOSWORTH, D. and DAWKINS, P. (1981) *Work Patterns: an Economic Analysis* (London: Gower).
DENISON, E. F. (1974) *Accounting for US Economic Growth 1929–1969*, The Brookings Institution.
FELDSTEIN, M. (1967) 'Specification of labour input in the Aggregate Production Function', *Review of Economic Studies*.
FOSS, M. (1963) 'The Utilization of Capital Equipment', *Survey of Current Business* 43.
GOLLOP, F. and JORGENSEN, D. (1980) 'U.S. Productivity Growth by Industry 1947–73', in Kendrick, J. W. and Vacarra, B. N. *New Developments in Productivity and Measurement Analysis* (Chicago: NBER).
HAMLIN, A. P. and HEATHFIELD, D. F. (1983) 'Shiftwork and the Choice

of Technique Under Alternative Maximands', *Scandinavian Journal of Economics* 85.

HEATHFIELD, D. F. (1972) 'The Measurement of Capital Utilisation Using Electricity Consumption Data' *JRSS* 135 (Series A).

JORGENSON, D. W. and GRILICHES, Z. (1967) 'The Explanation of Productivity Change', *Riview of Economic Studies* XXXIV.

KENDRICK, J. W. (1980) *Post-War Productivity Trends in the US 1948–1969* (Chicago NBER).

——— and VACCARA, B. N. (1980) *New Developments in Productivity and Measurement and Analysis* (Chicago: NBER).

MARRIS, R. (1964) *The Economics of Capital Utilisation* (Cambridge: Cambridge University Press).

MUELLBAUER, J. (1984) *Aggregate Production Functions and Productivity Measurement: A New Look*, CPER discussion paper 34.

WINSTON, G. C. and McCOY, T. D. (1974) 'Investment and the Optimal Idleness of Capital', *Review of Economic Studies* XLIII.

14 Electricity-based Measures of Capital Utilisation by United Kingdom Manufacturing Industry

Derek Bosworth and Tony Westaway

INTRODUCTION

The degree to which the productive capital of the economy is utilised is now recognised as an important dimension of production and a potentially significant influence on other factor demands, such as the demands for employees and hours, as well as the level of investment activity.[1] The empirical finding of increasing returns to hours in the employment function literature was, in part, argued to be a consequence of the misspecification of the model, associated with the omission of capital utilisation.[2] A more recent concern has been the extent to which the demands for hours and capital utilisation are separate influences on production.[3] Each requires empirical validation, which, in turn, necessitates the construction of accurate and meaningful measures of capital utilisation.

A wide range of alternative measures are, in principle, available. These include series based on electricity consumption; all fuel consumption; the number of hours that capital is operated; output per unit of capital (relative to some peak); and business survey data of capital utilisation. In practice, each series is characterised by important theoretical shortcomings, by a lack of published statistics available for their construction, and by a diversity of results which is difficult to explain if they represent the same phenomenon.[4] Of the various measures constructed and tested, the electricity based series has perhaps been among the most widely used and accepted.[5]

This chapter focusses on the problems of constructing electricity-based measures of utilisation. Although it retraces some of the ground covered in a previous paper,[6] it also extends the earlier work in a number of important ways. In particular, the indices of capital utilisation are constructed for seven manufacturing industries. The next Section attempts to review the relevant strands of the literature linking fuel consumption and capital utilisation. It develops a theoretical model which is tested in subsequent sections. The third Section outlines the data and sources used in the empirical work. The fourth Section reports the regression results for seven industry groups within manufacturing and, also, provides some additional results by disaggregating one of these industries further. The fifth Section uses these regression results to construct indices of capital utilisation for each of the industries covered and discusses some of their more obvious similarities and differences. The final Section draws together the main arguments and conclusions of this study, outlining the weaknesses of the measures presented here, but also considering their potential for the future.

FUEL CONSUMPTION AND CAPITAL UTILISATION

(a) Strands of the Literature

The main theme of this chapter is that capital services are released from the stock of capital only by the application of energy or power. Two closely related aspects of the literature have evolved. The first, and principle avenue of research, uses fuel consumption *in conjunction with* estimates of the stock of capital, to calculate the extent of capital utilisation. The second approach uses data on fuel consumption, *independently* of measures of the capital stock, as a proxy for capital services (both stock and utilisation dimensions). However, a further, related area of research with important implications for the design of measures of capital utilisation is the work on input demands, in particular the demands for energy.

(b) Overall Capital Services

The problems of measuring the stock of capital have given rise to a considerable degree of anguish in empirical work. Official, government estimates of the capital stock in many European countries, as well as the United States, are based on the perpetual inventory method.[7] At least three problems can be distinguished. First, the general approach requires a number of heroic assumptions which, in themselves, give rise to a considerable degree of scepticism about the usefulness of the resulting estimates in empirical work. Second, official measures are generally available only at fairly high levels of aggregation. Third, the estimates are of stocks and in no way reflect the degree to which the stocks are utilised.

Fears about the estimates have led some authors to adopt time trends in place of the official measures of the capital stock.[8] Other authors have argued that as the application of energy is required to release the services of capital, fuel consumption can be used as a proxy for capital services,

$$F = f(KS) \qquad (14.1)$$

where:
  F denotes an appropriate measure of fuel consumption
  KS are the overall capital services.

This approach has been used with some success in a number of studies[9] and is perhaps most easily justified at the more detailed industrial level, where official measures are either not available or not published. However, there are a number of reasons why the use of a simple fuel proxy of this type may prove inappropriate. We deal with these in the remainder of this Section.

(c) Fuel/Capital and Capital Utilisation

Given that the main applications of these measures will be in the production function/factor demand areas, there may be strong grounds for separating the stock and utilisation dimensions of the capital input.[10] It should be recognised that equation (14.1) can be rewritten:

$$F = g(K, U) \qquad (14.2)$$

where:
  K denotes the stock of capital
  U = capital utilisation.

If we know the instantaneous relationship between fuel consumption and capital stock (e.g., how much fuel each unit of capital consumes if it is used for a single instant), then it becomes possible to derive a measure of capital utilisation. In the very simplest case,

$$U = h(F/K) \qquad (14.3)$$

However, even where there is a fixed technical link between the amount of fuel consumed and each unit of capital utilised, this relationship may be altered over time because of technical change.

(d) Exogenous Information about Technical Change

Probably the single most important breakthrough in this area of study came in the pioneering work of Foss (1963), for the United States. The idea was developed further by Jorgenson and Griliches (1967) in the United States and then by Heathfield (1972) in the United Kingdom. This work linked the use of plant and machinery with electricity consumption. Electricity has a number of advantages over other fuels and the 'all fuel' measures: (i) it is a particularly important source of power for plant and machinery; (ii) it is homogeneous; (iii) it cannot generally be stored or hoarded by the user company; (iv) it is of invariant quality.

The principle underlying the approach is that plant and machinery are generally powered by electricity. Each unit of capital has an associated installed rated wattage, which defines a maximum amount of electricity that can be consumed, E°. The index of capital utilisation is taken as the ratio of actual electricity consumption, E, to the maximum consumption, E°. If technical change takes place, the approach appears to presume that it affects the actual and maximum electricity consumption equally, thereby leaving the calculated index unaffected, other things being equal.

Heathfield (1972) discovered that annual information on installed rated wattage was not available in the United Kingdom. In fact, only two observations of E° could be obtained for the whole of the period. Heathfield (1972, p. 210) thus compared the maximum consumption to the stock of plant and machinery:

$$(E^\circ/K) = e \tag{14.4}$$

for years in which both are available. For the years in which E° are not present, a constant incremental wattage–capital ratio is assumed in order to construct intermediate values of e. Given actual values of the capital stock and actual or interpolated values of the ratio, e, it is thus possible to construct an estimate of the maximum potential electricity consumption:

$$E_t^\circ = e_t K_t \tag{14.5}$$

where t denotes time. Given a value for actual electricity consumption, the index of utilisation is thus constructed as:

$$U_t = E_t/E_t^\circ \tag{14.6}$$

Intuitively, the accuracy of this index is likely to be greater the more important is electricity within the total of all fuels[11] and the greater the number of observations of $E°$. While we deal with both of these points in more detail below, it is informative to note that Heathfield (1972) had access to only two observations of $E°$, one close to the beginning and the other approximately in the middle of the sample period. As a consequence, technological (and other changes) are effectively approximated by a simple time trend.

(e) Inter-fuel and Fuel/Capital Substitution Effects

One other relevant strand of the literature that can throw light on the construction of fuel based indices is the work on input demand models, in particular the research which focusses on fuel demands. The trend in the 1970s was towards factor demand systems increasingly based on the 'flexible' functional forms derived from the theoretical work on duality between the production and cost functions.[12] These estimates give rise to information about either 'own-price' and 'cross-price' elasticities or (partial) elasticities of substitution between inputs. In this Section, we attempt simply to highlight the potential importance of substitution; no attempt is made at this stage to provide a systematic review of the elasticities isolated in the large and growing empirical literature. The general approach and the existing empirical findings may eventually provide important insights in the calculation of indices of capital utilisation. We return to this theme in the concluding section.

The general approach suggests that the production function can be expressed as:

$$Y = i(K, L, F_1, \ldots, F_n, M) \qquad (14.7)$$

where:
Y = gross output
F_i denotes the ith type of fuel input
M refers to raw materials.

Certain studies have attempted to characterise equation (14.7) by a flexible form of the production function.[13] More generally, however, if factor prices and output are exogenously determined, the underlying production structure has more often been described by a cost function:

$$C = j(P_K, P_L, P_{F(1)}, \ldots, P_{F(n)}, P_M, Y) \qquad (14.8)$$

where: C = total cost
P_j denotes the price of the jth input ($j = 1, \ldots, n+3$).

Equation (14.8) is thus commonly characterised by the translog cost function, of the form

$$\log C = a_0 + a_Y \log Y + \sum_i a_i \log P_i + \tfrac{1}{2} b_{YY} (\log Y)^2$$
$$+ \tfrac{1}{2} \sum_i \sum_j b_{ij} \log P_i \log P_j + \sum_i b_{Yi} \log Y \log P_i \qquad (14.9)$$

From Shepard's Lemma, the derived demand functions are found by differentiating the cost function with respect to prices, yielding share equations:

$$S_i = a_i + b_{Yi} \log Y + \sum_j b_{ij} \log P_j \qquad (14.10)$$

where:
S_i is the share of the ith input ($S_i = \delta \log C / \delta \log P_i = P_i X_i / C$, given that X_i is the quantity of the ith input.

Since the shares must add to unity, only $j+2$ of the $j+3$ equations are estimated. The parameters a_0, a_Y and b_{YY} cannot be identified from the share equations alone, they require the estimation of the cost function.

The cost function must be homogeneous of degree one in prices, as well as satisfying the conditions associated with a 'well behaved' production function.[14] Nevertheless, the cost function represented by equation (14.9) is a general function, it is non-homothetic and exhibits non-constant returns to scale. Homotheticity requires equation (14.9) to be a separable function of output and prices, implying the restriction $b_{Yi} = 0$. Homogeneity requires that the elasticity of cost with respect to output is constant throughout, implying the restriction that $b_{YY} = 0$. Finally, the function collapses to Cobb–Douglas form if $b_{ij} = 0$ throughout.

While there are strong grounds for estimating a system of equations such as those represented by (14.9) and (14.10), it should be recognised that the data demands are likely to be large. If four different types of fuel are distinguished, equation (14.10) has eight independent variables and equation (14.9) has a total of 26! Excessive data demands have invariably resulted in a number of further restrictions, applied to equations (14.9) and (14.10) prior to estimation. One simplification is to assume that the capital, labour, energy and materials aggregates are homothetic in their components and, in particular, that the energy input is homothetic in its oil, gas, coal and electricity inputs.[15] This enables a two-stage optimisation procedure:[16] (i) first isolating the optimal mix of fuels within the aggregate energy input; (ii) then choosing the optimal levels of capital, labour, energy and raw materials.

Even if (for reasons of data demands, for example) a 'flexible' function-approach is not adopted, the empirical work[17] highlights a number of factors that should be taken into account in the construction of fuel-based indices of capital utilisation:

1. The consumption of energy relative to capital is affected by the relative prices of the two types of inputs.
2. The consumption of one fuel relative to the total of all fuels will be affected by the relative prices of the different types of fuels (*re* own price and cross price effects).

Although we do not undertake a systematic review of existing studies in this chapter, they do indicate that different results are obtained for different industries and countries. It should also be borne in mind that the principle feature of this approach is that it does not place *a priori* restrictions on the elasticities of substitution *between fuels*. This is particularly useful in appreciating the limitations of the approach adopted in the empirical work reported in this chapter.

(f) A Multi-tier CES Approach

A cursory glance is sufficient to indicate that the wholly unrestricted forms outlined above are unlikely to be estimated from the (generally annual) data published in official United Kingdom sources. It was argued above that one method of reducing the data requirements was to place further restrictions on the form of the production function. At the same time, the chosen form of function would need to take into account at least the interfuel and energy/capital substitution possibilities outlined above. As a compromise approach therefore, this study adopts a multi-tier CES function that at least allows for these two dimensions of substitution and which can, in principle, be extended further (to allow for different elasticities of substitution between different pairs of fuel inputs, for example).[18] The derivation of the estimating equations from a three tier production function is described in the Appendix.

If we accept that the construction of the index should be based on electricity consumption, rather than one or more of the other types of fuels (for the reasons given in (d) above), the multi-tier CES suggests that:

$$(E/KU) = Ee^{nt}(P_F/P_K)^{-\sigma_2}(P_E/P_F)^{-\sigma_3} = k(t, P_E, P_F, P_K) \qquad (14.11)$$

where:

P_E, P_F and P_K are the prices of electricity, energy (e.g., all fuels) and capital

KU denotes capital services (e.g., the stock of capital multiplied by the degree of utilisation)

$n =$ the rate of technological change, formed as the net effect of the various dimensions of factor augmenting technological change (e.g., electricity saving, energy saving and capital saving).

In principle, equation (14.11) allows the hypothesis that $\sigma_2 = \sigma_3$ to be tested, as well as testing whether the separation of the two price components adds to the overall explanatory power of the model.

(g) Problems Inherent in the Approach

Examination of equation (14.11) reveals the essential problem with this approach: capital utilisation, U, is obtained as a residual. Unfortunately this means that equation (14.11) is estimated with (E/K) as the dependent variable and, by implication, there is an omitted variable problem. As U is likely to be cyclical, this means that there will be autocorrelation in the estimated equations. As a consequence, although we obtain unbiased estimates of the parameters, the precise forms of the t and F statistics are not strictly valid. Applying the usual least squares formulae for the sampling variances of the regression coefficients leads to serious underestimation of the variances and, therefore, an increased probability of wrongly accepting coefficients to be significantly different from zero.

In principle, several tactics might be employed. First, some other (e.g., non-fuel-based) proxy for capital utilisation might be tried (such as the CBI index). This would enable the robustness of the parameter estimates to be checked (though they should be unbiased anyway) and their significance to be tested. This type of approach has been tried elsewhere.[19] The problem is that other indices of utilisation are presumably considered to be inaccurate for some reason (otherwise, why are we trying to construct the fuel-based index in the first place?). This approach is likely to replace an omitted variable problem with a measurement of variables problem. Second, an alternative approach might be to use an autoregressive scheme of some type.[20] The usefulness of this approach depends on its empirical success in removing autocorrelation. Again, it is a means of checking the empirical results from the least squares equation, it is not possible to isolate a measure of capital utilisation directly from the residuals of the autoregressive scheme.

The accuracy of any measure of capital utilisation will always be affected by the problems inherent in measuring the capital stock. Even measures based on the operating hours of capital[21] in principle require estimates of the capital stock to use as weights in aggregation. There are some important question marks against the perpetual inventory method and the accuracy of the resulting estimates of the gross stock of capital. This approach, in common with every other method of constructing an index of capital utilisation, thus suffers from a measurement of variables problem, which in this instance may again result in a problem of autocorrelation. Other problems of a similar kind are dealt with below.

(h) Other Exogenous Variables

It is worth asking whether there are any other exogenous variables that should be incorporated in the relationship. At this stage, only one other variable was included, average annual temperature, T:

$$(E/KU) = d(t, P_E, P_F, P_K, T) \tag{14.12}$$

While temperature is a fairly obvious exogenously determined variable to include in the regression, it is associated with a number of important problems. First, it is recognised that this variable may not have a unidirectional effect on electricity consumption for all plant in a given industry. Certain types of plant may be harder to keep warm when the temperature is low, other types of plant may be harder to keep cool when the temperature is high, yet other types of plant may exhibit *both* characteristics. The net effect of variations in temperature may, therefore, not have a significant effect on the ratio of electricity to capital services. By implication, variations in temperature may have different effects in different industries. Second, it is possible that the overall annual average is too crude a measure: variations in temperature, or the duration of hot and cold spells might prove to be important. These questions are left to future research.

DATA AND SOURCES

Table 14.1 summarises the variables used in the empirical work reported below, giving the notation used and the definitions of the variables. All of the series are annual. A complete set of data can be constructed for the period 1960–82, giving a maximum of 23 observations. Because of the limited and inconsistent industrial breakdowns of the two primary sources, it was possible to construct the complete data set for only

Table 14.1 Notation and definitions

Notation	Definition	Source
Dependent variable E/K		
E	electricity consumption (million therm)	*Digest of UK Energy Statistics*
K	gross capital stock (£000 million)	*National Income and Expenditure*
Independent variables $t, P_E/P_F, P_F/P_K, T$		
t	net effects of factor augmenting technological change	Time trend
P_E	price of electricity	*Digest of UK Energy Statistics*
P_F	price of energy ('all-fuels')	*Digest of UK Energy Statistics*
P_K	price of capital (implicit deflator)	*National Income and Expenditure*
T	average annual temperature	*Digest of UK Energy Statistics*

seven industry groups: (i) food, drink and tobacco; (ii) iron and steel; (iii) chemicals; (iv) engineering; (v) textiles and other manufacturing; (vi) paper and board; (vii) bricks, pottery, glass and cement. However, some attempt is made further to disaggregate the last of these industries, providing results separately for: (vii.a) bricks; (vii.b) china; (vii.c) cement. There are a number of important problems with the data. These are worth discussing in some detail as they give a clear indication of the limitations to the empirical study reported below.

1. The difficulties associated with measuring the capital stock have already been mentioned. In particular, the need to make fairly heroic assumptions in order to construct a perpetual inventory measure (see p. 381 above).
2. A simple exponential time trend is adopted to represent the net effects of factor augmenting technological change. While this is the form traditionally chosen in economic textbooks, there is no *a priori* evidence that technological change enters the system in this manner.
3. The price of capital is taken to be the implicit deflator used to translate between the current and constant price investment series published in the 'Blue Book'. This has obvious limitations, not least of which is its

failure to incorporate investment grants, tax incentives, etc. A more fundamental problem, at this juncture, is the fact that the price of capital index is not published by industry. The choice is between an index relating to all capital, but for the manufacturing sector; and an index relating to plant and machinery, but for all industries (not just manufacturing). We opt for the former, though in practice – as far as the empirical results are concerned – it makes little difference which is chosen.
4. The price of electricity is published for 'major industrial users'. However, it must be stressed that this price is almost certain to differ between industries, if only because the very largest users are able to negotiate more favourable rates than the smaller ones.
5. The overall price of energy is constructed as a weighted average of the prices of the individual fuels, using the relative weights characteristic of each of the industries. However, no suitable index of petroleum prices was published, and the weighted average had to assume that petroleum prices could be represented by the index for 'heavy oils'.
6. The temperature variable has already been discussed. We have already argued that a simple annual average may not be the only possible influence on fuel consumption. One other dimension, which has not been mentioned to date, is that certain industries are concentrated in particular regions. Again, a national average will tend to gloss over any regional effects that might influence consumption.

EMPIRICAL RESULTS

(a) Alternative Models

Given the problems of measurement outlined above, the empirical results are quite interesting. Table 14.2 presents the results of the two-tier CES model, which assumes that the elasticity of substitution between electricity and other fuels is the same as between all fuels and capital. Table 14.3 reports the analogous results, where these two elasticities are allowed to differ. We consider each set of results in turn, before considering whether the more general three-tier function is a significant improvement over the two-tier function.

(b) Two-tier CES Results

The two-tier CES results are highly consistent insofar as they yield the anticipated sign for each of the variables in every industry. The

Table 14.2 Regression results: two-tier CES

Industry	Constant	P_E/P_K	Time trend	Temperature	$\bar{R}^2$	F	DW	SEE
Food, etc.	3.7383[a]	−0.6901[a]	−0.0092[a]	0.1066	0.77	25.1	0.6211	0.0428
Iron and steel	4.6559[a]	−0.7246[b]	−0.0109[a]	−0.0704	0.34	4.7	1.0009	0.1101
Chemicals	3.4117[a]	−0.5359[a]	−0.0192[a]	0.5863[c]	0.86	47.2	1.5161	0.0555
Engineering	3.5924[a]	−0.6891[a]	−0.0026[b]	0.0146	0.53	9.4	0.7210	0.0432
Textiles	5.5896[a]	−0.5492[a]	−0.0115[a]	−0.2682[b]	0.90	66.7	1.4934	0.0283
Paper and board	3.7298[a]	−0.1580	−0.0003	−0.1492	−0.08	0.4	0.8622	0.0424
Bricks, etc.	6.1081[a]	−0.2164	−0.0275[a]	0.0845	0.95	128.3	0.9842	0.0448

Notes:
[a] Significant at the 99 per cent level.
[b] Significant at the 95 per cent level.
[c] Significant at the 90 per cent level.

Table 14.3 Regression results: three-tier CES

Industry	Constant	P_E/P_F	P_F/P_K	Time trend	Temperature	$\bar{R}^2$	F	DW	SEE
Food, etc.	3.3079[a]	0.1450	−0.1817	−0.0049[a]	−0.0083	0.88	43.1	1.4304	0.0301
Iron and steel	3.8127[a]	0.6377	0.1736	0.0003	−0.2379	0.46	5.6	1.3385	0.0994
Chemicals	3.5536[a]	−0.7721[c]	−0.6642[a]	−0.0202[a]	0.6061[c]	0.86	35.0	1.5763	0.0559
Engineering	3.5148[a]	−0.4942	−0.5855[a]	−0.0018	−0.0108	0.83	7.0	0.8255	0.0439
Textiles	5.5085[a]	−0.4212[c]	−0.4783[a]	−0.0109[a]	−0.2795[b]	0.90	49.0	1.6800	0.0287
Paper and board	3.6013[a]	0.0644	−0.0138	0.0015	−0.1866	−0.08	0.6	1.0615	0.0423
Bricks, etc.	5.9088[a]	−0.0663	−0.1306	−0.0256[a]	0.0770	0.94	94.3	1.1124	0.0453

Notes:
[a] Significant at the 99 per cent level.
[b] Significant at the 95 per cent level.
[c] Significant at the 90 per cent level.

inconsistent sign on the temperature variable was always a possibility (see the discussion above): Table 14.2 shows that its coefficient is negative in three industries and positive in four. Further statistical interpretation of the results is hampered by the evidence of positive autocorrelation, which pervades the majority of the equations. Nevertheless, the overall fit of the equations, as shown by the R^2 and F statistics, is not high in every case. One industry – paper and board – appears to perform particularly badly in this respect, although it is largely out of keeping with the remainder of the results.

If we take the estimated coefficients and their significance levels at face value, a number of important features can be discerned. The relative price variable, P_E/P_K, appears to be significant at the 90 per cent level or higher in five of the seven cases. In these five cases, it takes a value of between 0.52 and 0.72, considerably lower than the Cobb–Douglas value of unity, but also some way away from the case of perfect complementarity. The remaining two regressions – those of paper and board and bricks, pottery, glass and cement – exhibit values insignificantly different to zero.

The other principal explanatory variable, the time trend, indicates net electricity saving technological change in every industry. It appears to be significantly different from zero in six of the seven cases. In every case, it indicates quite slow rates of electricity saving change: all cases are less than 3 per cent per annum and six out of the seven cases are less than 2 per cent per annum.

(c) Three-tier Results

The use of a three-tier function, distinguishing P_E/P_F and P_F/P_K, helps to reduce the problem of autocorrelation. Nevertheless, as we would expect given the potentially cyclical nature of the omitted variable, this problem is not completely removed. The overall fit of the equations appear to be improved somewhat by the separation of the two price variables, although the improvement is not statistically significant at the 95 per cent level, except in the case of food, drink and tobacco (iron and steel is close to being significant at this level). The regression equation for the paper and board industry remains particularly poor, and still seems out of line with the other results.

Four of the seven results have the anticipated negative signs on both the price variables, and only two of these industries appear to have both coefficients significantly different from zero. The chemicals industry result reaffirms earlier findings for this industry.[22] The textiles industry has: lower elasticities; a slower rate of electricity saving change; and an opposite sign on the temperature variable. The results for engineering and bricks, etc. are also broadly consistent with the previous two cases, although bricks, etc. appears to have a considerably lower pair of elasticities. However, the remaining three cases appear far from satisfactory.

Before leaving the three-tier approach, it is perhaps worth pointing out that, in the four cases where both price variables have the anticipated (negative) signs, the two coefficients in each pair are similar in magnitude. In these four cases, the two elasticities are, very broadly, of the same order of magnitude as before, lying between the special cases of zero and unitary elasticities.

(d) Some Additional Results

The results for bricks, pottery, glass and cement were among the more disappointing of those reported above. One obvious possibility is that this is a heterogeneous group of industries, where the aggregate does not reflect the individual component parts. In this instance, although capital stock data are not available for each industry, electricity and other fuel consumption can be separately distinguished. Bearing in mind the potential problems of using the same aggregate capital stock data for each component industry, the two- and three-tier versions of regression equation (14.11) were estimated for the three sub-groups: bricks, china and cement. The results are shown in Table 14.4.

It is difficult to tell from just looking at the disaggregated results whether the aggregation to a single industry group (e.g., bricks, etc.) was the underlying cause of the problem. It is interesting to note, however, that there are very different rates of technological change in the three industries. In particular, at over 6 per cent per annum, the rate of change for bricks was substantially higher than for any other industry. In addition, tests on the contribution of separating the two price components reveal significant F values at the 95 per cent level in both china and cement (although not in bricks, where the two coefficients are almost identical in magnitude). The F statistic in the case of china was, in fact, the only one which was significant at the 99 per cent level.

(e) Some Concluding Comments on the Empirical Results

Our views of the results are somewhat ambivalent. Given the imperfections of the data and the inherent omitted variable problem, the

Table 14.4 Two- and three-tier results for components of bricks, pottery, glass and cement

Industry	Constant	P_E/P_F	P_F/P_K	Time trend	Temperature	$\bar{R}^2$	F	DW	SEE
Two-tier results									
Bricks	6.5769[a]		−0.6993[b]	0.0638[a]	−0.0077	0.94	115.50	1.5087	0.2298
China	4.2816[a]		0.2003	−0.0048[a]	−0.0955	0.29	3.99	1.2686	0.0481
Cement	5.3906[a]		−0.8426[a]	−0.0442[a]	0.4250	0.95	128.37	0.8217	0.0736
Three-tier results									
Bricks	6.5340[a]	−0.7506	−0.7316[b]	0.0642[a]	0.0368	0.94	82.22	1.4609	0.1129
China	4.6471	−0.7734[a]	−0.4822[c]	−0.0110[a]	0.0323	0.60	9.31	1.5412	0.0360
Cement	3.0273[a]	−0.1782	−0.6085[a]	−0.0285[a]	0.6781[c]	0.96	150.12	1.4937	0.0595

Notes:
[a] Significant at the 99 per cent level.
[b] Significant at the 95 per cent level.
[c] Significant at the 90 per cent level.

regressions give some support for the approach suggested on p. 000. At this stage, however, there are no real indications that the three-tier function consistently 'outperforms' the two-tier function: while it is true that the problem of autocorrelation is lessened, of the aggregate industry groups only textiles (and perhaps iron and steel) exhibits a significant improvement in overall explanatory power, and where both price coefficients have the same sign, their magnitudes tend to be similar. However, at this stage, we would not place great store by the accuracy of measures of capital utilisation constructed on the basis of these results. While this seems to be a potentially important approach, accurate measures of capital utilisation are unlikely to be derived until some of the problems of measuring the variables are solved.

INDICES OF CAPITAL UTILISATION

(a) Comparisons of Capital Utilisation

Despite a number of reservations about the measures constructed from the equations reported above, we go on to calculate indices of capital utilisation on this basis. It is of some interest to establish whether the resulting series show some consistency, either across industries or between the two- and three-tier cases. The results for the seven industries are presented in Tables 14.5 and 14.6: the former is based on the two-tier and the latter on the three-tier function.

(b) Index Construction

From equation (14.11), it can be seen that the difference between the theoretical specification,

$$(E/K) = m(t, P_E, P_F, P_K, U) \qquad (14.13)$$

and the estimated equation,

$$(E/K) = n(t, P_E, P_F, P_K) \qquad (14.14)$$

is a measure of utilisation. Hence, if all the residual variation in the regressions can be attributed to the omitted variable, then U can be estimated as the difference between the actual and predicted values. Given the log linear form of both equations, indices of capital utilisation are constructed directly from the regression results as the antilog of the residual. The results are reported in Tables 14.5 and 14.6.[23]

Table 14.5 Index of capital utilisation: two-tier CES

Year	Food, drink, and tobacco	Iron and steel	Chemicals and allied	Engineering	Textiles	Paper and board	Bricks, pottery and glass
1960	91.34	94.06	105.80	98.21	99.19	98.08	97.98
61	94.82	89.24	103.83	98.90	101.01	100.89	100.41
62	100.19	85.54	102.19	98.62	100.22	99.63	97.65
63	102.98	95.93	94.26	100.00	99.82	96.36	95.33
64	100.90	101.81	91.46	102.40	97.15	97.63	99.62
65	102.04	110.73	98.07	102.45	98.45	100.40	101.37
66	102.17	108.31	96.79	100.65	99.00	102.06	100.87
67	102.68	104.98	96.02	99.90	99.44	100.00	104.01
68	103.59	114.72	105.94	101.14	102.99	103.73	108.42
69	104.39	117.65	107.57	100.84	104.09	106.65	104.19
70	101.59	112.51	102.28	96.34	104.10	105.40	98.74
71	99.44	99.78	100.52	99.00	101.61	99.63	100.92
72	96.68	92.25	96.31	96.74	95.55	94.24	98.10
73	96.28	91.56	97.21	99.25	100.67	98.72	101.14
74	99.98	92.79	100.30	96.04	94.66	95.50	94.22
75	103.75	94.19	93.76	100.88	99.99	96.32	91.22
76	109.32	103.93	102.60	104.71	100.46	99.95	99.48
77	101.67	99.66	107.77	106.28	101.10	100.62	101.57
78	100.64	114.26	100.11	104.93	102.11	103.97	104.73
79	99.64	116.34	111.48	105.89	104.77	107.77	106.99
80	95.49	82.83	94.60	103.38	98.57	104.97	103.54
81	97.20	96.05	95.69	98.00	96.30	95.39	95.05
82	94.95	92.46	98.38	88.03	99.58	93.81	96.38

Note:
Constructed from the regressions reported in Table 14.2.

Table 14.6 Index of capital utilisation: three-tier CES

Year	Food, drink and tobacco	Iron and steel	Chemicals and allied	Engineering	Textiles	Paper and board	Bricks, pottery and glass
1960	96.69	103.03	103.91	99.29	100.08	99.92	99.72
61	98.36	94.08	102.99	99.60	101.63	102.18	101.44
62	101.72	86.98	102.25	98.68	100.53	100.10	97.90
63	102.66	94.86	95.10	99.68	99.85	96.12	95.31
64	102.72	104.57	91.55	102.85	97.43	98.01	99.78
65	100.86	108.66	98.47	102.17	98.34	100.00	100.94
66	99.96	105.83	97.13	100.14	98.51	101.37	100.22
67	97.76	98.35	97.25	99.29	98.57	98.60	102.87
68	98.15	106.78	106.66	100.38	102.16	101.97	107.08
69	100.48	110.46	107.16	100.22	103.29	105.40	103.04
70	101.70	112.97	100.68	96.17	103.91	105.58	98.29
71	98.31	98.05	99.79	99.02	101.37	99.42	100.71
72	96.28	92.72	96.31	96.89	95.18	94.17	98.26
73	100.92	99.94	96.59	100.30	101.45	100.19	102.29
74	97.91	84.52	101.79	95.28	94.66	94.91	93.61
75	100.55	89.99	95.82	99.00	99.92	95.49	90.73
76	109.43	102.58	103.76	104.21	100.40	99.44	99.33
77	101.21	99.11	108.38	105.98	101.10	100.33	101.69
78	101.05	116.77	100.32	104.98	102.29	103.79	104.95
79	98.98	116.20	111.33	105.88	104.83	107.63	107.19
80	98.26	88.85	93.59	104.42	98.97	106.11	104.31
81	99.82	98.77	94.61	98.60	96.46	96.16	95.48
82	97.05	94.85	97.42	88.39	99.81	94.72	96.70

Note:
Constructed from the regressions reported in Table 14.3.

(c) Indices of Capital Utilisation

There is no reason to expect that the index for one industry will show exactly the same pattern over time as other industries. Nevertheless, there are a number of similarities, such as the peak in utilisation around 1968-9, shown in Table 14.5. There are, however, equally important differences, such as the different patterns for chemicals and engineering during the early part of the period. This is only to be expected, different industries are influenced to some extent by different factors which move their cycles out of phase. More interesting from a purely measurement point of view is whether the two- and three-tier equations yield different results. The extent of the impact caused by the change varies from industry to industry: while there are differences, the principal features of the engineering series remain largely unaffected; while there are important similarities, the series for food, drink and tobacco appears to be more radically affected.

CONCLUSIONS

This chapter examines the use of published electricity consumption data to construct measures of capital utilisation. In reviewing the relevant literature it considers the role played by technological change, relative factor prices and other exogenously-given variables, such as variations in temperature. The discussion stresses the potential importance of factor substitution for the measures of capital utilisation. In the light of this, one important task, which is beyond the scope of this chapter but which may be crucial to the design of such measures, is to review the existing literature on input demand models, particularly relating to fuel inputs.

Given the data limitations faced in this study, it does not appear possible, at least at this point in time, to adopt a regression equation based on a 'flexible' functional form. A much more restrictive version underlies the regressions reported here. Nevertheless, data problems notwithstanding, some interesting results were obtained. Both sets of estimated elasticities lay between zero and unity. In the light of the more aggregate industry results, it was difficult to make a convincing case for the more general, three-tier, production function over the two-tier case. Electricity saving technological change – often of around 1 to 2 per cent per annum, was isolated. Temperature appeared to play a significant role in one or two industries, but not consistently across all groups.

Despite certain fears expressed about the problems associated with the regression results, the study went onto construct indices of capital utilisation. The resulting indices were clearly cyclical: a characteristic we would expect of capital utilisation. They also exhibited (again, as we might expect) important differences across industries. However, there were also differences between the two- and three-tier model indices, although the differences here were perhaps less significant than the cross-industry variation.

The important question is whether, at this juncture, the electricity-based indices as constructed here can be relied upon to yield an accurate and reliable index of capital utilisation. Here we hold conflicting views: on the one hand (given the problems of measurement), the results are encouraging; on the other, the problems of measurement (as well as the inherent difficulties of the methodology) are formidable. Perhaps the safest conclusion is that the approach promises to yield useful results when improvements to the data base can be made. In particular, more detailed and accurate measures of capital stock and capital prices are required. If this is a criticism of the methodology adopted here, however, it is equally applicable to all the other, alternative measures of capital utilisation.

Appendix

THE MULTI-TIER CES FUNCTION

The production function can be built up in the following manner. The 'top tier' is obtained by allowing fuel services, FS, to be formed from the n different fuel inputs,

$$FS = \zeta_3 (\sum_i \phi_i F_i^{-\rho_3})^{-\theta_3/\rho_3} = \zeta_3 (V)^{-\theta_3/\rho_3} \tag{A14.1}$$

where:
ζ_3 is the technical efficiency parameter
$\phi_1, \ldots, \phi_n$ are the distributive parameters
θ_3 denotes the returns to scale effect in the provision of fuel services
$\sigma_3 (= 1/(1+\rho_3))$ is the elasticity of substitution between fuels.

In a similar way, fuel services and capital utilisation, KU, combine to form capital services, KS:

$$KS = \zeta_2 (aKU^{-\rho_2} + bFS^{-\rho_2})^{-\theta_2/\rho_2} = \zeta_2 (W)^{-\theta_2/\rho_2} \tag{A14.2}$$

where:
$\zeta_2, \theta_2, \sigma_2$ and ρ_2 are interpreted analogously to the parameters described in equation (A14.1) above.

Finally, capital and labour services are combined to yield output, Y:

$$Y = \zeta_1 (\alpha KS^{-\rho_1} + \beta LS^{-\rho_1})^{-\theta_1/\rho_1} = \zeta_1 (X)^{\theta_1/\rho_1} \tag{A14.3}$$

where the technology parameters are again given analogous interpretations.

Substitution of equation (A14.1) into (A14.2) and then, in turn, equation (A14.2) into (A14.3) yields a three-tier CES:

$$Y = \phi(KS, LS, FS) = \phi(KS, LS, F_1, \ldots, F_n) \tag{A14.4}$$

with three distinct elasticities of substitution, σ_1, σ_2 and σ_3. While this function does not exhibit the generality of the 'flexible' functional forms, nevertheless it encompasses the two-tier and single-tier CES, as well as the Cobb–Douglas functions as special cases. In particular, the single-tier CES is obtained by setting

$$\theta_2 = \theta_3 = 1 \quad \text{and} \quad \rho_1 = \rho_2 = \rho_3.$$

The problem faced by the firm attempting to minimise the costs of production subject to an output constraint can be represented by the Lagrangian expression,

$$LG = \sum_k P_k X_k + \Lambda (Y - \zeta_1(X))^{-\theta_1/\rho_1} \tag{A14.5}$$

where P_k denotes the user cost of the kth input and X_k is the quantity of that input.

It can thus be shown that, for a minimum,

$$(\partial LG/\partial F_i) = P_i - \Lambda (\partial Y/\partial KS)(\partial KS/\partial FS)(\partial FS/\partial F_i) = 0 \tag{A14.6}$$

and
$$(\partial LG/\partial F_j) = P_j - \Lambda(\partial Y/\partial KS)(\partial KS/\partial FS)(\partial FS/\partial F_j) = 0 \quad (A14.7)$$
where i and j refer to the ith and jth types of fuels.

Hence, from (A14.6) and (A14.7),
$$(F_i/F_j) = (\phi_i/\phi_j)^{\sigma_3}(P_j/P_i)^{\sigma_3} \quad (A14.8)$$
where $\sigma_3 (= 1/(1+\rho_3))$ denotes the elasticity of substitution between types of fuels.

In a similar manner, it can be shown that,
$$(FS/KU) = (b/a)^{\sigma_2}(P_K/P_F)^{\sigma_2} \quad (A14.9)$$
where σ_2 is the elasticity of substitution between capital utilisation and fuel services.

Thus, from equations (A14.8) and (A14.9),
$$(F_i/F_j)(FS/KU) = (b/a)^{\sigma_2}(\phi_i/\phi_j)^{\sigma_3}(P_K/P_F)^{\sigma_2}(P_j/P_i)^{\sigma_3} \quad (A14.10)$$
In order to simplify the analysis, it is assumed that, at any given point in time, attention can be focussed on a particular type of fuel, F_i, and the remaining fuel inputs can be amalgamated within F_j. In addition, it is assumed that the ith fuel forms a small part of total energy consumption and, hence, $F_j \approx FS$. Thus:
$$(F_i/KU) = \xi(P_K/P_F)^{\sigma_2}(P_j/P_i)^{\sigma_3} \quad (A14.11)$$
where: $\xi = (b/a)^{\sigma_2}(\phi_i/\phi_j)^{\sigma_3}$, a constant.

Notes

1. See Nadiri and Rosen (1969); Briscoe and Peel (1975); Nickell (1978, pp. 136–46); Bosworth (1981); Harris (1983).
2. See in particular, Nadiri and Rosen (1969); Ireland and Smyth (1970); Hazledine (1974, 1979).
3. See Hazledine (1978); Betancourt and Clague (1981), Bosworth (1981), Harris (1983), Bosworth and Pugh (1984).
4. See Bosworth and Westaway (1984).
5. See Bosworth and Westaway (1984); Bosworth (1985).
6. See Bosworth (1985).
7. See Griffin (1976, 1979); Hibbert, et al. (1977); Miller (1983).
8. For example, Ball and St Cyr (1966).
9. Bosworth (1974, 1976), and Moody (1974); Shastry (1984).
10. Nadiri and Rosen (1969); Ireland and Smyth (1970); Hazledine (1974).
11. Bosworth (1979) attempts to link different types of fuel with different types of capital and finds some support for the hypothesis that electricity and plant and machinery are closely connected.
12. For a very useful review of the general approach, see Wilson (1984). However, the review of the empirical work contained in this source is biased strongly toward the labour input and does not directly consider the question of fuel demands.
13. Wilson (1984).
14. In particular: $\Sigma_i a_i = 1$; $\Sigma_i b_{Yi} = 0$; $b_{ij} = b_{ji}$ (for $i = j$); and $\Sigma_i b_{ij} = \Sigma_j b_{ij} = 0$.
15. See, for example, Pindyck (1979, p. 170)
16. Denny and Fuss (1977).
17. See, for example, Uri (1979); Halvorsen and Ford (1978); Pindyck (1979).
18. Bosworth (1985).
19. Bosworth (1985).
20. Bosworth (1985); Bosworth and Westaway (1984).
21. Bosworth (1987); see also Foss (1981).
22. Bosworth (1985); Bosworth and Westaway (1984).
23. The results are the simple antilogs of the residuals. They have *not* been adjusted to equal 10 in any particular base year. However, our calculated index must have an expected or mean value of 100 to fulfil the *OLS* requirements for the error term – e.g., $E(u) = 1.0$ in a multiplicative (log/log) equation. The variance of u is not constrained.

References

BALL, R. and St CYR, E. (1966) 'Employment Models in UK Manufacturing Industries', *Review of Economic Studies* 33, pp. 179–207.

BAUTISTA, R. (1974) 'The Electricity Based Measure of Capital Utilisation in Philippine Manufacturing Industries', *Philippine Review of Business and Economics* 11, pp. 13–33.

BETANCOURT, R. and CLAGUE, C. (1981) *Capital Utilisation: a Theoretical and Empirical Analysis* (Cambridge: Cambridge University Press).

BOSWORTH, D. L. (1974) 'Production Functions and Skill Requirements', in Wabe, J. S. (ed.) *Problems in Manpower Forecasting* (Farnborough: Saxon House).

—— (1976) *Production Functions: a Theoretical and Empirical Study* (Farnborough: Saxon House).

—— (1979) 'Capital Stock, Capital Services and the Use of Fuel Consumption Proxies: an Appraisal', in Patterson, K. D. and Schott, K. (eds) *The Measurement of Capital: Theory and Practice* (London: Macmillan), pp. 246–61.

—— (1981), 'Shiftworking and the Specification of Factor Demand Models', *Scottish Journal of Political Economy* 28, pp. 256–65.

—— (1985), 'Fuel Based Measures of Capital Utilisation', *Scottish Journal of Political Economy* 32, pp. 20–38.

—— (1987) See chapter 15 below.

—— and PUGH, C. J. (1984), 'Production and Maintenance: Joint Activities of the Firm', *Scandanavian Journal of Economics* 85 (1983), pp. 267–82; (reprinted in Forsund, F (ed.) *Topics in Production Theory* (London: Macmillan), pp. 167–82).

—— and WESTAWAY, A. J. (1984), 'The Theory and Measurement of Capital Utilisation and its Role in Modelling Investment', paper presented at the *EIB Conference on Investment in Europe* (University of Louvain, Belgium).

BRISCOE, G. and PEEL, D. (1975), 'The Specification of the Short Run Employment Function', *Oxford Bulletin of Economics and Statistics* 37, pp. 115–42.

DENNY, M. and FUSS, M. (1977), 'The Use of Approximation Analysis to Test for Separability and the Existence of Consistent Aggregates', *American Economic Review* 67, pp. 404–18.

Department of Energy, *Digest of UK Energy Statistics* (London: HMSO).

FOSS, M. (1963), 'The Utilisation of Capital Equipment', *Survey of Current Business* 43, pp. 8–16.

—— (1981), 'Long-Run Changes in the Work Week of Fixed Capital', *American Economic Association*, papers and proceedings 71, pp. 58–63.

GRIFFIN, T. J. (1976), 'The Stock of Fixed Assets in the United Kingdom: How to Make Best Use of the Statistics', *Economic Trends* (October), pp. 130–43.

—— (1979), 'The Stock of Fixed Assets in the United Kingdom: How to Make Best Use of the Statistics', in Patterson, K. D. and Schott, K. (eds) *The Measurement of Capital: Theory and Practice* (London: Macmillan), pp. 99–132.

HALVORSEN, R. (1977), 'Energy Substitution in US Manufacturing', *Review of Economics and Statistics* LIX, pp. 381–88.

—— and FORD, J. (1978), 'Substitution Among Energy, Capital and Labour Inputs in US Manufacturing', in Pindyck, R. S. (ed.) *Advances in the Economics of Energy and Resources* (vol. 1) (Greenwich, Conn.: JAI Press).

HARRIS, R. (1983), 'Specification of Factor Demand Models and Shiftworking: an Extension to the CES Case', *Scottish Journal of Political Economy* 30, pp. 170–4.

HAZLEDINE, T. (1974), 'Employment and Output Functions for New Zealand Manufacturing Industries', *Journal of Industrial Economics* 22, pp. 161–98.

——— (1978), 'New Specifications for Employment and Hours Functions', *Economica* 45, pp. 179–93.
——— (1979), 'Employment Functions and the Demand for Labour in the Short Run', in Hornstein, Z., Grice, J. and Webb, A. (eds), *The Economics of the Labour Market* (London: HMSO).
HEATHFIELD, D. (1972), 'The Measurement of Capital Usage Using Electricity Consumption Data', *Journal of the Royal Statistical Society* (Series A) 135, pp. 208–20.
HIBBERT, J., GRIFFIN, T. J. and WALKER, R. L. (1977), 'Development of Estimates of the Stock of Fixed Capital in the United Kingdom', *Review of Income and Wealth* (Series 23), pp. 117–35.
IRELAND, N. J. and SMYTH, D. J. (1970), 'Specification of Short Run Employment Models', *Review of Economic Studies* (April), pp. 281–5.
JORGENSON, D. and GRILICHES, Z. (1967), 'The Explanation of Productivity Change', *Review of Economic Studies* 34, pp. 249–83.
MILLER, E. M. (1983), 'A Difficulty in Measuring Productivity with a Perpetual Inventory Capital Stock Measure', *Oxford Bulletin of Economics and Statistics* 45, pp. 297–306.
MOODY, C. E. (1974), 'The Measurement of Capital Services by Electrical Energy', *Journal of Industrial Economics* 36, pp. 45–52.
MORAWETZ, D. (1976), 'The Electricity Measure of Capital Utilisation', *World Development* 4, pp. 643–53.
NADIRI, M. and ROSEN, S. (1969), 'Inter-Related Factor Demand Functions', *American Economic Review* 59, pp. 457–71.
National Income and Expenditure (various) (London: HMSO).
NICKELL, S. (1978), *The Investment Decisions of Firms* (Cambridge: Cambridge University Press).
PINDYCK, R. S. (1979), 'Interfuel Substitution and the Industrial Demand for Energy: an International Comparison', *Review of Economics and Statistics* LXI, pp. 169–79.
SHASTRY, D. U. (1984) The Cotton Mill Industry in India, Institute for Economic Growth, *Studies in Economic Development and Planning* 34, (Bombay: Oxford University Press).
URI, N. D. (1979) 'Energy Demand and Interfuel Substitution in India', *European Economic Review* 12, pp. 181–90.
WILSON, R. (1984), The Impact of Information Technology on the Engineering Industry, research report (University of Warwick: Institute for Employment Research).

15 Capital Utilisation: Time Intensity Utilisation Rates in the United Kingdom Chemicals Industry

Derek Bosworth

INTRODUCTION

Capital utilisation is extremely difficult to define and measure but, analogous to labour utilisation, it has two essential dimensions: (i) the number of hours that it operates per period; (ii) the intensity that the plant is used for any given length of operating day. The majority of measures combine these two dimensions in a single index of capital utilisation. Indices of this type include the electricity, the 'all-fuel' per unit of capital and the output per unit of capital measures.[1] All of these have some merit but, equally, all have important theoretical and empirical problems.[2] A second group of measures concentrate on the operating hours of capital and, for want of a better title, they are termed 'time intensity utilisation rates' (TIUR). Perhaps the most obvious method of collecting information on TIUR is by asking for information about operating hours in business surveys. Such surveys are extremely rare at the present time.[3] An alternative method, with associated theoretical problems, is the approximation of operating hours of capital using shiftwork data.[4]

There may be important grounds for attempting to obtain measures that distinguish between the length and intensity of capital utilisation. If, for example, they are considered to be differently productive at the margin, then they should be included separately in production functions and factor demand models. There are, however, no direct measures of the intensity dimension currently available, but if an accurate overall index of capital utilisation could be obtained by means of the first group of measures and an accurate TIUR is available (or could be constructed), then comparison of the two indices should reveal the variation in capital utilisation associated with utilising the machines more intensively for any given length of operating week.[5]

The isolation of an index of the intensity of utilisation is, however, a longer-term objective. Its success appears to depend crucially on first obtaining a measure of the operating hours of capital. The remainder of this chapter focusses on the difficulties faced in obtaining an accurate TIUR measure where no direct survey of operating hours is undertaken. Hence, it sets out the theoretical and empirical problems that arise in constructing a TIUR index using information about shift working and hours of work.

The second section reviews the TIUR that have been constructed in the literature. The third section examines the theoretical problems associated with such measures. The fourth section outlines the data available and reports on the construction of shiftwork-based TIUR measures for the United Kingdom Chemicals industry. It looks at the results based on shift work data and investigates the role played by weekly and annual hours of work. The final section draws some conclusions about the general importance and usefulness of this approach to measuring capital utilisation.

TIUR MEASURES: A REVIEW OF THE EXISTING LITERATURE

A number of earlier studies have examined capital utilisation, using direct measures of the number of hours that the capital stock has been operated. TIUR have been constructed by Foss (1963, 1981) for the United States. These measures are available across manufacturing industries for several, widely separated points in time, enabling long-run changes in the work week of capital to be examined. While the use of shift work data for this purpose has been suggested by Foss (1963), the main information source comes from answers to survey questions about operating hours of capital. Using an analogous approach, Bautista (1974) calculated the percentage of potential working time that capital was operated, based on the results of a survey of 400 manufacturing firms in the Philippines. Finally, Morawetz (1976) used a survey approach in an attempt to establish the length of time and the intensity with which capital was utilised in both Israel and the Philippines.

Direct observations of capital hours are not generally available in the United Kingdom[6] – or, indeed, in many other countries. Even in the United States, direct survey data are sparse. It is hardly surprising, therefore, that researchers in this area have resorted either to collecting business survey data or constructing approximations based on shift working and hours data. The idea that TIUR can be constructed using information about work patterns appears to have been originated by Foss (1963, p. 16). An exercise of this type, using shift work data across manufacturing industries to look at long-term changes in capital utilisation and their implications for the growth in capital intensity, can be found in Bosworth and Dawkins (1981, pp. 203–14). This work has since been extended in Bosworth (1984, 1986), in a comparison of the main alternative indices of capital utilisation. While this work included the shift work-based measure, it did not attempt to discuss the construction of the index in detail. The only other work which has made use of the shift work data is that of Harris and Taylor (1984). While this study uses the stock of capital as a proxy for the full capacity input of capital services, allowance is made for the increasing utilisation rate due to the increase in shiftworking during the study period.[7]

THEORETICAL CONSIDERATIONS

(a) Shiftwork-based Measures and Continuous Manning

In this Section, we explore the conditions under which the shift work-based TIUR measures are a close approximation to their directly observed, survey-based, operating hours counterparts. The essential difference between the two approaches is immediately obvious: a measure based on shift work and hours per person is a labour-side measure, which must imply something about the way in which capital is manned. It is fairly clear that the two measures will generally differ whenever the most extreme case of continuous manning does not take place. In this instance, continuous manning not only implies that: (i) workers are present whenever capital is being operated; but also, (ii) capital is being operated whenever workers are present. By implication, the two measures will differ: in the case of automated machinery, which is simply loaded, left to run unaided and unloaded; where workers are present in the factory, but the machinery is lying idle (e.g., during maintenance of the machinery or when meal breaks, etc. are taken, which are included in reported working hours).[8]

(b) Homogeneous Shift System: Employment and Hours

The shift work-based TIUR measure requires information about the number of hours per day (week or year) covered by each type of shift system, U_j, where j denotes the jth type shift system, and $j = 1, 2, \ldots, n$ implies that there are n different types of shift system in use. Based on the continuous manning assumption, the length of operating period of a particular item of capital, U_j, can be constructed using information about the number of crews involved with that piece of capital, S_j, and the average number of hours worked per crew per shift, H_j. Thus, if day work (e.g., no shifts) is labelled as $j = 1$, then:

$$U_1 = S_1.H_1 - 1.H_1 = H_1 \tag{15.1}$$

where H_1 denotes the average hours of work for normal day workers.

In the case of two shift workers:

$$U_2 = S_2.H_2 = 2.H_2 \tag{15.2}$$

where H_2 denotes the average hours worked per crew by two shift workers.

Analogous calculations yield U_3 and U_4 for three- and four-crew systems.

(c) Capital Weights

If all the workers in a given firm or industry are employed on the same work pattern, j, then U_j represents the shift work-based TIUR measure. However, a significant proportion of firms (and all industries) work with a mix of shift systems, and some means of combining together the various U_j to yield some overall average value must be found. Ideally, each of the U_j should be weighted by the relative sizes of the capital stock employed on each shift, K_j.[9] The TIUR would thus appear as:

$$U = \sum_{j=1}^{n} U_j.(K_j/K_M) \tag{15.3}$$

where K_M denotes the total amount of capital available on the main shift.

In practice, however, K_j is not known, and some other form of weighting must be applied.

(d) Employment Weights

The only alternative appears to be to construct employment weights. The weight for the *j*th system can thus be written:

$$E_j/(S_j . E_M) \tag{15.4}$$

where:

E_j denotes total employment on the *j*th shift

S_j refers to the number of crews on the *j*th system

E_M = employment on the main shift (e.g., the total number of employees appearing within the factory during the busiest time of the day):

$$E_M = \sum_{j=1}^{n} E_j/S_j \tag{15.5}$$

where E_j/S_j is an estimate of the number of individuals from the *j*th shift who appear in the factory during the busiest time of the day.

Substitution of the employment weights for the capital weights will cause no change to the measure of capital utilisation if, and only if:

$$E_j/S_j = a . K_j \tag{15.6}$$

where *a* is a technically given constant for all *j*.

This is a strong assumption: it implies the same fixed coefficient technology on all shift systems. If the assumption holds, then it also implies an analogous fixed coefficient relationship between total employment on the main shift and capital on the main shift, independent of the mix of work patterns used:

$$E_M = \sum_{j=1}^{n} E_j/S_j = a . \sum_{j=1}^{n} K_j = a . K_M \tag{15.7}$$

and, hence,

$$E_M/K_M = a \tag{15.8}$$

It is then possible to write,

$$\frac{K_j}{\Sigma_j K_j} = \frac{E_j/(a . S_j)}{(1/a) . \Sigma_j E_j/S_j} = \frac{E_j/S_j}{E_M} \tag{15.9}$$

and it makes no difference whether capital or employment weights are used in the calculation.

In general, however, it appears likely that the shift work-based approximation to the level of operating hours of capital will tend to have an inherent negative bias whenever employment weights are applied. The reason for this lies in the fact that more capital-intensive systems tend to be operated more intensively. This bias can be illustrated using the example of a firm operating both a single- and a two-shift system (e.g., $j = 1$ and 2 respectively). Some capital is thus operated on a one-shift basis, K_1, and the remainder on a two-shift basis, K_2. Utilisation, U, can be calculated as:

$$U = (U_1 . K_1 + U_2 . K_2)/K_M \tag{15.10}$$

Using the alternative, employment weights, this can be written as:

$$U = \frac{(U_1 . E_1/a_1 . S_1) + (U_2 . E_2/a_2 . S_2)}{E_M/a} \tag{15.11}$$

where a is an average of a_1 and a_2.

If there are no differences between capital intensity on the main shift for the one- and two-shift systems, then $a = a_1 = a_2$, and these constant terms cancel in equation (15.11) and no bias is introduced by using employment weights. If, however, capital which is worked for two shifts (as we might expect) is more capital-intensive than the equivalent capital which is worked for just one shift, then $a_1 > a > a_2$, and, by implication, $(1/a_1) < (1/a) < (1/a_2)$. Hence, the implicit assumption of the simple employment weights (e.g., that $a = a_1 = a_2$), effectively weights the one-shift utilisation too heavily (as $(1/a) > (1/a_1)$) and the two-shift system too lightly (as $(1/a) < (1/a_2)$), causing an overall negative bias to the calculated measure of U.

TIUR MEASURES FOR THE UNITED KINGDOM CHEMICALS INDUSTRY

(a) Weekly v. Annual Series

The results of calculating the shift work-based TIUR for the United Kingdom chemicals industry are reported in this section. This task is undertaken in two stages: first, the construction of a TIUR measure using the data relating to a single operating week; second, an equivalent annual measure. In doing so, the implications of moving from a weekly to an annual basis are considered. In particular, the annual period raises some important questions about the practical difficulties of dealing with holiday periods. Nevertheless, despite these problems, it is fairly clear that the weekly index may give a significantly different picture of trends in capital utilisation during periods when holiday entitlements have increased, as they have in recent years.

(b) Data Sources

At the heart of the calculations reported below are the data on work patterns. Information about shift working and hours are taken from the twice-yearly survey of earnings and hours of adult male manual workers in the United Kingdom chemicals industry.[10] Although a number of other industries were included in the survey[11], the questionnaires were quite different, and the chemicals industry was the only one to report data by type of shift system. Five types of shift pattern were distinguished, including normal day working.[12] As restrictive as the source is, as far as can be ascertained, this is the only regular survey of any of United Kingdom manufacturing industry that gives information about shift working by type of system.[13] The first observation relates to June of 1963, first reported in the *Ministry of Labour Gazette* in November of that year.[14] Data were published in the same source[15] on a twice-yearly basis until the observation for June 1979. A further single observation relating to June 1980 was published, before the series was discontinued.[16]

The principal source of annual data on holidays over this early period is also the *Gazette*. It publishes the percentage distribution of employees across various lengths of holiday, excluding public customary holidays.[17] However, the information refers to all employees covered by national collective agreements,[18] and orders under the wages councils. The data therefore refer to a much broader group than just employees in the chemicals industry. In order to obtain an impression of the possible consequences of using the 'all-agreement' data, rather than information specifically for chemicals, comparisons are undertaken using data available for certain years in the Department of Employment *New Earnings Survey*.[19] Data on public or customary holidays are taken from the agreements associated with the chemicals industry and published in *Time Rates of Wages and Hours of Work*.

(c) TIUR Based on a Typical Working Week

Using the theory developed above and the data reported in (b) above an overall TIUR index of capital utilisation (e.g., estimate of capital operating hours) is constructed for a 'typical' working week, centered on the weeks of the Department of Employment Survey in January and June of each year (denoted by Roman numerals I and II respectively). The resulting series, based on 1970 (II) = 100.0, is reported in detail in Table 15.1 and in Figure 15.1.

The weekly series shows a marked difference between the highest and lowest values of capital utilisation: the index took a value of just over 95 in 1963 (II), compared with over 107 in 1967 (II). However, the overall picture is certainly not one of a steady increase in utilisation. Even ignoring the half-yearly fluctuations, the longer-term trend appears to indicate a fairly rapid rise in utilisation up to 1965 (II), followed by a much more steady increase over the remainder of the period, and even a slight downturn at the end.

Superimposed on this trend are quite marked short-term fluctuations

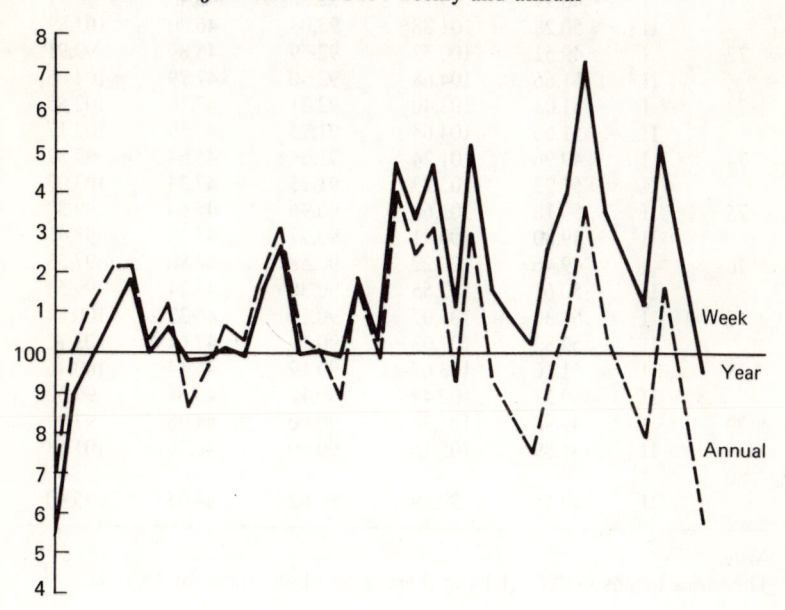

Figure 15.1   TIUR : weekly and annual

Table 15.1 Weekly and annual TIUR series

Year	Half	% week worked	Index (weekly)	% weeks worked in year	% year worked	Index (yearly)
1963	I	–	–	–	–	–
	II	47.09	95.42	94.23	44.37	96.60
64	I	48.83	98.95	94.23	46.01	100.18
	II	49.34	99.98	94.23	46.49	101.22
65	I	49.78	100.87	94.23	46.91	102.13
	II	50.25	101.82	94.04	47.25	102.14
66	I	49.03	99.35	94.04	46.11	100.38
	II	49.65	100.61	93.65	46.50	101.24
67	I	48.39	98.05	93.65	45.32	98.67
	II	48.83	98.95	93.65	45.73	99.56
68	I	49.40	100.10	93.65	46.26	100.72
	II	49.30	99.90	93.46	46.08	100.32
69	I	50.13	101.58	93.46	46.85	102.00
	II	50.68	102.70	93.46	47.37	103.13
70	I	49.32	99.91	93.46	46.10	100.36
	II	49.35	100.00	93.08	45.93	100.00
71	I	48.91	99.11	92.88	45.43	98.91
	II	50.28	101.88	93.08	46.80	101.89
72	I	49.51	100.32	92.69	45.89	99.91
	II	51.66	104.68	92.50	47.79	104.05
73	I	51.03	103.40	92.31	47.10	102.55
	II	51.66	104.68	91.73	47.39	103.17
74	I	49.96	101.24	91.35	45.64	99.37
	II	51.93	105.23	91.15	47.34	103.07
75	I	50.18	101.68	90.96	45.64	99.37
	II	49.80	100.91	90.77	45.20	98.41
76	I	49.46	100.22	90.58	44.80	97.53
	II	50.61	102.55	90.38	45.74	99.58
77	I	51.36	104.07	90.19	46.32	100.84
	II	52.82	107.03	90.19	47.64	103.72
78	I	51.16	103.67	90.19	46.14	100.46
	II	50.57	102.47	90.19	45.61	99.30
79	I	49.98	101.28	90.00	44.98	97.93
	II	51.89	105.15	90.00	46.70	101.68
80	I	–	–	–	–	–
	II	49.15	99.59	89.62	44.05	95.90

Note:
The series begins in 1963 (II) and there is no observation for 1980 (I).

in activity, with important and prolonged troughs in at least three or four periods (e.g., 1966 (I)–1968 (II), 1970 (I)–1971 (I), 1975 (I)–(1976) (I) and (possibly) 1968 (I)–1969 (I)). The start and end points of the series are also relatively low, and the first observation appears to play a particularly important part in establishing the overall large range of observations. If there is any seasonal effect, it is not sufficiently large to produce a consistent 'sawblade' effect in the series throughout. On balance, the first half observations (e.g. for January of each year) appear to be somewhat lower than the second half.

(d) Estimates of Holiday Entitlements

An index of operating hours based on a typical working week is, of course, of interest in its own right. However, the annual picture will be affected by other factors, in particular, the changing pattern of holiday entitlements and the extent to which plants are kept operating even when certain individuals (or crews) are on holiday (e.g., by means of additional crews or by overtime working). Data on holiday entitlements are far from comprehensive, however, and this section attempts only to obtain some idea of the broad order of magnitude of holidays and their potential importance in constructing TIUR measures.

Figure 15.2 illustrates the three primary series constructed in the Appendix (Table A.15.5), corresponding with average holiday entitlements $A(2)$, $A(3)$ and $A(4)$. Briefly, the three series are broadly as follows: $A(2)$ relates to basic holiday entitlements, excluding long-service and public holidays (interpolating the upper interval reported in the official holidays data); $A(3)$ also takes into account long-service holidays; finally, $A(4)$ also incorporates public and customary holidays. While too much should not be read into the detailed results, it is fairly clear from Figure 15.2 that all three series show a strong upward trend over the period as a whole. However, the growth is particularly strong between the years 1971 and 1976, and between 1979 and 1981.

(e) TIUR: Annual Series

If it is assumed that capital is laid up during the whole of the holiday period, then the annual TIUR can simply be calculated as the weekly TIUR multiplied by the proportion of the year which is worked.[20] The

Figure 15.2 Annual holiday entitlements

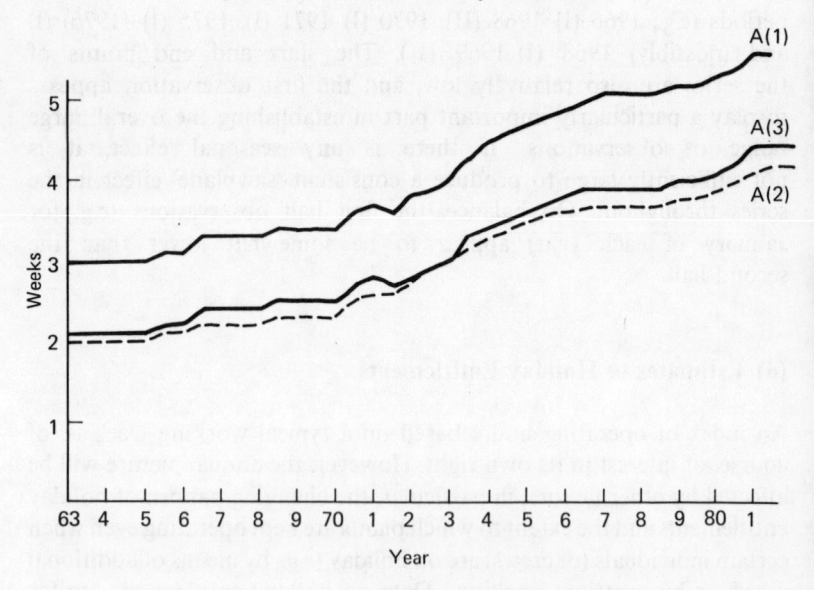

proportion of weeks worked is shown as column (3) of Table 15.1, the proportion of the year worked is shown as column (4) and the corresponding index (1970 (II) = 100.0) is shown in the final column. The annual index reported in Table 15.1 thus forms a lower bound of the TIUR measure. The degree to which the true series approaches this bound depends on the extent to which the factories continue to operate through holiday periods.[21] The degree to which the series is biased upwards or downwards depends on at least two factors: (1) the degree to which capital intensity has grown in the industry (affecting the accuracy of the employment weights);[22] (ii) the extent to which there have been changes in the degree to which factories shut down operations during worker holidays.

(f) Comparisons of the Weekly and Annual Indices

Following the discussions contained in (c) and (e) above (pp. 413–6), it is possible to compare the results for the weekly and annual TIUR measures, as shown in Figure 15.1. The weekly series cannot be considered as an upper bound insofar as it is biased downwards because it fails to allow for the growth of capital utilisation in the chemicals industry. If however, we assume that the weekly index approximates to the upper bound and the annual index to the lower bound, then the overall trend in TIUR is certainly not strongly upwards. The likelihood seems to be that there is no significant long-term trend in operating hours. Given the highly trended nature of the holiday entitlements, it is none too surprising that the short-term fluctuations shown in the two series are very similar.

CONCLUSIONS

The discussion in this chapter has shown that fairly heroic assumptions have to be made in order to construct an index of the operating hours of capital (e.g., a time intensity utilisation rate). In summary, the main problems are as follows: (i) the bias caused by adopting employment weights in times when capital intensity is growing; (ii) the assumption of the extreme version of continuous manning (or, at best, a fixed coefficient technology);[23] (iii) the lack of data on the extent of holidays; (iv) the lack of information about the degree to which one worker's holidays might be covered by either overtime working or by a member of a 'spare shift crew'; (v) the absence of data on female manual workers and their associated work patterns.

If it can be assumed that the assumptions and approximations adopted in the study do not invalidate the resulting series reported above, then they indicate that the long-term trend in operating hours of capital is certainly not strongly upwards. While the annual TIUR reported may be close to a lower bound, this index actually shows a long-term decline. The short-term fluctuations are quite marked, with strong peaks in the annual index occurring in 1965, 1969, 1972 and 1977. Most of these peaks are also apparent in the weekly TIUR series.

It is difficult to judge how useful this exercise has been overall. Other evidence is probably required before a final judgement can be made, perhaps relating to the performance of such indices in empirical work. On the other hand, the experience of constructing shiftwork-based TIUR does give rise to a degree of disquiet about the theoretical and empirical problems encountered. There is little doubt that there is a need, for quite separate reasons, for a series of employment data which distinguishes shift systems.[24] If this need were met, then shiftwork-based TIUR indices could be constructed at little cost. However, if the main aim is to produce series relating to the operating hours of capital, then it might be better to think in terms of a business survey questionnaire, which collects information directly on operating hours. Perhaps the ideal solution would be to collect both work pattern and operating hours data for a variety of industries in a single year. This would enable many of the assumptions outlined above to be rigorously tested.[25]

Appendix

An impression of the possible consequences of applying the 'all-agreement' data to the chemicals industry can be obtained by comparing the NES information available for: (i) the Chemical and Allied Industries Agreement with that for all such agreements (available for the years 1968, 1970, 1974 and 1981); (ii) the Chemicals industry, all manufacturing and all industries and services (available in 1974 and 1981). The data are set out in detail in Tables A15.1 and A15.2. Both sets of data appear to indicate that the chemicals industry has somewhat higher holiday entitlements than the overall average, for at least a part of the period. The collective agreement data indicate that chemicals may have experienced as much as three days per year higher holidays in the late 1960s and early 1970s, rising to around five days per year in the mid-1970s and early 1980s. This is contradicted somewhat by the industry results, which seem to indicate that chemicals perhaps had two extra days holiday in the mid-1970s, but, by the early 1980s, it had the same holiday entitlements as all manufacturing and all industries and services.

Despite the differences, both comparisons appear to indicate that a series based on the average entitlements for all agreements, rather than just chemicals, should not be too inaccurate. Thus, Table A15.3 reports the percentage distribution of employees by length of holiday entitlement (excluding both public/customary holidays and additional holidays through length of service). Half-yearly observations have been obtained by interpolation between annual observations in each interval. The upper band of four weeks and over was not further disaggregated until 1981. In order to avoid a downward bias to the estimate of average holidays during the latter end of the period used in this study, a broadly linear interpolation of the 4 + category is also reported from 1974 to 1981 (broadly in the sense that the 4 + and 4–5 categories were restricted to be non-negative in all periods).

Table A15.1 Comparison of Holiday Entitlements of Workers Covered by the Chemical and Allied Industries Agreement an All Workers Covered by Collective Agreements

Year	Agreement	% of employees with annual holiday entitlements of (weeks):								
		2–	2	2–3	3	3–4	4	4–5	5–6	6–8	Average
1968	Chemicals	1.9	8.5	81.5	7.8	0.4	0.0	0.0	0.0	0.0	2.5
	All agreements	60.0		34.0	6.0	0.0	0.0	0.0	0.0	0.0	2.2
70	Chemicals	4.5		82.8	10.8	0.5	1.4	0.0	0.0	0.0	2.5
	All Agreements	50.0		35.0	14.0	1.0	0.0	0.0	0.0	0.0	2.3
74	Chemicals	1.7	0.1	0.4	8.8	20.4	67.1	0.7	0.7	0.0	3.8
	All Agreements	1.0		2.0	38.0	52.0	7.0	0.0	0.0	0.0	3.3
81	Chemicals	0.3	0.0	0.0	0.0	0.3	8.4	78.3	10.3	2.4	4.6
	All Agreements	0.0		0.0	2.0	24.0	22.0[a]	52.0[a]	0.0	0.0	4.1

Notes:
[a] Estimated values.
Sources: NES (various dates).

Table A15.2 Holiday Entitlements by Industry: Chemicals, Manufacturing and All Industries and Services

% of employees with annual holiday entitlements of (weeks):

Year	Industry	0–2	2–3	3	3–4	4	4–5	5–6	6–8	8+	Average
1974	Chemicals	3.1	1.4	17.8	21.3	54.3	1.4	0.6	0.1	0.0	3.6
	Manufacturing	2.8	1.6	30.1	41.6	17.8	5.2	0.8	–	0.1	3.4
	All industries/services	4.4	1.5	39.7	31.3	13.2	8.5	1.0	0.3	0.3	3.4
81	Chemicals	0.5	0.3	1.6	1.5	21.6	66.1	7.9	0.8	0.0	4.4
	Manufacturing	1.0	0.4	2.6	2.8	23.0	56.3	12.4	1.5	0.0	4.4
	All industries/services	2.0	0.7	4.9	5.4	25.5	43.4	16.7	1.2	0.3	4.4

Sources: *NES* (1974), Table 166, p. F36 and *NES* (1981), Table 188, p. F105.

Table A15.3 Basic Holiday Entitlements, Public and Customary Holidays, and Long-service Holidays (Weeks Per Annum)

| Year | Half | % of employees by length of holiday entitlement ||||||| Percentage of employees with long-service holidays || Public Holidays |
		2	2–3	3	3–4	4+	4–5	5+	Reported	Actual	
1963	I	97	2	1	0	0	0	0	10	9	0
	II	97	2	1	0	0	0	0	10	9	0
64	I	97	2	1	0	0	0	0	10	9	0
	II	95	5	1	0	0	0	0	15	13	0
65	I	92	7	1	0	0	0	0	20	18	0
	II	84	15	2	0	0	0	0	21	19	0
66	I	75	22	3	0	0	0	0	22	20	0
	II	69	28	4	0	0	0	0	25	22	0
67	I	63	33	4	0	0	0	0	27	24	0
	II	62	34	5	0	0	0	0	27	24	0
68	I	60	34	6	0	0	0	0	27	24	0
	II	58	34	8	0	0	0	0	27	24	0
69	I	56	34	10	0	0	0	0	27	24	0
	II	53	35	12	0	0	0	0	29	26	0
70	I	50	35	14	1	0	0	0	30	27	0
	II	46	21	32	2	0	0	0	28	25	0
71	I	41	7	49	3	0	0	0	25	22	0
	II	35	6	56	4	0	0	0	21	19	0
72	I	28	5	63	4	0	0	0	17	15	1
	II	18	11	51	19	2	0	0	15	13	1
73	I	8	16	39	33	4	0	0	12	11	1

423

Year											
74	I	5	9	39	43	6	0	0	0	16	14	1
	II	1	2	38	52	7	0	0	0	19	17	1
75	I	1	2	34	46	18	0	0	0	20	18	1
	II	1	1	30	40	28	(24)	0 (4)	0	20	18	1
76	I	1	1	24	46	29	(21)	0 (8)	0	23	21	1
	II	1	1	17	51	30	(18)	0 (12)	0	26	23	1
77	I	1	1	18	49	32	(16)	0 (16)	0	30	27	1
	II	0	0	18	47	34	(14)	0 (20)	0	33	29	1
78	I	0	0	18	47	34	(10)	0 (24)	0	33	29	1
	II	0	0	18	47	34	(6)	0 (28)	0	32	29	1
79	I	0	0	17	47	35	(2)	0 (33)	0	34	30	1
	II	0	0	12	47	35	(0)	0 (35)	0	36	32	1
80	I	0	0	7	42	43	(4)	0 (39)	0	37	33	1
	II	0	1	5	33	50	(6)	0 (44)	0	38	34	1
81	I	0	0	2	24	62	(14)	0 (48)	0	39	35	1
	II	1	0	2	18	74	(22)	0 (52)	0	40	36	1
82	I	0	0	2	—	74	(24)	0 (57)	0	39[a]	35[a]	1
	II	0	0	—	11	87	(25)	0 (61)	1	37[a]	33[a]	1

Note:
[a] Deletion of certain wages councils provisions; all published figures relate to end of December and so are used as the January figure for the following year; June figures are interpolated within each heading.
Source: Department of Employment Gazette (various dates).

Table A15.4 Public and customary holidays in the chemicals industry

Year	Industry/Agreement										
	(1)	(2)	(3)	(4)	(5)	(6)	(7)	(8)	(9)	(10)	(11)
1963	6	–	–	6	6	–	–	6	6	–	–
64	6	–	–	6	–	–	–	6	6	–	–
65	6	–	–	6	–	–	–	6	6	–	–
66	6	–	–	6	–	–	–	6	6	–	–
67	6	–	–	6	–	–	–	6	6	–	–
68	6	–	–	6	–	–	–	6	6	–	–
69	6	–	–	6	–	7	–	6	6	–	–
70	6	–	–	6	–	7	–	6	6	–	–
71	6	–	–	6	–	7	–	6	6	–	–
72	6	–	8.5	6	–	7	–	6	6	–	–
73	6	6	8.5	6	7	7	6	6	6	6	6
74	7	7	9.5	7	7	7	7	7	–	7	7
75	7	8	9.5	7	7	7	7	7	–	7	7
76	7	8	9.5	7	7	8	7	7	–	7	7
77	8	9	10.5	8	7	9	8	7	–	8	8
78	8	9	10.5	8	8	9	8	8	–	8	8
79	8	9	10.5	8	8	9	8	8	–	8	8
80	8	9	10.5	8	8	8	8	8	–	–	8
81	8	9	10.5	8	8	8	8	8	–	–	8

Notes:
Industry/Agreements: (1) Joint Industrial council; (2) Imperial Chemical Industries; (3) British Nuclear Fuels; (4) Drug and fine chemical; (5) Paint, varnish and lacquer; (6) Match manufacture; (7) Printing ink; (8) Soap, candle, etc., (9) Polish; (10) Gelatine and glue; (11) Surgical dressings.
Source: *Department of Employment Gazette* (various dates).

Table A15.5 Average holiday entitlements (weeks per year)

Year	Half	A(1)	A(2)	A(3)	A(4)
1963	I	–	–	–	–
	II	2.0	2.0	2.1	3.0
64	I	2.0	2.0	2.1	3.0
	II	2.0	2.0	2.1	3.0
65	I	2.0	2.0	2.1	3.0
	II	2.0	2.0	2.1	3.0
66	I	2.1	2.1	2.2	3.1
	II	2.1	2.1	2.2	3.1
67	I	2.2	2.2	2.4	3.3
	II	2.2	2.2	2.4	3.3
68	I	2.2	2.2	2.4	3.3
	II	2.2	2.2	2.4	3.3
69	I	2.3	2.3	2.5	3.4
	II	2.3	2.3	2.5	3.4
70	I	2.3	2.3	2.5	3.4
	II	2.3	2.3	2.5	3.4
71	I	2.5	2.5	2.7	3.6
	II	2.6	2.6	2.8	3.7
72	I	2.6	2.6	2.7	3.6
	II	2.7	2.7	2.8	3.8
73	I	2.9	2.9	2.9	3.9
	II	3.0	3.0	3.0	4.0
74	I	3.2	3.2	3.3	4.3
	II	3.3	3.3	3.4	4.5
75	I	3.4	3.4	3.5	4.6
	II	3.5	3.5	3.6	4.7
76	I	3.5	3.6	3.7	4.8
	II	3.5	3.6	3.8	4.9
77	I	3.5	3.7	3.9	5.0
	II	3.6	3.7	3.9	5.1
78	I	3.6	3.7	3.9	5.1
	II	3.6	3.7	3.9	5.1
79	I	3.6	3.7	3.9	5.1
	II	3.6	3.8	4.0	5.2
80	I	3.6	3.8	4.0	5.2
	II	3.7	3.9	4.1	5.3
81	I	3.8	4.0	4.2	5.4
	II	3.9	4.1	4.4	5.6
82	I	3.9	4.2	4.4	5.6
	II	3.9	4.2	4.4	–

Source: Department of Employment Gazette (various dates).

This information is also incomplete, however, as it excludes both additional holidays from long service and public/customary holidays. The Department of Employment series provides information about the incidence of additional holidays from long service, again reported in Table A15.3. This figure is again an average of both manual and non-manual workers, while our basic data set relates to manual workers. In this instance, however, there may be a greater difference between the long service entitlements of these two groups which may give rise to some inaccuracy. Using data on additional holidays obtained from a special question in the (NES) for 1970, it was possible to obtain an estimate of the bias for that year. As a consequence, the incidence of additional holiday entitlements series was adjusted downwards by about 10 per cent to allow for this effect.

Finally, an adjustment is made for public and customary holidays. Data on the numbers of days of public holidays per year are published in *Time Rates of Wages and Hours of Work* as shown in Table A15.4. While the data are incomplete, with a number of changes to the agreements covered, it is possible to piece together a fairly accurate view of public holidays, shown as the final column of Table A15.3.

An attempt is thus made to calculate the total holiday allowances for the chemicals industry. The main variants are reported in Table A15.5. Average A(1) refers to the unadjusted series (e.g., with no interpolation of the upper bands between 1975 and 1981) and A(2) allows for the interpolated revaluation of the upper interval. As it seems likely that A(1) is biased downward in the latter part of the period, A(2) is preferred. A(3) allows for the existence of long-service holiday entitlements. It is an average formed by weighting and summing the holidays of the two groups (e.g., those who are and are not in receipt of long-service entitlements). Adding public holidays in with other holiday entitlements yields a revised average, A(4), which is taken as the best estimate of total holiday entitlements in the chemicals industry.

Notes

1. The electricity based measures include those of Foss (1963, 1981), Heathfield (1972) and Bosworth (1984a, 1985).
2. For a review and a comparison between all of the main alternative measures, see Bosworth (1979, 1984a) and Bosworth and Westaway (1984).
3. This technique has been used to collect data for the United States, Israel and the Philippines, see Foss (1981), Bautista (1974) and Morawetz (1976).
4. This was suggested in Foss (1963) and has been used in Bosworth (1984a, 1984b). The general principle is also taken up in constructing measures of capacity utilisation in Harris and Taylor (1984).
5. In practice, the separation of the two indices is not without its problems, see Bosworth (1985).
6. With the exception of the textiles industry, see Bosworth (1984b).
7. Harris and Taylor (1984, p. 8).
8. It may be possible to relax the continuous manning assumption if only a relative index is required. This will still involve the assumption of some fixed coefficient relationship.
9. See Morawetz (1976, p. 647).
10. In practice, the survey covered only MLHs 271-2 and 276, whereas chemicals as a whole relates to all of the 270s.
11. The other industries covered by the survey varied over time, but, at various points, they included: engineering, shipbuilding and iron and steel.
12. The shifts were distinguished consistently over time according to the following classification: (i) day workers; (ii) continuous three-shift workers; (iii) non-continuous three-shift workers; (iv) two-shift workers; (v) others, including night workers.
13. A review of the other main sources of shift work data, and the sorts of information contained, can be found in Bosworth and Dawkins (1981, pp. 84-9), and this is updated in Bosworth (1984c).
14. The results of the survey were first reported under the title, 'Occupational Earnings in Engineering, Shipbuilding and Chemical Manufacture, June 1963', *Ministry of Labour Gazette* (November 1963), pp. 426-32. The title of the report changes over time, but it can be traced fairly easily from the initial publication in 1963. The Gazette also changed name, as the associated Ministry changed from the Ministry of Labour, to the Department of Employment and Productivity and the Department of Employment.
15. The 1963 (II) survey, for example, collected information about those at work during the whole or a part of the pay week that included 19 June 1963. In instances where an establishment was stopped for the whole or a part of the specified week, information for the nearest ordinary week was used in its place – see note 21 below. The survey involved 2500 questionnaires, of which 2400 were returned in a form suitable for tabulation.
16. Some parts of the survey were taken over by the Engineering Industry Training Board in 1980, but the information on work patterns, which was always limited to the chemicals industry, was lost.
17. See, for example, Department of Employment, British Labour Statistics, Yearbook (1976) (London: HMSO), Table 48, p. 114.
18. As set out in DE, *Time Rates of Wages and Hours of Work*.

19. DE, *NES*.
20. In other words (52 − number of weeks holiday)/52.
21. It should be remembered that the assumptions adopted in the theoretical section assume a continuous manning assumption, so the assumption of the shut-down of processes during holidays is perfectly consistent with this. It could be argued, however, that missing workers could be covered by overtime working, insofar as the overtime already in the model only relates to normal working weeks and not holiday weeks, when the average hours of overtime per worker on overtime could be higher (see Bosworth and Westaway, 1984). No information is available about holiday overtime or the existence of 'spare crews' – see note 15 above.
22. See the theoretical discussion on pp. 410–11.
23. Note that there may be a further problem insofar as the assumptions adopted in the construction of the capital utilisation measure may not be consistent with those of the models in which it is applied (e.g., when it is used in the estimation of production functions or factor demand models).
24. The only major source of data at the present time is the NES, which gives information only about individuals in receipt of a shift premium. At the time of writing there were no data about employment by type of system. See notes 11 and 12 above.
25. One possibility would be to include a question on types of system in the NES, as this could be used to put some flesh around the bones of the 'shift premia' questions in earlier years. The information on the operating hours of capital could then be undertaken in a separate survey, drawing on the same population of firms. If, in addition, questions could be obtained about data used in the construction of other measures of capital utilisation, comparisons of alternative measures could be undertaken and an index relating to the 'intensity' dimension could be separated.

References

BAUTISTA, R. (1974) 'The electricity based measure of capital utilisation in Philippine manufacturing industries', *Philippine Review of Business and Economics* 11 (June), pp. 13–33.

BOSWORTH, D. L. (1979) 'Capital stock, capital services and the use of fuel consumption proxies', in Patterson, K. and Schott (eds), *The Measurement of Capital* (London: Macmillan).

——— (1984) 'Capital utilisation: empirical evidence for the UK chemicals industry', discussion paper, Department of Economics, Loughborough University.

——— (1985) 'Fuel based measures of capital utilisation', *Scottish Journal of Political Economy* 32, pp. 20–38.

——— (1986) *Work Patterns and Capital Utilisation in British Manufacturing Industry*, research report, Institute for Employment Research, University of Warwick.

——— and DAWKINS, P. J. (1981) *Work Patterns: an Economic Analysis* (Aldershot: Gower).

——— and WESTAWAY, A. J. (1984) 'The Theory and Measurement of Capital Utilisation and its Role in Modelling Investment', paper presented to the Conference on Investment in Europe (Catholic University of Louvain, Belgium, September).

——— (1986) 'Machine Utilisation in the British Textiles Industries', *Textiles Horizons* (forthcoming).

FOSS, M. F. (1963) 'The Utilisation of Capital Equipment', *Survey of Current Business* 43 (June), pp. 8–16.

——— (1981) Long Run Changes in the Work Week of Fixed Capital', *American Economic Association* papers and proceedings 71 (May), pp. 58–63.

HARRIS, R. and TAYLOR, J. (1984) 'The Measurement of Capacity Utilisation', discussion paper, Queen's University, Belfast and the University of Lancaster (May).

HEATHFIELD, D. F. (1972) 'The Measurement of Capital Usage Using Electricity Consumption Data', *Journal of the Royal Statistical Society* (Series A) 135, pp. 208–20.

MORAWETZ, D. (1976) 'The Electricity Measure of Capital Utilisation', *World Development* 4, pp. 643–53.

NES (New Earnings Survey) Department of Employment (London: HMSO) (various dates).

Time Rates of Wages and Hours of Work Department of Employment (London: HMSO).

URI, N. D. (1979) 'Energy demand as interfuel substitution in India', *European Economic Review* 12, pp. 181–90.

Author Index

Aarts, L., 135
Ansar, J., vi, x, xxiii, 79
Antos, 141, 149, 212
Artus, J., 23, 43
Autorengemeinschaft, 248

Bach, H., 120, 250
Baille, R., viii, x, xxiv, xxvi
Ball, R., 282, 382, 403
Ballance, D., 4, 46
Bancroft, G., 131, 154, 157, 212, 250
Barrett, W., 131
Bautista, R., 406, 407, 427
Bax, E., 135
Beach, C., 314
Bednarzik, R., 126, 145, 212
Beenstock, M., 98
Bennett, A., viii, x, xxiv, 326, 358, 363
Berg, D., 224, 240, 242
Berndt, E., 79, 308
Betancourt, R., 317, 325, 368, 380
Bewley, R., 235, 243
Bhattacharjee, G., 51
Blazejczak, J., 274
Boothe, P., 59
Bosworth, D., ix, x, xxv, xxvi, xxvii, 29, 43, 276, 277, 278, 279, 280, 282, 368, 380, 381, 382, 384, 386, 387, 388, 394, 403, 406, 407, 408, 412, 416, 427, 428
Bowen, W., 130
Bowers, J., 234
Brinkman, C., 252, 274
Briscoe, G., 380, 403
Brown, A., 225
Bruche, C., 168, 212
Bruno, M., 308
Bruinsma, H., 135
Buddenberg, F., 225, 234
Butler, A., 130
Burton, C., 4, 46
Buxton, A., 314

Cadwell, M., 326, 358
Cain, G., 127, 147, 148, 164, 165, 166, 212
Carlson, J., 6
Casey, B., 212

Chamberlin, E., xxi, 368
Cheshire, P., 234
Chow, G., 288
Christensen, L., 312
Christiano, L., 23, 43, 45, 56
Clague, C., 368, 403
Clarkson, R., 136
Clegg, H., 277
Cobb, C., 29, 33, 34, 35, 59, 82, 88, 110, 280, 281, 305, 312, 315, 369, 370, 371, 385, 393
Cohen, M., 135
Craine, R., 278, 279, 291, 305
Cyr, E., 282, 382, 403

de Jong, P., 135
de Neubourg, C., vi, vii, xi, xxiv, xxvi, 119, 120, 171, 212, 234, 235, 240, 243, 246, 247, 249, 250, 252, 255, 256, 263, 274
den Hartog, J., 227, 231–234, 240
Dawkins, P., 280, 368, 408, 412, 427
Dalziel, A., 98
Demopoulos, G., 130
Denison, E., 31, 32, 304, 368
Denny, M., 385, 403
Denton, F., 174, 213
Department of Employment, 314
Dernburg, T., 128, 130
Deroose, S., 168, 212
Desai, M., 29
Dewhurst, J., vi, x, xxii, 8, 45, 50, 53, 56
Diewert, W., 308
Douglas, P., 29, 33, 34, 35, 59, 82, 88, 110, 280, 281, 305, 312, 315, 369, 370, 371, 385, 393
Driehuis, W., 234
Dunlop, J., 131
Durbin, J., 34, 37, 94

Easterlin, R., 144, 212
Enzler, J., 45

Feaver, C., 174, 213
Feldstein, M., 278, 279, 291, 305, 371
Finegan, T., 130
Flaim, P., 123, 135, 136, 147, 212
Forbes, D., 50, 53, 56

Author Index

Ford, J., 385, 403
Forster, J., 234
Foss, M., 375, 383, 406, 407, 408, 427
Friedman, J., 126
Fuss, M., 81, 88, 110, 308, 385, 403

Gallop, 367, 368
Gastwirth, J., 130, 153, 160, 212, 248, 249, 250
Gilbreth, F., 354, 363
Gilroy, C., 154, 155, 157, 159, 212, 250
Gollop, F., 368
Gordon, M., 250
Gordon, R., 250
Gorzig, B., 252, 274
Granier, R., 135, 137, 170, 250, 253, 254
Gregory, P., 79, 80
Green, C., 128, 160, 165
Griffin, J., 79, 80
Griffin, T., 31, 43, 381, 403
Griliches, Z., 375, 383
Gross, J., 252, 274
Gujariti, D., 234

Hall, B., 34
Hall, R., 34
Halvorsen R., 385, 403
Hamlin, A., 368
Hansen, B., 223, 224, 225, 226, 242
Hansson, A., 59
Harris, R., v, x, xxii, 23, 38, 43, 135, 380, 403, 408, 427
Hart, R., 279, 281, 284, 287, 288
Hausman, J., 87
Hazledine, T., 283, 284, 305, 380, 382, 403
Heathfield, D., ix, x, xxv, xxvii, 314, 367, 368, 375, 376, 383, 384, 406, 427
Hedges, J., 135
Heijke, J., 234, 235, 243
Helliwell, J., vi, xi, xxiii, 58, 59, 60, 61, 64, 78
Hibbert, J., 381, 403
Hitch, T., 152, 212, 250
Hochkonjunkturjahr, 252
Holden, K., 235, 243
Holt, C., 174, 213, 224
Hughes, B., 279

Industrial Facts and Forecasting (IFF), 42
Ingham, A., vi, xi, xxiii, 79, 80, 98
Institut fur Arbeitsmarkt- und Berufsforschung (IAB), 119, 138, 174
Institut National de la Statistique et des Etudes Economiques (INSEE), 45, 53
International Labour Office (ILO), 123, 134, 175, 211, 212, 213
Ireland, N., 383, 403

Johansen, L., 86, 115
Jorgenson, D., 312, 367, 368, 375, 383

Kabaj, M., 317, 325
Khaled, M., 308
Klauder, 248, 251, 252, 274
Klauderu, W., 119
Klein, L., 23, 25, 30, 43, 145, 212
Kendrick, J., 367
Keynes, J., xxi, 120, 374
Killingsworth, C., 128
Kloek, T., 234
Knight, K., 279
Knox, F., 134
Kok, L., 249
Kooiman, P., 224, 234, 242
Kreijger, R., 224, 234, 242
Kuhlewind, G., 251
Kuipers, S., 225, 228, 231–4, 237, 240, 242, 243

Lal, D., 250
Laing, C., 305
Lau, L., 312
Lebergott, S., 123, 128, 152, 212, 250
Leon, H., vi, xi, xxiii, 79
Leon, L., 128, 160, 161, 164, 212
Leslie, D., 276, 277, 278, 279, 280, 281, 282, 283, 304, 305, 306, 307, 312, 315
Levitan, S., 127
Lindley, R., 120, 171, 212

McCoy, T., 79, 368
McRae, R., 59
McFadden, D., 308
Maandschrift Economie, 219, 242
MacGregor, M., 59
MacKinnon, J., 314
Maddison, A., 119, 134, 135, 137, 138, 140, 170, 172, 206, 212, 249, 250, 253, 254
Malcolmson, J., 87, 88, 89, 90, 91, 92, 98, 107
Margolick, M., 59
Marie, S., 126
Marris, R., 368
Meijers, H., 230, 242

Author Index

Meiners, H., 136
Melese, F., 80
Mellow, W., 141, 149, 212
Mendis, L., 312, 332
Mertens, D., 119
Miller, E., 381, 403
Mincer, J., 128, 130, 153, 160, 212, 248, 249, 250
Ministerie van Sociale Zaken, 219, 234, 235, 242
Ministry of Labour, 42
Mizon, G., 87, 88
Moll, R., 203
Moody, C., 382, 403
Moore, G., 123, 155, 160, 250
Morawetz, D., 406, 407, 409, 427
Mordasini, B., 120, 174, 213
Moy, J., 124, 125
Muellbauer, J., 12, 308, 312, 314, 332, 371
Muysken, J., vii, xi, xxiii, 219, 224, 228, 230, 231–4, 235, 240, 242, 243

Nadiri, M., 280, 284, 380, 382, 403
National Bureau for Economic Research, 164
Neale, A., viii, xi, xxiv, xxvi, 276
Nickell, S., 87, 8, 380, 403

OECD, 170, 212

Padmore, T., 59
Paish, F., 23, 43
Panić, M., 27, 43
Parihk, A., 235, 243
Parkin, M., 6
Parrillo, S., 50, 53, 56
Pearce, D., 23, 43
Peel, D., 235, 243, 380, 403
Perry, G., 126, 147, 152, 212, 250
Petersen, C., 135
Phan-Thuy, N., viii, xi, xxv, xxvi, 317, 325
Phelps, E., 174, 224
Phillips, A., 123, 149, 165
Pindyck, R., 385, 403
Plourde, A., 59
Plummer, R., 59
Preston, R., 23, 30, 43
Price, R., 46
Prior, M., 87, 88, 89, 90, 91, 92, 98, 107
Pugh, C., 380, 403

Reyher, L., 120, 174, 250
Robbins, Lord, xxi

Robinson, G., 7, 131
Rosen, S., 280, 284, 380, 382, 403
Rosenberg, P., 252, 274
Rosewell, B., v, x, xii, xxii, 3
Ruist, E., 45, 46

Salou, G., vi, xii, 58, 59, 60, 61, 64, 78
Salter, W., 80, 84
Sarrazin, T., 252, 274
Scanlon, W., 174, 213
Sharot, T., 279, 281, 284, 287, 288
Shastry, D., 382, 403
Shepard, R., 385
Shiskin, J., 119, 126, 127, 128, 152, 153, 154, 156, 160, 161, 164, 167, 212, 248, 250, 274
Shorey, J., 281
Silver, M., viii, xii, xxiv, xxvi
Sims, C., 305
Simler, N., 130
Small, S., 135
Smith, R., 135
Smith-Gavine, S., viii, xii, xxiv, 326, 358
Smyth, D., 382, 403
Sneesens, H., 224, 242
Sonderstrom, H., 45, 46
Sonnet, A., 174, 213
Sorrentino, C., 122, 124, 125, 135, 148, 160, 212, 248
Steinberg, E., 160, 161, 164, 212
Stone, R., 306
Strand, K., 128, 130
Sturm, P., vi, xii, xxiii, 58, 59, 60, 61, 64, 78

Taggart, R., 127
Taylor, F., xxii, 43, 234, 354, 363
Taylor, J., v, xii, 23, 29, 38, 43, 130, 250, 408, 427
Tella, A., 123, 130, 131, 135
Theil, H., 6
Tiokka, R., 174, 213
Tjan, H., 227, 231–4, 240
Toker, M., vi, xii, xxiii, 79
Triplett, J., 141, 212

Ullman, L., 277
Ulph, A., vi, xii, xxiii, 79
United Nations, 171, 213
Uri, N., 385, 403

Vaccara, B., 367
van Sinderen, J., 228, 231–4, 240, 242, 243
van Zon, A., 231–7, 240, 243

van den Berg, H., 234, 235
van den Bosch, F., 135
van der Burg, H., 240, 224, 242
Vandeweghe, R., 168, 212
Vroman, C., 168, 212

Walker, R., 381, 403
Warburton, P., 98
Warren, R., 235, 243
Watcher, M., 144, 147, 212
Watson, G., 34, 37, 94
Webb, A., 234
Weiserbs, D., 80
Westaway, A., ix, xii, xxv, 276, 277, 278, 279, 280, 282, 380, 387, 394, 403, 406, 427, 416, 428
Whybrew, E., 277, 283
Whitley, J., 294
Wilson, R., viii, xii, xxiv, xxvi, 276, 277, 279, 284, 294, 301, 384, 403
Winston, G., 79, 317, 325, 368
Winter, D., 23, 43
Wise, J., 277, 278, 279, 304, 306, 307, 315
Wood, D., 79
Wren-Lewis, S., 6

Zellner, A., 308

Subject Index

absenteeism, 157, 159, 171, 179, 199, 253, 256, 262
accelerator, 326, 338, 360
added workers, 127–30, 150, 160, 247, 250 (*see also* discouraged workers)
adjustment, 64, 130–1, 228, 279, 280, 283, 284, 285–302 (*see also* distributed lags, error correction)
aggregation, 224, 242
algorithms, 51, 109
attitudes, 352
automation, *see* technological change

bankruptcy, 341
bargaining, *see* collective agreements
basic hours, *see* hours/normal hours
basic pay, 276, 283, 286 (*see also* wages)
batches, 328, 355, 356
Belgium, 249
birth cohort, *see* demographic/birth cohort
bonus pay, 277, 323, 326, 331, 353, 354, 359 (*see also* overtime premia *and* shiftwork/shift premia)
bottlenecks, *see* shortages
Bureau of Labour Statistics (BLS), 128–9, 157, 158
business cycles, 23–44, 52, 60, 72, 119–245, 219–45, 247, 258, 259, 260, 261, 262, 264, 265, 306, 327–63, 393–400
Business Statistics Office, 5
Business survey data, xii, xxvi, 3–22, 23, 45–57, 320–1, 323, 327–63, 380, 406, 418, 374–5, 376 (*see also* CBI)
index of utilisation, 45, 46, 50, 53, 57
Scottish Business Survey, 23

Cambridge Growth Project, 285
Canada, 59, 66–78, 119–245, 246, 263, 264
capacity and capacity utilisation, xxi, xxii–xxiii, xiv, xxvi, xxvi–xxvii, 3–22, 23–44, 45–57, 58–78, 79–116, 219–45, 317–25, 427 (*see also* output)
intended and unintended idleness, xxi, xxii, xxv, xxvi–xxvii, 24, 79
social capacity, 320–5
capital costs (and prices), xxvi, 75, 79–116, 278, 282, 322, 323, 389 (*see also* prices/market versus shadow)
savings, 280
setting up and close-down costs, 278, 305 (*see also* adjustment)
capital goods, 13–14, 26, 326, 327, 334, 338, 349, 360 (*see also* investment)
capital intensity, 321, 408, 409–10
capital productivity, 23–44 (*see also* returns to one factor)
capital savings, *see* capital costs
capital services, xv, 28–31, 34, 43, 367–79 (*see also* capital stock *and* capital utilisation)
capital stock, 8, 9, 12, 13–14, 26, 27–44, 59–78, 79–116, 171, 280, 282, 284, 290, 305–15, 317–25, 338, 340, 355, 356, 367–79, 381, 382, 383, 384, 387, 388, 403, 408
capacity, 367 (*see also* shortages)
depreciation, 10, 31–33, 43, 60, 84–85, 91, 93, 98, 99, 103, 373, 339–40
effective capacity, 320
life, 31–3, 88, 95, 96, 107
net *versus* gross, 31
perpetual inventory method, 10, 32, 373, 381, 388
plant and machinery, 27, 29, 33, 42, 43, 383, 384, 390, 403
rate of return on, 88
scrapping, xxv, 9–14, 26, 31–3, 43, 60, 75, 86, 92, 220, 367, 373, 374, 375, 378
capital utilisation, xxiii, xxv–xxvi, 29–31, 33, 42, 53, 79–116, 113, 260, 278, 317–25, 367–79, 380–405, 406–29
annual, 411–29
length of operation, 29–31, 33, 113, 368, 369, 371, 380, 388, 406, 407, 417
idle capital, xxv–vi, 86, 100–3, 367, 373, 374, 375, 376, 378 (*see also* capital utilisation)
intended and unintended idleness, xi, xxi, xxii, 79, 115, 318–21

435

capital utilisation (*contd.*)
  intensity of operation, 371, 406, 407, 418, 428
  measurement problems, 317–21, 367–79, 380–405, 406–29
  weekly, 411–29
Central Planning Bureau, 220, 227, 230, 237, 239, 243
Central Statistical Office (CSO), 6, 7, 31–3
Centre for Latin American Development Studies, 317
chemicals industry, 406–29 (*see also* manufacturing)
Chow test, 288
Cobb-Douglas function, *see* production functions
collective agreements, 131, 276, 282, 314, 420
competition, 339, 352
computerisation, *see* technological change
Confederation of British Industries (CBI), xxii, 3–22, 24, 45–6, 49–53, 56–7, 332, 387, 374–5, 376 (*see also* business survey data)
  monthly survey, 3, 5
  quarterly survey, 4–5, 7, 9, 10, 11, 12, 13
consumer goods, 13–14, 327, 334, 338, 339, 349
continuous manning, xvi, 408–11, 416, 417, 427, 428
continuous processes, 282
contractual arrangements, *see* collective agreements
costs (and cost minimisation), 24, 60, 62–78, 82, 84, 89, 95, 99, 100–2, 103, 104, 106, 110, 112, 113, 115, 278, 281, 282, 284
  variable cost, 84, 85, 86, 99, 100–2, 103, 104, 106, 110, 112, 115
costs of adjustment, *see* adjustment
crews, *see* shiftwork

death, 141
demand (for labour), xxi, xxiii, 79–116, 159, 168, 219–45, 276, 320, 324, 351 (*see also* factor demands)
demographic factors, xxvii, 119–245, 248, 249, 255, 264 (*see also* labour force *and* population)
  age (and young workers), 144–8, 150, 153, 154, 155, 171–98, 207

birth cohort, 140–50, 178
crowding effect, 144, 212
gender, 145–9, 150, 153, 154, 155, 161 166, 168, 169, 171–98
Department of Employment, 285, 286
Department of Energy, 79, 115
Department of Labour, 126
depreciation, *see* capital stock/depreciation
deterioration, *see* capital stock/depreciation
developing countries, xxi, xxv, xxvi, 317–25
disability, 134–5, 157, 159, 173, 179, 196, 199, 203, 220, 221, 228, 230, 235, 243, 255, 256, 263, 274 (*see also* mental health)
discounted cash flows, 82–3, 90, 91, 95
discouraged workers, 127–30, 144, 150, 153, 154, 155, 156, 160, 161, 168, 247, 248, 250 (*see also* added workers)
displacement effects, 321
distributed lags (and lag structures), 287–301
distributive shares, 307 (*see also* production functions)
dualist theories, 134
dual cost function, 76, 308, 384–6

earnings, *see* pay
economic activity, xxi, 4, 130, 253, 254, 284, 327–63 (*see also* output)
economic hardship, *see* poverty *and* welfare
Economic and Social Research Council (ESRC), 23, 43
education (learning by doing and training), 91, 95, 131, 134–5, 166, 172, 173, 178, 194, 203, 249, 252, 255, 256, 280, 284, 304
efficiency, *see* productivity
effort (intensity of work effort), xxiii, xxiv–xxv, 34, 284, 327–63 (*see also* labour utilisation/PUL)
electricity-based measures, xv, 29, 43, 314–15, 380–405, 406
  homogeneity of electricity, 376, 383
electricity generation, 88, 110
employers, *see* management
employment (employees and labour demand), 28–44, 59–78, 79–116, 119–245, 246–75, 276–303, 327–363, 369, 370, 371, 380
  casual workers, 323

Subject Index 437

female, 252, 281, 283, 285–302, 312–15
guest workers, 206
male, 126, 252, 281, 285–302, 314–15
occupations, 148, 224, 234–5, 242
operatives, 327–63; direct, 326, 359; indirect, 326, 359
regions, 224, 234–5, 242
self-employed, 134
staff, 326, 331, 359
employment functions, *see* factor demand functions
employment promotion, 317–325 (*see also* government policies *and* work sharing)
energy, 59–78, 79–116 (*see also* electricity *and* factor demands)
engineering, xxvii, 32–41, 376, 412, 427 (*see also* manufacturing)
Engineering Industry Training Board, 412, 427
error correction mechanism, 289 (*see also* adjustment *and* distributed lags)
Europe, 136, 172, 381 (*see also individual country names*)
European Economic Community (EEC), 124
European Production Study Group (EPSG), xxi, xxvii, 29, 43
European Statistical Offices (Eurostat), 124
expectations, 4, 72, 78, 80, 81, 83, 86, 88, 89, 95, 98, 99, 107, 291 (*see also* adjustment, discounted cash flows *and* distributed lags)
exports, *see* trade

factor demand functions (and employment functions), 58, 85–86, 93, 104, 105, 106, 107, 110, 219–45, 276–303, 380–405
'factory summary sheet' (and time sheets), 211, 331, 356
female workers, 417
firing, 130–1, 224, 234, 280, 323, 357
fixed coefficient technology, *see* production function
fixed costs, 282 (*see also* quasi-fixed labour costs)
flexibility, 352
food, drink and tobacco, 25, 32–41 (*see also* manufacturing)
forecasting, 6, 103, 106, 107, 130–1, 349, 350–1

France, 45, 53–6, 66–78, 119–245, 249, 253
Fraser of Allender Institute, 23
fringe benefits, 277
fuel based measures, *see* electricity-based measures
full employment (and natural rate of unemployment), xxiii, 62, 67, 74, 130, 147, 219–45, 254, 255, 261 (*see also* labour utilisation)
full-time equivalents, 250, 257 (*see also* part-time workers)
full-time workers, 178, 281, 285–302, 312–15 (*see also* full time equivalents *and* part time workers)

Gallop, 6
Germany, 66–78, 119–245, 246, 248, 249, 250, 251–3, 255, 263, 264
Gordon Committee, 123
government policy, xxiv, xxv, 23, 58, 119, 120, 123, 127, 134–6, 147, 150, 151, 166, 167, 168, 170, 172, 219, 234, 247, 252, 258, 263, 274, 305, 317–25, 344 (*see also* taxes)
'big push' versus 'selective push', 322–3
fine tuning, 332
Great Britain, 92, 125, 327–63 (*see also* United Kingdom)
growth accounting, 304

health, *see* disability and mental health
Heath, 332
hidden reserve, 250–5
hidden unemployment, 127–130, 175 (*see also* hidden reserve, hoarding, labour utilisation *and* unemployment)
hiring, 130–1, 224, 280, 304, 323, 356
hoarding (fuels), 376, 383
hoarding (labour), xxii, xxiv, 130–1, 150, 152, 219–45, 247, 279, 305 (*see also* labour utilisation
holidays, xxvii, 121, 136–40, 159, 168, 173, 179, 192, 194, 199, 211, 249, 252, 256, 411–29
public, 412, 415, 419, 422–4, 426
long service, 415, 419, 422–3, 426
hours of work (labour), xxiv, xxv, xxvi, xxvii, 29–31, 33, 34, 42, 119, 130–1, 135–6, 136–40, 150, 152, 154–5, 156–60, 164, 168, 170–1, 172–3, 177–8, 179, 180–1, 196, 204–5, 207–10, 211, 246–75, 276–303,

Subject Index

hours of work (*contd.*)
　　304–15, 327–63, 368, 369, 370, 371, 380, 407–29 (*see also* labour utilisation)
　　normal hours, xxi, 42, 137, 159, 173, 178, 192, 211, 276–303, 304, 312–15
　　overtime, xxiv, xxvi, 27, 42, 113, 138, 152, 157, 159, 168, 173, 211, 230, 258, 277, 278, 282, 283, 286, 290, 294, 300, 301, 303, 305, 350, 356, 415, 416, 428 (*see also* overtime premia)
　　short time, xxiv, 25, 130–4, 138, 152, 157, 159, 168, 173, 199

illness, 121 (*see also* absenteeism, disability *and* mental health)
imports, *see* trade
incentive pay, *see* bonus pay
income, 276, 277, 283, 345, 363 (*see also* pay)
incomes policy, 283
incremental capital-installed rated wattage ratio, 375–7 (*see also* installed rated wattage)
inflation, 4, 6, 23, 147, 149 (*see also* Phillips curve)
installed rated wattage, 375–7, 383
interest rate, 92, 93
intermediate goods, 326, 327, 334, 338, 349, 350, 360
International Labour Office (ILO), xxvi, 121, 124, 126, 152, 211, 317–25
Institut fur Arbeitsmarkt und Berufsforschung (IAB), 250–3, 255
Institut National de la Statistique et des Etudes Economique (INSEE), 45, 53–56
Institute for Employment Research (IER), xxi, xxvii
institutionalists, 277, 283, 286, 290, 307
instrumental variables, 93–4
inventories, *see* stocks
investment, xxvi, 4, 26, 60, 72, 79–116, 220, 317–25, 328, 329, 336, 337, 340, 341, 345, 354, 357, 360, 363, 375, 376 (*see also* capital stock/perpetual inventory method)
　　plant and machinery, 329
involuntary unemployment (labour), 374
iron and steel, 412, 427 (*see also* manufacturing industry)
Israel, 406, 407, 427
Italy, 66–78

Japan, 66–78, 119–245
'Jobs', 328, 355

labour costs, 62, 74, 356, 357 (*see also* wages)
labour demand, *see* employment
labour force, 67, 119–245, 225, 242, 246–75, 301, 328, 344, 361, 362
　　registered labour force, 151, 156, 159, 160, 161, 167, 169, 172 (*see also* unemployment/registered)
　　youth labour force, 141 (*see also* demographic/age)
labour market, xxvii, 74, 160, 167, 301 (*see also* demand *and* supply)
　　market imperfections, 219–45
labour market accounts, 119–245, 246, 250, 255, 256, 257, 274
　　monitoring account, 172
　　'use of potential' account, 172
labour services, *see* labour utilisation
labour slack, *see* labour utilisation
labour utilisation, xxiii–xxv, 12, 28–31, 34, 96, 119–245, 246–75, 279, 327–63, 370 (*see also* hours of work *and* shortages)
　　hours measure, 154–5
　　labour slack, xxiv, 119–245
　　percentage utilisation of labour (PUL), xxiv–xxv, 327–63
　　tight labour market, 123, 127, 140, 149, 165 (*see also* inflation *and* Phillips curve)
　　under-employment, 324
labour services, *see* labour utilisation
labour slack, *see* labour utilisation
lagged adjustment, *see* adjustment
lay-offs, 152 (*see also* short time)
leading indicators, 350
learning (by doing), *see* education
leisure, xxvii, 276, 277

macroeconomic models, 58, 59, 72
maintenance, 373, 408, 352
management, xxvi, 282, 326, 339, 342, 348–358, 359, 363
manual workers, 281, 285–302, 314–15, 417, 426
manufacturing industries, 3–22, 23–44, 50–7, 79–116, 131, 276, 289–301, 304–15, 320, 327–63, 380–405, 408, 412, 421 (*see also* chemicals, iron and steel, shipbuilding; public utilities *and* services)
market share, 357

Subject Index

materials, 82, 92, 115
materials handling, 352
maximum likelihood techniques, 314, 108–10
mental health, 255, 256 (*see also* disability)
migration (emigration and immigration), 141, 171, 172, 175, 207, 248, 249, 254
mobility, 169, 224
monetarism, 326, 332, 333, 336, 337, 338, 345
monopoly, xxi, xxiii, xxiv
Morocco, 320, 325

National Insurance contributions, 279
'net work put in', 327–63 (*see also* employment, hours *and* PUL)
Netherlands, 119–245, 219–45, 246, 249, 258, 259, 260, 261, 262, 263, 264, 270–3
new international economic order, 317
Nigeria, 320, 325
non-manual workers, 285–302, 314–15, 426
non-market work, xxvii, 147–8, 157, 194, 196
North Sea oil, 283 (*see also* prices)

obsolescence, 10, 373
official reserve, 130 (*see also* labour force)
operatives, *see* employment
order books, 4, 328, 331
ordinary least squares, 93, 243
organisational change, 326–63
Organisation for Economic Cooperation and Development (OECD), xxiii, 58, 59, 72, 78, 206
 INTERLINK model, 59
output (demand, demand pressure and deviations from desired output), xxi, xxv, 3–22, 53, 58–78, 79–116, 131, 171, 219–45, 277, 280, 281, 282, 284, 285–302, 305–15, 323, 327–63 (*see also* economic activity, inflation *and* Phillips curve)
 homogeneity, 87
output per unit of capital measures, 380
overtime premia, xxi, 277, 283, 323

participation, xxiii, 127–30, 140–50, 153, 160, 162, 164–5, 167, 172, 173, 179, 194, 248, 250, 251, 252, 255, 256, 262, 263

part-time workers, 130–4, 138–40, 150, 152, 154–5, 156–60, 169, 171, 175, 179, 192, 194, 196, 199–200, 203, 207–10, 247, 249, 253, 256, 259, 281, 283, 285–302, 312–15 (*see also* hours)
pay, 121, 152, 199, 277, 278, 283, 326, 356, 358, 359 (*see also* bonus pay *and* wages)
peak load demands, 283
peak-to-peak, xxii–xxiii, 7, 23–46, 56, 221, 252, 265, 283–4 (*see also* Wharton School)
percentage utilisation of labour, *see* labour utilisation
 index, 327–63
 panel, 326, 331, 333, 334, 346, 348, 357, 358, 359, 363
perpetual inventory method, *see* capital stock/perpetual inventory method
Philippines, 406, 407, 427
Phillips curve, 123, 149, 165
population (of working age), 130, 140–50, 160–7, 169, 171–98, 247, 253, 254, 255
poverty, 127, 150, 155–6, 164, 317
prices and price elasticities, 4, 27, 58, 59–78, 81, 92, 95, 96, 98, 99, 103, 104, 106, 110, 111, 115, 130, 281, 282, 283, 354, 368, 373, 374, 375, 376, 377, 378, 380–405 (*see also* expectations)
 market versus shadow prices, 73, 320–5 (*see also* natural rate of unemployment)
 oil shock, 12, 14, 32, 43, 54, 60, 74, 80, 98, 332
product demand, *see* output
production function, xxii–xxiii, xxv, xxvi, 23–44, 28–44, 58–78, 277, 278, 279, 281, 282, 284, 304–15, 332, 369–73, 375, 382, 384
 CES technology, xxiii, xxv–xxvi, 28–44, 59, 60, 75–7, 78, 369, 370–1, 386–405 (*see also* MACE *below*)
 Cobb-Douglas (log-linear), 28–44, 59, 82, 84, 88, 280, 281, 305–15, 369, 370, 371, 372, 385, 393
 factor shares, 96
 fixed coefficient (Leontief), 82, 369–70, 382, 410, 427 (*see also* vintages/clay-clay and substitution)
 flexible functional forms (and Generalised Leontief), 110, 312–15, 384, 385, 399 (*see also* dual cost

production function (*contd.*)
functions and translog functions)
frontier, 24
isoquant, 82
Johansen schema, 86, 115
Macro Energy (MACE), 58–78
neoclassical, 79, 80
returns to one factor, xxiv, xxvi, 34, 67, 75–7, 90, 96, 278, 279, 280, 282, 304–15 (*see also* prices/market and shadow)
returns to scale, 59, 72, 75–7, 78, 280, 281, 370, 371, 372, 377, 378
substitution between inputs, xxiii, xxv–xxvi, 59, 60, 75–7, 79–80, 81, 82, 112–13, 148–9, 371, 381–405 (*see also* vintages)
translog function, 312, 385
vintage, xxiii, xxiv, 75–7, 79–116, 219–45: clay-clay 227, 231–235 (*see also* fixed coefficient); *ex ante/ex post*, xxiii, 79–116; marginal vintage, 85, 86, 99, 102, 104, 106, 110, 115; putty-clay, 80, 81, 82, 87, 110, 231–5; putty-putty (putty-semi-putty), xxiii, 80, 81, 105–15
productivity, xxii, xxv, 59–78, 171, 253, 255, 257, 263, 265, 278–9, 282, 283, 291, 304, 306, 323, 327–3, 367–9, (*see also* production functions/returns to one factor, production functions/returns to scale *and* technological change)
labour efficiency index, 59–78
profits (and profit maximisation), 62–78, 81, 82, 86, 88, 95, 99, 103, 105, 110, 121, 130, 152, 199, 278, 328, 350, 351
psychophysiological quanta, 331, 353, 354, 355, 363 (*see also* 'standard minute')
public utilities (and other non-manufacturing producing industries), 285–302, 303–15 (*see also* manufacturing industries *and* services)

quality of products, 322 (*see also* technological change)
quasi-fixed costs (of employment), 64, 67, 72, 279, 282, 304
quasi-rents, 80, 88, 90, 91, 92, 95, 97–105, 374, 375 (*see also* prices)
zero quasi-rent line, 86 (*see also* marginal vintage)
quits, 153, 169, 174

rated wattage, *see* installed rated wattage
recruitment, *see* hiring
recursive system, 281, 287
redundancy, *see* firing
region, 334
retirement, xxiii, xxiv, xxvii, 134, 135, 166, 169, 171, 173, 194, 196, 199, 249, 252, 255, 256, 259
returns to one factor, *see* production functions
returns to scale, *see* production functions

salaries, *see* income and pay
savings, 345, 363
school leaving age, *see* education
Scotland, 23, 45, 50–3, 55
scrapping, *see* capital stock
seasonal variations, 54, 413–5, 417
secondary workers, 130, 147, 148, 160, 248
services, 283, 289–301, 419, 421 (*see also* manufacturing industries *and* public utilities)
Shepard's lemma, 385
shiftwork, xxv, xxvi, 27, 33, 42, 110, 280, 286, 317–25, 369, 371, 372, 378, 406–29
  alternating day and night, 42
  double day shifts, xxv, 322, 323, 324
  laws, 323–4
  rotating, 323
  shift premia, xxi, 277, 283, 322, 323, 418, 428
  three shift, 42
  weekend work, 27
shipbuilding, 412, 427 (*see also* manufacturing industry)
shortages, xxi, xxvi, 4, 7–22, 23, 27, 28, 53, 167, 211, 290, 295, 320, 321, 322 (*see also* labour utilisation)
  financial, 8
  labour, 8, 9–10, 23, 27, 28
  materials, 8
  orders, 8–9 (*see also* order books *and* output)
  plant and machinery, 8
shorter working week, 304 (*see also* work sharing)
short-time working, 277
size (of plant or firm), xxv, 3, 49, 281, 322, 334
social security benefits, 124, 127, 134–5, 149, 150, 151, 169
standard industrial classification, 5, 19–21

Subject Index

statistical distribution
  normal, 6
  rectangular, 6
strikes, 159, 173, 199, 206, 283, 334
Sri Lanka, 320, 325
staff, *see* employment
'standard minute' (hour, week, etc.), 327–63
stocks (work in progress and finished goods), 4, 64
sub-contracting, 322
substitution between inputs, *see* production functions
supply (of labour), xxi, 8, 23, 34, 166, 168, 169, 219–45, 276, 278, 283, 286, 290, 320, 324
SURE estimator, 308–15
survey data, *see* business survey data
Sweden, 46, 119–245, 246, 249, 264

taxes, 99, 249, 259, 323, 324 (*see also* government policy)
  credits and allowances, 75
technological change (and technology), xxv–xxvi, xxvii, 29, 31, 60, 75–7, 92, 98, 278–9, 284, 306–15, 327–63, 357, 383–405
  automation, 357
  computerisation, 331
  Harrod neutrality, 60
  technological necessity, 280
technology, *see* production function *and* technological change
temperature, 388, 389, 399
textiles industry, 32–41, 427 (*see also* manufacturing industries)
Thatcher, 332
third world, *see* developing countries
time intensity utilisation rate, xxvi, 406–29
trade, 3, 5, 58, 59, 321, 322, 324
trade unions, 282 (*see also* TUC)
Trade Union Congress (TUC), 304 (*see also* trade unions)
training, *see* education

unemployment, xxii, xxiii–xxiv, 27, 119–245, 219–45, 246–75, 279, 306–15, 317, 322, 324, 328, 361
  benefits, *see* social security benefits
  cyclical, xxiv, 219–45
  demand deficient, xxiv, 219–45
  disequilibrium analysis, 223–4, 235
  disguised, 131–4, 150
  duration, 155, 156, 175 (*see also* poverty *and* welfare)
  employment/population ratio, 160–7, 179
  frictional, 199, 220, 221, 224, 230, 242
  involuntary and voluntary, xxiii, 219–45 (*see also* part-time work)
  measurement, 119–218: errors (of omission and commission), 126–36; registration, 122, 123–6, 130, 150; sample survey, 122, 123–6, 128, 130
  natural rate, *see* full employment
  search (and search theory), 121, 126, 128, 130, 135, 151, 153, 154, 155, 159, 160, 161, 169, 174, 223–4, 235, 242
  seasonal, 220, 221, 228, 230
  structural, xxiv, 219–45
UV (unemployment/vacancy) curve, xxiv, 219–45
United Kingdom, xxvi, 23–44, 56, 66–78, 79–116, 119–245, 253, 282, 285–302, 304–15, 375, 376, 380–405, 406–29
United States, 60, 66–78, 88, 119–245, 246, 248, 255, 263, 264, 274, 305, 354, 363, 381, 383, 406, 407, 427
utility function, *see* welfare function

vacancies, 171, 219–45
vehicles industry, 32–41 (*see also* manufacturing)

wages, 27, 28, 60, 62, 67, 73, 79, 95, 96, 111, 126, 130, 169, 224, 277, 278, 282, 304, 314, 322 (*see also* basic rate of pay, overtime premia, pay *and* shiftwork/shift premia)
  minimum wage, 135–6, 149
  rhythmically varying wages, 79, 110
  rigidity, 224
Wages Councils, 314 (*see also* collective agreements)
'waiting time', 338, 339
welfare (and welfare function), 126–7, 135–6, 157, 166, 276, 277, 281
western economies, 122 (*see individual country names*)
Wharton School, 23–44, 45, 53, 56 (*see also* peak-to-peak)
work measurement, xxv, 331, 353, 354, 355, 356, 357, 358, 363
work patterns, xxii, 287, 288 (*see also* hours of work, part-time working *and* shiftwork)
working age, 122

Subject Index

'workpost' (workpoint), 331, 338, 355, 356, 357
work scheduling, 356

work-sharing, 140, 169, 170, 249, 259
(*see also* shorter working week)
World Bank, 317